Library user education

# DATE DUE

# Library User Education

## *Powerful Learning, Powerful Partnerships*

Edited by
Barbara I. Dewey

The Scarecrow Press, Inc.
Lanham, Maryland, and London
2001

SCARECROW PRESS, INC.

Published in the United States of America
by Scarecrow Press, Inc.
4720 Boston Way, Lanham, Maryland 20706
www.scarecrowpress.com

4 Pleydell Gardens, Folkestone
Kent CT20 2DN, England

British Library Cataloguing-in-Publication Information Available

**Library of Congress Cataloging-in-Publication Data**

Library user education : powerful learning, powerful partnerships / edited by Barbara I.
Dewey.
    p.   cm.
    Contains chapters based on 43 presentations given at a conference held Nov. 11–12,
1999 at the Iowa Memorial Union.
    Includes bibliographical references.
    ISBN 0-8108-3897-4 (alk. paper)
    1. Library orientation—Congresses. 2. Information services—User
education—Congresses. 3. Information technology—Study and teaching—
Congresses. I. Dewey, Barbara I.
Z711.2 .L7339  2001
025.5'6—dc21                                            00-058334

# Contents

## Information Literacy

## Web-Based Library Instruction

## Specialized User Populations

## Partnerships with Health Sciences Communities

# Introduction

*Barbara I. Dewey*

The importance of user education for library users within a technology-based context has never been greater for colleges and universities. The significance of acquiring superior information-seeking, analytical, and application skills for one's life journey has never been more critical. At risk is the commitment of universities to fulfill their mission (in the words of the University of Iowa strategic plan) "to advance scholarly and creative endeavor through leading-edge research and artistic production; to use this research and creativity to enhance undergraduate, graduate, and professional education, health care, and other services provided to the people of Iowa, the nation, and the world; and to conduct these activities in a culturally diverse, humane, technologically advanced, and increasingly global environment."[1] Also at risk is lifelong success in one's career, home, and personal life. The premise of *Library User Education: Powerful Learning, Powerful Partnerships* is that the successful acquisition of information literacy or information-fluency skills cannot be accomplished by librarians alone. It must be done through partnerships with teaching faculty and other colleagues who play a role in advancing teaching and learning.

## A POWERFUL BLEND

Partnerships of faculty, librarians, and technologists result in a powerful blending of knowledge navigation, subject expertise, and pedagogical mastery. In order to broadly explore the partnership concept, the University of Iowa Libraries hosted an international conference on educational strategies and programs that support faculty, students, and staff in teaching, learning, and research. "Powerful Learning, Powerful Partnerships: Educating the University Community in a Dynamic Information Environment" was held on November 11–12, 1999, at the Iowa Memorial Union.[2] The University of Iowa Center for Teaching cosponsored the conference. Institutions represented included eighty universities, twenty colleges, and four community colleges. Librarians, technologists, administrators, and faculty attended from twenty-nine states, the U.S. Virgin Islands, the United Kingdom, and Canada. Conference plenary speakers were Brian Hawkins, president of EDU-CAUSE, and Lizabeth Wilson, associate director for Public Services, University of Washington Libraries. Papers and poster sessions were given by librarians and faculty from more than fifty institutions on various topics related to library user education focusing, in particular, on programs featuring academic partnership. *Library User Education: Powerful Learning, Powerful Partnerships* contains chapters based on forty-two presentations given at the conference that focused on library user education employing academic partnerships.

## THE MIRAGE OF CONTINUITY

Brian Hawkins, an internationally known higher-education scholar, writes in the area of information resources, libraries, academic planning, and the use of technology in higher education. His plenary presentation, "The Mirage of Continuity: Matching Realities and Aspirations," set the stage for lively discussion about the impact of major change in libraries serving institutions of higher education because of irreversible and fundamental transformations occurring in the academy.[3] He talked about the historic illusion of libraries in chains and how, although libraries no longer use physical chains to secure books, they are still intellectually, economically, and structurally chained in a way that will not allow transformation to occur. Hawkins used the model "fire, fuel, and focus" to illustrate his presentation, quoting William Butler Yeats, who said that education is not the filling of the pail but the lighting of a fire. Hawkins talked about three independent components—content, access, and guidance—necessary to bridge what he termed the "digital divide." His last component, guidance, describes the core content of *Library User Education: Powerful Learning, Powerful Partnerships*. Guidance through partnerships with librarians, faculty, and technologists is fundamental to the powerful partnership model so that students will reap the benefits of a truly integrated education drawing from a variety of media, no longer "chained" to a linear or traditional format. The chapters in this book reflect concrete strategies to unchain libraries and educational methods to effectively harness all forms of information and scholarly production through partnerships.

## INFORMATION FLUENCY

The conference's second plenary speaker, Lizabeth Wilson, publishes and presents widely on learning technologies, educational collaborations, and assessment. She has held many leadership positions in the American Library Association (ALA) and the Association of College and Research Libraries (ACRL), and is ACRL president for 2000. She is a well-known expert on information literacy programs.[4] In her chapter "Information Literacy: Fluency Across and Beyond the University," she stresses that because students face diverse, abundant choices, information literacy is a critical survival skill. Her chapter sets the stage for the rest of the book by concluding that collaboration and integration of different approaches is the key to advancing information literacy progress on college and university campuses.

## LIBRARY USER EDUCATION IN PARTNERSHIP

*Library User Education: Powerful Learning, Powerful Partnerships* consists of ten sections dealing with partnerships and library user education. The first four sections deal with campus-wide strategies, faculty-focused programs, and high tech venues—Campus Strategies, Faculty Development Programs, Faculty–Librarian Partnerships, and Partnering with Technology Centers. The next three sections include programs and strategies for library user education and information literacy in different formats—Instruction and Faculty Outreach, Information Literacy, and Web-Based Library Instruction. Two sections address specific audience needs—Specialized User Populations and Partnerships with Health Sciences Communities. The book concludes with the section on Program Assessment and Modeling.

## WHY IOWA?

The University of Iowa Libraries has intensified its efforts in advancing library user education and outreach over the past decade. As with other research libraries, it became increasingly clear that exploding numbers and complexity of information resources in all formats, along with the emergence of new learning technologies, required more comprehensive programs on effective use and application of scholarly materials for teaching and research. Thus, major effort was expended at the University of Iowa to increase faculty and students' understanding of research processes and scholarly communication through a wide range of strategies and partnerships. The University of Iowa Libraries is now considered to be a leader in library user education and was cited recently in a major research library journal as one of six institutions demonstrating the best practices and models for information literacy in the United States.[5]

An idea for a major conference on user education with a partnership theme developed in early 1998 to both showcase Iowa's experiences and bring together educators from other colleges and universities to present and discuss their advances in developing and promoting library user education across the curriculum.

## THE INFORMATION ARCADE: A BREAKTHROUGH

In 1992, the University of Iowa Libraries opened the Information Arcade, a unique groundbreaking facility founded on the philosophy of collaboration between librarians, faculty, and technologists, and designed to support the use of electronic resources in research, teaching, and independent learning.[6] Since its opening, the Arcade has been the focus of intense worldwide attention, including winning the 1994 Meckler/ALA Library of the Future Award.

Development of a physical space such as the Information Arcade, visually and actively demonstrating action based on an education philosophy (interactive learning combined with rich connections to networked information resources), remains a critical element in the success of current Iowa partnerships and future development of others. Established with a $750,000 grant from the Roy J. Carver Charitable Trust, the Arcade consists of an electronic classroom and clusters of multimedia workstations and information stations. Most importantly, the Information Arcade features human expertise and support for its users.

The creation of the Information Arcade provided a dynamic way for librarians to work directly with early innovators on campus. When taught in the Arcade's electronic classroom, courses were transformed into a hypertext-guided tour of subject matter using documents, images, and photographs. From the research library perspective, the Information Arcade provided a focus for bringing together the resource navigation expertise of librarians needed to support emerging interactive learning environments and the application of new technologies. What occurred was a fundamental change in the way librarians and faculty worked with students and with each other. Important for librarians, the facility provided a new way to use their expertise to integrate information resources (in all formats) into courses, along with the information-seeking and problem-solving skills needed to sort out and apply the vast body of information resources. The opportunity to experiment with emerging learning technologies and create information resources for research and teaching with Arcade technology and staff expertise was a major advancement.

Using the Information Arcade as a model, the University of Iowa Libraries, in collaboration with academic colleges and departments, has built or is planning similar facilities throughout the campus. The Information Commons and the Information Commons West electronic information and multimedia teaching facilities at the University of Iowa Hardin Library for the Health Sciences opened in August 1996 and February 2000 respectively.[7] Jim Duncan's chapter discusses further Commons services and activities.

ARTIC (Advanced Real Time Information Center) is an electronic teaching facility located in the Marvin A. Pomerantz Business Library. ARTIC's purpose is to incorporate state-of-the-art technologies for all kinds of dynamic (real-time) business information sources, especially global financial trading markets, into a teaching venue for College of Business Administration faculty and librarians. ARTIC extends the collaborative and innovative philosophies of the original Arcade concept by providing an actual space for librarians and faculty to improve students' ability to compete in our real-time, global, information-driven economy through effective navigation of business information sources.

Ongoing building projects for the Engineering Library and the Biology Library include Arcade-inspired smaller electronic teaching facilities within their walls. These facilities enable greater access to electronic multimedia resources, which are so important in these disciplines, and bring together more students and faculty in subject-specific interactive learning environments. The facilities, planned in close collaboration with the College of Engineering and the Biological Sciences Department, provide yet more venues for dialogue with faculty regarding collaborative ventures for integrating electronic resources into their curriculum.

Extending our reach to thousands of students in a large university setting is simply not possible in classrooms (electronic or otherwise) or through regularly scheduled educational sessions held in the library. Although engaged in user education programs for some years, it was clear that at the University of Iowa, we were not reaching large numbers of students and faculty. For example, in 1990, a total of 393 user education sessions were held reaching 6,678 students. By 1999, the number of sessions increased to 542 reaching 11,708 students. However, this falls far short of the campus population of 28,000 students. And it was also clear from user needs assessment surveys that faculty and students had ever-increasing needs in learning how to effectively use the more complex and numerous information resources available at a large research university.[8]

## COMPUTER-BASED USER EDUCATION EFFORTS

One way research libraries can hope to scale user education programs in a truly exponential way is through the implementation of broadly accessible Web-based tutorials and information packages that may be used twenty-four hours a day by many individuals at one time. *Library Explorer*, developed initially as a hypercard program, now Web-based, is a computer instruction program designed to help students learn to choose information sources and find tools appropriate for their work. Using the book as a metaphor, *Library Explorer* directs users to a variety of "chapters" and allows them to search the Libraries' on-line catalog at any point in the program <http://www.lib.uiowa.edu/libexp/>. A specialized information package, *Engineering Reference Assistant* provides students "virtual" assistance locating engineering information resources appropriate to their needs and class projects. The *Engineering Reference Assistant* can be accessed via the Web<http://www.lib.uiowa.edu/eng/robo/robo1.htm> and is available anytime the student needs help.

## TWIST

Another way the University Libraries decided to expand its reach to large numbers of students is through an initiative called TWIST (Teaching with Innovative Style and Technology). TWIST <http//twist.lib.uiowa.edu> originally was a three-year project funded by a $370,000 grant from the Roy J. Carver Charitable Trust. TWIST's primary goal is to assist faculty to incorporate new technologies and information resources into their courses and thus reach students. Initial TWIST projects include assisting a Latin American media scholar to construct a Web page for two courses providing students with information about traditional and electronic information sources, and working with a cross-cultural communication scholar to develop an experimental course using electronic communication tools to link students from Iowa to students at the University of Jyvaskyla in Finland.

As with user education programs described earlier, reaching large numbers of faculty and, consequently, students in courses via the faculty was unrealistic through traditional methods. Thus, TWIST also completed a series of Web-based learning guides <http://twist.uiowa.edu/tutorials/> that can be used at the users' convenience or point of need.

During the 1997–98 academic year, TWIST focused on developing partnerships of librarians and faculty in a program called TWISTed Pairs to explore the use of Web-based learning environments for specific classes. A general process for implementation of the TWISTed Pairs model is that TWIST staff (1) meet with the librarians and show options they can use with faculty, (2) survey the librarians involved to determine current skill levels and develop a training needs assessment, (3) meet with librarian–faculty pairs to develop individualized plans, (4) continue training librarians (and faculty), and (5) work directly with faculty offering assistance as needed <http://twist.lib.uiowa.edu/projects/>. The TWISTed Pairs model has proven to be the most successful strategy and continues today.

## UIII—UNIVERSITY OF IOWA INFORMATION LITERACY INITIATIVE

Further scaling is being accomplished with UIII (University of Iowa Information Literacy Initiative), a program in partnership with faculty to achieve greater information literacy for University of Iowa students. Application of the UIII approach to the international health curriculum is described in this book in the chapter titled "Information Literacy and International Health Topics." The program is based on the assumption that the best way for students to become truly information literate is for information skills to be integrated into the university's curriculum. Ideally, students need to practice and immediately apply information skills if they are to deepen their competencies. Faculty and librarians discuss course goals and the skills the faculty would like to emphasize in a particular course. Different approaches can be used including developing a guide for students to use for resource evaluation, creating a course Web site giving students a guided jumping-off point for searching the Web, developing an assignment where students work on a search strategy appropriate to a problem statement, or presenting a class session on one or more of the information literacy skills. The Science Information Literacy Initiative also described in this book is a specific outgrowth of the UIII effort.

## POWERFUL PARTNERSHIPS—NEXT STEPS

Next steps in advancing library user education and information literacy in an age of transformation involve concentrated efforts to establishing even greater credibility with academic partners as described in the following chapters. Librarians need to gain the confidence of faculty, and technologists need to communicate more effectively with both librarians and faculty. Purposeful and well-planned programs need to be put in place to expand the integration of information literacy or information fluency throughout the curriculum and as a basis for lifelong learning.

The ability to strategically develop and place effective partnerships within the new learning communities emerging from our colleges and universities is increasingly critical if universities and colleges continue to believe that "deep" research and critical thinking remain important outcomes for graduates. The alternative is that future generations of college graduates will be content to skip on the surface of information and knowledge as they make major decisions for life and career. *Library User Education: Powerful Learning, Powerful Partnerships* provides a wealth of innovative ideas and resources for librarians and faculty who are serious about educating library users in truly comprehensive and long-lasting ways.

## NOTES

1. University of Iowa. Next Century Iowa: Bridges to the Next Horizon. A Strategic Plan for the University of Iowa, 2000–2005 <http://www.uiowa.edu/president/strat_plan.html> [accessed 30 August 2000].

2. The conference planning committee consisted of library staff including Barbara I. Dewey, conference convenor, Jim Duncan, Marsha Forys, Carol Ann Hughes, Neville Prendergast, and Karen Zimmerman. Many other staff worked as volunteers throughout the conference. Additional information may be found on the conference Web site <http://www.lib.uiowa.edu/symposium99/>.

3. See also Brian Hawkins and Patricia Battin, eds., *The Mirage of Continuity: Reconfiguring Academic Information Resources for the Twenty-First Century*, (Washington, D.C.: Council on Library and Information Resources and American Association of Universities, 1998).

4. American Library Association, Association for College and Research Libraries, "Institute for Information Literacy Program Initiatives" <http://www.ala.org/acrl/nili/initiatives.html>.

5. Cerise Oberman, Bonnie Gratch Lindauer, and Betsy Wilson, "Integrating Information Literacy into the Curriculum: How Is Your Library Measuring Up?" *C & R L News* (May 1998): 347–52.

6. Anita Lowry, "The Information Arcade at the University of Iowa," *CAUSE/EFFECT* 17, no. 3 (Fall 1994): 38–44.

7. J. M. Duncan, "The Information Commons: A Model for (Physical) Digital Resource Centers," *Bull Med Libr Assoc* 86, no. 4 (October 1998): 576–82.

8. The University of Iowa User Needs Assessment Web page with results of the comprehensive needs assessment surveys is located at <http://www.lib.uiowa.edu/unag/> [accessed 30 August 2000].

# 1

## Information Literacy: Fluency Across and Beyond the University

*Lizabeth A. Wilson*

### WHY SHOULD WE CARE ABOUT INFORMATION LITERACY?

No other change offers greater challenges than the emergence of the Information Age. Information is expanding at an unprecedented rate. Enormous strides are being made in the technology for storing, organizing, and accessing the ever-growing deluge of information. As we increasingly rely on global networks for the dissemination of knowledge, a new information literacy has emerged. While providing access to information used to be our primary challenge, we now face a formidable task: coping with an excess of information and ensuring that our students succeed in this information-saturated world. What used to suffice as literacy no longer suffices. What used to be considered as effective knowledge no longer is sufficient.

Our information environment is changing dramatically. Internet watchers estimate that the number of Web sites doubles every forty to fifty days. Computers today are one million times more powerful than those in 1979. Technologists project that in twenty years, computers will be one million times more powerful than today. The U.S. Department of Labor Secretary's Commission on Achieving Necessary Skills (SCANS) recommended in 1991 that all entry-level employees must be able to acquire and use information and work with a variety of technologies.[1] There is even a sickness caused by information overload, which canbe hazardous to your health. Getting physically sick as a result of the stress caused by information overload now has an official name—Information Fatigue Syndrome.

Information literacy has become a survival skill. Students face diverse, abundant information choices. Information is available through libraries, community resources, special interest organizations, media, and the Internet. Information comes increasingly in unfiltered forms. The uncertain quality and expanding quantity of information pose large challenges. The sheer abundance of information will not in itself create a more informed student body without a complementary cluster of abilities necessary to use information effectively. At the core of information literacy are skills that have always been a part of our teaching. We have always sought to help our students become critical thinkers.

What do students tell us about their ability to use information? At the University of Washington, we surveyed incoming freshmen, graduating seniors, alumni five years out, and alumni ten years out.[2] Each group was asked to identify which skills it valued most highly. All four groups ranked the following as their top priorities: problem solving, information use and management, technology use, writing, and reading. The percentage of freshman who rated their own competence as "very good" or "excellent" in the top-valued skills were

**49.8 percent.**  Defining and solving problems
**41.5 percent.**   Locating information needed to help make decisions or solve problems
**38.7 percent.**  Working effectively with modern technology, especially computers
**36.8 percent.**  Critically analyzing written information
**49.6 percent.**  Writing effectively

When graduating seniors rated their own competence as "very good" or "excellent" in the same top-valued skills, there is growth in confidence, but not as much as desired.

**68.5 percent.**  Defining and solving problems
**63.6 percent.**   Locating information needed to help make decisions or solve problems
**50.1 percent.**  Working effectively with modern technology, especially computers
**59.6 percent.**  Critically analyzing written information
**64.1 percent.**  Writing effectively

University of Washington students are not unique. If the survey were replicated at other universities, the results probably would be similar. Students recognize that information, technology, and thinking skills are important, and that they are not confident, even upon graduation, of their competencies in these areas. Given that the life span of a college degree is fifty-five years, we must ask ourselves, have we prepared our graduates to continue learning into the twenty-first century? Have we prepared our students for a world we can't even begin to imagine?

## What Is Information Literacy?

There are many definitions of information literacy, all variations on a common theme. Information literacy forms the basis for lifelong learning. It is common to all disciplines, to all learning environments, and to all levels of education. Lifelong learning is becoming a way of life. The demarcations between K–12, higher education, and the workplace are increasingly artificial and antiquated.

The American Association of School Librarians and the Association of Educational Communications and Technology define the goal of information literacy as ensuring that K–12 students are effective and efficient users of ideas and information.[3] According to the report of the American Library Association Presidential Commission:

> To be information literate, a person must be able to recognize when information is needed and have the ability to locate, evaluate, and use effectively the needed information.[4]

In 1999, the National Research Council (NRC) published its report on "what everyone should know about information technology."[5] The NRC advances FITness (fluency in information technology). The NRC dismissed the term literacy because it can connote rudimentary skills and knowledge. Fluency requires the acquisition of three kinds of knowledge: concepts, skills, and capability. They are interdependent, co-equal, and cannot be taught in isolation. According to the NRC, information technology fluency is the basic knowledge necessary for a lifelong quest to acquire new skills, understand the foundational technology concepts, become progressively more capable with information technology, and apply information technology optimally to meet one's needs.

Another variation comes from Jeremy Shapiro and Shelley Hughes in their article "Information Literacy as Liberal Art" in *Educom Review*.[6] They suggest that the saturation of our daily lives with information organized and transmitted via technology and the way in which public issues and social life are increasingly being shaped by issues such as intellectual property and privacy require an information and knowledge curriculum that is multidimensional. Shapiro and Hughes define information literacy comprising interrelated facets:

- Tool literacy: the ability to understand and use the tools of current information technology including software, hardware, and multimedia
- Resource literacy: the ability to understand the form, format, location, and access methods of information resources
- Social-structural literacy: knowing that and how information is socially situated and produced

- Research literacy: understanding and using information technology tools relevant to a researcher's work
- Publishing literacy: the ability to format and publish research and ideas electronically in multimedia forms, and to introduce them into the electronic realm and the community of scholars
- Emerging technology literacy: the ability to adapt to, understand, evaluate, and use emerging innovations in information technology
- Critical literacy: the ability to evaluate critically the strengths, weaknesses, potentials, and limits of information technologies

Anne Zald and Mark Donovan in "Defining Moments: The Role of Information Literacy in the Twenty-First Century Construct of Education" encourage us to expand our notion of information literacy:

> By expanding our concept of information literacy to encompass the production and ratification of knowledge rooted in scholarly communities (and elsewhere) we can create a conception of information literacy that is both extraordinarily powerful and fits well with the practices and expectations of the college and university faculty who must be our allies. Although we approach it from different perspectives, information literacy is the educational ground shared by faculty and librarians.[7]

There are many ways to define information literacy, but regardless of the definition chosen, there is much work to be done. No one department or institution can go this alone. The multidimensional nature of information literacy requires broad-based educational collaborations.

## Where Are We Now with Respect to Information Literacy?

In an effort to assist institutions in evaluating their information literacy readiness, Cerise Oberman and I developed the Information Literacy IQ test (appendix 1). The IQ in this test stands for Institutional Quotient, not Intelligence Quotient. The test is designed to measure an institution's readiness for integrating information literacy into the curriculum.

To take the test, answer all the statements with true or false. Total the number of trues marked and match the total score with the corresponding stage. The first two stages, "First Steps" and "On Your Way," are critical foundational stages in preparing an institution to understand and embrace information literacy. The "Experimenting" and "Full Speed Ahead" stages are the realization of the earlier conceptual stages. The last stage, the "Model Program" stage, is the penultimate accomplishment. Under each of the five stages, a series of strategies are suggested to assist institutions with moving to the next stage.

How are colleges and universities across the nation stacking up when it comes to addressing information literacy? What are the best practices? The institutional approaches are as diverse as the thousands of institutions of higher education. However, there are defining characteristics of the best practices. I have found five common characteristics of such institutions.

## INFORMATION LITERACY IS INTEGRATED INTO THE EDUCATIONAL MISSION OF THE INSTITUTION

In model approaches, information literacy is prominent in mission and vision statements, strategic plans, and program descriptions. Information literacy is an institution-wide agenda and part of the president's and the provost's vocabulary. Information literacy is not viewed as one department's purview. The faculty recognizes that information literacy matches the educational goals of the institution, that it adds value to learning, and that it is complementary to discipline-based goals. While an integrated curricular approach is a best practice, we must realize that change in higher education is also a long process. I heard a state senator remark, "The hallmark of higher education is the ability to resist change." And he meant it as a compliment.

### Collaboration among Educators Is Key

Best practices are collaborative efforts and involve the broadest range of educators. A climate of collaboration exists at best-practice institutions. Collaboration is something much different than cooperation. It is much more powerful because it fundamentally changes roles, relationships, and structures and moves us out of our "functional silos." Programs that work bring together those who share the same educational goals, although they may have different perspectives.

### Technology Is Brought into the Service of Information Literacy Education

Model programs do not confuse information literacy with technology literacy. This is a challenge because we teach in an era of technology lusting. There is a lot of talk of how technology will allow us to educate students faster and more cheaply. Expectations about technology have grown to almost mythic proportions. Stephen Ehrmann asks many of the right questions:

> if we rush out and buy new technologies without first asking hard questions about appropriate educational goals, the results are likely to be disappointing and wasteful.[8]

If you are headed in the wrong direction, technology will only get you there faster. Approaches that work have been able to maintain a sense of reality as the hype has grown. Best practices know what they want to accomplish educationally before employing technology. They pay attention to what is known about learning.

Arthur W. Chickering and Zelda Gamson have summarized many years of research in articulating seven principles for good practice.[9] They tell us if you want to increase learning: encourage student/faculty contact, enable collaboration among students, use active learning techniques, give prompt and rich feedback, provide more time on task, communicate high expectations, and support diverse ways of learning. Can we use technology to enable learning and engender good practice?[10]

Can we use technology to encourage contact between learners and instructors? There are many success stories of asynchronous communication. E-mail, computer conferencing, and the Web allow students and faculty to exchange ideas faster and more often. Interaction increases, and learning increases.

Can we use technology to facilitate collaboration among learners? Networked technology enables distributed study groups, collaborative learning, and group problem solving. The extent to which the Internet encourages spontaneous collaboration was one of its earliest surprises.

Can we use technology for active learning? Learning is not a spectator sport. Technology provides almost limitless possibilities to facilitate active learning. Networking supports learning by doing, time-shifted interaction, and productive engagement.

Can we use technology to provide rich and prompt feedback? The ways in which new technologies can provide feedback are many, and we've just begun to scratch the surface. As colleges and universities move toward capstone experiences and outcomes assessment, networks can provide storage and easy access to student processes.

Can we use technology to allow more time on task? When learning is limited to the classroom, Monday, Wednesday, and Friday, 9 A.M., at Padelford Hall, learning is constrained. Learning can now be carried on twenty-four hours a day, seven days a week.

Can we use technology to communicate high expectations? Many have experienced, firsthand, heightened expectations from self-publishing on the Web. Standards rise when students share work that was previously seen only by the instructor with peers and the world.

Can we use technology to support diverse ways of learning? The visual, the accelerated, the plodding, the linear, the nonlinear learner can all be accommodated. Great gains are possible for those with different physical constraints or cognitive processes.

## BEST PRACTICES ARE STUDENT CENTERED

Information literacy approaches that work keep the student at the center. Teaching must be within the context of each learner's needs and experience. All of the best practices employ resource-based or problem-based learning. Students are adept at collaborative and active learning. Best practices take assessment and evaluation seriously and keep in touch with students.

## BEST PRACTICES SUPPORT
## FACULTY LEARNING AND DEVELOPMENT

Faculty development is a visible commitment of model institutions. An environment that encourages instructors to keep learning is critical. This commitment often is manifested in faculty development and curricular redesign efforts such as the Faculty Development Partnership at the University of Arizona, the TWIST Program at the University of Iowa, or Catalyst at the University of Washington.

## MODEL PROGRAMS

What are some of the model programs and what might we all learn from them? In reviewing models of successful integration, the richness of approaches and the diversity in size and mission of the institutions is impressive. Four such approaches are highlighted in the following sections of this chapter.

**California State University, San Marcos, California**
<http://www.csusm.edu/library/ILP/>

Information literacy is identified as one of the five areas required within the general education program of study. General education courses include an information literacy component. The Information Literacy Program supports these courses. The program's mission is to infuse throughout the curriculum the teaching of information theory, concepts, skills, and use of the library to the community and formal outreach programs, focusing on those skills necessary for accessing, retrieving, evaluating, and using information.

**Florida International University, Miami, Florida**
<http://www.fiu.edu/~library/ili/>

FIU's Information Literacy Initiative is a partnership of the libraries, the Academy for the Art of Teaching, and individual faculty. FIU focuses on "changes in the way they teach students and support their learning that can make a significant difference in students['s] technological sophistication and critical thinking skills." The Information

Literacy Initiative helps faculty find ways to provide information literacy skills to students within the context of individual courses and disciplines. FIU sequences information literacy experiences into the curriculum, providing workshops and year-long working sessions for groups of faculty and entire departments.

**University of Iowa, Iowa City, Iowa**
<http://www.lib.uiowa.edu/info.html>

As a large institution with the challenge of student numbers, the University of Iowa uses information technology and interactive instructional programs to support the information literacy of the greatest number of students and faculty. Current efforts include

**Library Explorer.** A Web-based tutorial that includes interactive segments dealing with all aspects of library research
**Information Arcade.** A prize-winning advanced facility for using electronic information and multimedia for teaching, research, and independent learning
**TWIST.** A three-year project to create a model training program for librarians and faculty on networked information resources
**UIII.** The University of Iowa Information Literacy Initiative

**University of Washington, Seattle, Washington**
<http://www.washington.edu/uwired/>
The UWired Collaboration

In 1994, at the behest of the provost to "do something" about information and technology, the UWired partnership was forged among the University Libraries, Undergraduate Education, and Computing and Communications. Each unit saw collaboration as the only way to support information and technology in teaching and learning. Each knew it was competing for the same scarce resources.

UWired provides access to the tools and resources that students and faculty need to use technology to enhance teaching and learning, promotes fluency with information and information technology, and fosters innovation in technology-enabled teaching and learning. UWired reflects the University's mission to provide an undergraduate education that emphasizes inquiry and fosters those qualities of mind that encourage independent judgment.

*The Challenge and Value of Technology*

UWired agrees with Brian Hawkins that the networked environment is transforming higher education. The future of higher education will be determined by how institutions respond to networked technology and the demands for student fluency with information and technology. Technology can not or should not replace the efforts of faculty. Rather, UWired seeks ways to give faculty access to technologies and assist them in making use of these in ways that increase learning. UWired works with its partners to address policy issues such as intellectual property, copyright, and classroom support of technology that, unless resolved, will continue to hamstring learning.

Technology has the potential to transform teaching and learning in at least four major ways. It can promote curricular integration, engage disengaged fields of study, facilitate active and collaborative learning, and extend learning opportunities to new populations of students. Traditionally, the challenge of technology has been understood as integrating technology into the curriculum. UWired supports another view—curriculum integrated through technology.

*Partnerships and Infrastructure*

UWired has expanded to include five primary partners—the libraries, campus computing, educational outreach, educational partnerships, and undergraduate education. Each partner has contributed substantial resources and expertise to the collaboration. There are numerous affiliates and their number continues to grow. Affiliates include such units as the office of educational assessment, classroom support services, the College of Arts and Sciences, intercollegiate athletics, the School of Medicine, and most recently, the School of Library and Information Science.

UWired has three management groups. The Executive Committee is made up of opinion makers from the five partner organizations. Each can commit resources on behalf of its unit. The Steering Group is made of "anyone who needs to be there," and is largely self-defined by initiatives and issues. It flows and ebbs between fifteen to twenty-five people. The Lab Management Board is made up of individuals from across campus and focuses on computer lab policy, planning, and funding. Working groups carry out the initiatives. The focus of these groups changes with the strategic directions and needs of UWired. Currently the groups are focused on information literacy, training and support, evaluation and usability, faculty development, and emerging technologies.

*Facilities, Operations, and Initiatives*

UWired manages a number of facilities and is responsible for all open-access computer labs on campus. UWired has built two innovative learning and teaching spaces called collaboratories. These collaboratories are located in the undergraduate library and are designed to facilitate collaborative learning in a networked environment. The UWired Center for Teaching, Learning, and Technology provides assistance, workshops, and consultation for educators.

Many curricular initiatives come under the UWired umbrella. Information literacy and technology instruction is part of the freshman learning group experience and transfer student curriculum. Upper-division classes and entire curriculums have been reshaped to leverage networked technology for course delivery and content. Intercollegiate athletics became a partner in UWired, providing student athletes laptops and the skills to stay connected while on the road.

In the beginning, UWired's first effort was to distribute laptops to freshmen in small learning communities and provide them with instruction and a plug-and-play space. The students, faculty, and librarians were transformed by the experience. One UWired student, addressing a group of spellbound faculty at a campus symposium, held his laptop over his head and said, "This is the future. Either get on the bus, or get out of our way."

But the laptop approach was not scaleable or sustainable at a large institution and in some ways missed the point. UWired needed to create a transformational infrastructure for faculty as well as students. UWired now supports opportunities for curriculum integration among entire departments and between academic disciplines. UWired has moved from the early adopter (Johnny Appleseed) approach to the collective department level to ensure long-term systemic change.

The university does not operate in an educational vacuum. UWired is connected with the state's community colleges, K–12, the other baccalaureates, and the business community. Teams from the thirty-two community colleges participated in a weeklong UWired symposium on teaching and technology. The symposium included sessions on the use of technology in training, facilities issues, and planning for interinstitutional collaboration. UWired hosted an in-service day for 700 Seattle public school teachers titled "Educating the Citizen for the Twenty-First Century: Information Literacy and Service Learning." During the summer of 1999, supported by funding from the Gates Foundation, our state's principals and superintendents attended a Smart Tools Academy and were given a laptop and training on using technology to transform their work and their schools.

UWired has entered into several collaborations aimed at using our state's K–20 high-speed network. The libraries have taken the lead in building the Digital Northwest. From scanned manuscripts from the Japanese-American relocation and internment in the Pacific Northwest to photographs from the Klondike gold rush to the archives of the Canwell Red Scare hearings at the University of Washington, the unique resources of a research library are being extended over the state's K–20 network.

## Information Literacy and Linked Courses

One of UWired's primary goals is the promotion of information literacy and it has found linked courses particularly productive. Four types of linked courses offer students the opportunity to learn information and technology skills in classes that are linked to courses in a disciplinary field.

The first type of linked course provides an opportunity for undergraduate students to take an information seminar in conjunction with a large lecture class. Librarians collaborate with faculty to deliver instruction in locating, evaluating, and using information in the context of a particular subject. Seminars may use such tools as on-line discussions and peer reviews, and cover topics such as evaluation criteria, copyright issues, use of library databases, and Web searches.

A second variation of the linked course is being offered collaboratively by the School of Library and Information Science, the University Libraries, UWired, and several other academic departments. This first undergraduate offering under the aegis of the library school provides an introduction to the intellectual and pragmatic abilities of information fluency. During the fall of 1999, librarians taught four pilot courses linked to geography, history, forest resources, and environmental studies.

The third type of linked course is the Freshman Interest Group (FIG) program introduced in 1987. First-quarter freshmen enroll in clusters of courses organized around themes. Each FIG includes a resource seminar taught by an upperclassman. In 1994, information and technology topics were added to the seminar curriculum. The two thousand freshmen enrolled in FIGs develop basic competencies in electronic communication, the Web, and library resources.

The final example of linked course is UWired's collaborative effort with the Interdisciplinary Writing Program. Librarians provide instruction in the use of information resources in a way designed to complement assignments. A writing link to an American history course may involve students in historical research with primary source materials. Students in a writing course linked to geography may be asked to use observational field methods, GIS, and statistical data sets to examine urban phenomena.

Many lessons are generated from the linked courses. Information literacy is learned best if taught in a disciplinary context. Complex skills require a substantial response, not just adding something on top of a course. It's all so new that strategies are evolving and a flexible approach is required. What are considered best practices today might not work tomorrow. Linked courses add coherence to education, letting students see how the sum is greater than the parts. Collaboration among different educators is required. Faculty, teaching assistants, writing instructors, librarians, technologists, and instructional and Web designers are all key players. While programs such as linked courses are one way, information literacy can not be taught through these efforts alone. Across the university, faculty are recognizing the challenges posed by the information flood.

## Individual Faculty Efforts

In the School of Medicine, Dr. Edward Walker's students are learning how their study and practice of medicine depends on being fluent with information. In his course Systems of Human Behavior and Developmental Medicine, students study how the complex interaction of biology, developmental history, environment, and behavior results in disease. His course is not about information technology, yet he impresses upon medical students how their practice will be dependent on their ability to know how to find information, how to evaluate its credibility, and how to use it to solve patient cases.

Students are assigned to "virtual clinics" that meet on-line weekly. Students are presented with clinical situations that are difficult to capture in a lecture or textbook. For example, a patient with fibromyalgia prompted students to search the Web for information and set up a discussion of how, particularly in the context of medicine, the Web can be both useful and dangerous. Walker and students discuss how to evaluate sites and other information. Students examine how to assess peer review, scientific validity, the credentials of the Web author, and any apparent conflicts of interest. In another case, students are presented with a Cambodian patient, speaking to them through an interpreter, who reports signs of depression. In order to approach this case, students learn how to use on-line resources that provide them with information to practice medicine that is sensitive to cultural differences. Walker has recognized the intimate links between his fields of study, information technology, and information literacy.

## Catalyst

The centerpiece of UWired's current faculty development efforts is the Catalyst Web site.[11] While the early technology adopters often placed a premium on finding allies and receiving in-person assistance, as more and more faculty move on-line, they look for convenient, just-in-time support. Catalyst provides this support and does so in a way that puts pedagogy at the center of the discussion about technology. The Web-based tools that are part of the site each had their origins in collaborations with instructors. For example, the UWired Peer Review tool facilitates student-based, asynchronous collaboration and was designed in collaboration with a campus writing center. This tool was then bundled on the Catalyst Web site with support materials that provide an instructional framework for faculty who wish to use the tool. Through

Catalyst, UWired identifies promising practices that address enterprise-wide educational needs and then provides support to the entire campus community. Catalyst not only extends UWired's reach, but also improves the overall quality of faculty support, providing department support personnel with a set of resources they can draw on, freeing them up to provide services individually tailored to their faculty. By aggressively profiling the efforts of campus educators, Catalyst makes faculty innovation visible and directly contributes to the vitality of the teaching community on campus.

## What Are the Lessons Learned from UWired?

The "vision thing" is critical. UWired's vision is one where teaching and learning is infused with the best technology, and "technology" becomes just another tool. This will only be realized through efforts that support systemic change. We advocate for this vision and work to support activities that will make it a reality. We don't, however, presume to know exactly how this will happen. If we thought we had the answer, we would probably be wrong.

**Think strategically.** Operating in an environment with constrained resources forces us to continually reexamine our use of time, people, and money. We all encounter organizations that seem to be either trying to do too much with too little or too little with too much. There are many things we would like to do that we can't. The number of good ideas always exceed the resources available.

**Accept uncertainty.** Embrace experimentation. The only way to realize our vision and make good strategic choices is to accept the fact that we are operating in a highly uncertain environment. Such flexibility is only possible when an organization creates a culture of experimentation that generates ideas and approaches, discards most of them, and embraces the ones that best advance their goals.

**Collaborate. Often.** It is far too easy at our institutions to become isolated. UWired was founded as a partnership, and as the organization has grown, this partnership as flourished up, down, and across the administrative hierarchy. Certainly relationships such as this are complex and are not always easy, but the prevailing ethos is worth the work.

## CONCLUSION

In concluding this chapter, I bring the reader full circle—back to the student. We know from the surveys of students and alumni that being able to locate and use information is ranked at the top of their list of lifelong skills. Are we positioning our graduates to succeed in the next century? We know from leaders in industry that an information literate workforce is critical for our economy. The expectations are high. Are we addressing these twenty-first century needs? We learned from our library surveys that undergraduates place a high priority on instruction in the use of information.[12] We also know that students are looking to the faculty, librarians, their departments, and anyone who will listen for help. Are we answering the call? Our students come prepared to take advantage of the instruction we can provide. Eighty percent of our entering freshmen expected to have a computer in their residence. Ninety percent had used a word processor at least weekly during the past year, and 76 percent had used the Internet at least weekly. Although the majority of our students have good access to computers and experience using them, there remains the minority that do not. These students are in critical need of additional support.

There is no blueprint to follow to integrate information literacy across and beyond the institution. There are many models. Each environment is different with its own history and culture, people and personalities, resources and requirements. Although each institution presents unique circumstances, best practices described in this chapter can be used as models. In building integrated and collaborative approaches to information literacy, the following questions should guide implementation:

- How and with whom might you share the responsibility for the information literacy of your students?
- Where and how might you infuse your university and community with information literacy education?
- How can you build information literate communities?
- What approaches will be integrative and scaleable?
- What partnerships are needed?
- How can you articulate your work with K–12 and others?
- How will you know when your students have attained information fluency?
- Lastly, and perhaps most importantly, how can you prepare yourself for these responsibilities?

The need is great. The stakes are high. There is much to do. We will only be able to further the information literacy of our students and our communities through collaboration.

## Appendix 1
### Information Literacy I.Q. (Institutional Quotient) Test

This "I.Q." test is designed to help you determine the readiness of your institution in integrating information literacy into your curriculum. Respond to each statement by circling True or False. Total the number of true statements you have circled and compare your rating with the chart on the reverse side.

Librarians at your institution
- Librarians are teachers at my institution    True   False
- Librarians are engaged in curriculum planning
  (e.g., serve on institutional curriculum committees)   True   False

Recognition of the importance of information literacy
- My campus has developed a definition of
  information literacy    True   False
- Information literacy is evident in our campus
  planning documents, such as strategic plans   True   False
- Campus administrators are committed to the
  importance of information literacy   True   False
- Faculty accept/partake in responsibility for
  information literacy education   True   False
- There are support and rewards for faculty who
  develop and redesign curriculum to include
  concepts of information literacy   True   False

Learning/teaching infrastructure
- My institution engages in resource-based or
  problem-based learning   True   False
- My campus encourages a climate of collaboration   True   False
- Teaching modalities are student centered, with
  an emphasis on active learning   True   False
- Collaboration exists among curricula designers,
  faculty, librarians, academic advisors, and
  computing staff   True   False

Information infrastructure
- My campus is fully networked   True   False
- The library offers a variety of digital and print
  information resources in quantity and scope   True   False

*Total Number of True Responses*    _____

*Your I.Q. score (sum of all the statements marked True) provides a relative ranking of where your institution may be in terms of developing an information literacy program. The following chart is prepared to assist you in moving your institution forward with an information literacy program, based on your I.Q. score.*

*If your total score is:*

1–3     You are taking "First Steps." Why not initiate a local discussion about the value and role of information literacy on your campus?

- Invite someone from a model program to assist you in beginning the discussion.
- Identify and share some articles on information literacy.
- Consult selected Web sites on information literacy.
- Survey what's being done at your institution.
- Learn about your regional accreditation requirements for information literacy.
- Articulate information literacy as a top priority.

4–6     You are "On Your Way." Why not form a campus committee or utilize an existing committee, such as a teaching, learning, and technology roundtable, to address information literacy?

- Define information literacy in your environment.
- Develop a program proposal for information-literacy education.
- Identify faculty–librarian development opportunities or propose them.

7–9     You are "Experimenting." Why not implement a pilot assessment project?

- Examine "best practices" at institutions similar to your own.
- Construct an assessment tool.
- Consider scaleability.
- Develop cost models.

10–11   You are "Full Speed Ahead." Why not consider establishing a fully developed information-literacy program?

- Provide an evaluation of the pilot program.
- Clearly articulate the goals of a fully developed information-literacy program to faculty and students alike.
- Construct a mechanism for continual evaluation and renewal.
- Establish and/or reallocate permanent resources and staffing.

12+     You have a "Model Program." Why not consider sharing your information literacy program as a model program?

- Give a paper at a professional meeting (e.g., AAHE, EDU-CAUSE, ACRL, a conference in a discipline).
- Write an article on both your successes and failures.
- Maintain a Web site that is linked to the Institute for Information Literacy (IIL) Web site <http://www.ala.org/acrl/nili/>.
- Publicize your success and share your experiences.

Designed by Cerise Oberman, Plattsburgh State University
of New York, and Lizabeth A. Wilson, University of Washington
©1998

# NOTES

1. Department of Labor, Secretary's Commission on Achieving Necessary Skills. *What Work Requires of Schools: A SCANS Report for America 2000* (Washington, D.C.: U.S. Department of Labor, 1991).

2. Gerald M. Gillmore, "Ratings of Competence: From New Freshman to Ten-Year Alumni." *OEA Research Reports, 1999* <http://www.washington.edu/oea/9912.htm> [accessed 13 February 2000].

3. American Association of School Librarians and the Association of Educational Communications and Technology, *Information Power: Building Partnerships for Learning* (Chicago: American Library Association, 1998).

4. American Library Association, Presidential Commission on Information Literacy. *Final Report* (Chicago: American Library Association, 1989), 1.

5. National Research Council, Commission on Physical Sciences, Mathematics, and Applications; Committee on Information Technology Literacy; Computer Science and Telecommunications Board, *Being Fluent with Information Technology.* (Washington, D.C.: National Academy Press, 1999) <http://www.nap.edu/readingroom/books/BeFIT> [accessed 13 February 2000].

6. Jeremy J. Shapiro and Shelley K. Hughes, "Information Technology as a Liberal Art," *Educom Review* (March–April 1996): 31–35. The same article can be found on the *Educom Review* Web site under the revised title of "Information Literacy as a Liberal Art," <http://www.educause.edu/pub/er/review/reviewArticles/31231.html> [accessed 13 February 2000].

7. Mark C. Donovan and Anne E. Zald, "Defining Moments: The Role of Information Literacy in the Twenty-First Century Construct of Education," presented at the Association of College and Research Libraries, Instruction Section Think Tank III: Information Literacy and the Technological Transformation of Higher Education, New Orleans, June 24–25, 1999.

8. Stephen C. Ehrmann, "Asking the Right Questions: What Does Research Tell Us about Technology and Higher Learning?" *Change* (March–April 1995): 21–27.

9. Arthur W. Chickering and Zelda Gamson, "Seven Principles for Good Practices in Undergraduate Education," *AAHE Bulletin* (March 1987): 3–7.

10. Arthur W. Chickering and Stephen C. Ehrmann, "Implementing the Seven Principles: Technology as Lever," *AAHE Bulletin* (October 1996): 3–6.

11. Catalyst can be viewed at <http://www.washington.edu/uwired/catalyst> [accessed 13 February 2000].

12. Complete survey results are available at <http://www.lib.washington.edu/surveys/> [accessed 13 February 2000].

# 2

# Strategies to Make the Library an Instructional Partner on Campus

*Sally Kalin and Loanne Snavely*

Among several challenges facing academic/research libraries, one of the greatest involves ensuring that libraries have a prominent place in higher-education institutions. This challenge has been greatest during efforts to improve and promote information literacy. Higher education's transformation by technology has led to new models of instruction. As these develop, libraries cannot afford to be complacent; they must be partners in this process.

Our institution, Penn State University, is very large, with twenty-five campuses, a student enrollment of 80,000, and 4,000 faculty. To position the University Libraries as a visible partner in the university's changing educational mission, librarians are learning to be politically savvy, proactive, and more assertive about exploring new partnerships on campus.

Have we been successful? Not every time, far more so than if we had waited—possibly forever—to be asked for our ideas or for contributions. We'd like to share some of our experiences.

## FINDING THE LIBRARY'S PLACE IN THE UNIVERSITY'S STRATEGIC PLAN

Daily activities so involve us at times that we miss opportunities to examine the broader institution and how we fit into it.

For example, while working on the libraries' self-assessment document for an accreditation review, we sought wording in official university documents to which we could relate our statements. During

18

this process, we discovered something that we had overlooked before. Inside the front cover of the university's *Strategic Plan* was a list of goals for Penn State. The fourth goal was to create "world-class teachers and learners." This wording has been used frequently since its discovery, for it is clear that a "world-class learner" must know how to learn and therefore must be information literate. The corollary, then, is that the librarians, in partnership with university faculty, students, and staff, have a vital role to play in the educational process. Using the wording in the *Strategic Plan* has helped others to better understand our role in Penn State's educational process and mission. Every institution of higher education has statements about mission, goals, and strategic directions. Examining these for wording that supports the library's goals is an essential effort. Further, we should engage our administrations and faculty colleagues in active discussions on these goals. One of the ways to achieve this is by identifying our "shared" language.

## COMMUNICATING WITH CAMPUS COLLEAGUES

***Via raising visibility.***    Librarians need to explore every avenue that promotes their visibility. Again, this requires assertiveness. To develop recognition for the concept of information literacy and to ensure that faculty associate the term information literacy with the library, we mailed every faculty member a one-page newsletter entitled *Information Literacy and the Library*. It was brief and to the point, and offered information and assistance. We've also taken every opportunity to show off our Web-based instructional modules. For example, the Center for Academic Computing sponsors an annual Teaching and Learning Conference, which is an ideal opportunity for librarians to network with other instructional leaders on campus.

***Via networking.***    Personal networking also is critical. Librarians must get out into the campus community, talk to people, and take advantage of opportunities to gain recognition for the library's programs and initiatives. For example, a Penn State Faculty Senate committee authored a report that inadequately addressed the issue of information literacy. We sent a letter expressing our concerns but also invited the committee chair to lunch. This action provided an opportunity to discuss the issues in depth, and to establish a closer bond than a letter or phone conversation could have.

As librarians, we must interact with campus faculty and administrators and establish ourselves as fellow colleagues and professionals. We must be evangelists, participating in the instructional dialogue so that we can inform the teaching faculty of the realities and dispel the myths about the libraries.

## BEING PART OF WHAT'S HAPPENING ON CAMPUS

***Locate and become involved in initiatives.***   Librarians should track new instructional initiatives and become involved in what's happening. Two years ago, Penn State initiated a major revamping of its general education requirements. Fortunately for the libraries, a librarian was appointed to the General Education Task Force. She was successful in getting information literacy on the committee's agenda, which opened the door for further involvement by the libraries. We moved proactively, appointing an Information Literacy Task Force to parallel efforts in other colleges. When the university asked colleges to prepare an implementation plan, we did too—even though no one expected the libraries to respond. Our plan outlined the challenges we would face with several hundred new first-year seminars and the new emphasis on information literacy. When a general call went out for comments on a white paper on general education, we not only commented but requested changes. We made phone calls, pushing to have a library representative named to the General Education Implementation Team. Throughout this process, we did not wait to be asked to participate, but assumed that we were part of the new initiative and acted accordingly. Did our approach work? For the most part, yes. One positive outcome was funding from the provost for two new library faculty positions that were to be committed to instructional programs.

***The Libraries and the World Campus.***   Penn State, long a national leader in continuing and independent learning, founded a World Campus to develop new Web-based distance education programs for a burgeoning and competitive market. No librarians were appointed to the curricular teams. We visited the director of the World Campus to offer him *resources*—library faculty who would willingly contribute their expertise and time to making the World Campus successful. A director charged with starting a major new undertaking has difficulty turning down resources. He accepted our offer, enabling librarians to become involved in creating the nascent World Campus and accompanying Web-based courses. Clearly, a proactive approach nets positive results.

## INITIATING PARTNERSHIPS ON CAMPUS

***Colloquy.***   Each year Penn State holds a forum for 250 faculty, students, and staff to come together to explore instructional issues and share ideas. This "colloquy" occurs on a day between semesters when classes are not in session. Opportunities to engage in dialogue across the entire educational community are not common in our large university, so the community looks forward to this special day all year long.

When the 1999 program was announced, we were thrilled to see information literacy as one of three topics selected for the day's discussion. Unknowingly, we had set the stage for this. During the previous semester, we met with the director of the Center for Excellence in Learning and Teaching (CELT), who also happened to be the chair of the colloquy planning committee. We had discussed information literacy, its importance for the students, and the critical need to have a dialogue with faculty on these issues. While the purpose of that meeting was to see how CELT and the libraries could work together, it clearly had planted a seed in the director's mind.

The surprise was that we were not invited at first to play a role in the colloquy, so we approached the program chair to let her know how delighted we were to have information literacy as a topic, and asked to be involved. The result? Ten librarians were asked to facilitate the information literacy sessions. This gave us lots of visibility, credibility, and the opportunity to introduce and guide a discussion with many campus faculty on integrating information literacy into the curriculum.

***Establishing partnerships is key.***   We've forged other partnerships. A librarian has been a member of the Educational Technology Services Advisory Board and the Schreyer Institute for Innovation and Learning Advisory Board, and a librarian occupies a permanent position on the Faculty Senate Curricular Affairs Committee. With the dean's support, we successfully lobbied to have a librarian appointed to the Steering Committee for Penn State's new Teaching and Learning Consortium. She, in turn, was able to involve another librarian on an influential group. Librarians voluntarily teach sessions for the Center for Academic Computing's annual "Summerfest" and "Winterfest" technology course offerings for faculty and successfully compete to present at the annual Teaching and Learning with Technology Symposium. Librarians also participated in planning, implementation, and curriculum development for Penn State's new School of Information Science and Technology.

## OBTAINING FUNDING IN AN ERA OF CUTBACKS

It's a fact that many of our best ideas require money. As budgets shrink, we need to aggressively seek new sources of funding.

***Internal funding initiatives.***   To implement new programs, many universities establish funding initiatives to entice participation and support from faculty. These incentive grants, although often small, can provide seed money for libraries to try new and different approaches to academic programs and services. Announcements of these grants are sent to colleges in anticipation of applications from teaching faculty and administrators.

Penn State has established several incentive grant programs to encourage innovative teaching, undergraduate education, and the integration of technology into instruction. Because information literacy is integral to the changing educational environment, the libraries have been assertive about applying for these grants and have been very successful. Grants have been received to support the design of an educational program for teaching faculty; design a credit course for an honors program; pay for a graphic designer for our tutorials; scan archival resources for use by first-year seminars; create tutorials in business, music, and legislative research; and redesign a course on chemistry resources. We believe that our success resides in proposing different approaches to instruction and in attuning projects to serve the broadest audience possible.

But we must be diligent about keeping our eyes open for any and all funding opportunities. In another case, a major corporation gave Penn State a substantial grant to fund innovative projects in distance education. A form letter sent to all deans, including the dean of libraries, invited applications. We responded with a project proposal. The unit administering the grant indicated that the libraries were not eligible because the grants were only for teaching faculty. We countered by arguing that our dean had received a letter of invitation and insisted that librarians were faculty who made important contributions to distance education and could make more. Finally, the unit acquiesced and allowed us to participate. We proved our importance to the project through our commitment, high level of participation, and the quality of our product. We have done things that would not have been otherwise possible without this funding.

**Fund-raising.**    In addition to internal university funding, librarians should consider fund-raising as a means of supporting instructional programs. Working with the libraries' development staff has been another important avenue for generating support. Informing the development division thoroughly about the value of instructional programs and information literacy enables it to represent these ideas and needs to potential donors.

People who give to higher education like to support learning, so these can be appealing areas for contributions to the library. Prior to Penn State's $1 billion campaign effort, a consulting firm conducted a survey to determine what potential donors preferred to support financially. Survey results indicated that undergraduate and graduate education were the most favored areas for contributions.

These results have proven correct in donations to the libraries' instructional programs. Our most successful effort in securing donor funding for instruction has led to graduate assistantships and a faculty associate. A young Penn State graduate who started a very successful software consulting company loved the idea of having an impact on student learning, and so funded graduate assistantships in information literacy. In the first year, two graduate assistantships were devoted to the development of instructional modules called "Information Literacy and You." The modules are currently in the final stages of completion.

The other aspect of this particular gift has been periodic six-week visits to the libraries by employees of the donor's company. We call them "faculty associates." These intelligent young people, mostly new Ivy League graduates at the top of their class, receive a great deal of training from their company. Their technical expertise is then partnered with that of librarians on instructional projects that can take advantage of each member's unique skills. For example, one faculty associate developed a Web-based program to collect instruction statistics utilizing his ColdFusion software expertise.

***Foundations.*** Another major source of funding is foundation grants. We have found that a close working relationship with the development staff is critical to seeking such funding when the opportunity arises. As a result of such exchanges between development and the libraries, for example, a major foundation is providing funding for equipment for the instructional technology classrooms in the new Paterno Library.

## CONCLUSION

Achieving visibility on a university campus requires a series of small successes, inevitably peppered with some setbacks. At Penn State, we are constantly looking for ways involving technology to achieve our ultimate goal of information literacy for all Penn State students.

We have also learned that we must continually engage the university so that we play a significant role in meeting Penn State's instructional mission. While this is sometimes difficult, we cannot afford not to do it. In describing some of our experiences, we hope to inspire other librarians to explore new avenues, take risks, and become partners in their institutions' instructional missions.

# 3

## The Principle Is Partnership: General Education Library Instruction at Illinois State University

*Lisa Janicke Hinchliffe and Patricia Meckstroth*

### INTRODUCTION

General education courses provide an excellent opportunity for reaching undergraduate students and providing them with basic library and information skills and instruction. Unfortunately, in many cases, students may delay enrollment in basic general education courses, preferring instead to take classes in their chosen major fields. As a result, library instruction designed for the new first-year student is given to the second-semester senior who rightfully observes that "I should have learned this when I was a freshman." For many years, librarians at Illinois State University struggled with this scenario. Fortunately, the implementation of a sequential, integrated General Education Program has now enabled the development of a sequential, integrated General Education Library Instruction Program.

### GENERAL EDUCATION AT ILLINOIS STATE UNIVERSITY

For the past several years, Illinois State University has been involved in an effort to strengthen undergraduate education by redesigning the university's general education program. Like many other universities, for nearly twenty years Illinois State had a distribution-style program that required students to choose 15 courses across 8 categories out of nearly 300 possible courses. In contrast, the new program, which was implemented in fall 1998, is a structured, integrated program divided into three "cores."

In the Inner Core, students take courses that develop their writing, communication, and reasoning skills and their science and mathematical literacy. In the Middle Core, the courses are nontraditional interdisciplinary courses built around five different category themes. Outer Core courses introduce students to methods and ideas in several academic disciplines. This new program is coordinated horizontally: courses in each core reinforce skills students are learning in other courses in that core. A prerequisite structure for courses also contributes to the vertical integration of the program: courses in the Middle Core build on what students have learned in the Inner Core, and the Outer Core in turn builds on the Middle Core.

Overall, the general education program not only has a new structure, but also is characterized by new teaching and learning dynamics. General education courses do not use textbooks but instead are resource-based. Teachers employ new pedagogies that contribute to active learning by students. Students write often and work on projects in small groups. At this public university with about 20,000 students, nearly 3,000 of whom are freshmen, general education is a large-scale undertaking. Yet nearly all general education courses are taught in small classes or in lecture/breakout–discussion-group formats.

Developing this new program was an extended campus-wide process occurring over a period of many years. In the early nineties, the academic senate of the university adopted a new general education philosophy statement and a set of student learning objectives that formed the basis for the new program. A faculty/administrative committee developed a detailed proposal for the new program, and the senate approved a three-year pilot for the proposal. A university faculty Pilot Implementation Committee, which included a librarian, was established to oversee course development and the piloting process. The pilot program was initiated with faculty committees developing proposals for each of the Inner Core courses that were then offered to students on an experimental basis. Course development committees articulated specific goals and objectives for each course, planned course content, and identified appropriate pedagogies. During the three-year piloting process, many Middle Core and some Outer Core course proposals were also developed and piloted.

After extensive evaluation by students, faculty, and administrators, the program was modified slightly and then approved by the academic senate for full implementation in fall 1998. The program is administered by a director of General Education working with two advisory faculty committees: the Council on General Education, which serves as the curriculum review committee and determines policy, and the General Education Coordinating Committee, which addresses coordination of courses within and across categories of the program and deals with practical implementation issues. A librarian sits on each of these committees.

## LIBRARY INSTRUCTION PROGRAM

Built into the sequenced and integrated General Education Program is a sequenced and integrated library instruction program. If the General Education Program did not have the structure that it has, the success of the General Education Library Instruction Program would not be possible.

Five of the courses or course categories in the General Education Program have an information literacy objective:

> Students will be able to collect, analyze, synthesize, and evaluate information and argument from a range of sources appropriate to specific problems.

The courses/course categories are

- Foundations of Inquiry (Inner Core Course)
- Language and Composition (Inner Core Course)
- Language and Communication (Inner Core Course)
- Language in the Humanities (Middle Core Category)
- Quantitative Reasoning (Middle Core Category)

These five courses/course categories have been targeted for library and information literacy instruction. The resulting General Education Library Instruction Program is integrated into the General Education Program as well as customized to the circumstances of specific courses.

All Foundations of Inquiry classes have one or more course-integrated instruction sessions to develop basic information literacy skills and competencies. The students are also required to take an in-person or virtual tour of the library to develop familiarity and comfort with the library facilities. Instruction for Language and Communication is a course-related, outside-of-class workshop focusing on the research process. Research instruction for Language and Composition is course-integrated but only offered on an as-requested basis. The library instruction coordinator directly coordinates and manages these instructional offerings.

Library instruction for Language in the Humanities and Quantitative Reasoning courses is also offered on an as-requested basis; however, teaching faculty work directly with the subject librarians to arrange the needed sessions.

## PARTNERSHIPS

Two types of partnerships have developed in the General Education Library Instruction Program. First, coordinator–coordinator partnerships, in which a course/course category coordinator and the library instruction coordinator work together to develop programmatic approaches.

Second, faculty–librarian partnerships, in which faculty members teaching classes work with a librarian to develop assignments and instruction to meet the needs of a particular class.

The most successful component of the General Education Library Instruction Program is the Foundations of Inquiry library instruction. The Foundations of Inquiry course, the cornerstone of the new general education program, is required of all entering freshmen in their first semester and is designed to introduce students to college-level intellectual inquiry. It focuses on the development of critical thinking; analytical and reflective reading, speaking, and writing; and skill application in addressing topics in several disciplines. Students practice reasoning by participating in discussions, debates, and symposiums, and completing numerous writing assignments. They must do research to obtain supporting evidence for the arguments they present in any of these activities. The course is taught in small sections of thirty students, and faculty interact extensively with students.

Foundations of Inquiry library instruction has been overwhelmingly successful. One hundred percent of the faculty teaching in fall 1998 and 97 percent in fall 1999 brought their classes for library instruction. A substantial chapter on library research is included in *The Foundations Book*, the required text for all Foundations of Inquiry classes. Foundations of Inquiry library instruction is supported by both a strong coordinator–coordinator partnership and highly collaborative faculty–librarian partnerships.

Language and Communication and Language and Composition library instruction is characterized by coordinator–coordinator partnerships with very limited faculty–librarian contact. Partnerships in Language in the Humanities and Quantitative Reasoning are still developing but will likely have both coordinator–coordinator and faculty–librarian partnerships, though less strong than those relationships supporting Foundations of Inquiry.

## FACTORS INFLUENCING DEVELOPMENT

Five factors influenced the development of the partnerships in the General Education Library Instruction Program: course planning, course goals and objectives, course instructors, administrative structure, and instructor training and development.

The interdisciplinary course development committees for Foundations of Inquiry, Language and Communication, and Language and Composition all included at least one librarian, which allowed librarians the opportunity to work with the teaching faculty to develop course goals and objectives that specifically related to aspects of information literacy. Because these specific goals and objectives were then integrated into course documents (e.g., syllabi, outlines, and assignments), library instruction is also integrated into the fabric of the courses. Librarians were not formally involved with the development of the courses in the Language in the Humanities and Quantitative Reasoning categories and thus, although the courses adhere to common course category goals, these goals are very broad and lack explicit linkages with library instruction services.

When the course instructors are tenured, tenure-line, or full-time adjunct members of the faculty, faculty–librarian partnerships have developed or are developing. However, in cases where the course instructors are primarily teaching assistants, only coordinator–coordinator partnerships have developed. Similarly, the coordinator–coordinator partnerships have been affected by the administrative structure of a course/course category and the strength of the partnership parallels the leadership strength of the course/course category coordinator.

Finally, both coordinator–coordinator and faculty–librarian partnerships have been stronger in circumstances in which instructor training and development is provided to the instructors and in which the librarians participate as either presenters or participants.

## ORGANIZATIONAL EFFECTIVENESS

For three years, Lisa Janicke Hinchliffe, a member of the Pilot Implementation Committee (one of the authors of this chapter) also served as an assistant to the dean of undergraduate studies and then in the newly created position of acting director of general education. From this campus-wide and administrative perspective, she was able to observe the ways in which the General Education Program and the related General Education Library Instruction Program have evolved and to identify some of the librarian behaviors that contributed to the unusually high degree of successful integration of library instruction into general education: (1) library faculty advocated before the senate and the deans the creation of library positions on all key program and course development committees and filled each of these positions with a librarian with relevant experience or academic subject expertise; (2) librarians participated at the earliest stages in defining goals and learning objectives for the program and sustained that participation throughout the long process of determining what would actually be taught in courses; (3) librarians on committees kept their sights on "the big picture" and rose above territorial disputes to facilitate workable compromises while retaining the integrity of the program; (4) librarians presented themselves to faculty as partners in the teaching endeavor, as information and research experts who had crucial skills and knowledge to offer in support of faculty teaching and student learning. For all faculty members teaching the Foundations of Inquiry course, for example, the library offered a "personal librarian" to work with them and their students; (5) Milner Library, just like the other colleges, also contributes its share of faculty to teach Foundations of Inquiry sections. Library faculty who teach Foundations of Inquiry and librarians who serve as "personal librarians" to Foundations of Inquiry faculty participate and serve as presenters in faculty development workshops; (6) the library instruction coordinator, Patricia Meckstroth, makes use of her position on the administrative General Education Coordinating Committee to establish and broaden positive working relationships with other faculty and to further develop the library instruction program.

As a result of these kinds of proactive efforts on the part of librarians, it is clear at the campus level that library faculty at Illinois State are respected by other faculty and that the appropriate climate has been created for continued faculty–librarian partnerships.

## FUTURE DEVELOPMENTS

The new General Education Program has brought about many opportunities for the General Education Library Instruction Program at Illinois State University. Further developments are, however, necessary and likely. In particular, the planned strengthening of the administrative structure and the instructor training and development in the Middle Core course categories will further strengthen existing, though in some cases fledgling, partnerships. Likewise, efforts will continue to expand and refine library instruction offerings for Language and Communication and Language and Composition. Current emphasis on assessment in both the General Education Program and the Library Instruction Program is also expected to provide additional information about areas for improvement and areas of strength in current offerings.

# 4

# Navigating Knowledge Together: Faculty–Librarian Partnerships in Web-Based Learning

*Joyce A. Meldrem, Carolyn Johnson, and Carol Spradling*

A multilevel partnership strategy builds successful collaborations between faculty and librarians in academic communities. With the growing range of information retrieval products, librarians have the perfect opportunity to demonstrate the educational benefits of librarian–faculty cooperation. Faculty members welcome and need guidance regarding copyright issues, credible Web sites, and searching for precise, accurate, and relevant information. Especially in regard to the Web, many faculty members "feel overwhelmed by the size and complexity of the Internet and are reluctant to spend their valuable time making sense of it."[1]

Course content and student learning increases in value through the information literacy knowledge and skills that a librarian shares with faculty and students. It is beneficial for librarians and faculty to develop partnerships where librarians become an integral part of the electronic teaching and learning process. As a result of these partnerships, librarians and faculty codevelop and design effective course materials, such as on-line research tutorials, on-line assessments, and course Web pages.

Electronic learning environments increasingly provide new partnership opportunities to foster collaborative alliances between faculty and librarians.[2] Partnering strategies include informal dialogues with faculty, formal presentations at departmental meetings, faculty–librarian teaching teams, freshman year experience participation, university committee appointments, and cutting-edge working group memberships.

## INFORMAL DIALOGUES

Informal conversations are often ignored when developing partnership strategies but should not be overlooked or underestimated in value. Everyday, casual conversations build trust with faculty. Conversing before university committee meetings, at campus lectures, in the student union, before department and/or college meetings, and at social or athletic events can foster working relationships. In addition, at Northwest Missouri State University, a Faculty Office Call service is offered in which librarians will visit faculty members' offices and informally talk with them about information literacy and retrieval strategies to enhance their research and teaching. Conversely, during the librarians' office hours, faculty often drop by or call with information requests or questions about curriculum development. Once a librarian has assisted with a request, the faculty member recognizes the value of the contribution and often returns with additional requests.

## FORMAL PRESENTATIONS

Faculty and librarian partnerships can also be encouraged through formal presentations. During Northwest faculty development days, librarians have offered Web page creation workshops, Internet and database searching techniques, and brainstorming sessions about Web-based curriculum materials. They have also provided campus sessions on copyright and intellectual property issues, team management, and Web-based instruction. The librarians are asked to participate in biannual college meetings and other departmental meetings where the library's services and resources are marketed. This arrangement began through contacts the library director made with college deans.

Traditional and on-line library instruction is conducted in class sessions upon request and for targeted classes where a need for improved information literacy skills is recognized. Campus faculty have also attended summer library workshops that are offered for our regional business and education community. Through this exposure to our instructional expertise, librarians have received additional requests for formal library instruction.

## ACADEMIC COURSES

Collaborative alliances can also be built through course development. Northwest librarians have taught both entire courses and modules within a course. For example, because a Northwest librarian taught

Freshman Seminar (our freshman orientation course), the library staff was requested to assist in integrating information research skills into the required freshman seminar curriculum. A library representative has also been added to the Freshman Seminar planning committee because of the contributions of this librarian. A similar experience occurred in Northwest's required general education computer literacy course. The computer literacy faculty recognized the benefits of consulting with the library staff in planning the course curriculum and materials and began consulting them and requesting their assistance on a regular basis in developing course materials. For additional examples of this practice at other universities, see Wade Kotter's article on librarian–faculty relations.[3]

As librarians become an integral part of the teaching and learning process, team teaching becomes a natural outcome. An instructor who was developing a new course entitled Web-Based Teaching requested assistance from an information librarian. During this consultation process, the instructor recognized the librarian's expertise on certain Web-based content areas and invited the librarian to team teach the new course. The students also appreciated the unique perspective that the librarian brought to the Web-Based Teaching course.

Participation in the development and delivery of course modules is another successful method for partnering. At Northwest, librarians have created information literacy modules for English Composition, Freshman Seminar, Fundamentals of Oral Communication, and Using Computers. Through brainstorming sessions the librarians have developed many imaginative presentation methods to introduce their educational objectives for information literacy to key faculty members. For example, to initiate contact with English Composition faculty, librarians hosted a high tea complete with scones and cucumber sandwiches. From the discussion during the event, librarians then developed a library research strategy module for the English Composition course. The librarians gather information annually from faculty focus groups, surveys, and discussions to improve the instructional content and delivery of the modules.

## UNIVERSITY COMMITTEES

University committee appointments are essential for improving visibility and fostering peer relationships between teaching faculty and library faculty. Even librarians who do not have faculty status can increase their visibility by participating in university committees in an ex officio capacity. Conversations between colleagues can lead to an enhanced understanding of student needs, assessment strategies, and instructional methods.

## WORK GROUPS

Many ad hoc work groups form on university campuses in addition to official university committees. On Northwest's campus, several of these groups touch on technology and information literacy issues. Librarians offer a unique perspective to issues such as distance education, modular learning, quality processes, copyright, intellectual property, and on-line learning. For example, Northwest librarians are asked on a regular basis to share their knowledge regarding copyright resources and issues with the university administration and faculty. In particular, partnerships are formed with instructional technologists when planning for on-line learning or developing curriculum. Copyright information is also delivered to these constituencies through presentations, bibliographies, and webliographies.

## INSTRUCTIONAL PRODUCTS

As a result of many different department and faculty partnerships, Northwest librarians have developed the course-related and educational materials listed below. They also work to maintain and nurture partnerships to continually improve the quality of these instructional materials.

### Both Sides of the Issue
<http://www.nwmissouri.edu/library/courses/speech/procon.html>

This Web site is used in English and Speech general education courses and provides information on how to research controversial or pro/con topics. It covers both print and Web sources and suggests keywords for periodical article searches.

### Computer Science Senior Seminar Research Guide
<http://www.nwmissouri.edu/library/courses/computers/csis.html>

This Web site contains links that are pertinent to research in the field of computer science, such as on-line searching strategies, on-line resources, and citing Internet sources. The research guide was developed by a librarian and is used by computer science faculty in their curriculum.

### Copyright Resources
<http://www.nwmissouri.edu/library/courses/copyright/resources.html>

This Web site supplies references to print materials and annotated hyperlinks to Web sites regarding copyrighted materials and educational fair-use issues. Faculty preparing on-line curriculum materials use this Web site. When coupled with copyright scenarios prepared by the librarians, it is used in courses and presentations to empower faculty members to locate their own answers to copyright questions.

### Course/Subject Resources
<http://www.nwmissouri.edu/library/courses/courses.htm>

Features of this Web page include subject bibliographies of print and electronic resources, Web-based instructional resources for selected courses, and research guides for specific fields of study. The librarians use this Web page as the library's curriculum clearinghouse Web page. It is used for undergraduate and graduate instructional sessions, for reference services, for research consultations, for faculty office calls, and for presentations.

### Distance Education <http://www.nwmissouri.edu/library/courses/education2/distance.htm>

This page features links to distance education resources, journals, associations, and institutions; Web sites regarding evaluation and assessment of on-line learning; and Web sites covering academic freedom, intellectual property, faculty workload, and copyright. It also includes access to authoring, programming, and page maintenance tools, and educational software; Web sites regarding learning styles, learning style tests, and learning theories; Web sites for library programs and librarians; and examples of higher education and K–12 instructional pages. As teaching faculty become involved in distance education, this resource is used to provide answers, examples, and background information.

### Evaluating Web Site Criteria and Assignment <http://www.nwmissouri.edu/library/courses/usingcomputers/eval.html>

This on-line tutorial allows students to develop special skills needed when evaluating Web sites. It was developed by Owens Library and is used in a computer literacy course taken by all Northwest students.

### Faculty Office Calls
<http://www.nwmissouri.edu/library/services/officecalls.htm>

Public services staff at Owens Library provide one-on-one reference assistance to Northwest faculty members. During a personalized "office call," librarians explore academic library resources from the faculty member's office.

Hot Paper Topics <http://www.nwmissouri.edu/library/courses/
english2/termindex.htm>

This Web site is used in English and Speech general education courses
and is designed to help students generate ideas for position or persuasive papers or speeches. Topics and issues related to the curriculum
topics are listed.

Intellectual Property Resources <http://www.nwmissouri.edu/
library/courses/copyright/ipresources.htm>

This Web page supplies annotated hyperlinks to Web sites, sample institutional policies, and print materials regarding intellectual property
issues. As teaching faculty become involved in creating on-line course
materials, this resource is used to provide answers, examples, and
background information.

Research Tutorial
<http://www.nwmissouri.edu/library/courses/english/research.html>

The Web site features a tutorial used in English composition courses to
introduce users to basic information about research. The English Department and composition students provide librarians with feedback
on an annual basis.

SearchHut Tutorial
<http://www.nwmissouri.edu/library/search/hut/tutorial.html>

The Search Hut is an on-line tutorial about using specific keywords and
other search elements to locate text, visual, or audio sources on the
Web. The tutorial includes interactive quizzes and practice searches. It
was developed by a librarian and is used by the computer literacy
course taken by all Northwest students.

Web-Based Teaching <http://cite.nwmissouri.edu/courses/4459007/>
At the "Enter Network Password" window, type guest for both the
username and password.

This Web-based course investigates the pedagogy of Web-based
teaching, learning, and classroom materials. This course assists faculty in developing the necessary Internet skills and resources for
Web-based teaching. This one-hour course was team taught by faculty members in the Department of Computer Science/Information
Systems and Owens Library.

## CONCLUSION

The explosion of the information age and the Internet has encouraged librarians and faculty to develop partnerships that focus on common electronic learning environments. Faculty often need guidance regarding new information literacy issues. Librarians have a unique opportunity to provide workshops for faculty about new information literacy skills, to collaborate with faculty when integrating information literacy skills into the curriculum, and to participate in faculty work groups when planning new electronic learning environments. If faculty members are approached with creative and multifaceted partnering opportunities, faculty–librarian partnerships are not difficult to foster. The advances made in course content and student learning directly support the mission of higher education.

## NOTES

1. Deborah Wills, "Internet Tutorials for Faculty: Meeting Academic Needs," *RQ* 36, no. 3 (Spring 1997): 360.
2. Aletha D. Stahl, "What I Want in a Librarian," *Reference and User Services Quarterly* 37, no. 2 (Winter 1997): 133–35.
3. Wade R. Kotter, "Bridging the Great Divide: Improving Relations between Librarians and Classroom Faculty," *Journal of Academic Librarianship* 25, no. 4 (July 1999): 299–300.

# 5

# Anatomy of an Outreach Program: Outreach at the UCSD Libraries

*Maggie Houlihan and Duffy Tweedy*

In August 1997, the University of California, San Diego (UCSD) Library established a formal outreach program to meet goals and objectives related to library services to undergraduates. This has presented the library with a powerful opportunity to try new ideas and initiatives, identify key areas for further action, and measure results. The outreach program is a work in progress, and outreach staff look forward to expanding and refining efforts to increase effectiveness.

## BACKGROUND

Historically, the UCSD library system has not had a systematic, coordinated outreach program. Outreach was sporadic at best and was never addressed on a library-wide level. Library campus-wide visibility has never been strong, in spite of the fact that the image of the main library building serves as the campus logo.

In 1994, a campus-wide Task Force on Library Services to Undergraduates, made up of faculty and librarians, was formed and concluded that (1) the library was doing some outreach, (2) large segments of the library's clientele were unaware of services, and (3) the library should try to identify ways to improve outreach and visibility to build upon their already strong base of services. Subsequent library discussions established the following objectives regarding outreach: a clearly articulated level of support for outreach, an active public relations/outreach program, coordination with other campus resources, and timely delivery of instruction. Although there was strong support for the establishment of an overall coordinator of outreach and instruction, the library management group opted for the establishment of three separate outreach positions—one each for the biomedical, science and engineering, and social sciences and humanities libraries. Only the biomedical position did not include an undergraduate outreach component. Between August 1997 and November 1998, the three positions were filled.

Another product of library-wide discussions was a campus-wide student survey conducted in 1996 to find out what students thought of the UCSD library system, its staff, and services. Students found the large, architecturally impressive Geisel library building (that houses the Social Sciences and Humanities Library and the Science and Engineering Library, among others) intimidating, the flickering lights a nuisance, and the temperature too cold. For the most part, students didn't think they needed library instruction. It was interesting to note, however, that students found instruction useful once they experienced it.

The job description for the Social Sciences and Outreach coordinator position was finalized six months after the incumbent started. As this was a brand-new position based on new concepts, it was felt that it would be most effective to develop the position on previously articulated priorities coupled with needs identified during the initial months. This turned out to be an extremely effective approach, as possibilities were kept wide open and the experience gained in these early months presented a clear idea of how the position should be structured.

Within months, outreach efforts were well under way, with great results. Networking extensively with other student service providers on campus was invaluable in gaining insight into the student culture and developing partnerships to work collaboratively to promote student academic enrichment.

## INITIAL CHALLENGES

The outreach positions were funded without a budget for corresponding activities, which made planning for and implementation of outreach initiatives difficult or impossible during the first year. A budget was developed for the second year and approved as a one-time allotment, but not until late October, a full month after the start of the fall quarter. This seriously curtailed fall outreach planning. In fiscal year 99/00, permanent funding was requested and granted during the summer. This fiscal accomplishment signaled that outreach and instruction was valued and becoming an integral part of the organization.

In addition to a lack of budget, coordination of outreach activities was lacking. The Social Sciences and Humanities Library Undergraduate outreach coordinator initially took this role through the Instruction and Outreach Committee to ensure that materials appropriate to all undergraduates were available at all events and represented in all outreach materials. Beginning fall 1999, the three outreach positions are coordinating their efforts and are providing full coverage for students from all majors.

Instruction and outreach have always been hampered by a lack of graphics expertise. Newsletters, ads, handouts, and other materials require the application of sophisticated graphics software, some of which, like PageMaker, have a very high learning curve and require creativity and knowledge of layout and graphics design. It was impossible to find all of this expertise within existing library staff, so we began investigating contracting this work. Based on recommendations from other campus colleagues, we have succeeded in contracting the layout of the *Navigator* (the library newsletter) and the creation of the *Guardian* (UCSD's student newspaper). Outsourcing has proven to be a cost-effective way to get projects completed.

Perhaps the most difficult and pervasive challenge, however, was entrenched attitudes about instruction and outreach. Comments such as "undergraduates are not the focus of an academic research library," "it won't work," "I don't have time to work on this," "the faculty will never give up class time for library instruction," were not uncommon. In addition, excellence and innovation in instruction does not always result in recognition and/or reward, nor does lack of outreach to faculty and graduate students necessarily result in discussion or concern.

This has contributed to a lack of overall coordination of the outreach efforts by subject bibliographers to their respective faculty and graduate students. Bibliographical responsibilities are highly decentralized and are performed with autonomy, and no forums exist to discuss and coordinate outreach and instruction to faculty and graduate students. It is almost impossible to get an accounting of who is doing what with their faculty and grads and what kinds of contacts are made. This has made it difficult to organize broad-based events for sharing information about new and existing library services and resources, which is extremely important when so much research and teaching is interdisciplinary. In addition, outreach efforts can be negated when a contact is made and a request for instruction is received, but the relevant bibliographer doesn't follow through. A mechanism needs to be developed for follow-up.

More generally, there seemed to be a lack of acceptance for the efforts required by all involved to make the library's programs successful. A great outreach program takes the support and participation of a lot of people. Many instruction and outreach professionals share the same experience: a lot of support exists for the effort, but the work falls on the shoulders of a very few. This includes things like writing articles for newsletters, participating in outreach events (that sometimes are held on weekends and evenings), making discipline-specific presentations on campus, and preparing discipline-specific handouts for various campus events that are suitable for outreach.

## ACCOMPLISHMENTS

The library's outreach program has grown quickly into a thriving, popular, visible part of campus life. The UCSD Library participates in a myriad of campus events, including the Welcome Week Student Services Fair, the Cross-Cultural Center Block Party, Admit Day, Preview Day, individual college orientations for new students and their parents, student forums, and various individual college fairs. Participation in these events has increased the library's visibility immensely. A substantial and attractive table covering/banner emblazoned with "UCSD Library" and the library logo is used at all tabling events. This combination table covering/banner creates a very professional and visible announcement of the library presence.

In addition to in-person presence, the library now uses campus media extensively. An advertisement is placed in the fall orientation issue of the *Guardian*, which is distributed widely throughout campus; in the campus-wide poster calendar; and the *Student Organizations and Leadership Opportunities Handbook*. Each year, all incoming students receive the calendar and the handbook. Feature articles about new library electronic resources, written by library staff, appeared in the *UCSD Times* (newsletter sent to all staff and faculty) and in *Grad-to-Grad* (newsletter sent to all graduate students each fall).

Aside from established campus publications, the library's own newsletter/calendar called the *Navigator*, launched in fall 1998, has been very well received. Articles highlight new databases, services, and programs, and instruction schedules for all the libraries are featured. The *Navigator* is important not only for its content, but also as a very professional and attractive publication. Anything the library can do to elevate its staid image is a bonus.

Recently the library staged a very successful first annual "Library Open House" for faculty and graduate students, featuring information on new resources and services, a chamber music miniconcert provided by talented musicians from UCSD's Music Library, and an opportunity to meet the new university librarian. Approximately 110 faculty and graduate students attended. This demonstrated the breadth of the outreach program; undergraduates are not the only ones on campus who need attention.

A "Welcome Students" banner is hung above the entrance to the Geisel library building every fall, and a"Good Luck with Finals" banner is put up during finals week each quarter. Each banner cost $125 for a total $250 investment, which has more than paid for itself in positive public relations.

Networking and collaborative relationships with various campus service providers are well established. These groups include the Women's Center, Cross-Cultural Center, OASIS (tutoring services), Center for Teaching Development, and the Career Services Center. Areas of common concern have been identified and reciprocal support provided. For instance, the library presented a program on Designing Effective Library Assignments for Teaching Assistants in a special teaching enhancement effort offered through the Center for Teaching Development. Mailing lists have been shared. Some student services staff now make focused referrals to individuals in the library rather than just sending students "to the library, " and we advertise each others' services whenever feasible.

Customized On-Line Research Skills sessions are held for staff from various campus offices, including Student Affirmative Action, Office for Sexual Harassment Prevention and Policy, Staff Affirmative Action, Human Relations Advisory Board, and Dean's Office. The sessions have been well received as participants have learned how to use myriad library resources and services from their office and home workstations, most of which were new to them. They have also become advocates for the UCSD Library.

The undergraduate outreach coordinator participated in a campuswide forum for students to share their campus experiences with key student service providers. This event was organized by the vicechancellor for student affairs, the Associated Students of UCSD, and the Graduate Student Association. The library and the need for mandatory library research skills training were discussed at length. An advertisement for this event was placed in the *Guardian*, but the library was not listed as a participant. The vice-chancellor sponsoring the forum was called and welcomed library participation. (Outreach staff read the *Guardian* every week to see what's going on with students and have found great opportunities there). The discussion resulted in a commitment from the vice-chancellor to work together for student academic enrichment. This turned out to be an excellent opportunity for networking and gaining library visibility.

Library participation is now a part of Homecoming—a big campuswide event involving current and past students, faculty, and staff, and the community. A social sciences and humanities librarian presented a session on the on-line reference shelf he created, which was well attended and received.

All this activity has led to increased requests for library instruction for students from faculty and teaching assistants teaching core undergraduate courses and upper division courses. These workshops have been well received and we are providing instruction to thousands of students per year.

Outreach was incorporated into the Instructional Services Advisory Action Committee, resulting in a new title, Instruction and Outreach Committee (IOC), and a new focus on outreach. This group manages the new, permanent budget. As stated above, the significance of having a permanent budget cannot be exaggerated. However hardworking the outreach staff, money changes everything.

## FUTURE PLANS

While outreach has had success using campus media, more could be done in this area. The library should be in the calendar section in the *Guardian*, on the marquee at the Price Center Theater (also used to advertise campus events), on the electronic billboard in the campus shuttles, and in public service announcements on the student-run radio station. In particular, there may be an opportunity for collaboration with the editorial staff of the *Guardian*. The editorial staff has been approached with an idea to let the library contribute a monthly column featuring information about new electronic resources available through the library and other related items. In addition, outreach staff will be in contact with the *Guardian* and the *UCSD Times* with library-related news of interest to students, staff, and faculty. Both publications have indicated an interest in featuring stories about new developments in electronic resources and services made available by the library.

Similarly, while a start has been made regarding outreach to campus staff, a sustained effort needs to be made. The library needs to advertise its services and classes available to campus staff through campuswide electronic mailings. It is hoped that those who attend will become allies of the library and recommend library programs and classes to students and faculty.

One interesting idea for increasing the quality, as opposed to the quantity, of the library's media presence involves having the library become a class project for a marketing class at a local college or junior college. This would result, hopefully, in ideas for a multifaceted media campaign from students for students. Likewise, outreach staff would like to solicit input from student focus groups to find out what incentives would be the most attractive and then implement a program of incentives to encourage undergraduate participation in our training sessions. Increasing the library's visibility does little good if the image is not one that appeals to students, and only students can judge that.

A new development being pursued is quarterly "Research in Focus" forums in the library that will feature a faculty member's latest research in an area of interest to UCSD students, staff, and other faculty. We already have commitments from three faculty members for the upcoming calendar year. As part of each event, outreach staff will coordinate the creation of a Web page that will highlight library resources relevant to the topic.

The instruction and outreach staff need to improve existing Web pages and develop new ones to more effectively advertise our services. On-line tutorials are needed so that students uncomfortable with computers and who want to learn to use library resources outside a classroom at their own pace and time can do so. The program has hired a student with substantial computer skills to provide both the needed technical ability and the student perspective as to what works.

The main effort will be to continue to increase contact with faculty and teaching assistants who are teaching core undergraduate courses and with staff in mentoring and tutoring programs to gain acceptance and support for the library's instructional programs. Three of the five colleges' writing programs require attendance at the library research skills orientation session created specifically for their college's writing assignments. The library is in negotiation with the other two colleges' writing program coordinators.

## CHALLENGES BEING ADDRESSED

One of the common challenges in library instruction is discovering the right mix of library classes for undergraduates. Instruction staff may know very accurately the skills students need, but that knowledge does no good if sessions are not packaged and marketed so that students will actually come in. Currently the library offers Library Survival Skills and On-Line Research Skills during Welcome Week and for the first seven weeks of each quarter. Attendance dies off after the first two weeks of the fall quarter, and is practically nonexistent at any time during the other quarters. The focus is on contacting faculty teaching high- and low-volume undergraduate classes to collaborate on designing a library session to support class research assignments. The literature and common sense agree that students are more motivated to learn research skills if they have a class paper requiring those skills.

Of course targeting lower-division research assignments will not be productive if these assignments become scarce. Some professors and one of the five colleges at UCSD are reducing or eliminating research paper assignments. It is not uncommon to find juniors and seniors who have yet to write a substantial research paper requiring synthesis of information in books and journals.

The greatest challenge, as with all library instruction units, is finding enough time to do all the work that could be done. Surely no library is well enough staffed and funded to do everything it would like to do for its patrons: on-line and paper guides, classes, appointments, and so on. The difficulty then is deciding which projects to take up and which to defer. By making greater use of focus groups and evaluation forms, UCSD Library hopes to be able to focus its outreach efforts where they are most effective.

## SUMMARY OF KEY POINTS TO SUCCESS

Certain themes stand out as key points in the success of outreach so far. It is essential to have acceptance from key library administrators, and at some point this needs to translate into a permanent budget controlled by the instruction/outreach personnel. An attractive library presence, on paper, on-line, and in person, is expensive. Nonetheless, outreach units must have adequate graphics support; if outreach looks bad, the library looks bad. Getting this financial and graphic support has allowed our library to produce a useful, valued product (a newsletter/calendar) consistently enough that it is now an accepted and expected part of campus.

Before cooperation can be sought among nonlibrary units, it must be solid in-house: it is important to have library-wide cooperation among outreach staff, and then work for cooperation with other campus student service providers and campus media. Outreach is everybody's business, and the more people involved in the library, the better. The library must become an integrated, normal part of campus life. Those involved in outreach need to think and work outside the library, to become familiar faces at campus events. Finally, they must not be afraid to make cold calls. Nothing ventured, nothing gained.

# 6

# Training College Faculty to Use World Wide Web Technologies in the Classroom

*Leslie Czechowski and R. Cecilia Knight*

Grinnell College is a small, highly selective, liberal arts college in central Iowa with approximately 1,300 undergraduate students and about 135 faculty. The library had seven faculty and fourteen full-time equivalent staff (eighteen people) in the fall of 1993. We now have one additional library faculty member.

In the fall of 1993 the Mellon Foundation invited many liberal arts colleges to develop proposals for how they would use Mellon monies to integrate technology into classroom activities to increase teaching efficiencies and to bring librarians and computer specialists together with classroom faculty in this effort. Grinnell's proposal included six different projects from different faculty groups, all of which included a librarian in the development. Two of the projects originated in the library, created with groups consisting of one librarian and several classroom faculty members.

This chapter examines the portion of the grant that involved using the Internet in teaching. The group, convened by a librarian, consisted of a political scientist, a sociologist, an economist, and a computer scientist/linguist. When we began to develop this proposal in the fall of 1993, we were talking about Gopher and FTPing datasets. We drew pictures illustrating the organization of the Internet and how it worked, and shared stories of hours wasted attempting to get data from FTP sites into our own computers in some sort of usable format. By the time we had rewritten the proposal a half dozen times in the fall of 1995, Mosaic, a graphical user interface that would facilitate work via the Internet, was available. The pace of change was almost incomprehensible.

## INITIAL STEPS, 1993-1995

The proposal comprised a variety of elements, including hiring an additional library faculty member to share the extra workload of doing week-long faculty workshops during the summers of 1996 and 1997, and becoming more active in collaborating with faculty in the classroom in using the Internet. The grant also included funding to hire an Instructional Multimedia Technology Specialist (IMTS). We currently have four of these positions on campus, one for each of the three divisions (Sciences, Humanities, and Social Studies), with an additional one for Fine Arts.

The grant was awarded late in the fall semester of 1995 and planning began on how we would meet our commitments under the grant. Over January break of 1996, the six librarians involved in the grant learned what we needed to know in order to be able to teach the identified skills to others (see table 1). Each librarian took one or two topics from the outline and learned how to teach it. Each morning for a week we had internal workshops where we either taught or learned a new skill, and then spent the afternoon practicing it or reading more about it. We felt that this pace would also work for most faculty members and we found that we could also trade off and fill in as needed in teaching the workshops. At this point Mosaic was left behind and Netscape became the graphical user interface for the project.

Table 1

# Skills to learn and teach

- Netscape set up
- Searching the WWW
- Creating WWW pages using the campus system
- HTML
- Web page design
- Copyright

## SPRING AND SUMMER 1996

Although the grant started in the summer of 1996, we offered our first pair of half-day workshops the week before classes started in mid-January. We repeated this combination three other times over the course of the semester on Saturday mornings and during spring break. We covered configuring Netscape for individuals' computers, using search engines to identify resources, deciphering URLs and domain names, and creating Web pages using basic HTML codes. We also offered the same sessions without pedagogical discussions for faculty secretaries and administrative staff. By summer, 75 of Grinnell's 135 faculty had attended the workshops, including emeritus faculty.

Initially one weeklong workshop for eight faculty members was scheduled for the summer, but because the interest in this topic was high, we had two separate weeklong workshops for twelve faculty members each. Faculty members received a stipend for attending summer workshops and the faculty development budget made up the difference between the available Mellon monies and the reality of the interest level. We felt that we should act quickly and meet the existing need.

It was suggested by participants that the sessions be divided up according to academic divisions, with science meeting one week and humanities and social studies the other. Our numbers of interested faculty would have justified this type of split. However, we were looking for a chance to bring people together and share ideas. So, instead of using the divisional model, we divided the groups by experience level. This made it easier to meet the participants' technical needs while bringing together a more discipline-diverse group. Having a mix of faculty in the workshops, facilitated building relationships across departmental and divisional lines, which is a general goal for our faculty development program.

We covered most of the material we had addressed in the half-day workshops but emphasized pedagogical applications and added such topics as listservs and newsgroups. We did much more with images and color (but not sound) and had background readings on most of the topics we covered. For this summer's workshops, we followed the traditional model of having a folder with agenda, background readings, informational sheets, and so on. This worked well and was familiar to the participants.

During the academic year 1996–97, we continued offering the half-day workshops, always modifying the content to keep up with changes in Internet technologies. We taught more staff, both administrative and academic, and did a bit of consulting around campus to help people smooth out rough spots with Web page development and use of the Internet.

The libraries' administrative assistant began working with the librarians in early 1996 on the development and maintenance of the libraries' Web site. Initially she participated in the workshops by doing the keyboarding; eventually she answered the more complex HTML questions. She took on a regular instructor's role in the staff workshops and provided a great deal of support to the offices around campus as the staff developed the Web pages for the academic departments.

## SUMMER 1997

We provided one weeklong workshop in the summer of 1997. Eleven classroom faculty from all divisions participated. We assessed the experience level of faculty with regard to their knowledge of and experience with Internet and computer technologies, but all faculty were included in the same workshop. The workshop was in a chemistry classroom with only display hardware and we allowed time at the end of each morning's session for the faculty to work in a computer lab. They were able to develop their course Web pages or locate needed Web resources with the help of the librarians.

Two innovations improved the workshop that year. First, we started using an on-line syllabus for the class (see table 2). We had

Table 2

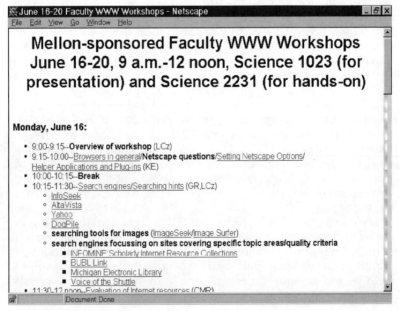

been teaching the faculty to do this, but hadn't used the technology ourselves. We discovered the dynamic nature of a Web syllabus: as the faculty created and updated their Web pages, we could all see their work immediately; when faculty located useful Web resources, links to the Web page could be quickly added; syllabi and course readings for a traditional set of handouts no longer needed to be printed. Second, a faculty member from the Political Science Department joined us as a presenter. She had been collaborating with a librarian to locate statistical information on the Internet for course and research use and learning how to download the statistics into a spreadsheet program. Her experiences informed the other classroom faculty about advantages and drawbacks of using Internet resources.

As the faculty and librarians evaluated the workshop, we were reminded that different levels of experience with computer and Web technologies could be a barrier to learning. For example, in the summer of 1997, we had a Russian faculty member who could barely navigate on her computer and a psychology faculty member who was more expert at HTML than the librarians were in the class. How could we develop experiences that would benefit both? But serendipity provided a wonderful opportunity for these two faculty members to work together, one learning by doing, one learning by teaching. We again realized that trying to cover course Web page design, how to search the Web and evaluate Web sites, discussion of other technologies, and pedagogical uses of technology constituted too much material for five, half-day sessions. Now that most of the faculty on campus had attended at least one of the workshops, we decided to focus on the pedagogical aspects of technology in the classroom rather than teaching the faculty how to use the technology.

## SUMMER 1998

Although the Mellon grant had ended, there was continued interest in Web workshops from college administrators and the faculty, so the librarians taught one more weeklong workshop in the summer of 1998. Sixteen faculty members, five librarians, several computer services staff, a few faculty presenters, and one Instructional Multimedia Technology specialist found themselves in a small classroom crowded with old-fashioned wooden chairs and one monitor mounted on the ceiling. By this point in the development of technology at Grinnell College, additional people had been hired to support technology. We believed that a workshop in which we worked with our new partners in these areas would provide the classroom faculty with the opportunity to meet and interact with the many people on campus who shared our enthusiasm for the new technologies. The computer services' staff focused on teaching PageMill and techniques for transferring Web pages to the new server. Faculty presenters showed their course Web pages and discussed their use. We demonstrated techniques for searching the Web and discussed the value of using the Web in research. Having a balanced number of faculty from each division provided glimpses of the varying challenges and opportunities posed by technology for the humanities, sciences, and social studies.

It was an invigorating week for all involved. We had useful discussions regarding the level of support on campus for technology. The faculty were interested in adopting Web technologies in their classes, but had neither the time nor the interest to create Web pages themselves. The IMTSs would provide needed assistance, but faculty believed that more support was necessary.

The librarians realized that the time had come for us to move on. We no longer needed to teach the classroom faculty how to design Web pages; many already had that expertise and we now had IMTSs to assist faculty. We developed a new model for library-related, technology-based workshops. Later that summer, we led a workshop for the Economics Department regarding use of Web technologies specifically designed for research in economics. Two librarians, the libraries' administrative assistant, and one of the IMTSs researched and developed a Web page (see table 3) and two-day workshop for the economics faculty. The workshop

Table 3

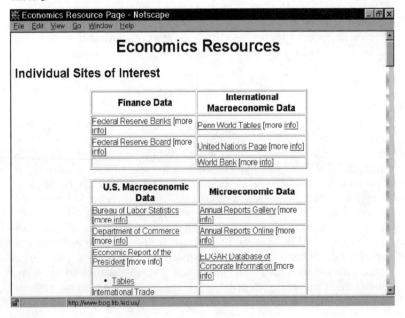

focused on locating and evaluating Internet sites for financial data, micro- and macroeconomic data, and metadirectories of economics sites on the Web. Extensive time was spent on downloading, formatting, and transferring files from the Web into Excel, and there were other technical issues relating to use of economic statistics. The classroom faculty members were delighted with the workshop. The librarians learned that this type of workshop worked very well for us at this point. The focus on one discipline provided a cohesive framework that was missing in our previous workshops and strengthened the liaison relationships that the librarians have been working to build. It also brought together the traditional and technological expertise of the librarians in an exciting new structure. The collaborative work between the librarians, IMTSs, library staff, and classroom faculty provided an excellent model for future work.

## SUMMER 1999

Building on our success with the Economics Department, we developed a workshop for faculty in the French Department in the summer of 1999. They wanted to learn about a variety of research technologies for their own work, for their students in a senior seminar, and for a new capstone course on postcolonial French literature. Two librarians developed a Web page (see table 4) for the workshop that included

Table 4

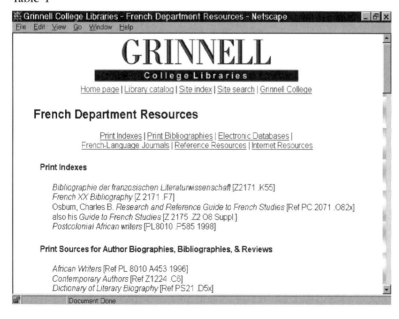

traditional print resources, electronic bibliographic databases, and Web resources. During the two half-day sessions, we presented resources, taught the faculty about the potentials for searching on-line databases, and evaluated Web sites. Because the faculty wanted to use this resource for their students in the coming year, we asked for their input in critiquing the sources chosen. Working collaboratively, we revised the resources page, adding, discarding, and fine-tuning the lists and links. They were pleased with the results and currently link to this page from their departmental home page and use it for their courses. We were glad to know that our new model for collaboration between classroom faculty and library faculty was workable and useful.

## COLLABORATION AMONG CAMPUS PARTNERS

Things have changed at Grinnell as a result of the librarians taking a leadership role in the use of the World Wide Web. One of the goals of the Mellon Grant program was to increase collaboration among librarians, classroom faculty, and between computer specialists and classroom faculty, and this has happened. During the first year of the grant, everything that was accomplished could be attributed to the librarians, and while we stretched ourselves to teach HTML and Web-authoring software and to set up listervs, we did not offer or indicate in any way that we would continue to teach software packages. The IMTSs have filled that role, as well as many others, as their presence has become greater on campus, and librarians have collaborated with them on many workshops. We have also been involved with some semester-long collaborations with faculty members emphasizing information technology. These include team teaching a music and multimedia course with a member of the music faculty and a first-year tutorial with a computer science professor.

Looking back at 1993, our approach to dealing with the integration of the Internet into academic life was appropriate to our setting. Most faculty now use the Internet as naturally as they use the telephone, E-mail, and the photocopy machine. Not all have Web-based syllabi for their courses, but it is just a matter of time before the infrastructure will be in place to facilitate the creation of course Web pages without needing to know HTML. More extensive pedagogical use of the Web will increase as professors develop applications that enhance their students' learning.

Being leaders in the use of educational technology strengthened the libraries' position on campus. The use of the Internet as a component of the research process is a continuing educational opportunity for the librarians as we work with both faculty and students. As the Internet is normalized into our social fabric, we will continue to maximize its usefulness in the campus setting as an extension of the physical library through the design of our Web page and information literacy efforts.

# 7

# New Developments
# in the Learning Environment:
# A Partnership in
# Faculty Development

*Tom Rocklin*

New technologies always carry with them new challenges to match the new opportunities they present. Deploying networked computers on college campuses has certainly presented teaching and learning opportunities. With those opportunities have come serious faculty development challenges. In this chapter, I describe the ways in which a partnership, which we call nTITLE (New Technologies in the Learning Environment, <http://www.uiowa.edu/~ntitle/>), among our Center for Teaching, libraries, and Information Technology Services (ITS) has successfully addressed some of these challenges at the University of Iowa. I begin by describing enough of the history of nTITLE to identify the forces that led to nTITLE and then in turn describe the program as it has evolved, comment on what we know about its effectiveness, and finally identify some of the lessons we have learned.

## HISTORY

Early in 1996, members of the Faculty Senate Budget Committee developed an initiative they called the Technology Based Teaching Initiative. In broad outline, they described a program that would combine infrastructure development with faculty training to make real the teaching and learning promises of networked computers. This initiative was included in the university's budget request to the legislature, and by November 1996, it began to appear likely that the initiative would be funded. The provost asked the Center for Teaching to take the lead in organizing the faculty development effort that came to be known as nTITLE. Near the end of 1996, the Libraries and Information Technology Services agreed to join the partnership. The first workshops were offered in August 1997, with additional workshops each summer since.

In retrospect, the key elements of this history are two. First, the program began not as an administrative mandate but as a grassroots initiative on the part of the faculty. nTITLE has remained very much a faculty-driven effort. Second, from the time nTITLE first began to take shape, it was conceived as a partnership. From the beginning, it was clear that each of the three units had an interest in seeing the program succeed and none of the three had the resources to conduct the program on its own.

## WHAT DOES nTITLE LOOK LIKE?

In describing nTITLE as it now exists, it will be helpful to (artificially) separate my description of the philosophy, goals, and practices of the program.

### Philosophy

The cornerstone of the nTITLE philosophy is a trust in faculty. We believe, and act on the belief, that faculty members who are well informed are capable of making good decisions. This means that (as will be discussed below) the participants in nTITLE are given a great deal of freedom. They choose, to a great extent, what skills they learn and what equipment and software they acquire.

The only real constraints we want to place on faculty participants flows from a second element of our philosophy: a focus on teaching and learning. Every faculty development program involving learning technologies has to deal with a natural temptation to focus on taming the technology. That is, it is tremendously tempting to make sure that each participant knows what every menu selection of every piece of software does. We resist this urge in favor of creating a climate in which as much of the discussion as possible centers around how technology features fit into teaching and learning environments.

Because we trust faculty members to want to do their jobs well, our philosophy focuses more on removing barriers than on creating incentives. That is, we are more interested in directing our efforts and resources to making it easier to create effective teaching and learning environments than we are in creating incentives for faculty members to heroically overcome structural barriers. For example, the equipment grants that faculty members receive probably do function as an incentive, but that is not how we arrived at the decision to use our resources to provide the grants. Had we been simply looking for incentives, we might have given stipends instead of equipment grants. Either would have worked as an incentive, but with the equipment grants, we were able to avoid the situation in which a faculty member learns a host of new skills but is unable to implement them because of a lack of equipment.

## Goals

Consistent with our nTITLE philosophy, we pursue three kinds of goals in the program. First and foremost, we seek to create a forum for the consideration of the ways in which we teach and our students learn. The fact that faculty members are learning new technical skills and trying to imagine how these skills might help them teach means that they are unusually open to reconsidering all of the processes involved in their teaching. Second, we seek to provide a way for faculty members to increase their technical skills relevant to teaching. This inevitably means different things for different workshop participants and different things from year to year. Our goal, then, is to meet faculty members where they are as learners and make as much progress with each as we can.

Finally, as I have suggested, nTITLE is about both faculty development and infrastructure development. Our third goal is to make continual progress toward an environment free from barriers to the realization of the promises of learning technologies. Brian Hawkins noted five kinds of institutional motivation for deploying learning technologies.[1] Institutions invest in learning technologies to meet student demand, to meet statutory objectives and budget constraints, to create efficiency in delivery, to make money, and to enrich the learning environment. The last motivation, to enrich the learning environment, is far and away the dominant motivation behind nTITLE.

## Practices

Over the three-year history of nTITLE, we have evolved a set of practices to meet our goals. These practices fall into three areas. The most visible component of the program is the *workshops*, but our practices concerning *continuing support* and *infrastructure development* are equally important to the success of the program.

## Workshops

Each workshop lasts four full days and enrolls twenty-four participants. The workshops are held in the University Libraries' Information Arcade, which is equipped with a workstation (high-end Macintoshes with Virtual PC for Windows emulation) for each participant and an instructor's station with dual projectors and screens. A faculty member experienced with learning technologies and acknowledged as an excellent teacher leads each workshop.

Our instructional strategies have evolved to honor participant autonomy as much as possible. We begin the workshop by explaining to participants that we expect them to make active choices about how to use their time and that they are free to work on anything at any time. We reserve "front of the room" instruction for brief demonstrations of pedagogically useful ways to apply various technologies and presentations designed to provoke discussion of issues related to using learning technologies (e.g., copyright). In addition to demonstrations of the software participants are learning to use, we invite "pioneer presentations" from faculty members who are exploring unusual uses of learning technologies.

The skill instruction that participants receive comes in the form of supported hands-on practice with authentic materials. Participants bring materials to work on and we provide them with both a reference manual and a project manual. The project manual suggests projects to try with their materials and guides them through the projects with step-by-step instructions and specific references to the relevant sections of the reference manual. As the participants work, they are assisted by coaches (normally we have between four and eight coaches in the room at a time) and by their fellow participants. Thus, we use presentations from the front of the room to provoke interest, but the basic pedagogical model is learning by doing, with discussion to spark further reflection.

The topics covered in the workshops evolve from year to year. Generally, we have given participants the opportunity to learn to use a WYSIWYG HTML editor, WebCT (an integrated Web-based course development tool set), the Acrobat tools for document distribution, a presentation tool (PowerPoint), an image editing tool, and more recently, video and audio editing tools. We also provide introductory instruction on intellectual property issues, privacy and security, evaluation, and resource identification. No participant is interested in all of these topics and we recognize that no participant will master even those skills he or she practices the most. The format does, however, give people the opportunity to get a good start on the skills most important to them.

## Support

Because the workshops can only be a start for the participants' skill development, ongoing support has been an important concern in nTITLE's development. The structure of the workshops allows faculty members to become very familiar with resources available for continuing support. In addition to holding the sessions in the libraries' facility, we arrange a visit to the Information Technology Services facility dedicated to faculty support and take our breaks in the Center for Teaching. We go out of our way to make sure that participants meet staff from each unit and understand that these staff members are available for postworkshop support. We also sponsor listservs for support and maintain Web sites for support.

## Infrastructure

Each of the 120 participants directs the spending of $3,000 for what we think of as "faculty-directed" infrastructure development. Given the diversity of the participants' circumstances and teaching responsibilities, it is no surprise that their purchases are quite diverse. They include a variety of software in addition to computers and peripherals (primarily printers, scanners, and cameras).

In addition, nTITLE funds are spent on classroom improvements and ongoing support for classroom operations. A classroom committee organized by the provost's office directs these funds. The bulk of these "administratively directed" funds go to adding and replacing computers and projectors either fixed in classrooms or mounted on carts serving several classrooms. Between these two kinds of spending, we seek to ensure that faculty members have the resources in both their offices and their classrooms to implement the skills they have acquired.

## HAS nTITLE BEEN EFFECTIVE?

Our limited information indicates that over the first three years of nTITLE, we have been successful in addressing our goals. One indicator of our success comes from faculty reactions. On the last day of each workshop, participants rate the value of the experience, their enjoyment of the experience, and the difficulty they experienced. For our most recent workshops, participants rated the value 3.5 (on a four-point scale, where 3 was "valuable" and 4 was "very valuable"). Participants rated their enjoyment 3.6 (also on a four-point scale, where 3 was "quite a bit" and 4 was "very much"). Finally, they rated the difficulty 2.3 (also on a four-point scale, where 2 was "not so difficult," 3 was "difficult," and 4 was "very difficult"). We also ask whether participants would recommend the workshops to a similarly situated colleague. Of the 332 participants in nTITLE workshops, 331 have responded "yes" to this question. The final piece of evidence concerning faculty reactions is that we receive almost twice as many applications for the program as we can accommodate.

We can also measure, to some extent, the impact of nTITLE on the learning environment by examining the use of technology in teaching and learning. In 1996, we identified approximately two dozen course Web sites on campus. In 1999, we identified 810. Some of this growth would have taken place no matter what. The fact that nTITLE was in place, though, encouraged faculty members to think about using technology in their teaching. It also catalyzed a number of infrastructure and process improvements that made it easier for faculty members to use the Web in teaching.

Driven by demand from faculty members, we have progressed from a handful of classrooms equipped with computers and projectors to 172 of our 200 general assignment classrooms having technology available to faculty members. Of these, 63 are fixed installations and the rest are served by carts.

## LESSONS LEARNED

We have learned innumerable lessons as we have developed and nurtured nTITLE. The most important of these lessons can be grouped into lessons we have learned about *collaboration* and lessons we have learned about *faculty as learners*.

### Collaboration

nTITLE has become a very high visibility success on campus. Each of the three units involved routinely features its participation in nTITLE in publicity both on and off campus. Reading the publicity emanating from any one of the units might lead to the inference that that unit deserved the lion's share of the credit for nTITLE's success. None of this reporting is dishonest. In the context of describing our unit's accomplishments, we naturally focus on our contributions. It has been important to the success of nTITLE that each unit is both able to use the success as an indicator of the unit's success in accomplishing its mission *and* been tolerant of the ways in which other units have described their contributions.

This is just one of the ways that the units' interests are as important as the abilities they bring to the effort. At a simple level, we all contribute to the program because it is an important program for the university. It is important to our success, though, that we recognize that the program can further more parochial goals that each of us have and that we attend to those goals as well. One simple example is that all of us want to use the program to help let faculty members learn about the services we offer. In other cases, we have unique interests.

One final lesson about collaboration has been important to our success. Things change. For example, when nTITLE began, ITS was organized in a way that made it difficult for ITS to provide ongoing postworkshop support for participants. Because of that, the Center for Teaching hired and trained graduate assistants to provide that support. Now, ITS has a unit dedicated to academic technologies that *can* provide that support and the Center for Teaching no longer provides it. Our partnership does not have a formal document governing it, but we do understand the need, from time to time, to renegotiate the ways in which we work.

## Faculty as Learners

Participants in the nTITLE workshops come from all colleges of the university. Some teach large undergraduate courses taken primarily by students in their first or second year of university life. Others' teaching is limited almost exclusively to residents and fellows in the College of Medicine. In theory, we could try to group participants by discipline as we schedule workshops. In practice, adding another constraint to scheduling would create a nightmare. We would not want to, even if we could, though. The diversity among faculty members in the workshops serves two very useful purposes. First, most obviously and most importantly, the diversity enriches the conversations that participants have about teaching. There are approaches to teaching that are more prevalent in one discipline than in others and the workshops have proven to be productive arenas for exposing participants to thinking about teaching that is different from their own. Second, in these workshops, we present a wide range of technological possibilities. Occasionally, a participant wonders out loud what possible use a particular possibility could have. The workshop leader could answer, but it is much more compelling when, as often happens, a fellow participant answers.

In our first workshops, we were concerned that faculty members demonstrate mastery of a set of common objectives. We have become much less concerned with that sort of goal as we have seen the benefits of granting faculty members a great deal of autonomy. One of the pleasures of faculty development work is that faculty members are nearly universally highly skilled learners. They were successful students and since then have generally taught themselves a great deal. We have found that interesting faculty members in the possibilities of technology, providing them with immediate access to skilled coaches, and then getting out of their way has been very effective. This approach also resolves the issue of trying to match curriculum to the groups' interests. In effect, each participant constructs his or her own curriculum.

The final lesson we have learned is to never miss the opportunity to be a good model. Our workshop leaders are all excellent teachers and the design team has put a lot of thought into how to provide effective instruction in our context. In the workshops, it is possible for participants to see how much they can learn without having been lectured to, for example. We also try to think very critically about whether the ways we are using technology in our instruction makes sense—because we know that our faculty participants will.

## FINAL THOUGHTS

nTITLE has been a catalyst for our three units to evolve ways to work together on other projects. It was a high-stakes initiative with a lot of attention focussed on it from the beginning. What we learned about collaboration in developing nTITLE has served us well in other projects as well. Our ability to collaborate effectively on nTITLE is one of several developments that nTITLE has catalyzed. In the end, these peripheral developments may be as valuable as the direct results of nTITLE.

## NOTE

1. Brian Hawkins, "The Mirage of Continuity: Matching Realities and Aspirations," presented at the Symposium on Powerful Learning, Powerful Partnerships, University of Iowa in Iowa City, November 11–12, 1999.

# 8

## Development of a Faculty Web Training Program at George Washington University

*Scott Stebelman*

Providing instruction to faculty is more complex than other user groups. Librarians at George Washington University (GW) have often found that faculty perceive their own research knowledge and skills to be adequate and hence are resistant to instructional overtures, especially from people who may lack advanced subject degrees, such as librarians. Busy professionals, faculty frequently have competing demands on their time, demands ranging from creating lesson plans to grading papers, meeting with students, and working on academic committees. Older than most of their students, and probably educated before computers were commonplace in most classrooms, faculty often manifest skepticism about the relevance of computers to research and teaching, and fear learning a skill that is more mechanical than conceptual.[1] To reach and train faculty successfully, librarians must be cognizant of the following needs and issues: the characteristics of faculty as a user group, methods of marketing workshops to faculty, developing and promoting teacher partnerships, identifying topics of interest to faculty, methods for increasing attendance, and developing Web resources to assist with training.

### CHARACTERISTICS OF FACULTY AS A USER GROUP

Although computers have become an essential part of much scientific and social science research, their importance in other disciplines—particularly the humanities—has been less pronounced. Many English professors still teach Shakespeare and Milton without introducing electronic texts or even bibliographic databases into class discussions. Even those faculty who use computers to analyze data or to enhance instruction (either through PowerPoint presentations or multimedia simulations) may not use the Web to identify or gather relevant information and data. As experienced researchers, faculty have developed years—perhaps decades—of fixed information-seeking habits that are resistant to change. Telling a faculty member that the Web contains unique information that cannot be found easily in print sources, or that this information exists only in electronic form, is not always persuasive. What is persuasive is personal experience, that is, not finding demographic or economic data in a familiar print resource, or being questioned by colleagues and graduate students who cannot believe the faculty member has not developed more modern research skills.

In some cases, skepticism about Web research is valid. Several years ago, student reporters from our campus newspaper asked faculty if they used the Web in their research or teaching. Some faculty understood the growing importance of the Web, but acknowledged that they rarely used it. One English professor explained that few literary editions on the Web were textually reliable and hence he would not recommend them to his students. Another professor feared that her students would stumble upon sites that contained questionable information, or highly biased analysis, and that students would not be discerning enough to realize the problem. Until more information was vetted, or better screened, both of these instructors preferred to rely on print resources.

Finally, because faculty are often viewed as intellectuals with specialized expertise and knowledge, many feel self-conscious and threatened about being placed in a learning environment where they may look "stupid."[2] If the librarian trainer is demonstrating the virtues of search engines and asks the participants to compare Alta Vista with Northern Light, the faculty member may be frozen because he or she does not know how to enter a URL into the browser location box. Obviously a good trainer would require a certain skills level for all registrants, but it is likely that many faculty members have stayed away for fear they would be humiliated in front of their peer group. This leaves open the option of "house calls" to such faculty, where the librarian works one-on-one with them in the privacy of their office, but that is a strategy supplemental to workshop instruction.

## MARKETING WORKSHOPS TO FACULTY

Based on responses from our focus groups, we learned that many faculty do not regularly visit the library or its Web pages and hence are unaware of what training workshops are offered. In the case of workshops, as with most instruction, the library needs to use a variety of publicity mechanisms to reach this audience. If the department has an electronic mail list (E-list) for its members, a message should be sent announcing the workshops, the topics to be covered, dates and time, and prerequisites for registration. If a departmental mailing list does not exist, or is not accessible to the library, then the library will need to create departmental faculty mailing lists. These are time consuming, primarily because they need frequent updating, but E-list distribution is one of the most effective publicity vehicles. At George Washington University, we have created a separate E-list called INTQUERY, which is restricted to faculty and higher-level administrators. The list not only publicizes our workshop schedules but also provides instruction on narrow topics, such as finding biographical information on the Web. In an effort to accommodate those faculty who are still more print than electronic focused, we send individual fliers to all full- and part-time faculty, and to departmental office staff, requesting that the fliers be placed on bulletin boards. The library's home page, although not necessarily the first place faculty will go for instructional information, can be useful if the workshops are prominently advertised on the first page. In addition to the textual information, the library can include a registration form that can be submitted in lieu of an E-mail or telephone registration.

## DEVELOPING AND PROMOTING TEACHER PARTNERSHIPS

There is one paramount reason why librarians need to partner with other campus units: nonlibrarians often provide the credibility and expertise that librarians lack. When we teach a workshop in a specific discipline, such as the social sciences or English as a Foreign Language, we may seek out a faculty member to serve as a co-teacher. As mentioned earlier, when a librarian argues that the Web is indispensable to research or teaching, faculty often wonder how someone outside their discipline could state this with certainty. However, if one of their own colleagues makes the same claim, they are more likely to listen. While the librarian can concentrate on the skills portion of the presentation, the faculty member can provide case studies, usually from his or her own research and teaching.

This was done most effectively with our Web publishing workshops. Faculty members who had mounted course Web pages illustrated the kinds of information they placed on these pages: syllabi, biographical information, student projects, and hyperlinks to relevant Web sites. In one case, an economics professor demonstrated how he had published the class textbook on his course page. This had several advantages that were not lost on the faculty audience: students could read selectively from the hyperlinked table of contents, resources that were mentioned in the text could be linked, and material on this Web page (unlike a print text) could be updated at any time.

In addition to co-teaching with faculty, librarians occasionally have teamed up with computer center staff. For several years, we provided a "Basic Web Workshop" that taught participants how to navigate the Web and identify resources germane to a particular discipline.

The computer center staff member would focus on functional skills, such as printing, saving, and bookmarking a page, while librarians concentrated on research skills, such as how to use search engines and evaluation clearinghouses (e.g., Britannica and Argus) to identify the best sites. We also offered "Web Page Creation" workshops: the computer center staff taught HTML codes and editors, while librarians covered how a page—through uploading curriculum vitae, original research, and committee documents and drafts—could be used for professional advancement. A third partner was the University Teaching Center, which did not participate in the teaching but was quite helpful in publicizing the workshops through its E-list and informal campus networks.

## IDENTIFYING TOPICS FOR FACULTY WORKSHOPS

Perhaps one of our most difficult challenges was identifying what we thought would be the most useful and popular Web workshop topics. Over the years, the following topics have been included: economic and demographic data; primary resources (heavy on the humanities but included some numeric data sites); education; political science; public policy; government documents; English and American literature; social sciences; utilizing the library's subscription and full-text databases; advanced Web searching techniques; evaluating Web resources; and cybercheating. To our surprise and chagrin, the workshops that were least popular were the disciplinary workshops—the low attendance (four to six people) perhaps validates an earlier point made, that faculty see themselves as the experts in a discipline and are wary of others making similar claims. More popular were those workshops that taught skills the faculty knew they lacked, such as using advanced search engines to find relevant information, or techniques for establishing the authority and credibility of a Web site. Most popular of all has been our workshop on cybercheating: faculty are becoming increasingly tired of and irritated with students who plagiarize from the Web, and appreciate techniques for documenting cheating.

## METHODS FOR INCREASING ATTENDANCE

In spite of the energy and time librarians have expended in developing the workshops, attendance is sometimes sparse. We attribute this to several factors: (1) faculty who were interested in learning about the Web have done so and moved on to other projects, such as multimedia course development; (2) many faculty uninterested in the Web three years ago are still uninterested today; (3) our topics, although constantly changing to reflect new scholarly trends, still don't resonate with our audience; and (4) the days of the week and times chosen for the workshops are inconvenient for some faculty.

Rotating the times of workshops has not made much difference. They are normally scheduled on Friday, when few classes are in session; however, because the environment is largely a commuter campus, many faculty stay away because they do not want to travel ten to thirty miles merely to attend a library workshop. In an attempt to increase attendance, we have opened the workshops to graduate students. This appeared to have been a mistake, because faculty attendance dropped off even more noticeably, perhaps further evidence that faculty are self-conscious when trained in a group that includes students. Attrition rate has been very high—from 50 percent to 60 percent of all registrants fail to attend, in spite of reminder E-mails sent at least forty-eight hours before each workshop. Some libraries have discouraged no-shows by charging registrants a small fee, then reimbursing them if they attend or, inversely, charging them or their department a fee if they fail to attend.[3] Our library, cautious about the negative public relations such a policy might engender, has decided against implementation.

For those faculty preferring workshops tailored to the needs of their specific departments, we offer workshops that can be scheduled during a regular departmental meeting. Working with the chair and the department's library representative, we can ensure that Web resources supporting the specialized research interests of faculty are covered. These meetings are also opportunities for enhanced collegiality, as participants all know each other and have developed in many cases social as well as professional relationships

## DEVELOPING WEB RESOURCES TO ASSIST FACULTY

Although attendance has been modest at times, those who do attend usually give favorable evaluations. Two resources have significantly contributed to these positive attitudes: providing terminal assistants (approximately one for every five participants) to help faculty who are floundering at a lab computer, and producing detailed, clearly written user aids. The user aids are first produced in HTML and printed out for the workshops; they are also mounted on the library's Web training page for those faculty who could not attend and for faculty who want to consult them again at a later time. In fact, the user aids are part of a larger series of Web pages we designed specifically to support faculty learning.[4] In addition to the user aids, these pages also include the semester schedule of Web workshops, a research consultation form for faculty needing to conduct Web research or utilize the Web in teaching; announcements about our annual information technology symposium; links to HTML development sites; and instructions for subscribing to INTQUERY, our faculty/administrator E-list. Because faculty are important as a political constituency as well as a user group, we believe the special attention devoted to them is good for public relations and for increasing their willingness to be advocates for the library's long-term agenda, which includes increases in the materials budget as well as in our instructional activities.

## CONCLUSION

Faculty Web workshops can be successful if librarians address key issues before the workshops are given. These issues include understanding some of the anxiety faculty bring to computer training, their perception of themselves as the primary experts within their disciplines, and their need for a variety of marketing and publicity vehicles. Libraries that partner with other administrative units in delivering instruction will probably have stronger presentations as well as solidify their working relationships with these units. Finally, offering workshops that focus on nontraditional scholarly topics, such as cybercheating, can be just—if not more—successful than workshops restricted to single disciplines.

Our library is in its sixth year of offering Internet and Web workshops. We have evolved from teaching E-mail, FTP, and Gopher to Web page design and Web research. Of current interest to faculty are computer applications that can assist them with teaching; our institution has developed its own courseware, called Prometheus, which allows faculty to create attractive, multifaceted Web pages (e.g., they include E-reserves, group E-mail, and chat) without having to learn HTML. The library is exploiting this interest by creating Web pages designed to support individual courses; these pages, accessible through the library's home page, have strengthened faculty beliefs that the library has a prominent role in facilitating learning.[5]

## NOTES

1. A survey of Mississippi State University faculty revealed that, although most faculty felt confident in their use of computers, older faculty were less confident than younger faculty, and confidence levels varied among disci-

plines. See Lee, Kuang-Wu Johnny. "Faculty Utilization, Attitudes, and Perceptions Regarding Computer Technology at Mississippi State University." (Ph.D. diss., Mississippi State University, 1998.)

2. For a discussion of factors influencing faculty anxiety with computers, see Steve Gilbert, "An 'On-line' Experience: Discussion Group Debates Why Faculty Use or Resist Technology," *Change* 27, no. 2 (March–April 1995): 28–45; and D. M. Dusick, "What Social Cognitive Factors Influence Faculty Members' Use of Computers for Teaching? A Literature Review," *Journal of Research in Computing in Education* 31, no. 2 (Winter 1998): 123–37.

3. This information came from responses to a message, posted by the author, to NETTRAIN in May 1997.

4. The URL for the faculty training page is <http://www.gwu.edu/~gelman/train/index.html> [accessed 5 January 2000].

5. The URL for the library Web pages supporting individual courses is <http://gwis2.circ.gwu.edu/~train/> [accessed 5 January 2000].

# 9

# Building Bridges with Faculty through Library Workshops

*Julie Chapman and Michelle White*

## INTRODUCTION

Valdosta State University (VSU), located in southern Georgia, is a liberal arts university offering degrees at both the undergraduate and graduate level. The university comprises approximately 9,000 students who are served by 500 faculty members. The faculty became the focus of a series of outreach workshops that taught tips for creating effective library research assignments and for mastering on-line searching techniques for Georgia Library Learning On-Line (GALILEO).

GALILEO is a collection of more than 250 on-line databases available to a variety of user groups. The user groups include public libraries, public K–12 school libraries, technical school libraries, private academic libraries, and the University System of Georgia libraries. In the fall of 1998, the GALILEO Steering Committee created the GALILEO Training Grant, which was available on a competitive basis to each user community. We wrote the grant to hold workshops to teach VSU Faculty and VSU's Consortia Faculty (Abraham Baldwin Agricultural College, Waycross College, and Bainbridge College) how to search GALILEO and how to create effective library research assignments that incorporated those skills during two six-hour workshops offered on a Saturday. The $1,000 grant was received later in the fall of 1998.

## FUNDING AND MARKETING

The grant funds can be divided into the following four main categories: publicity, support materials, catering, and compensation. The workshops were publicized with printed flyers stating the dates and times of the workshops along with the topics that were to be covered. The bottom half of the flyer asked for the faculty person's name, department, phone number, E-mail address, experience level with GALILEO, and questions. Approximately one-third of the workshop participants responded through the printed flyers. The best response came from E-mail invitations with the same information sent through the faculty listserv and from personal invitations. Support materials included color-coded handouts, name tags, and folders. The handouts, produced at a professional printing office on high-quality paper, gave the workshop a polished appearance and saved time for us to plan the workshops. Name tags were used during the first workshop; in subsequent workshops, name tents were used because they were easier to read from a distance. Participants greatly appreciated the catered breaks, especially in the morning of the all-day workshops. They consistently remarked that these times to mingle helped them feel welcome and gave time to socialize. The final category of the funds was used to compensate us for the extra time spent creating and giving the workshops.

## LITERATURE

Once the workshops were funded through the GALILEO Training Program Grant, our task was to create an agenda, handouts, PowerPoint presentations, and exercises in detail. Thus, a literature search was conducted in LibraryLit, ERIC, and Education Abstracts. Since the library already had a strong instruction program with a heavy emphasis on GALILEO, the main search was to find information on how to teach faculty the elements of effective library research assignments. The most useful article was "Creating a Library Assignment Workshop for University Faculty," written by Pixey Mosley of Texas A&M University. We modeled our first workshop on the one described in this article and included much of the information in our PowerPoint presentation covering effective library research assignments. We also found many libraries across the country offering similar workshops and tip sheets to their faculty when the same search was conducted on the World Wide Web. Some of the libraries we looked to for inspiration were University of Minnesota, Texas A&M University, and Queen's University.

## WORKSHOP GOALS

Workshop goals are divided into two main categories—goals for the faculty and goals for the library. The faculty wanted to know how to get the most out of GALILEO and were interested in learning more complex searching techniques. Thus, the main focus of the first half of the workshops was on search strategies covering Boolean operators, limit commands, proximity commands, field-specific searches, and truncation. These skills were reinforced with hands-on examples and exercises. Faculty members were also interested in the background of GALILEO and its organization. The faculty wanted to know not only how to use GALILEO for their own research, but also how to better help their students find information during research consultations. Finally, there was a great interest in learning tips that would allow faculty to create better research assignments in the hopes of getting better results from their students.

The goals of the library were just as complex. We wanted an integration of the assignment tips into the faculty's thought process so that when they sat down to create an assignment, they would have the library's resources in mind. We also encouraged consultations with the library when the assignments are created. This consultation could have been as involved as the librarian and instructor sitting down to create an assignment together, or as simple as sending the assignment to the library so we would be aware of the students' needs. The promotion of the Library Instruction Program seemed a natural goal of the workshops. The attendees were given a brochure of the program and examples of how the library instruction sessions would enhance the faculty's research assignments throughout the workshops. We also wanted to create an open atmosphere that would encourage interaction between the VSU faculty and the library. Finally, one of the most rewarding goals was to reach a variety of faculty. Faculty from fourteen departments attended the workshops.

## FIRST WORKSHOP

The first workshop was held on March 20, 1999, a Saturday, from 9:00 A.M. to 4:00 P.M., with a one-hour lunch break and two ten-minute breaks. Each participant received a name tag and folder containing library brochures, worksheets, tip sheets, printouts of PowerPoint presentation slides, an evaluation form, and the librarians' business cards. The morning session activities included an overview of GALILEO databases and Internet resources, a presentation on constructing a search strategy, sample searches to work through as a group, and GALILEO search exercises to be completed individually.

At the end of the session, there was time scheduled for the participants to work on the search exercises and to ask questions.

The afternoon session focused on designing successful library research assignments. We started with two role-playing skits of a student approaching a reference librarian for help with a research assignment. Next was a PowerPoint presentation covering types of library assignments (pros, cons, and examples), phrasing of library assignments, elements of good library assignments, and quick tips for developing Web assignments. After PowerPoint, participants worked on an interactive group assignment on evaluating and comparing pairs of library assignments. Finally, participants worked in pairs or individually to create library assignments that incorporated GALILEO. We wrapped up the workshop with a discussion of the newly created assignments, a question-and-answer session, and time to fill out an evaluation form.

After the first workshop, we sat down to discuss the comments from the feedback forms, as well as our impressions and evaluations of the workshop format, pace, and content. We also began planning for the second workshop and incorporated into the agenda changes based on feedback and our evaluation.

## CHANGES MADE BASED ON FEEDBACK

Several workshop participants commented that basic information about Odum Library would have been helpful, so we decided to start the second workshop with an overview of the Odum Library Web page and the services and resources offered. A number of faculty stated that they wished we had gone into a more detailed description of the GALILEO databases and bibliographic databases in general. Based on these comments, we added a more detailed explanation of the scope and coverage of the GALILEO databases, as well as a discussion of how and by whom bibliographic databases are compiled, and how they are different from Internet search engines. Finally, several participants suggested that more time be scheduled to work through the GALILEO search exercise questions. We added some additional time and also made an effort to walk around the room and be more available for questions.

## CHANGES MADE BASED ON EVALUATIONS

The biggest changes made involved handouts. Three handouts were added to the packets, including Citing Electronic Sources and Evaluating Internet Resources. The Constructing a Search Strategy sheet was expanded into a PowerPoint presentation, which included more detail on Boolean searching, proximity operators, and limiting a search. We then decided to upload the handouts and PowerPoint presentation to the Web <http://books.valdosta.edu/ref/fachandouts.html>. At the ensuing workshops, participants were able to follow along with the search strategy with PowerPoint on their terminals, instead of watching a small, fuzzy screen at the front of the room. Once the handout Web pages were on-line, we created a Library Services and Resources for VSU Faculty site around them, <http://books.valdosta.edu/ref/faculty.html>.

Modifications were also made to the format of the second session. Role-playing skits were eliminated and the session started with a discussion of the participants' examples of types of library research assignments. We hoped this would increase interaction and participation and reduce the lecturelike aspect of the subsequent PowerPoint presentation. This Designing Successful Library Research Assignments PowerPoint presentation was shortened for several reasons. First, we noticed that some participants in the first workshop had seemed to get restless during the twenty-minute presentation. Second, we felt that too much theory was included. Third, we were responding to feedback that the entire second session seemed too long.

## SECOND WORKSHOP

The changes were incorporated into the second workshop, which was held in June 1999. Unlike the first all-day Saturday workshop, this one was split into two sessions and held on two consecutive evenings from 6:00 to 9:00. Thirteen faculty members attended the first session, while five attended the second.

Evaluation forms were reviewed at the workshop's conclusion and the third workshop, to be held in September, was planned with fewer changes.

## CHANGES MADE IN THIRD WORKSHOP

Based on participants' feedback, in the third workshop, we eliminated the GALILEO video shown at the beginning of the first session and provided even more information about the Odum Library Web page and services. We were able to talk in detail and answer questions about the library instruction program and services for distance learning students and faculty. The Search Techniques portion of the workshop was restructured. Instead of going through the PowerPoint presentation and then working through examples, we alternated between presenting search strategy components and corresponding examples. This seemed to reduce the problem of participants falling behind and increased understanding of the concepts.

## FUTURE DIRECTIONS

The experience of and response to the first three workshops exceeded our expectations, and we plan on continuing and expanding the sessions. The library will schedule at least one workshop every semester, alternating times and days and trying weekday sessions. We hope that other interested librarians will lead future workshops and suggest other possible workshop topics. In addition, brown bag lunch sessions for faculty are being developed. Topics include Searching the Internet, Evaluating Internet Resources, Introducing New Databases, and Subject-Specific Databases.

## RIPPLES AND CONTACTS

A number of ripple effects and contacts, foreseen, hoped for, and unexpected, resulted from the three workshops. First, two of our main goals were met on a small scale: more faculty consultation with librarians when creating assignments and generally more interaction between faculty and librarians. Several workshop participants have returned to discuss the creation of library research assignments, one of whom has contacted us at least twice a semester. In addition, a Library Research Guide for Nursing was collaboratively developed for an instruction session held for the classes of two faculty members who attended the first workshop.

A number of unexpected outcomes also occurred. A workshop participant approached a librarian to co-teach a two-credit Perspectives course on Internet Technology, which is being held in spring semester 2000. Several school, community college, and college librarians from south Georgia and north Florida have contacted us about using the handouts and PowerPoint presentations to design their own faculty workshops. The library also received a letter of appreciation from the university's vice president of academic affairs.

The workshop handouts are on the Web and are being used by librarians during instruction sessions, as well as by a number of teaching faculty. According to internal library Web counts, the Library Services and Resources for VSU Faculty Web page is being used steadily.

## HELPFUL HINTS FOR FACULTY WORKSHOPS

In summary, we would like to share some helpful hints for the development of workshops for faculty. First, market in a variety of formats and often. We received the best response from posting and reposting messages on the campus faculty listserv; other possibilities include flyers, campus newspaper ads, table tents in faculty lounges, and personal contacts. Second, plan to hold workshops on various days and at different times. All-day Saturday and evening sessions were successful for us, and we plan on offering one during a week day. Third, incorporate a variety of presentation styles and tools to address different learning styles and to help avoid boredom. We used discussions, lecture, group work, PowerPoint presentations, color-coded handouts, Web pages, and written exercises. Fourth, offer refreshments and breaks. Finally, include an evaluation/feedback form with plenty of space for comments. In addition to writing positive comments about our teaching and the amount learned, our participants took the time to suggest how things could be done differently or other items/topics we should/could have covered. We incorporated many of these suggestions into subsequent workshops.

# 10

# What One Person Can Do: A Theory of Personal Involvement in Establishing Library–Faculty Partnerships

*Bruce Gilbert*

Author's note: Slides and notes from the original presentation are available at <http://www.brucegilbert.com>. The description of Drake University's information literacy program is available at <http://www.lib.drake.edu/assist/instruction.html>.

This essay will center on some of the theoretical and philosophical concerns that are encountered in the process of establishing librarian–teaching faculty relationships. These thoughts should be of interest to those (particularly librarians) who wish to establish such relationships, or those who wish to rethink and revitalize existing relationships.

Let me stress that this is no "ivory tower" think piece; the thoughts expressed herein stem not only from personal reading and research on the topic, but also from the ongoing process of establishing new relationships at Drake University. It should be helpful, then, to briefly review my own experience working with teaching faculty–library faculty partnerships at Drake.

## TEACHING–LIBRARY PARTNERSHIPS: PERSONAL EFFORTS

I would like to begin with a moment of personal hubris. I am proud to have something of interest to say about teaching–library partnerships even though this is not my primary duty. Since my arrival at Drake eight years ago, when I was initially hired as the systems librarian, I have taken an interest in wider issues than the latest software release. I do this for two reasons: first, because my own personal interests are varied; and second, because by greater involvement in these areas, my work as a "computer person" is better informed and guided.

There was, of course, considerable instructional faculty–librarian interplay before my arrival at Drake in early 1992. Certain classes had strong library components, and certain teaching faculty were strong proponents of the library. There was, however, no formal library program that attempted to reach every student in a classroom setting.

Nor can I take credit for that; Karl Schaefer is the first coordinator of Library Instruction at Drake (appointed in 1996), and deserves the bulk of the credit for our improved offerings. Those offerings now include a closer link with the Drake General Education curriculum, as well as mandatory library instruction for all First Year Seminar courses.

A brief review of my own efforts includes working with Drake's School of Education to co-teach one of Drake's first for-credit courses that was taught entirely on the World Wide Web, serving as a faculty co-advisor for (to date) four different doctoral dissertation candidates, and working with Dr. Schaefer in his early efforts to establish library instructional "beachheads" by team-teaching sessions of selected courses. These early efforts oriented me, I believe, toward a more productive relationship between teaching faculty and librarians.

## THEORETICAL AND PHILOSOPHICAL ASSUMPTIONS

What are the theoretical and philosophical assumptions that underlie increasing partnership between librarians and teaching faculty? A definition is in order before this question is parsed further. To begin with, what are "partners?" I would argue that traditional, "I'll call you when I need you" librarian–faculty relationships should not be called partnerships. A "partnership," for example, should include elements such as the active involvement of librarians in curricular discussions, and the active involvement of instructors in discussions regarding service provision by libraries. In my view, there clearly must be a symbiotic, mutually beneficial relationship existing before it can be called a "partnership."

## RATIONALE FOR EXISTENCE OF PARTNERSHIPS

Why, then, librarian–instructional faculty partnerships? Because both groups are "where the students are." Both groups have long histories of providing out-of-class consultations. In-class participation for the academic librarian is also nothing new. What is new is the relative increase in quantity and quality of that participation.

The reasons driving increased interaction are clear. They are the increase in information skills that is required by the mass introduction of the personal computer into education as well as everyday life, and the hugely increased amount of information that is available on the Internet (at Drake, we use the catch-all term "electronica" to refer to this new environment). We possess the common experience of sailing on uncharted seas.

The rest of this chapter centers on the "librarian" portion of this emerging relationship, but should be of interest to teaching faculty as well.

A few general words about "traditional" classroom–library efforts are appropriate. For many years, librarians have pursued a process referred to as "bibliographic instruction," or BI, generally designed to teach users the basics of information and item search and retrieval. Topics covered typically included library orientation, the Library of Congress (LC) Subject Headings, as well as LC call numbers. Most academic instructors happily steered their students (particularly first-year students) toward these courses even as they themselves avoided them.

Collection development, or the purchasing of library materials in various formats, is another area where teaching and library faculty have had interaction; sometimes cooperatively, sometimes not.

Yet these efforts, important as they are, are not, I would argue, enough to deserve the term "partnership" as we defined it earlier. Moreover, "electronica" forced librarians to look at not only these earlier efforts but also other services such as interlibrary loan and cataloging in new ways (the MARC record in cataloging, for example, is more than twenty years old). Less use of print collection and more dependence by users upon Internet sources of varying ranges of quality, as well as demands from these users for even more of this kind of information, made us realize that "doing old things in new ways" by trying to apply strategies developed in the print world to this new, untamed, and unorganized world, was not going to work. Our efforts, therefore, including seeking new partnerships, must recognize the radical nature of this sea change.

## FORMAT WARS

Thus, we see librarians were deluged by the backwashes of electronica before it became a widely recognized concern in the rest of academia. Unfortunately, some librarians chose to fight the "format wars," saying that print would always be preferable to electronic access, despite increased demands by users for electronic information. This was a mistake, albeit a somewhat understandable one. This is especially true given that the librarian is charged with supporting lifelong learning, that is, helping the user at whatever point he or she may be in the learning process. Teaching users about computers, how to use them and their vagaries is not what most librarians prepared for; yet, given this "lifelong" commitment, that is pretty much where they ended up.

Now we find the modern academic librarian in the position of defending what I call the "radical middle ground," a shifting and seemingly shrinking piece of turf wherein we defend the value, in certain educational contexts, of access to both electronic and nonelectronic formats of information.

## PARTNERSHIPS AND EDUCATIONAL PARTNERSHIPS

How do we hold that middle ground? Only by personal involvement and initiative. We must stake out, as individuals, our role in any partnership with teaching faculty via a process of educational transformation. To make this point clear, note that a transforming process must include three things: an ending of something, a beginning of something new, and a "transforming agent" that exists both before and after, but appears in new and unexpected ways in the transformed entity.

This transformation must begin with "traditional" evaluation and classifying skills; but these skills must be reforged in order to fulfill their potential in this new world. If we are not willing to undertake this transformation, beginning on an individual level, then I argue that we are not deserving of the term "partner" in the educational process. Moreover, we will not be there for teaching faculty (not to mention our students!) as they undergo their own personal information crises.

How might we go about this process? I would begin by suggesting that we work on something librarians are good at anyway: asking the right questions, and shunning those with "easy answers." This process, I would argue, is illuminated better if we understand that much of what masquerades as "answers" in this brave new world are, in fact, the source of many of the problems of this electronic world.

## CASE STUDY OF A "WRONG ANSWER"

Let us begin with an analogy: one drawn between those who teach biological evolution, and those who teach about information. Those who teach evolution constantly have to fight against the familiar and traditional view of evolution that suggests that evolution is a linear, inevitable process (we are all familiar with the "evolutionary chart" that shows a fish emerging from the ocean to inexorably be transformed into a man, albeit through the many intermediate steps of reptile, mammal, monkey, and early hominid) when it is nothing of the sort; newer representations show evolution as a branching tree or bush, and students realize that chance and circumstance play major roles in determining what species survive and perish.

Similarly, those of us who work with information as a medium must deal with another common misconception. There are many different representations, but the underlying idea is usually the same: (Data) organized is (Information) understood is (Knowledge) leads to (Wisdom).

There are many different, yet similar, representations of this idea available on the Internet and elsewhere, but they share a common problem: they are nonsense. If we think about someone we think of as "wise," for example, perhaps our grandmother or perhaps the Dalai Llama or the pope or whomever, we certainly do not envision them having gone through a process similar to this. The idea that such people are wise because they have successfully assimilated the most data and information is ludicrous on the face of it. Wisdom comes from experience, thoughtfulness, and a probing mind; consuming or even understanding "facts" plays, at best, a small part in its accumulation.

## INFORMATION INFLAMMATION

In fact, *too much* information is more often the case today, and I would argue this hinders, rather than helps, the creation of knowledge and wisdom. We all know the terms: information overload, techno-stress, and so on. I sometimes refer to it as "information inflammation." Although a little hard to pronounce, I hope that if you think about it, you will see that this is an apt description for the overwhelmed user of information today. If you look at a situation such as the coverage of prominent, breaking events, from medical studies to the death of prominent individuals, we see a process where the event is quickly followed by an avalanche (a "groundswell," if you will) of information and analysis. This "inflammation" of the social organism is similar to the swelling that occurs in the body human when trauma occurs. The swelling has its initial utility (in both cases) but becomes detrimental and eventually crippling in the body human if not treated. In society, the long-term result is the opposite of "knowledge" or "wisdom," but instead, a bunch of accumulated facts and Web sites that resist any deeper understanding of the phenomenon.

The recent controversy over the Harry Potter books is, perhaps, an example of the results of the negative impact of this inflammation. Many parents (most whom, I suspect, have not read the books) objected to these wildly popular novels because they heard they contained references (however fanciful) to wizardry and magic (woe to these same parents if they ever discover that the local middle school "media center" carries *Macbeth* on its shelves!) A much-reproduced cartoon shows disapproving parents instructing their Potter-reading son to "Stop reading that and go play video games!"

This situation is instructive for a number of reasons. It demonstrates that although computer games and simulations may be "challenging," they are often not challenging that portion of our children and our students that we would most like to grow; for example, their imagination. It also reminds us that, for good or for ill, the book is still the ultimate "virtual reality" engine.

There are many similar examples of the dangers of this kind of "inflammation"; moreover, there are many on-line problems parading as answers beyond the "Data leads to Wisdom" error. I argue that librarians, particularly those who teach information literacy, are uniquely positioned to help our students recognize such errors, and engage their critical facilities in the process. In doing so, however, we must guard against certain inherent pitfalls that dot the path electronica.

## NATURE OF COMPUTER-MEDIATED LIMITATIONS

For example, as we peruse the nature of computer-mediated limitations, I want to stress that we should not focus on the all-too-common "hygienic" problems with computers, the common complaints about lack of network bandwidth, annoying bugs in software, and the like. Harping on these concerns will merely allow students to dismiss us as neo-Luddites whose concerns will be "fixed" by the next software upgrade or additional T-1 line. Instead, we need to focus on some of the inherent weaknesses of computers as educational tools that will *always* be present.

To start with the obvious, computers are logic machines. They can help us analyze problems to the extent that they are logical problems. Yet, if we turn to serious concerns such as, "Why don't American citizens vote?" we can see that thinking entirely logically is a hindrance to addressing this problem. For, if we, as individuals, address this concern in a strictly logical way, there is little reason to vote, since our one, single vote has little chance of influencing the outcome of any given election. What is missed by such an analysis, of course, is most of what makes us human, namely, that such notions as the problem of computers being "logic machines" is compounded by the fact that computers are, further, "abstraction machines." A child who views a triangle on the screen does not experience a triangle as a thing, the way one who constructs a triangle from three pencils does. To have to view everything at a two-dimensional, technologically mediated level is a unique development of the modern pathology. At the recent EDUCAUSE conference, for example, I attended the presentation of Colin Powell, who is a fine speaker. EDUCAUSE had provided large screens on which Powell's image was projected within the large arena. I was relatively near the erstwhile general, but I noticed that most of the people around me, including many even closer than myself, were watching not the general but his projected image. Such people will go home and say, "I've heard Colin Powell speak," but they have no more experienced him as a speaker than someone who saw him on Larry King.

With computers as abstraction machines, this problem is even worse; a computer program is a self-contained world that admits no outside world beyond its own predetermined rules. Reality is not allowed to impinge, unless it is introduced as a new variable. The oft-heard complaint (particularly in libraries), "Why can't everything be on the computer?" will soon have its answer: everything will be on the computer when we are nothing more than computer-logic and abstractions; that is, when the computer becomes us, and we become it.

## APPROACHES TO EFFECTIVE PARTNERSHIP

Faced with such limitations, just what can one person do? Well, we should do what we have always done, or else we will have lost the battle by letting someone else define the battlefield. We must simply do it with renewed vigor and determination. As educators and librarians, we must stay active and involved, particularly in the general education requirements; we must not let the demands for an "information literate" student supplant the need for a critically questioning, ethically involved student, for example.

We must be creative in how, and with whom, we form partnerships. There is an obvious need to partner with the technically savvy, and we have begun doing that. However, it is equally (if not more) important to partner with those who are not yet, or may never be, "computer literate" (such people represent, now and in the future, the vast majority of humankind!). Our creativity must be put to use to best help these individuals, as well as to realize that many, particularly in the academic community, bring special skills to this new arena. One example of this might be the philosophy faculty, particularly those involved in teaching ethics. (How many people, philosophers or otherwise, have considered how the choice to use a computer in the first place is, at its root, an ethical concern?)

Obviously, we must keep informed; not just on what is the newest and greatest, but on how people learn to cope with what's the newest and greatest.

Finally, the thread that has run throughout these remarks is that we must neither shrink from the tough questions, nor assume that a problem should be addressed, or even posed, in a certain way.

To do otherwise is to be unfaithful to the questioning spirit that called us to our profession of learning and teaching and helping. If we as librarians or teachers can not just espouse these values, but embody them for our students and our users, then we will have reached a level of awareness and coherent expression of an individual that anyone should be "proud to call a partner."

# 11

## Creating a Successful Faculty–Librarian Partnership for First-Year Students: Librarian's Perspective, Faculty's Perspective

*Susan Avery, Nancy DeJoy, and Virginia McQuistion*

### CREATING IS A PROCESS

Creating a successful faculty–librarian partnership for first-year students is a process. The steps that must be included in this process are: laying a foundation, building library–faculty cooperation, developing instruction, and assessing the program. The focus of this chapter will be the development of these partnerships at Millikin University (MU) after a program revision that mandated the incorporation of library instruction into core courses.

### ABOUT MILLIKIN UNIVERSITY

Millikin University is a four-year private, undergraduate institution in Decatur, Illinois, comprising the School of Arts and Sciences, the School of Fine Arts, the School of Nursing, and the Tabor School of Business. The fall 1999 enrollment was approximately 2,300.

### LAYING THE FOUNDATION

The foundation for the present program was laid beginning in the fall of 1978, when the university curriculum committee endorsed a plan presented by the librarian that created the course called Library Research Methods. This one-credit course was required of all incoming students. A proficiency exam was offered to exempt those who had good library research skills. Two librarians taught 3 sections of 30 to 35 students each semester, reaching the 450 freshmen who were enrolled at that time.

As 1978 was "BC" (before computers invaded libraries), the interdisciplinary course focused on concepts and skills related to print resources and tools. Pre- and posttest results published in *Research Strategies* in 1984 affirmed that the course was making a difference in students' research abilities.[1] Through the years, the credit course incorporated the emerging technologies as they were developed. Faculty became well acquainted with the course content and relied upon it to prepare their students for research. Many built upon it within their disciplines with their own assignments and/or invitations to librarians to give additional instruction.

In 1994 a new provost came with ideas for curriculum revision. A committee was formed to develop a new program. Because of their previous experience with library instruction, the committee members recognized its importance, and a mandate for instruction was written into the program.

There are only two statements within the planning document relating to library instruction. One is included among the "learning goals": "Required proficiencies in writing, oral communication, quantitative skills, library research and information technology . . . express the University's commitment to preparing capable graduates." The second statement elaborates on the concept of measuring proficiency. One sentence mandated that library research skills will be integrated into the first-year Critical Writing, Reading, and Research sequence. However, three sentences focused on the requirement for a proficiency exam at the end of the freshman year. This statement, in the opinion of the librarians, placed too much emphasis on the demonstrating of proficiency and not enough on the process of the instruction itself. The librarians had not been asked to participate in the formulation of this statement. We presented arguments against several of its components during the faculty deliberations, but these were lost in the larger discussion of the program as a whole. A request to the Curriculum Committee to waive the proficiency requirement was granted for the first year. We continue to wrestle with the concepts of "proficiency" and an "exam" to measure this.

It is important to emphasize the significance of writing the instructional component into the course requirements. This has been an essential element in our successful process. The instructors and librarians *must* include the instruction in their course development to provide all students with a common base of library skills and research concepts. This is a crucial element.

## MILLIKIN PROGRAM FOR STUDENT LEARNING

Planning for the new program, now titled the Millikin Program for Student Learning (MPSL), began in 1994. By 1996–97 a pilot program was in place. During that academic year, two librarians and four faculty members were involved in the freshman course, a two-semester sequence titled Critical Writing, Reading, and Research (CWRR). The librarians worked hard to "customize" the instruction and assignments for each class. However, we did not feel that we were a part of the team. The CWRR instructors gave varied acceptance to the library instruction, ranging from true course integration to reluctant course interruption. In fact, an early comprehensive plan for CWRR as presented by a faculty committee made no reference to library instruction.

Now with many more instructors (15 each semester), students (600), and sections (30) in the program, the three instruction librarians are able to customize the in-class exercises only with some preplanning with the instructors, but we cannot customize the homework assignments to the degree that we did in the pilot program.

This lesser degree of customization is offset by the development of shared goals, those shared by both librarians and faculty, which are: the student shall successfully outline a basic strategy to locate information; locate relevant materials using the several databases; and recognize and apply evaluative criteria to each source of information, including Internet sites. These shared goals help bring to light the "recognition that librarians and faculty are in the same business."[2]

The librarians and writing faculty have also worked together to define our unique roles. The librarians identify skills needed by students and provide instruction and assignments. For their part, the faculty members stress the importance of sessions and provide follow-up assignments that use library resources. The presence of faculty at the time of the library instruction is crucial to its success. We have consistently noted that those sections that score highest on library assignments are also the sections that have the highest degree of faculty–librarian collaboration.

## INSTRUCTIONAL PROGRAM COMPONENTS

| | |
|---|---|
| Self-guided tour | Internet evaluation |
| IBIS (the Wilson databases) | Is this a magazine or a journal? |
| ILLINET On-Line (the book catalog) | Search Strategy Checklist |

Each of these components has been a part of the instructional program since the pilot; however, some shifting of the components between semesters has taken place. The changes in the order of instruction have been altered based on both the librarians' observation of the students' research needs and concerns expressed by the faculty, such as student reliance on the Internet.

## ASSESSING THE EFFECTIVENESS OF LIBRARY INSTRUCTION

Assessing the proficiency of the library instruction that has taken place in the freshman core sequence is difficult. The mandate of the MPSL addressed the need for the demonstration of a library proficiency. However, the reality of accomplishing a level of proficiency in four actual instruction sessions can, in all probability, be viewed as impossible. The statement further indicates that this proficiency will be determined by a partnership of librarians and teaching faculty. But are writing faculty any more comfortable measuring a library proficiency than librarians are with grading writing assignments?

The goal of the library instruction, for both the librarians and the writing faculty, is to increase students' writing, reading, and researching capabilities. In a sense, we are striving to create a level of competency in the students. The role of measuring this competency falls on both the librarians and the writing faculty. Perhaps the most effective indicator of the success of the library instruction is measured by the faculty who observe the use of library resources by students in assignments that follow up the instruction.

## THE SEARCH STRATEGY
## CHECKLIST AS AN ASSESSMENT TOOL

The effectiveness of the library instruction that has taken place during the first year is best demonstrated when applied to the research paper that is the culminating activity of CWRR. The Search Strategy Checklist is the assessment tool designed for this purpose.[3] Success of this final measurement is highly dependent on strong faculty–librarian partnership. The role of the librarian is best served as a facilitator. Librarians meet with each class to share search strategies and discuss the checklist, a systematic approach to research, which guides the students through the use of a variety of resources.

The faculty use the checklist in the manner they feel best serves their class needs: it may accompany the final research paper, be completed prior to the research paper, or used in part for shorter papers. Faculty who are in the best position to note the correlation between the students' research, bibliography, and the paper's content are responsible for grading the checklist.

## BUILDING PARTNERSHIPS TO THE STUDENTS' ADVANTAGE

Library assignments are not isolated exercises. Yet for many first-year students, the correlation between a particular class assignment and the library instruction presented earlier in the semester is not evident. Building on the faculty–librarian partnership is a key in connecting the assignments and the instruction to the students' advantage. This can include things as simple as the librarian compiling suggested resource lists for student use, and faculty alerting librarians to upcoming assignments with heavy library usage. Faculty–librarian communication is paramount to the students' success in applying the library skills presented in the class sessions.

## LOOKING TO THE FUTURE

There is probably never a point at which librarians and faculty will feel that they have integrated library instruction into a course to its fullest advantage. The valid concerns of librarians that the instruction is not enough, and of the faculty that the instruction takes too much class time will undoubtedly persist to some degree. Continual review of what we are doing and how we are doing will lead us to new innovations.

One key to the awareness of where we have been and where we are going takes place at semester meetings of faculty and librarians involved in first-year instruction. It is through the interfaces in these settings that many of the changes in the integration at MU have taken place. This also provides a forum for faculty and librarians to discuss effective assignments that incorporate the library instruction in an individual class and once again reflect on the shared goals.

The transition from a credit course to integration has meant that the level of instruction and the students' proficiency have changed. Conveying this to other faculty on campus remains a challenge. Enthusiastic administrators and program coordinators can further the success in implementing an integrated library instruction program.

We all have made much progress from an initial uneven and somewhat disappointing start to the point where we find ourselves today. Creating a partnership is a *process* with many ups and downs, trials and errors. We have developed, and continue to develop, successful faculty–librarian partnerships that are advantageous to first-year students. It is, indeed, an ongoing process.

## THE FACULTY PERSPECTIVE, BY NANCY DEJOY

For many faculty, integration of library components into a first-year writing course requires rethinking a course that either one has been teaching for a long time or that one has just begun teaching but with little or no formal training to teach. Because this process of rethinking requires integration on a number of levels, it can be overwhelming at first. Additionally, what might seem like small issues in the noninte- grated classroom become important issues in the integrated classroom. For example, scheduling class sessions in ways that make organiza- tional sense is a skill many teachers employ automatically. But organ- izing class sessions for materials one may not be familiar with and/or that others will present takes on a new dimension. In fact, organizing a course in such a situation requires a level of collaboration that many teachers are not trained to expect and with which they have no expe- rience. Furthermore, if implementation plans do not include consider- ations for the time it takes to create a well-integrated course, all parties, in this case faculty and librarians, can end up knowing that they have not had the time to create the most effective approach possible and feeling that the teaching–learning interactions of the course were not as effective as they could have been.

Many teachers are as familiar with writing assignments as they are with organizing class sessions. However, integration of a new course component can present faculty with challenges in this area too. Our li- brarians have created an approach to integrated library sessions that in- cludes a follow-up worksheet. From the librarians' perspective, faculty should "provide follow-up assignments that utilize library resources." However, faculty who have not been included in the process of iden- tifying student needs and deciding upon the focus for instruction can perceive the follow-up component of library instruction as discon- nected from the realities of their classrooms. Again, the results empha- size the ways that attempts at integrated approaches to learning can create productive tensions that foster collaboration. The instance cited here by Avery and McQuiston in which librarians revised the order of session presentations because faculty needed librarians to address evaluation of Internet resources earlier than they had originally done so is a good example of how integration can lead to more effective ef- forts between and among instructors working together to meet shared student learning goals. Once sessions are reorganized to address learn- ing goals, identifying skills needed by students in relation to course goals as well as in relation to the skills required by the library culture in general, faculty find it easier to provide follow-up assignments that "utilize library sources" in ways that make sense both in relation to the library sessions and in relation to the reading, writing, and/or re- searching goals of the course.

As a process, then, integration of the library component of Critical Writing, Reading, and Researching problematizes the organization of course materials, assignment writing, and other common faculty ac- tivities in ways that emphasize the differences between courses with isolated content and courses with integrated content. The tensions that result can be productive if they are used to address the larger issues involved—workload issues, collaborative faculty development issues—and if they lead to faculty–librarian efforts to revise curriculum in pedagogically sound ways.

In my role as coordinator of first-year writing programs, and in a context in which higher education continues to demand more and more of first-year programs in general, I have found that integration of the library component into our Critical Writing, Reading, and Researching courses parallels, exemplifies, and mirrors the challenges and opportunities we face as educators generally. For example, staffing issues become important in new ways as integration occurs. What does it mean, for example, for a university to insist upon integration across areas in a course traditionally staffed by a large percentage of adjunct faculty with high attrition rates? One thing it means is that librarians must employ integration methods appropriate to this situation, still leaving room for deeper collaboration as opportunities arise. Furthermore, because we are just beginning to articulate and practice shared goals for the courses in question, and because we are in an institutional context not yet used to integrated and collaborative endeavors, we must be patient as faculty develop ways to write assignments that engage library instruction in integrated ways.

On the other hand, integrating library instruction has opened many possibilities for faculty. Including collaborative presentation opportunities like this one, yearly updates about our library systems as faculty attend class sessions (especially the way such sessions position faculty as lifelong learners), and opportunities for guided reflection on the effects of technology facilitates professional development. These opportunities can deepen the sense of partnership that defines approaches to integration, allowing them to model best practices for collaborative endeavors generally.

Formative assessment can also be an important part of deepening the significance of integrative efforts and collaborative endeavors. If assessment is to be formative, it must give information about the success level of the program and about opportunities for improvement. Formative assessment must continually identify learners' starting points so that program activities can create strong relationships between the known and the new for those learners. Furthermore, there must be some consistency between the assessment philosophy being used to evaluate students and the assessment philosophy being used to evaluate the program. Lastly, formative assessment must facilitate the development of strong partnerships. Conceived of this way, the assessment process itself can help us not only name and evaluate our expectations for this integrated and collaborative endeavor, but it can also help us create hope and open possibilities as we experience the exhaustion and challenges that define implementation of a program that problematizes the heart of many of the traditional teaching practices of higher education.

Faculty–librarian partnerships can take a leadership role as we move toward a focus on student learning and its place in the teaching–learning dialectic of education, and as we dare to take the risks posed by the necessities of integration and collaboration in that dialectic. Because faculty–librarian partnerships parallel, exemplify, and mirror the challenges and opportunities we face as educators generally, they can go a long way toward helping us and our students meet the literacy demands we face across academic, cultural, personal, and other contexts.

## NOTES

1. Virginia Frank McQuistion, "The Credit Course: Reaffirmation from Two University Libraries-Measurement: Millikin University," *Research Strategies* 2, no. 4 (Fall 1984): 166–71.

2. Christine M. Larson, "What I Want in a Faculty Member," *Reference and User Services Quarterly* 37, no. 3 (Spring 1998): 259–61.

3. "Search Strategy Checklist," *Staley Library* 1999, <http://www.millikin.edu/staley/searchcwrr.html> [accessed 20 December 1999].

# 12

# Going to (the Engineering) School: Strategies for Integrating Library Instruction in the Engineering Curriculum

*Joan D. Ruelle*

Like many academic engineering librarians, I am not an engineer. My area of specialization is instruction, and when I came to the Science and Engineering Libraries at the University of Virginia, one of my goals was to increase the integration of library instruction in the engineering curriculum. The library had existing instruction programs in the Engineering School, but our levels of instruction had reached a plateau and we were looking for ways to expand our teaching mission.

The Science and Engineering Libraries have a good reputation of public service with our users, and a strong collaborative history with some units within the Engineering School. One of these is the Division of Technology, Communication and Culture, which is a unique program that provides engineering students with instruction in the humanities and social sciences, and is home to most of the school's writing courses. For the first-year classes in this division, we offer library instruction sessions to between 300–400 students each fall, introducing them to the library building and services, searching the on-line catalog, and providing a very brief introduction to general science and technology databases. In their fourth year, students take a course in this division that leads them through the process of writing their fourth-year thesis. For this course, the library teaches sessions for 200–300 students focusing on in-depth instruction and hands-on searching of subject-specific databases. Neither the first- nor the fourth-year course instructors felt that they could spare class time for library instruction. Furthermore, the sections of these classes were often larger than our classroom could accommodate. To provide library instruction under these circumstances, the library offers large numbers of these classes at different times of the day, and students are directed to sign up for a session that fits their personal schedule. In the fall of 1999, we offered 38 sessions for 303 first-year students, and 31 sessions for 254 fourth-year students in the first two and a half weeks of the school year. Admittedly, this is no small task. But the benefit of reaching so many students is well worth the short period of very intensive teaching. This is a very strong instruction program and it has the support of the engineering faculty, most of whom require their students to attend the sessions. While we were committed to continuing this program, we were also concerned that we were only seeing students in their first and fourth years. What about the second and third years?

In search of an answer to this question, we met with engineering faculty representatives to discuss the lack of library instruction in the middle years. While they were supportive of the library in general terms, it was clear they had no interest in expanding library instruction to the second- and third-year courses in the curriculum. Most of their reasons were good ones; many of these courses are either text-based with one textbook, or laboratory-based courses where faculty did not feel that additional research was required. But they also gave us reasons that we perceived as problematic; the Engineering School is committed to maintaining a four-year curriculum, so the pressure to fit everything in does not allow room to include "extras" like library instruction. The library is located in a separate building from the Engineering School; not far, but far enough that the distance is perceived as a barrier to students and faculty. And finally, we sometimes encountered the idea that the students *should already know* how to do this kind of research, and there is no appropriate place in the curriculum for what is perceived as remedial instruction.

Meeting with the engineering faculty was very instructive, and caused us to rethink our strategies for increasing the integration of instruction in the curriculum. Rather than assuming that the plateau of instruction was merely a marketing issue (in the past we had tried various ways to advertise our instructional services and waited for the requests to come pouring in), we decided to take a broader view. The approach was revised and we worked to make the library a more integrated part of the *life* of the Engineering School *as a whole*. Many of the strategies we employed have been used in academic libraries to increase liaison activities, and certainly our liaison work benefited as well. However, what we believe is unique is that we took this approach with the goal of increasing our library instruction foremost in mind. Many of the strategies were based on individual conversations, being in the right place at the right time, and other opportunities for connection that are difficult to define and even harder to quantify. Our strategies are personalized and diverse, and rather than providing a road map, I hope that sharing them with colleagues will spark ideas for personalizing this approach in other institutions.

## REACHING THE FACULTY

Personal contact with faculty members has been very important to the success of our initiative. To guarantee consistent contact with engineering faculty members, the librarian liaisons meet to set faculty contact goals each semester. Typical goals include meeting with every new faculty member in the departments, meeting with the departments' library representatives and chairs each year, and also contacting two additional faculty members each year. In these meetings, we learn about the faculty members' research and teaching, inquire about materials they need to guide our selection, and learn about the work their graduate students are doing. In addition, these meetings often provide an opportunity to tell the faculty member about a new resource, help them with database problems, and inform them about the library's reserves program. During the visit, we outline the range of instructional services we provide, and suggest how library instruction might supplement the courses they teach, if appropriate. We also ask the faculty members if they would like to receive notice of new books in their subject areas, and when something relevant appears on our new books shelf, we send them an E-mail notice.

In addition to one-on-one contact with faculty members, we also tried to expand our level of participation in faculty programs. Since most of our librarians do not have educational backgrounds in the sciences and engineering, we were seldom seen attending technical lectures in the past. To broaden our involvement, we attend more of these events, increasing not only our knowledge of our subject areas, but also demonstrating our interest in and collegiality with the engineering faculty. We have also actively let the faculty know that we take notice of happenings in their professional lives. This can mean small things such as sending congratulatory notes when faculty members receive grants or teaching awards, or larger projects like interviewing faculty members for the library newsletter. While these activities do not appear to be directly related to library instruction, they do increase the sense of collegiality between librarians and academic faculty, and this can facilitate library instruction. As instructional librarians, our students are rarely our own, and it is only right that faculty are reluctant to share their students with colleagues they do not know or trust.

## REACHING STUDENT SERVICES

To further broaden our participation in the life of the Engineering School, we also made contact with services outside of the classrooms, such as Engineering Career Services, Orientation and Open Houses, and the Office for Minority Programs. As we learned more about the services these offices provided and told them about our own, we were often invited to add a library component to existing programs. The library now participates in every general orientation in the Engineering School, we have team-taught courses with Career Services staff about doing preinterview research on companies, and we offer library instruction as a part of the Summer Bridge program for incoming minority students in the Engineering School.

## REACHING STUDENTS

Reaching the engineering students seemed a daunting task—there are so many of them, and their needs and interests are so diverse. To make this outreach more manageable, we decided to start with smaller, easily identifiable groups of students. We contacted the presidents of student engineering organizations and asked to meet with them to discuss their mission and how the library might be supportive. Some of the groups never responded, but some were happy to meet with us and were pleased to see the library take an interest in their organizations. From these discussions came some of our most creative and interesting outreach programs. The Society for Women in Engineering needed a place to have lunch with the high school women they host on-grounds each year. This is now a yearly lunch in the library—giving us an opportunity to interact with current and future students, and giving the students a different view of the role of the library in their lives. The Solar Airship Team is always on the lookout for opportunities to advertise and recruit for its student-run programs, and the library is always searching for innovative programs to host during Parents' Weekend. We worked with the airship team members to create an airships history display, and they flew one of their smaller airships in the library reading room during our Parents' Weekend program.

In addition to our outreach to student organizations, we also have organized our own Student Advisory Group, a volunteer group of students we invite to meet and discuss issues relating to the library once a semester. If the volunteer students are unable to make the meeting, we ask them to pass the invitation along to an interested friend. We bring pizza and sodas to the meeting, which is always appreciated by the students, and a short agenda of topics. The students are very free with both their praise and criticism, and we have learned a great deal about our services and their needs from these discussions.

## THE UNIVERSITY

In addition to activities specific to the Engineering School, we have also participated more broadly in university-wide events. Specifically, regular participation in events sponsored by the University's Teaching Resource Center (TRC) has been a great way to identify ourselves as teachers, and meet with faculty members throughout the university who are interested in improving their teaching skills. Participating in the TRC's intensive teaching portfolio workshop was a great opportunity to talk about the library's teaching mission, albeit often in response to the question, "What's a librarian doing in this workshop?"

Beyond teaching programs, there are numerous other opportunities to participate in university-wide programs. Librarians were often not in attendance at these events because of various demands on our time, and sometimes because of our perceived outsider status as nonacademic faculty. By carving out the time and making it a priority to attend these functions, we have done significant networking and learned more about our faculty colleagues, and they perceive us as more involved and interested in their work.

## BUT WHAT ABOUT INSTRUCTION?

It is clear that by changing our approach and becoming more involved in the broader life of the Engineering School, we learned a great deal about the engineering faculty, students and student services. But what about instruction? Did we reach our goal of greater integration of library instruction into the engineering curriculum? We *are* doing more instruction for the Engineering School, and perhaps more importantly, we are doing more *types* of instruction for the Engineering School. In addition to increased numbers of traditional course-related sessions, we are receiving more referrals from both faculty and students, and we are teaching significantly more one-on-one research tutorials. Since changing our approach, we have actually taught library instruction sessions in response to requests *from students*. The real success has been the change in perception that instruction is not an anomalous "extra," but rather an integral part of the library's role in relation to the Engineering School.

As an indicator of this integration, I will end with the example of what I call my "mailbox presence." As a follow-up to meetings with faculty members, I send out E-mails about new books in their research areas. I have noticed since beginning this practice that many of the E-mail requests I receive for library instruction come with the subject heading *RE: New Book*. Whether they are asking me about a new database, referring a student with a research problem, or inviting me to teach in one of their classes, I am convinced that this contact is facilitated by my presence in their mailbox. Look at your own mailbox and consider who is represented there; people you know, people with whom you have a connection, people who are a part of your life and community. I believe that we are succeeding in reaching our goal of greater integration of library instruction in the engineering curriculum as a result of this type of increased presence of the library in the life of the Engineering School.

# 13

# Learning Centers as Library Partners

*Susan Deese-Roberts*

Learning centers providing academic support services to undergraduate students are found on most university and college campuses. These centers can become powerful partners with library instruction programs, providing library information services in formats familiar to students such as peer tutoring and small group workshops. Learning centers can also provide an infrastructure for the hiring, training, and evaluation of tutors; the scheduling of tutoring appointments and workshops; and the assessment of services. Libraries can provide the tutoring training curriculum for library research skills and can determine the scope of tutoring sessions and workshop content. New services not traditionally offered by the library or learning center can exist through creative collaboration.

Library instruction provided by tutors is not designed to transform tutors into amateur reference librarians but rather to bring the benefits of tutoring assistance to the acquisition of library research skills. Tutors can learn to assist students with use of hardware and software, with search strategies, and with evaluation of information. Tutors also receive training related to the tutoring relationship such as training in interpersonal communication skills and the ethics of the tutor–student relationship.

## LEARNING CENTERS AS LIBRARY PARTNERS

Though learning centers have not been regarded in literature as traditional library partners, library and learning centers have much in common. Both libraries and learning centers express support of the academic and/or teaching mission of the institution in their statements of purpose. Both libraries and learning centers value lifelong and independent learning skills and provide students with tools necessary for out-of-classroom learning. Student-centered services, active learning, and measurable outcomes are principles of instruction offered through libraries and learning centers. Librarians regularly assist students who are working on course-specific assignments and often work with faculty on the creation of those assignments. Tutors work with students on course-specific assignments; tutors and/or their supervisors often work with faculty on the interpretation of assignments. Students who regularly use learning center services have formed the habit of seeking out-of-classroom learning assistance. Library instruction programs can capitalize on that student behavior by collaborating with the learning center to create library-specific academic support services.

The administrative location of a learning center within an institution of higher education will vary from institution to institution. Some learning centers are units within student affairs divisions while others are incorporated into academic affairs. Academic departments may administer some learning centers such as an English department that provides a writing lab or a mathematics department that sponsors a mathematics tutoring program. Some learning centers are associated with developmental education programs and primarily serve students enrolled in remedial courses.

## PEER TUTORING SESSIONS

Tutoring is a service provided by most learning centers; peer tutoring is often the model at four-year institutions with professional tutoring more common at two-year institutions. Some centers provide computer assisted instruction and a growing number are using Web sites to mediate services. Many learning centers offer academic support for specific courses as well as reading, writing, and study skills development. Some learning centers target specific populations of students, such as first-generation college students, and provide services to those students regardless of course enrollment. Other centers focus services on specific courses and provide services to any and all students enrolled in those courses.

In addition to developing tutoring services for library research skills, possible collaborations between libraries and learning centers include providing library research strategies incorporated into writing services. Research paper clinics could include both writing strategies and research strategies. Also, tutors in writing labs could be trained in research and information evaluation skills so that students could receive research and writing assistance at one time. Students could receive tutoring services at the learning center for classes in which there are library assignments, including those in which library instruction is offered. Tutors could attend library instruction sessions for a specific course and then work with students on the completion of the assignment. This approach might work well in those courses in which students receive library instruction and have a significant, related library assignment.

Tutors could also provide hands-on assistance with use of on-line catalogs, periodical indexes, browsers and search engines, and E-mail. This assistance could be scheduled as a follow-up to library instruction sessions or could be work completed prior to a library instruction session. The former approach accommodates those students who need more one-on-one instruction or hands-on experience than can be provided during a group session. The latter approach allows the library instruction program to set consistent expectations concerning student knowledge of basic library tools before attending library instruction sessions.

Tutors could also work as library assistants in the library, helping students with specific hardware and software problems, helping with basic search strategies, and making referrals to reference assistance. Tutors could be assigned to information desks and could assist with hands-on portions of library instruction sessions.

## FORMAL PEER ASSISTANCE PROGRAMS

Though the examples are limited, formal peer assistance programs have been used in libraries. The Reference Assistant Project (RAP) at the University of Wisconsin–Parkside was started in 1980 with funding from the Minority Programs Office. Upper-division minority students were trained to provide assistance to students enrolled in two introductory English courses in which specific library assignments must be completed. The students in the courses were primarily freshmen. "The rationale for the project was to provide student-to-student interaction in order to encourage minority students to use library facilities and therefore not delay completing their library competency requirements during the normal time period."[1] The reference assistants primarily answered directional, factual, or research strategy questions. The assistants helped students use reference tools directly related to specific course assignments, including the completion of a library skills workbook. Evaluations of the service indicated that students found the service to be valuable. They noted that the reference assistants were very helpful in guiding students through the use of reference sources and were easy to approach.

The Peer Information Counseling Program (PIC) was established at the University of Michigan Undergraduate Library in 1985 to improve retention of undergraduate minority students. Three assumptions were used in designing the program. The first two were that library research and information management skills are essential for academic success and that minority students in particular may find using a large research library an intimidating process. The third assumption was "that one of the best resources for helping minority students succeed is the influence of successful minority students themselves."[2] Peer information counselors assisted students in the reference area of the library by conducting reference interviews; helping with selection of the proper library index, catalog or database; determining appropriate subject headings; and recognizing the need to make a referral to a librarian. Counselors also provided assistance with writing term papers and use of word processing software. Writing instructional materials and publicizing the PIC program were the other main duties of the counselors. Student users, peer counselors, and librarians rated the program as effective. Students who used the service found it to be very valuable and encouraged its continuation and growth. Counselors enjoyed the opportunity to help others and noted the benefit of greater expertise in computer use and library research for their own studies. Librarians were impressed with the performance of the counselors, especially in the area of positive public service attitude.

In 1993, Mercy College developed plans for three major information literacy initiatives.[3] The first two initiatives were directed at increasing the number of course-integrated instruction activities and developing an information literacy outcomes assessment plan. The third initiative was to develop an information literacy peer tutoring program. The peer tutoring job description included (1) assisting students and faculty in locating and using materials in the library, accessing sources of materials not owned by the library, and using on-line sources; (2) training students and faculty to use a variety of equipment in the library, finding answers to factual reference questions, and making appropriate referrals to reference librarians; (3) helping students to select appropriate search strategies and sources; (4) developing brief bibliographies and guides; and (5) assisting librarians with preparation of instruction sessions. Training was accomplished through a packet of materials aimed at orienting tutors to job duties and expectations and at helping tutors to develop expertise in automated library systems. Supervisors discussed worksheets and suggested readings with tutors. Librarians and tutors evaluated the program as positive with some reservations. The actual duties performed by tutors varied widely from location to location. Some performed routine library tasks associated more closely with other student jobs such as shelving materials, filing cards, and servicing copy machines. Most peer tutors did provide assistance to patrons using on-line workstations. Most librarians involved in working with tutors reported that the assistance with using computer terminals and in searching databases was the most important role of the tutors.

Reservations included assessment and training issues: "Librarians are particularly concerned with evaluation of the peer tutor's performance and impact on students' overall acquisition of information literacy skills. Since the underprepared Mercy student has special trouble in formulating a good question, can a peer tutor be trained to recognize and refer or sharpen unfocused or misleading questions—such as 'Help me get something about dreams'—when the amount of training time is limited?"[4]

Peer library assistance was provided at Binghamton University. Undergraduate students enrolled in a course in the School of Education and Human Development were required to research a contemporary social issue by using library periodical resources. While librarians had traditionally conducted one-hour instruction sessions for the students in the course, it was apparent that the sessions were not successful in meeting the needs of all students. Inquiries at the Reference Desks provided evidence that students with limited computer skills and those who were novice library system users needed more assistance. In 1993, a librarian and an academic advisor decided to train a group of peer advisors to be library instruction peer advisors as well. The Peer Advisor Library Instruction Program was first introduced during the fall 1993 semester. At that time, only one peer advisor was trained to provide library instruction assistance; the peer advisor attended instruction sessions conducted by librarians and offered to tutor students individually, encouraging hands-on practice. Only two students used tutoring services that semester. The program was expanded during following semesters with as many as seven peer advisors trained as library instruction advisors. Training was composed of learning to conduct searches using campus library resources and the Internet and to assess the appropriateness of library sources. Peer advisors were required to complete an annotated bibliography of sources on a topic of their choice with requirements tied to specific sources and types of information. "Providing library instruction through the use of the existing Peer Advisory Program was an effective means of reaching more students in need by offering instruction in a supportive, non-threatening environment. . . . As the number of nontraditional students continues to increase and the library's electronic tools continue to evolve, the Peer Advisory Library Instruction Program will continue to supplement the classroom instructional session with personalized library instruction."[5]

At the University of New Mexico, the general library and the campus learning center, the Center for Academic Program Support (CAPS), collaborated to create a library strategies tutoring program.[6] CAPS has been located in the largest campus library since 1979 but previously had not provided services related to library use. A librarian designed the training curriculum for the library information portion of the tutor training program and served as a tutor supervisor during the pilot project. Tutors provided assistance with searching the on-line catalog, selected periodical indexes, and the Internet. Tutors also gave tours of library facilities and explained library policies and services. The program has expanded to include tutors working with library faculty and staff during library instruction sessions offered to students enrolled in a freshman writing course; tutors assist with hands-on portions of the sessions. Also, students enrolled in credit courses offered by the general library receive tutoring assistance, as needed, with library research projects. Plans for the future include tutors providing assistance to students using workstations in the reference area and serving at the Microforms/Periodical Information Desk.

## CONSIDERATIONS FOR COLLABORATION

When considering collaborations with campus learning centers, librarians would benefit from a review of national standards for learning assistance and tutor training programs. Two national professional associations target learning center professionals in their membership and provide leadership in establishment of professional standards—National Association for Developmental Education (NADE) and College Reading and Learning Association (CRLA). NADE and CRLA are members of the Council for Advancement of Standards in Higher Education (CAS). CAS comprises thirty-one member associations representing higher-education student services programs and has released national standards and guidelines for the field of learning assistance. Those standards are available from the CAS Web site <http://www.cas.edu>. CRLA provides tutor certification through guidelines for tutor training programs. More than 300 institutions of higher education have a CRLA-certified tutor training program on campus. A CRLA-certified program meets specific guidelines governing the hiring, training, and evaluation of tutors. Additional information is available through the CRLA Web site <www.crla.net/Certification.htm> and through conference presentations and workshops held at chapter and national conferences of CRLA, NADE, and other professional associations. NADE Self Study Guides: Models for Assessing Learning Assistance Programs allow programs to evaluate their own work situations in terms of program factors influencing tutoring, adjunction instruction, developmental courses, and the teaching/learning process. The guides are available at each annual national NADE conference or from the NADE Web site <http://www.umkc.edu/cad/nade/nadedocs/certstan.htm>.

Campus learning centers are potential library partners for the development of effective library instruction programs for students. Libraries and learning centers support institutional learning and teaching goals, model excellence in instruction, maintain high service standards, and value development of lifelong learning skills. Libraries and learning centers are often sites of formal and informal student learning; services often include both planned and spontaneous interactions with individuals and groups. Libraries have experimented with peer assistance programs but efforts are not widespread. Partnerships with learning centers can assist libraries in developing effective peer assistance programs and with integrating library instruction opportunities into academic support services. These partnerships benefit learning centers by allowing them to expand services to include development of research and information literacy skills. Learning centers often do not have the personnel expertise to provide the tutor training needed to assure that library strategies tutors meet information literacy standards; learning centers benefit from the expertise of librarians in providing that training. Students benefit from learning center/library collaborations through new academic support services often not available from the learning center or library alone.

# NOTES

1. Willie Mae Dawkins and Jeffrey Jackson, "Enhancing Reference Services: Students as Assistants," *Technicalities* 6, no. 8 (August 1986): 4.

2. Barbara MacAdam and Darlene P. Nichols, "Peer Information Counseling: An Academic Library Program for Minority Students," *The Journal of Academic Librarianship* 15 (September 1989): 205.

3. Ann M. Klavano and Eleanor R. Kulleseid, "Bibliographic Instruction: Renewal and Transformation in One Academic Library," in *Library Instruction Revisited: Bibliographic Instruction Comes of Age*, ed. Lynne M. Martin (New York: Haworth Press, 1995), 359–83.

4. Klavano and Kulleseid, "Bibliographic Instruction," 375.

5. Prue Stelling, "Student to Student: Training Peer Advisors to Provide BI," *Research Strategies* 14 (Winter 1996): 54.

6. Susan Deese-Roberts and Kathleen Keating, "Integrating a Library Strategies Peer Tutoring Program: Pilot Project," *Research Strategies* 17, no. 2 (Summer 1999), in press.

# 14

# Bleeding Edge: Challenges in Delivering Educational Technology Services

*Jim Duncan*

I would submit that the range of expectations put upon librarians and support staff these days makes all of us not just busy, but frantic. For many of us who manage educational technology facilities, standard operating procedure involves a constant state of change. The bleeding edge. We are continually adapting in our job responsibilities and in the tools we employ. This is certainly impacting education services librarians too. How many of us were authoring Web pages in 1994? How many of us are doing it now? Is anyone besides me wondering how long we can maintain this pace amid such changes in technology and continue to apply the technology creatively to our work and our services?

I bet you thought you were going to read about how heavenly it is here in Iowa City, just seventy miles southwest of the Field of Dreams. Well, okay, maybe you'll read a little about our idyllic surroundings. But first, I'd like to share a story with you. It's about baseball.

*One dreamy, sun-soaked day several years ago, I took a day trip in my beat-up, rattletrap '79 Jeep Wagoneer. This piece of fine automotive machinery was so oxidized that it no longer had any visible color, or at least any color you would describe as factory standard. It was simply rust. But somehow, the Wagoneer was comforting to drive; you always knew you were still on the road when you could look down at the floorboard between the gas and the brake and see asphalt rushing past.*

*I drove north out of Dyersville, following the signs, admiring the lush fields of corn and beans, and settling into the curves of the gravel roads. And before I knew it, the place rose into view, like something out of a movie. The Field of Dreams.*

*It was noon, maybe one o'clock. The parking lot was empty, the field in need of a mow. I was the only person there. So I stood for awhile and looked at the house on the hill where Kevin Costner's movie family had spent evenings swinging on the porch, watching the sky fade to purple while the fireflies lit up like random sparks of fluorescent green-yellow. I sat in the stands next to the field, just a little disappointed. It had seemed bigger, more immaculate on the theatre screen, with clean lines and perfect blades of grass. Here, it looked just like any Little League field, in any town.*

*There's only so long that you can sit and look at an empty baseball field carved out of the corn somewhere in rural northeast Iowa. No sooner had I turned to walk to the Wagoneer when a station wagon roared into the lot, spitting gravel from beneath its wheels. All doors flew wide open and a horde of boisterous children with mitts and bats and balls poured out, shrieking in pure joy at their summer freedom. Within minutes, the game had begun. I watched and listened to their excitement and saw that the field had come alive.*

*Then somewhere in the middle of a rotation, an average-sized girl with average hair stepped up and swung her bat with a perfect arc. That sweet crack of wood rang true, and within seconds, the ball had soared out into left field into the tall corn.*

I got to thinking about that game the other day because I realized that there is a connection between baseball and the work we do in our educational technology facilities. If you'll bear with my extended metaphor, I'll give you a little play-by-play.

Initially, there's the investment. Often, it's capital spending on construction and computer hardware. In the movie, it was a bodiless voice whispering, "If you build it, they will come." In 1992, we carved out a section of our main library at the University of Iowa to build the Information Arcade. In 1996, we constructed what you could consider my playing field, the Information Commons, located in our health sciences library. In a visit to Hardin Library for the Health Sciences, you would see open-access computing areas, two electronic classrooms, and our multimedia development stations, a total of 10,000 square feet. We are fortunate to have this built, but like the baseball game in my memory, the setting is far less interesting than the action that takes place on the field. First base is our first goal: enhanced delivery of new media services.

What are new media services? I consider them similar to the traditional set of services offered in a traditional learning resources center, only with new media and new tools. In the Information Commons, for example, we don't have video and audio tapes, 35 mm slide collections, or medical models. We offer digital resources on CD-ROM or whatever is available on our servers. Our specialized collection of books largely support the use of our technology tools.

But, as we dash toward that first base, things can prevent a safe scamper down the path. I'll give you three: (a) patron access issues, (b) information service challenges, and (c) technical support issues.

## OBSTACLES IN PATRON ACCESS TO RESOURCES

In a facility like ours, hours of operation have an effect on access. We have collections of CD-ROM products available for checkout at our service desks. Their use requires retrieval by a staff member from our cabinets. Even for educational titles delivered from our servers, access is limited by our hours. In many ways this is a "closed stacks" system. We made this operational decision based on the complexity of our titles and the belief that many users need support to simply load and launch the executables for these CD-ROM titles. It's also a budget issue—we simply don't have the funds to staff our Information Commons and Information Arcade facilities anytime the libraries are open, nor do we have the budget to license individual CD-ROM titles for delivery on the Web, anytime, anywhere.

Let's look at collection development. Given the cost of these multimedia titles, I find it hard to justify purchases unless they are guaranteed to be used by students, and often that requires some integration with the curriculum. In my experience, if it isn't a required component or at least recommended in a course, it won't get used. But in basing my collection development approach on these cost-efficiency factors, by not purchasing certain top-quality educational multimedia titles, am I in a sense denying access to key resources that could have a positive impact on students' learning if only they were available? This begs a question; does serendipity still have a potential role in the learning process within our high-tech facilities?

Here's another access issue. When our patrons sit down in front of our computers, their access is complicated by a dizzying array of interfaces. You have the basic operating system with its file management scheme and collection of icons. Sometimes we try to enhance access in our facilities by purchasing application or menuing software designed to facilitate the quick access to our collections of educational software or electronic research resources. We try to standardize our screens. Unfortunately, on a large campus like ours, we often have different departments administrating different educational computing facilities and end up with different front ends.

And then you have the variety of educational software packages themselves, each offering its own flavor of interface. We often find ourselves doing quick instructional sessions when it's clear that the "intuitive interface" designed by the software author turns out to be not so intuitive. Such interfaces serve as barriers for delving in and accessing the relevant content. When you're dealing with a book or journal, you don't have to instruct the patron how to open the cover and turn the pages or consult the index to find a subject contained within that piece of bound media.

## REFERENCE AND INFORMATION SERVICE SHORTCOMINGS

How do users know what title they want to use? If a faculty member or instructor hasn't recommended or required the use of a particular title, then the student often asks us what to use.

One day I was passing by our service desk and I overheard one of our student staff members assisting a patron. He was friendly, stopped what he was working on at the desk, gave his full attention to the patron, and listened to the question. He turned, pulled one of our CD-ROMs from the collection, and pointed out an available computer nearby, saying "If you need any help getting started, just flag me." All in all, it was a great example of friendly, user-oriented service. But there was a problem. This patron was a second-year medical student who wanted to use something to supplement his studies for the upcoming board exam. We do have many titles, but some are better suited to nursing students or speech pathology and audiology students; other titles are more for reference than interactive, self-paced learning. The CD-ROM suggested by our staff member wasn't going to satisfy the medical student's needs, only neither of them knew it.

The real issue here is lack of reference experience and lack of knowledge of our collection. What if our student staff member had asked a few key questions? Even then, how would he have known which CD-ROM to pull? It's no surprise that our reference service within the facility may be lackluster, given that we staff our desk with undergraduate work-study and part-time students. Good service requires training and plenty of experience at the desk to learn the collection.

We operate in a diverse technological environment. This is what I worry about: our staff can handle questions related to E-mail, word processing, accessing Web sites, running software, scanning images, and digitizing video. That's of considerable value for our service reputation. But what about typical reference questions about searching MEDLINE or other biomedical literature databases, or searching the Web, or searching specialized resources such as statistical data sets? I'm concerned that our student staff members are so eager to help patrons that sometimes they don't always refer patrons to our information services desk when they're out of their depth of knowledge.

## TECHNICAL SUPPORT CHALLENGES

Here's another challenge. We are implementing electronic titles in stand-alone and networked environments and having to ensure ongoing operating ability over time. And it's impossible, sometimes. Think about the viable, well-designed instructional titles you used to run in your facilities that either weren't updated to run on Windows 95/NT or Mac OS 8.x and possibly never will be. We have one such product, Virtual Heart, which will run on Macintosh, but not a Power Mac, and will run on Windows 3.1 but not 95 or NT. The physiology department loves this simulation software, and has integrated it so fully into its lab sessions that replacement will be a project in itself. You just don't have that problem with a book or journal. Unlike an electronic textbook, a printed textbook doesn't suddenly stop functioning with the latest upgrade of an operating system or the achievement of a landmark date, like 01/01/2000. Can you imagine being unable to open a book's cover because of some conflict with a .dll file?

Negotiating license agreements has become a tangled mess. These agreements often restrict access and/or use in ways that are counter-productive to our delivery objectives. Some of you have run into this, where a given title would be better used if it were available to multiple users simultaneously, or at least accessible from multiple workstations. Unfortunately for us, some publishers have created licensing restrictions that limit our ability to provide good access. For example: (a) the publisher will allow you to load and deliver the title from an application server only if you pay through the nose for a facility or site license, despite your guarantee to limit the number of user launches through metering software; or (b) you cannot deliver the title in a library setting, period. Only individual users may purchase and use it. Can you imagine being told that a book cannot be purchased by a library, that only individuals can buy it? Some publishers even go so far as to package their software and license agreement statements in shrink wrap so that by opening it, the license agreement is put into effect before you've even had a chance to read it!

The technology itself, by constantly changing, has added further complexity and challenge to our services. We encounter corrupted files, macro viruses, operating systems locking up in mid-use, printer jams, confusion about downloading and saving information, poorly documented software, and many more problems. Good, problem-solving, technical support people are sometimes difficult to retain because of the widening salary gap between the commercial and academic sectors.

*At the Field of Dreams, the game was in progress. Somewhere out there, deep in the corn, was a boy, the left fielder, frantically hunting for the ball. Meanwhile, our runner was rounding first and barreling*

*like a little human steam engine toward second base, legs and arms*
*pumping like pistons. Several kids were calling to the fielder to hurry.*

Second base is our second goal: development of consultation services and educational training.

In our educational technology facilities, consultation services take
place primarily around our multimedia development workstations. We
rely heavily on undergraduate students, and many have become versed
in the use of the tools during the course of their employment. What we
can't train so well is an advanced knowledge of how the tools can be
applied to curricular needs.

This is where we involve our next level of staffing, our graduate assistants. These students (we refer to them as Commons Consultants or
Arcade Consultants) possess specialized skills or have been trained in
advanced technologies, ranging from Web-based course management
and delivery systems to multimedia development tools. Our graduate
students have a stronger understanding of pedagogy and are able to interact more comfortably one-on-one with faculty and staff. In the Commons specifically, faculty and staff are the primary users of our multimedia development area and the primary recipients of our consultation
services. Increasingly, we've been able to use graduate assistants as instructors for our small- and large-group training workshops.

Time is the biggest issue for delivering these services. One-on-one
consultations can last for thirty minutes or five hours, spread across
several days. It really depends on the patron's need and level of expertise with the technology. Technical hitches sometimes arise, which
adds further complexity to the interaction; sometimes a staff member
will schedule a follow-up time for a consultation in order to buy time
to troubleshoot a problem or learn a particular software technique.

Then what if a staff member solves a problem, but another staff
member encounters the same issue? Inadequate communication between staff members, or between management and staff can result in
inefficiencies.

We've put an enormous investment in staff training in order to create a system of qualified consultants. This is time intensive and can be
particularly problematic if turnover is high.

Finally, there is some question about the value of providing educational training to faculty on such topics as Web publishing, multimedia authoring, and other development topics. Within the University of Iowa Libraries, we've established a strong track record of
providing faculty with technology training, both campus-wide and
within individual units, like ours. One example is our nTITLE workshops, which bring together faculty from across campus for a week
to learn: PowerPoint; Web publishing; image scanning and opti-
mization; and WebCT, a Web-based course management and delivery system. We've seen faculty members become energized during

their weeklong training, and I'm sure it helps that they receive a $3,000 stipend that can be applied to the purchase of hardware or software used for preparing their on-line courses.

In the health sciences, I'm not convinced this is the most cost-effective approach—many faculty are too busy with research and clinical responsibilities to put time into producing and editing Web pages. They return from a week of training and put the hefty workshop training manual on their shelves, fully intending to implement some of their learning but never quite finding the time to spend pushing pixels. One can argue that it's important for faculty to receive such training in order to expose them to the possibilities of new educational technologies. But one also can question whether or not it's cost effective for the university to be investing in such exhaustive faculty training, particularly in techniques that instructional technologists and librarians are already best equipped to handle. After all, aren't our health sciences faculty members best qualified to conduct research and see patients? I often advocate the establishment of a service where faculty and librarians and technologists can come together as teams to produce such resources, each bringing a relevant skill set and thereby enhancing the cost effectiveness. In such a model, the faculty members would come with content knowledge, the librarians and instructional technologists would organize and direct the projects, and the graduate and undergraduate students would perform the lion's share of the production work.

In the Information Commons, we teach our own heavily attended sets of workshops. The Web publishing series (an eight-week set of workshops) was a real success the one spring in which we delivered it, but the effort required forty-two hours of staff time to plan and deliver. I've since evaluated the effectiveness of the series and determined that it was too time intensive for us to conduct such workshops when the primary attendees were general university staff interested in producing fancy Web pages showcasing their pets and hobbies. Our intention had been to empower staff members within the health sciences colleges and hospital who were responsible for some aspect of Web page development as part of their work. Since evaluating our series, we've offered short workshops targeted to specific colleges or departments. These workshops are not so comprehensive; they are reduced in scope and are structured to address specific curricular development needs, such as training in PowerPoint or in use of the university's WebCT system.

*The batter was running and craning her neck to see if she could press her luck. Rounding second base, she notched it into a higher gear and dashed toward third. Most of the kids were yelling with excitement at the action unfolding. The poor left fielder was a dim ghost out in the corn, rattling the stalks as he continued to search for the baseball.*

Third base is our third goal: production of multimedia resources for instruction and learning.

This is a role unfamiliar to many libraries. In the Information Commons, we've had some successes in this arena. But there is an underlying question: is this an appropriate role for us? As libraries we traditionally serve as information providers and collection managers—should we be moving toward a role of content creation and publication?

The requirements for doing multimedia production successfully are significant. Staff members must have a strong knowledge of development tools and their potential application to a range of instructional needs. Staff members must possess the skills to translate a faculty member's desired teaching outcomes into tangible, functional, educational software packages or on-line learning resources. The issue here is one of identity. Are we as librarians becoming instructional designers?

Publishing electronic content consumes a huge amount of time. In the Information Commons, we've been doing this—one example is our recent production of an educational CD-ROM title, *The Bones of the Skull: A 3-D Learning Tool*. It combines text and images in a format that includes interactions with users and the integration of media resources produced in a QuickTime VR format. Essentially, as the user works through the interactive content, exploration of associated virtual anatomical models provides a learning approach that simulates learning in a lab. Users can manipulate the models on screen by rotating or tilting, and we've added extra value by providing clickable hotspots pointing to labeled views, color correlations, and identification of landmarks.

Talk about bleeding edge. This project bled us for eighteen months, partly because the technology had not caught up to our ideas for its functionality and integration within core instructional content. A significant investment in staff time was required, but needed to be balanced with the ongoing demand for consultation services and for teaching small and large group educational workshops. These other services impacted our development time. To do such work in bits and pieces is difficult; at times we required intensive sessions with staff attention focused purely on production. The hardware and software necessary for the project had to be chosen carefully. We also needed to become intimate with copyright law and its application to the use of digital materials, but from a publisher's perspective. Our release for the product will likely occur in spring 2000, and we're currently grappling with our understanding of mass-publishing and distribution processes.

*The action had reached its zenith. Our batter veered outside the base path, still looking over her shoulder to see if the left fielder had emerged. The corn suddenly parted, and the fielder exploded from the field of green, waving the ball for everyone to see. He cocked back, nearly horizontal, and hurled it. I remember that moment as if it were frozen, a perfect white sphere hanging motionless in a perfect blue sky.*

## HOME PLATE: BACK TO THE FUTURE?

What is our future? If we've rounded the bases, are we just coming back to the same place? I like to think that our future is something different, but with many of the same characteristics of our present, that we will maintain our fundamental missions, philosophies, and ideas about service.

I'll wrap up by bringing us back to where I started, the demands on people who operate educational technology centers or similar library facilities.

In many institutions, one professional staff member is employed in these types of learning resource centers. There is an expectation that the person be available to handle reference questions; do specialized collection development in conjunction with curricular needs; attend and contribute expertise at meetings, particularly related to Internet and multimedia technologies; provide consultations regarding educational multimedia to faculty and staff; teach courses; direct the development of multimedia resources such as Web sites and CD-ROM titles (even to the extent of contributing with hands-on efforts); provide technical troubleshooting for software, computers and peripherals; manage student staff and perhaps merit and professional staff; write grant proposals; prepare snazzy conference presentations; and write articles for publication.

If there is just one theme to draw together the many issues described above, it's this: just as you can't play baseball without fielding a team, you can't run an educational technology facility without adequate staff. This issue stands at the core of everything we do within our libraries, from traditional services to new media services. Investment by our institutions in the staffing infrastructure of our libraries is critical to our ability to take on these evolving roles of librarian/instructional technologist/educator.

I'm sorry I don't have more space to write about some of the solutions that we've implemented at the University of Iowa Libraries. I wish I could provide more detail about our newest ball field, the 5,000-square-foot expansion of the Information Commons we recently completed. This project essentially doubled the size of our existing facility. It involves a second electronic classroom designed to be a flexible, learner-centered space, and a case-based learning and small-group study room partially designed as a result of our experiments with wireless networking. We are applying our experience on that pilot study to a research project we've planned in collaboration with the College of Dentistry. There we go again, more bleeding edge activity.

I'll leave you with the end of my story.

*As the runner rounded third and came sprinting down the home stretch, a chaperoning parent, who for some reason was not caught up*

*in the action on the field, called out, "Hey, anybody want ice cream?"*
*All motion stopped, as if the game were freeze tag instead of baseball.*
*The throw dropped into the infield, untouched. There were cheers; the*
*field was emptied in seconds, the station wagon crammed with little*
*sweating bodies, and in a cloud of dust, was gone. It was not a perfect*
*ending to the game, but for me a memorable one nonetheless.*

Thank you kindly for reading; I welcome your communication on
these and related issues via E-mail: jim-duncan@uiowa.edu. You can
visit the Information Commons on the Web at <http://www.lib.uiowa.
edu/commons/>.

# 15

# Powerful Partnerships: Cross-Campus Collaboration for Faculty Instructional Technology Education

*Susan Hollar, Laurie Sutch, and Darlene Nichols*

Developments in information technology continuously offer new opportunities for faculty to enhance their teaching, to provide creative learning experiences for students, and to enrich their scholarship. With the proliferation of information technology, faculty are faced with the challenge of finding time to experiment with new resources as well as knowing where to go on campus for assistance and guidance. In response to this faculty need, eight University of Michigan units have collaborated to create a network of technology support staff to share knowledge and resources and to offer Enriching Scholarship, an innovative weeklong series of seminars on the integration of technology into teaching, learning, and research. This grass-roots group is called the Teaching and Technology Collaborative (TTC). Despite a campus more typically characterized by decentralization and autonomy, it was clear that these units had a common ground and that cooperation would not only benefit the university teaching faculty, but the participating service units as well.

## THE ORIGINS OF THE TEACHING AND TECHNOLOGY COLLABORATIVE

In the fall of 1997, the University of Michigan Instructional Technology Division's Office of Instructional Technology (a department that supported advanced applications of instructional technology) took the first steps that led to the formation of the TTC. An Office of Instructional Technology (OIT) staff member proposed a meeting for campus units that offered technology training to faculty at the University of Michigan.

Units invited to the initial meetings included the university library, the Science Learning Center (a computing facility for science education), the Center for Research on Learning and Teaching (a unit that provides seminars and training on university teaching in general), the Faculty Exploratory (a technology training facility for faculty), the Language Resource Center (a facility for language learning), and the University Library's Knowledge Navigation Center (a technology training facility for students, faculty, and staff). The purpose of this meeting was to bring together units from across campus to share information about their services and programs, to discuss observations about campus needs, and to share details on the equipment and software that were available in different units for faculty. As a result of these meetings, the Teaching and Technology Collaborative was formed with the following goals:

- to raise faculty information technology literacy levels
- to increase visibility of campus units that support faculty use of information technology
- to establish an informal network for faculty who are interested in the integration of technology resources into their research and teaching

Since the TTC was an informal group, initially there were no criteria for membership. After an academic year of working together, the TTC set aside time to evaluate whether or not all of the right units were involved. Even though the most prominent campus units involved in technology and teaching were part of the TTC, it was important to make sure no unit was missing that should be involved. From these discussions, formal criteria for membership evolved and new units were invited to join. The membership criteria were (1) commitment to meetings, (2) real and in-kind contributions, (3) focus on faculty support, and (4) campus-wide or very large constituency.

Although it is the unit that is the member of TTC, the unit must send a representative who is able and willing to attend meetings. During the planning period for Enriching Scholarship, for example, the TTC meets weekly for as long as two hours and subcommittees may also have meetings. Other times of the year, meetings are less frequent, but still the commitment for the unit and for the individual representing that unit is significant. The activities of TTC need to be supported by staff time and in-kind contributions as well as by real monetary support. Fortunately, all of the units have been very supportive and willingly provide a range of resources, including direct financial contributions. Because the primary focus of the TTC has been on the work of faculty, it is expected that service to faculty is part of each unit's mission. Finally, services of each TTC unit must be available to faculty campus-wide or to very large-constituencies. Although most academic departments have information technology support staffs, the TTC functions on a broader scale.

In sharing observations about campus technology directions, members discovered some common themes. Probably the biggest issue, and the one that really galvanized the formation of the TTC, was the campus confusion over which units provided what services. Numerous departments appeared to offer similar services—it was not surprising that many faculty members were bewildered. Adding further confusion were the wide range of skill levels among faculty and the levels supported by the various units. Some units were the best choice for technology-savvy faculty, but not for novices, who were better served elsewhere. All of these faculty members, however, were experiencing the same thing—a campus culture that increasingly expected that technology would be used in delivering instruction—and overhead projectors just were not enough anymore. With limited time and ever-expanding expectations, faculty needed help. Finally, TTC members were observing a slow and steady shift toward more interdisciplinary research and interdepartmental cooperation, creating a positive climate for collaborative efforts such as the TTC.

## COLLABORATION AT WORK:
## THE ENRICHING SCHOLARSHIP PROGRAM

The TTC's first collaborative product was the TTC Matrix <http://www.umich.edu/~teachtec/TTC_table.html>, an attempt to organize a one-page guide to technology training and support services on campus. The next step was a more detailed road map describing these services. That project quickly evolved to a much more exciting plan, however, after much discussion and debate. Enriching Scholarship: Integrating Teaching, Information, and Technology was a weeklong series of workshops and seminars all related to incorporating technology into teaching. During this week, each unit would offer workshops—many of which were already offered throughout the year—that would be presented as a single, coherent package. The series included software-specific workshops such as PowerPoint or Claris HomePage and information resources such as Lexis-Nexis's Academic Universe and ISI's Web of Science. There were also more general programs on issues such as copyright, particularly as it related to using technology, and course assessment. There were workshops at different skill levels and repeated sessions for high demand topics, such as Web page design. Timing was also an important consideration—when were faculty members still on campus, but with time to attend? The month of May was selected as the best choice—shortly after commencement when faculty were generally still on campus, but after the heavy burdens of winter term.

The TTC had several goals for Enriching Scholarship:

- to increase faculty awareness of facilities and of services
- to provide instruction, information, and inspiration for faculty members on using technology in their research and teaching

- to provide opportunities for task-oriented, hands-on learning so that by the end of a session or the end of the week, the faculty member could have a basic Web page, PowerPoint presentation, or EndNote library
- to encourage faculty to return to TTC units for further instruction and assistance (Enriching Scholarship was to be a starting point, not an end)

In May 1998, the TTC offered fifty workshops as part of Enriching Scholarship. A total of 185 individuals participated, with over 900 registrations. Two-thirds of the participants were faculty, and other participants included graduate student instructors and university staff members. The series as a whole, as well as most of the specific sessions, received extremely high marks from program participants; sessions on Web page development and graphics and multimedia applications were especially popular. The faculty members appreciated the opportunity for hands-on, goal-oriented workshops that led them to a product. The program was such a hit that there was little question that the TTC would bring it back in 1999.

After reviewing evaluations from the first year, it was clear that organizers needed to allow for a broader range of skill levels. Descriptive materials needed to be more explicit regarding the skill level of each session and what the participants' experience should be. There was also a demand for more skill development sessions for novices. Finally, TTC members learned that faculty members had used Enriching Scholarship as an opportunity to network with faculty they would not have otherwise met. This last benefit could be better promoted in the following year.

In 1999, the Enriching Scholarship week was launched with a showcase of faculty projects. More than twenty faculty members were on hand to demonstrate ways they were using technology in their teaching. Other faculty members were free to browse through printed TTC materials from each TTC unit and to talk with each other and the showcase participants over a light brunch. For the hands-on training sessions during the remainder of the week, workshop offerings expanded to sixty-four. With more than 200 individuals filling almost 1,000 slots, Enriching Scholarship again received a very positive response. About two-thirds were faculty, as in the previous year, although a much larger number were junior faculty members. Further, 75 percent of faculty participants were new to Enriching Scholarship, meaning more faculty were developing their technology skills and more users were learning about the many services available to them.

## UNIVERSITY LIBRARY CONTRIBUTIONS

The University Library as a unit has been strongly committed to Enriching Scholarship and to the TTC. While the library already has a high profile on campus, faculty members do not typically think "library" when they think of technology. There is also a need to integrate information resources into other technology tools; for example, linking full text electronic resources into course Web pages, or downloading from electronic databases into bibliographic software programs. Thus, both the library and the campus gain from the library's participation in technology training for faculty. The library participated actively in planning and teaching sessions both years. In the first year, the library offered instruction on new information resources as well as presentations on library services. In 1999, the library offered sessions called "Scholar's Workshops" in the humanities, social sciences, arts, and science, in addition to instruction on software applications offered by Faculty Exploratory staff. (The Faculty Exploratory became part of the University Library in 1999.) Another contribution was instruction on the bibliographic database management software programs EndNote and ProCite.

## PLANNING ENRICHING SCHOLARSHIP

Planning Enriching Scholarship is a large task. To tackle the planning process effectively, the TTC formed five subgroups: scheduling, publicity, budget, registration, and evaluation/assessment.

### Scheduling Subgroup

The scheduling subgroup was responsible for developing a coherent, well-rounded offering of workshops within the framework of the week. To start the scheduling process, TTC units submitted a proposal for each workshop the unit wanted to offer. The proposal included a description of the workshop, as well as any special room or technical needs, such as a preferred platform (Mac or Windows) or a particular piece of software. The subgroup then set an initial program, striving for complementary workshop offerings and a range of participant skill levels, as well as selective repeat sessions for popular topics such as Web page development and scanning. The scheduling subgroup also identified campus facilities for workshops, and established standardized time slots in order to avoid overlap and to allow participants travel time and breaks. The initial schedule was then brought to the larger group for revisions and final approval.

### Publicity Subgroup

Publicity for Enriching Scholarship took three main forms: print, electronic, and word of mouth. Prior to producing this publicity, the subgroup worked with a graphic designer to create a logo, which was used in the print and electronic materials. Print material included postcards (see figure 1) that were sent to faculty via campus mail six to eight weeks prior to the event. The postcards were intended to get faculty to

Figure 1

start thinking about Enriching Scholarship, and included some examples of workshop titles and the URL for the Web site. Posters were also placed around campus, including academic departments, well-traveled areas, and campus parking structures. Text was also submitted for inclusion in campus news sources, such as the faculty/staff newspaper. Brochures with the complete workshop schedule and registration information were also available upon request prior to Enriching Scholarship and were available during the week.

Publicity in electronic format was an important tool for communicating Enriching Scholarship to the campus. Information was sent out via E-mail to TTC units' E-mail groups, as well as through the university's central administrative E-mail groups. The E-mail messages briefly explained Enriching Scholarship and pointed faculty to the Web site. The Web site <http://www.umich.edu/~teachtec/ES99/ES99index.html> was the central point for information on Enriching Scholarship, and included the complete workshop schedule and descriptions, as well as on-line registration. In addition, announcements about Enriching Scholarship were made at other events, including unit workshops, meetings, and interactions with faculty.

## Budget Subgroup

While the budget subgroup oversaw costs, the account was coordinated and managed by one TTC unit. Enriching Scholarship costs included publicity, special equipment (microphones, recording equipment), catering, room reservations, and in 1998, a special speaker from off campus. In addition to actual funds, TTC units made many in-kind contributions, particularly in staff time. In 1998, costs totaled $2,650, with in-kind donations of a graphic designer, staff preparation and teaching time, photocopying, and speaker fees. In 1999, costs totaled $4,112, with in-kind donations similar to those of 1998. The increase in cost was a result of more printed pieces including more posters and reusable signs.

### Registration Subgroup

In both years, the registration process for Enriching Scholarship was handled primarily on-line as well as by phone. In 1998, registrations were taken via a form on the TTC Web site and then manually added to a FileMaker Pro database. Confirmations were then manually sent to participants via E-mail. Because of the overwhelming response, this system was very labor intensive, and in 1999, the registration system was automated. Registrants entered data via a Web form <http://www.umich.edu/~teachtec/ES99/registration.html> that automatically wrote the information to a database. The database generated E-mail confirmations that were sent immediately to the registrants. Registrants were also able to log in to the Web site to view and change workshop selections, and instructors could view class lists via an instructor's Web page.

### Evaluation/Assessment Subgroup

The evaluation/assessment subgroup developed evaluations for distribution at each workshop. The goal of the evaluation was to acquire information about what worked and did not work for each session and Enriching Scholarship as a whole. The results were compiled in the Statistical Package for the Social Sciences, and the TTC drew upon the results to plan the next year's Enriching Scholarship. Relevant results were also included in reports to unit directors.

## FUTURE OF THE TTC AND ENRICHING SCHOLARSHIP

The TTC has proven to be a useful organization and resource for its members, as well as the campus as a whole. By combining forces, the TTC partners have been able to creatively address a number of campus issues related to instructional technology and develop a more supportive infrastructure for the faculty without considerable expense. At this writing, Enriching Scholarship 2000 is on the drawing board with plans for expanding faculty opportunities for networking and discussion along with an array of new training sessions. The TTC has made it possible for its members to better manage the escalating changes by creating an environment of mutual support for staff and faculty.

# 16

# Collaborating with Faculty to Enhance an Academic Research Library's User Education Program

*Jon R. Hufford*

This chapter examines the collaboration efforts of librarians and faculty to provide Web-based instruction in information literacy to Texas Tech University's students. The collaboration relates directly to the increasingly important role new technology and distance education play in higher education. The chapter includes a review of the missions, goals, and efforts of the university's Distance Learning Council; the Texas Tech University's Libraries' Distance Learning Team; and the Teaching, Learning, and Technology Center (TLTC), which among other things is responsible for preparing faculty to use new technologies in the classroom. These entities provide the motivation for the collaboration. Several collaboration efforts are discussed.

Though collaboration has always had an important role to play in academe's world of scholarship, teaching, and service, much more than usual has been written on this subject in recent years. This literature generally attests to the fact that collaboration plays a much greater role than formerly in accomplishing the diverse activities associated with the academic world. There are undoubtedly many reasons for the increasing emphasis on professional collaboration. Certainly, one of the most influential recent publications that have encouraged this trend is W. Edward Deming's *The New Economics for Industry, Government, Education*.[1] Steven Covey's *The Seven Habits of Highly Effective People* is another.[2] Covey's habit of synergy, which emphasizes the importance of creative cooperation, has influenced professionals across the country, encouraging them to collaborate with colleagues in the course of their professional lives.

Following the trend, professionals at academic research libraries have wholeheartedly embraced the idea of collaboration. This is especially the case for librarians responsible for user education programs. This chapter examines the extent to which members of the Texas Tech University Libraries' user education unit have collaborated with Texas Tech faculty in order to enhance the instruction offered library users. It focuses on user education through Web-based instruction and in an indirect manner on the increasingly important role played by new technologies, generally, and distance learning.[3]

## THE TRANSFORMATION TAKING PLACE IN HIGHER EDUCATION

A transformation is occurring in how universities teach students. New technology; increased collaboration among faculty, administrators, and support staff; changes in the makeup of student bodies, with adults, minorities, women, and foreign students participating in ever increasing numbers; and distance learning are major components in this transformation. The University Continuing Education Association published a report titled *Lifelong Learning Trends: A Profile of Continuing Education* in 1998. This report describes in detail some of the trends bringing about this transformation. One trend is the great potential for the adult population in the United States to participate in distance learning. According to the association's report, distance learning has become an appealing alternative for working adults with career and family responsibilities who want to enhance their education. Other trends include the fast and consistent growth of jobs in occupations requiring more education, and the increased number of American households that have access to technology-based instruction. Web-based instruction and collaboration in the work efforts of campus colleagues are flourishing under these circumstances.[4] The collaboration frequently relates to the production of Web sites.

## MOTIVATION FOR THE COLLABORATION AT TEXAS TECH UNIVERSITY

Three administrative units provide the motivation for the collaboration that takes place among faculty and librarians at Texas Tech University. They are the Distance Learning Council; the Teaching, Learning, and Technology Center; and the University Libraries' Distance Learning Team. The Distance Learning Council's mission is to provide leadership in determining distance learning policies, procedures, and priorities. The vice provost for outreach and extended studies is the council's permanent chair.[5] Members of the council represent all of the university's colleges, schools, and administrative units that have been identified as "stakeholders" in distance learning. The council's membership was established with the expectation that support, cooperation, and collaboration in the university's distance learning efforts would be assured. A major goal of the council is to create the Texas Tech University World Campus Web site. This site will facilitate the activities of academic departments and other Texas Tech units involved in distance learning.[6] Another goal is to establish a review process for distance learning courses and programs to ensure quality and compliance with standards and regulations.

The Texas Tech University Teaching, Learning, and Technology Center's two missions are to develop and apply appropriate technology to teaching and to foster a culture of teaching and learning on campus. It is primarily involved in assisting faculty in learning new instructional technologies and, in general, improving teaching and learning at the university. The center has undertaken several activities since its inception in the spring of 1997, including offering technology classes and workshops, faculty incentive grants, and teleconference and round-table series, and sponsoring a faculty Internet user group. Librarians are able to participate in all of these activities.

The third unit involved in facilitating collaboration among faculty and librarians is the Texas Tech University Libraries' Distance Learning Team. The libraries' associate dean created the team in early 1999 in response to the Distance Learning Council's efforts to gain campus-wide interest and support. The team's mission is to advise the associate dean of libraries on all matters relating to library services provided to students and faculty involved in distance learning and to recommend new library programs and services for distance students. Its chair functions as liaison to the Distance Learning Council. An early goal was to develop a page on the libraries' Web site that informs distance students about all relevant library services. This Web page has been completed and is now available to the public. An ongoing goal is to monitor and evaluate library services provided to distance students.

## COLLABORATION EFFORTS

### On-Line Tutorial for Freshmen

As early as the fall of 1995, librarians in the Texas Tech University Libraries' Information Services Department decided that the libraries' videocassette orientation needed to be replaced as soon as possible by a Web-based tutorial that would serve not only as an orientation for freshmen but also teach basic library research skills. The videocassette had been out of date for about two years. Actually, a portion of it explained how to use the card catalog; however, an on-line public access catalog replaced the card catalog within one year after the video began to be shown to freshman classes in 1992. Another factor that spurred the librarians to action was the fact that renovation of the library building was to begin in late 1996. The department staff felt that it would then be hard pressed to accommodate the large number of orientation tours regularly requested each fall and spring. Information Services staff hoped that by encouraging faculty and students to view an orientation/tutorial on the Internet, the number of students who came to the library for tours would decrease, thus alleviating congestion in the building during the renovation.

One instruction librarian volunteered to be responsible for creating the Web-based tutorial. This librarian selected Authorware as the software she would use to create it and met regularly with the associate director of the Teaching, Learning, and Technology Center so that he could teach her how to use the software.[7] She also collaborated with other librarians in writing a grant proposal for hiring a graduate assistant to help her do the work involved in creating the tutorial. A grant was awarded in early 1996. A research assistant was hired shortly after that, and the project was then begun.

The on-line tutorial was completed in late 1996 and has been in use ever since. Although it was meant to introduce undergraduates—especially freshmen—to the Texas Tech Libraries and to tutor them in basic library research principles, actually it is available to anyone who has access to the Texas Tech University Libraries' Web site. The statistical record for the 1998–99 academic year indicates that 2,334 people accessed the tutorial during that year. In the same year, the number of users who came to the library for a tour declined.

## On-Line Tutorials Oriented to Specific Academic Disciplines

The success of the on-line tutorial for freshmen encouraged library staff to consider creating tutorials oriented to specific disciplines. Those members of the Distance Learning Council who represented the colleges and schools became especially interested and supportive of discipline-oriented tutorials when they learned of the libraries' plans. In response to the coaxing of one particular council member, the liaison librarian responsible for the physical sciences wrote a grant proposal. He proposed that a research assistant be hired who would help create a Web-based tutorial designed to develop the research skills of faculty and students majoring in the sciences, especially the environmental sciences.

This second grant for the development of a Web-based tutorial was awarded in the summer of 1999. A team of three librarians began working with a research assistant in September of that year. This on-line tutorial, named "EVEN: Environmental Education On-Line," was completed in the spring of 2000. Additional discipline-related tutorials will be created over the next few years. The Information Services staff hopes these new tutorials will help reduce still more the number of users who come to the library for orientations. Staff members expect that users will find the on-line training much more convenient.

### Faculty and Graduate Student Workshops Sponsored by the Libraries and Teaching, Learning, and Technology Center

Beginning in the fall of 1999, the Texas Tech University Libraries and the university's Teaching, Learning, and Technology Center began to offer faculty and graduate student workshops together. The libraries had done faculty workshops in the past. Attendance at these earlier workshops dropped off not long after the center began doing workshops in the spring of 1997. However, the center's workshops were different in character and content from the libraries' workshops, and some faculty recently began asking TLTC staff for workshops that included demonstrations of bibliographic databases like those in the FirstSearch package. These are the kinds of workshops librarians had given two years previously. No one at the center felt qualified to talk about bibliographic databases and demonstrate them, and this led to librarians being asked to collaborate with TLTC staff in planning and participating in some of their workshops.

Two jointly sponsored workshops were given in the fall of 1999. Their titles were "Internet and Bibliographic Database Search Strategies and Techniques" and "Cyberplagiarism." Three or four presenters lectured on their topics and then demonstrated a handful of databases and Web sites. Attendees had opportunities for hands-on practice between each presentation. Electronic forums for continued discussion among participants and attendees followed each of the workshops. These librarian- and TLTC-sponsored workshops and electronic forums have become a permanent part of the center's roundtable series offered to faculty. Two or three workshops on different topics will be offered each semester, with hands-on practice, lectures, demonstrations, and electronic forums continuing to be a part of each workshop.

### Other Collaboration Efforts

Texas Tech University Libraries has a "Distance Learning Services" page on its Web site that provides information about services and library materials available for students who enroll in off-campus Texas Tech University courses or for research hours. The Web page, like the libraries' Distance Learning Team that created it, came about in response to the Distance Learning Council's effort to foster interest and support across campus for distance learning. The associate director of libraries and the assistant head of Information Services for Library Instruction are both members of the council and are particularly responsive to any suggestions from fellow council members concerning library support for distance learning. These two persons were responsible for the formation of the team and the Web page's creation.

Finally, in the near future, instruction librarians will begin collaborating with members of the Distance Learning Council and the Teaching, Learning, and Technology Center to develop a Web-based course. This course will be based on an existing classroom-taught one-hour credit course. A great deal of resource sharing, collaboration, and work will be needed before this goal is completed.

## CONCLUSION

Whatever directions collaborative efforts at Texas Tech University may take in the future, they will most definitely share three attributes. First, the development of new teaching and learning technologies will increase at an ever-faster pace and will be used on an ever-greater scale by instructors. This technology includes, but is not restricted to, the entire range of computer and audiovisual equipment. There will also be a greater role for distance learning in higher education, and a still greater degree of collaboration will take place across campus. All of these developments are interrelated. The new technology will spur growth in distance learning, and more distance learning will increase the demand for new technology. As the need to keep up with the new technology and with increased numbers of distance learning classes becomes prevalent, faculty and librarians will find it expedient to collaborate in their teaching on an ever-greater scale. Texas Tech University will share these attributes with many other universities around the world.

## NOTES

1. Deming advocates cooperation, as opposed to competition, in the workplace. Successful collaboration depends completely on a spirit of cooperation. W. Edward Deming, *The New Economics for Industry, Government, Education* 2d ed. (Cambridge: Massachusetts Institute of Technology, 1994), 121–22.

2. Stephen R. Covey, *The Seven Habits of Highly Effective People: Restoring the Character Ethic* (New York: Simon & Schuster, 1989), 262–84.

3. The Texas Tech University Distance Learning Council selected the term "distance learning" instead of "distance education" to describe itself and what it is doing because it wants to emphasize the learning part of the process that is taking place at a distance, not the teaching part. Though I decided to use "distance learning," it and "distance education" are synonymous.

4.  *Lifelong Learning Trends: A Profile of Continuing Higher Education.* 5th ed. (Washington, D.C.: University Continuing Education Association, 1998) 23, 79, 85.

5.  The Outreach and Extended Studies Division offers elementary, middle school, high school, continuing education, and college credit courses to around 70,000 people. The college-level courses and degree programs are offered through the campus academic departments. The Southern Association of Colleges and Schools is responsible for accrediting the Outreach and Extended Studies programs.

6.  The Texas Tech University World Campus will provide an institution-wide resource base to support academic and administrative units in achieving their goals in distance learning, including the application of distance learning information technologies.

7. The center's associate director is also a faculty member who teaches in the College of Engineering.

# 17

# What Is the Matrix? Constructing a Virtual Presence for the Library Instruction Program

*Angela E. Weaver*

I chose to use the metaphor of the matrix as the theme of this chapter because the concept itself is a rich one encompassing a range of key ideas that guided me during the creation of an on-line presence for the Library Instruction Program.[1] That is not to say that at the time I was aware of the concept as a guiding force, but upon reflection, I have realized that it is a useful way of organizing my thoughts regarding the process and its outcome.

Truthfully, it was only after having seen the movie *The Matrix* that the idea came to me, and even then I started on an entirely different track, the idea of reality versus virtual reality, one of the film's major themes.[2] It was only after looking up the definitions for the word matrix that I realized its significance went beyond that particular duality. Subsequently, I have extended the concept of a matrix to apply to the philosophy behind going on-line; the planning, execution, and continuing maintenance of the Instruction Program's Web site; as well as the actual structural format of the World Wide Web itself. This chapter will present an overview of the instruction home page in relation to some of those ideas and concepts, with the last section outlining future plans for the site in terms of assessment, growth, and new areas of exploration.

## PHILOSOPHY

Before writing even one line of code or sketching out the home page design, creating the instruction site required the formulation of a philosophy that would serve as a guide in subsequent activities. In order to develop this philosophy, I asked myself two questions. One, what general goals did I want to accomplish with the site? And two, given the medium, should technological changes, in part, drive decision making?

William J. Mitchell wrote in his book *City of Bits* that a revolution was taking place, a digital revolution, and that "the most crucial task before us is not putting in place the digital plumbing of broadband communication links . . . but rather one of imagining and creating digitally mediated environments for the kinds of lives we want to lead and the sorts of communities we want to have."[3] Beyond being a site that students can access in order to retrieve answers to specific questions or to fulfill classroom assignments, the instruction page should be a place where students feel that they are part of a learning community. Susan Jurist has written, "Students will look at a University's Web page to decide if it would be an exciting place to spend the next four years."[4] The idea of a Web site being a place is crucial to its development as a center of learning and not just a repository of answers. An Amazon.com warehouse is a storage facility; a library is a center of learning. However, the Amazon.com Web site could be perceived as a learning center.

Central to the development of the instruction page as a site for a community of learners is the task of involving students in the site. Ruth Small has engaged in interesting research looking at the motivational qualities of Web sites and has developed an instrument called Web-MAC.[5] WebMAC is based on a number of theories and models such as Keller's ARCS Model that looks at attention strategies, relevance strategies, confidence strategies, and satisfaction strategies. It is interesting to notice that these strategies take into account affective states of being, how a person's emotional state is effected by Web page design. In particular, it would be interesting to explore how different sensory information contributes to differing emotional states. There have been many anecdotes regarding the reader's satisfaction in turning the page of a book. It would be valuable to study how our spatial, tactile, visual, and temporal experiences of Web pages differ from print formats and whether or not these differences have any bearing on the degree of satisfaction we feel when accessing information in one format over the other, and the rate of recall.

Not only is it important to look at how we, by our design, influence emotional states in our users, but we should also examine how browsers contribute to these conditions by the way they interpret digital information. Shredder, Web Stalker, and Netomat are examples of browsers developed by visual artists to offer an alternative to the way traditional browsers present digital elements on a Web page.[6] These alternative browsers affect how we interact with the Internet by transforming individual pieces of digital material into visual elements. Of course, these programs are extreme examples, but they are representative of a growing body of work by designers who are challenging our perceptions by subverting and manipulating our expectations. In doing so, they are also calling attention to how browsers influence the on-line experience.

The second philosophical question focuses on the role of the technology itself as a change agent. In an interview with Jennifer Fleming, author of *Web Navigation: Designing the User Experience*, Kim Brown of *Webreview* asks, "Doesn't the medium itself partly dictate the users' behavior? How do designers effectively ride the line between giving users the information they need while pushing their edges a bit to get them to think and explore?"[7] Educators have an obligation to expose students to the kinds of technology they will encounter in the real world, in this case, the rest of the World Wide Web. Although it is tempting to want to create a safe haven for them among the often confusing World Wide Web environment, designers do them a disservice if they do not present students with real world challenges that force them to process what they are doing and how they are doing it. Of course, we have to remember the context in which we are operating. As Fleming cautions, we have to be careful to try and understand our users' points of view and to challenge users but not overwhelm them, not to spoon-feed them but to provide guidance in terms of overcoming obstacles, and to make overcoming obstacles a learning experience. Clearly, a balance has to be struck between presenting real world challenges to encourage independent learning and also providing the guidance needed for students to successfully meet those challenges.

## PLANNING

In terms of site planning, four issues were involved, including identifying the site's users, the kinds of pages and page design, level of skill needed to create the site, and selection of software and hardware.

Although my title is library instruction coordinator, I primarily deal with the first-year undergraduate writing program classes. So I made the decision to direct my efforts toward that group of users. In order to do this, I created User Profiles. User Profiles, as defined by Jennifer Fleming, "are brief studies of the sort of person who might visit your site."[8] A User Profile for the Instruction site's typical user is as follows:

Shannon is a freshman at the University of Mississippi in her second semester. She is currently enrolled in English 102 Writing Composition. Her only exposure to the library beyond course reserves and studying is one fifty-minute instruction session her class attended. Her instructor has assigned a short paper on a current topic of her choice. She has to cite five resources in her paper: one reference resource, one book, two articles, and one Web site. The only thing she remembers from her instruction session is what the librarian looked like and that all the answers were on the Web.

Although there was a great deal more that could have been included in the site, I tried to focus on the kinds of information students such as Shannon would need. I also had to be aware of the level at which I engaged students and to constantly monitor how I was presenting concepts and what prior knowledge was needed in order to make the concepts comprehensible. Additionally, there was the problem of accommodating different learning styles. There has been work done on the question of field dependence and independence as it relates to hypermedia. Field dependence and independence refer to the degree to which the contextual field affects an individual's processing of information. Jennifer Summerville has identified ways of engaging these different types of learners. Techniques of stimulating field-dependent learners include providing outlines or graphic organizations of content; graphic, oral, or auditory cues; orienting strategies; and embedded questions.[9]

Decisions also had to be made regarding the types of pages to include in the site. Luck and Hunter have documented six types of Web pages based on function and form: billboard, directory/index, text, graphic, input, and multipurpose.[10] Although pages may incorporate more than one function, care has to be taken to apply appropriate styles to the differing parts of the pages as needed. After the decision was made as to the types of pages that would be included, an overall design had to be created that looked at a user's entire experience of the site. As Fleming states, "It is less about decoration than it is about interpreting information for its intended audience."[11] She also goes on to say that "design on the Web is not considered related to how users find information—a serious misconception."[12] Although much has changed since 1997, examples of inadequate and ineffective design abound.

At the time I began planning the pages, I did have experience designing basic graphics. However, more was involved. Clark et al. have explored the idea of visual literacy, the ability to understand, create, and use visual images as applied to creating Web pages.[13] Visual literacy is composed of three parts: visual thinking, visual communication, and visual learning; and requires that designers think about how to translate ideas into visual information, how that information is received and processed, and what knowledge is constructed as a result of seeing the visual.[14] Exposure to the concept of visual literacy forces site builders to carefully evaluate their use of graphics.

## FUTURE PLANS

Three areas of interest will fuel the further development of the instruction home page including integrating CourseInfo into the site, adding more interactive content, and implementing a system of evaluation.

CourseInfo is a commercial product the University of Mississippi purchased from Blackboard, Inc., to enable instructors to build and manage virtual classrooms without learning HTML.[15] The system features synchronous and asynchronous communication, a means of generating and distributing content, and assessment tools. In anticipation of teaching the library's one-credit course, I created a CourseInfo page for EDLS101 Introduction to Library Research and Electronic Resources.[16] At present, the site includes a syllabus with an outline of classes; course documents including handouts and worksheets; in-class exercises, homework, and quizzes; and links to other World Wide Web sites. The intention is not for the CourseInfo module to supplant the instruction home page but for the two to work in tandem. An example would be a hyperlink from the instruction home page's OPAC (On-Line Public Access Catalog) tutorial to a quiz on the catalog that is housed in CourseInfo. Originally, I coded a quiz entirely in HTML with links to correct answers and feedback, a process that was time consuming. The same quiz took only a fraction of the time with CourseInfo. CourseInfo offers a way of incorporating interactive elements into the instruction home page from one source without having to develop them entirely from the ground up. Although certain features are restricted to students enrolled in a class, many can be opened to guest users.

Along those same lines, I would also like to incorporate more interactive content in the instruction pages irrespective of CourseInfo. Based on experience with offering E-mail reference service, I believe that introducing a chatroom or bulletin board for use by on-line patrons might prove a successful means of augmenting our traditional reference and instruction services. Currently we are planning to experiment with operating a chatroom during limited evening hours to supplement our E-Ref service. I even foresee a time when real-time video could be utilized in our interactions to provide point-of-need instruction. However, before such massive changes are initiated, an evaluation of existing services will need to be accomplished.

Outside of a general survey sent to faculty to gauge their satisfaction/dissatisfaction with library services, an evaluation of the instruction services has not been performed for the past three years. As a result of my research, I have identified a number of possible assessment strategies.

## WebMAC

Ruth Small's WebMAC "specifies four general categories of a motivational Web site: Engaging, Meaningful, Organized, and Enjoyable."[17] The instrument contains sixty items on which Web sites are measured, fifteen for each category. Within each category, strategies are identified on which sites are measured. For example, strategies for Engaging include: an eye-catching title and/or visual on home page, attractive screen layout, interesting content, occasional change of pace, and interactivity. Values are assigned for each strategy in separate columns marked P and E based on the presence of that strategy and its effectiveness. The scores for the P and E columns are totaled for the category and plotted on a graph for that category. Low scores on the graph indicate either the need for more strategies or a need for improving those strategies.

### Ethnographic Studies

A second means of assessment would be to perform ethnographic studies on the user population, which would involve spending time in the field (real or virtual), looking at users' on-line information contexts and how things happen, understanding people and their environment, and then designing products and services accordingly.[18] I feel that it is important to know what kinds of sites students are visiting, how they search for information on-line, and why they go on-line, in order to take advantage of possible educational opportunities and to increase the motivational value of our instruction sites. By knowing what kinds of navigational challenges students are already meeting, we can better plan our own navigational designs. Also, we can take advantage of their interests to draw them into our services. Clark et al. found that libraries were using traditional library icons to indicate resources online.[19] Libraries could also employ familiar icons from popular culture as metaphors for library services. An excellent example would be "Putting the First Pieces Together," an on-line tutorial at Wake Forest University that uses puzzles as a metaphor for information gathering.[20]

### Participatory Design

Participatory design also offers an interesting approach to assessing site effectiveness by actively involving the site users as team members in the design process.[21] The professional designers would perform user studies prior to developing prototypes, and once the prototypes are completed, students would be drawn from the university population and invited to participate in the design activities. Designers would benefit from having the intended population experiment with prototypes before they are available to the general public. Students would benefit from the feeling of ownership of the site, which would, hopefully, develop, and from the sense that they are vital participants in and contributors to an active community of learners.

## CONCLUSION

In the movie *The Matrix*, Morpheus says to Neo, "there is a difference between knowing the path and walking the path."[22] Whereas at first it may sound like a specious statement, beyond its Zen-like overtones there lies a truth. There is a difference between knowing about the Web and actually immersing oneself in the Web. In constructing the instruction home page, I have had to acquire knowledge by researching current instruction practices, learning about the technical aspects of the Web and its capabilities, and by actually surfing the Web the way a student would. In order to be successful, the instruction page must continue to take into consideration and strike a balance with the many assets, contradictions, and disadvantages of the Web while at the same time providing valuable information in a format that encourages learning and stimulates exploration. At last we come to the question with which we began: "What is the matrix?" This chapter has attempted to explore some of the answers to that question as it applies to the library instruction site. However, even more important than the question, "What is the matrix?" is the question facing the hero at the end of the film and myself at the end of this chapter, which is: "What do we do with it?"

## NOTES

1. J. D. Williams Library, "Library Instruction Homepage," *Library Instruction Homepage*, September 20, 1999, <http://www.olemiss.edu/depts/general_library/lip/home.html> [accessed 28 December 1999].

2. *The Matrix*, dir. Wachowski Brothers, Warner Brothers, 1999, videocassette.

3. William J. Mitchell, *City of Bits* (Cambridge, Mass.: MIT Press, 1996), 5.

4. Susan Jurist, "Top Ten Rules for Creating Graphics for the Web," *College & Research Libraries News* 57, no. 7 (1996): 418.

5. Ruth V. Small, "Assessing the Motivational Quality of World Wide Websites," ERIC ED 407 930, 1997.

6. Potatoland, "Launch Shredder," *Shredder*, 1998, <http://www.potatoland.org/shredder/> [accessed 29 December 1999]; "Backspace, Download I/O/D4: The Web Stalker," *Web Stalker*, <http://bak.spc.org/iod/iod4.html> [accessed 29 December 1999]; Netomat, "Download Netomat," *Netomat*, 1999, <http://www.netomat.net/data/1.1/install.htm> [accessed 29 December 1999].

7. Kim Brown, "An In-Depth Interview with Jennifer Fleming," *Webreview.com*, 1998, <http://webreview.com/pub/web98east/21/flemingiview.html> [accessed 21 August 1999].

8. Jennifer Fleming, "Crafting the User Experience," *Webreview.com*, 1998, <http://webreview.com/wr/pub/web98east/21/webnav1.html> [accessed 17 August 1999].

9. Jennifer B. Summerville, "The Role of Awareness of Cognitive Style in Hypermedia." Paper presented at the National Convention of the Association for Educational Communications and Technology, St. Louis, Missouri, 18–22 1998, ERIC, ED 423865.

10. Donald D. Luck and J. Mark Hunter, "Design Principles Applied to World Wide Web Construction." Paper presented at the annual conference of the International Visual Literacy Association, Cheyenne, Wyoming, October 1996, ERIC, ED 408985.

11. Jennifer Fleming, "In Defense of Web Graphics," *Webreview.com*, 1997, <http://webreview.com/pub/97/07/25/feature/index4.html> [accessed 17 August 1999].

12. Fleming, "In Defense of Web Graphics."

13. Barbara I. Clark, Nancy N. Knupfer, Judy E. Mahoney, Kevin M. Kramer, Hamed Ghazali, and Nabel Al-Ani, "Creating Web Pages: Is Anyone Considering Visual Literacy?" Paper presented at the annual conference of the International Visual Literacy Association, Cheyenne, Wyoming, October 1996, ERIC, ED 408990.

14. Mary H. Tipton, Cindy L. Kovalik, and Mary B. Shoffner, "Visual Literacy," *Visual Literacy* 1999, <http://www.educ.kent.edu/vlo/> [accessed 17 August 1999].

15. Blackboard, "Blackboard Products and Services," *CourseInfo*, 1999, <http://company.blackboard.com/CourseInfo/index.html> [accessed 19 December 1999].

16. J. D. Williams Library, "EDLS101," *EDLS101*, 1999, <http://www.olemiss.edu:8042/courses/EDLS101/> [accessed 29 December 1999].

17. Small, *Assessing the Motivational Quality of World Wide Websites*, 6.

18. Fleming, "In Defense of Web Graphics."

19. Clark et al., "Creating Web Pages," 357.

20. Z. Smith Reynolds Library, "Research: Putting the Pieces Together: An Interactive Tutorial," *Putting the Pieces Together: An Interactive Tutorial*, 1999, <http://www.wfu.edu/Library/referenc/research/index.html> [accessed 29 December 1999].

21. Jennifer Fleming, "Designing for Users," *Webreview.com*, <http://webreview.com/wr/pub/web98east/21/webnav3.html> [accessed 22 August 1999].

22. *The Matrix*, 1999.

# 18

# Scope and Sequence in Library Instruction: Getting the Most from Your Collaboration with Writing Programs

*James Elmborg*

Bibliographic instruction programs have unique institutional challenges not faced by other academic units. In determining curriculum, our colleagues in academic departments often talk of "scope and sequence." A program with scope and sequence has a clearly defined body of knowledge and theory to study (i.e., scope). It also presents concepts in an orderly fashion to allow students to progress from the simple to the complex as they move through the curriculum (i.e., sequence). In order to become full-fledged participants in the academic business of the university (which is teaching and learning), librarians need to move toward this kind of thinking. We need to begin to think in terms of coherent programs that have philosophical goals and that have logical development in complexity and breadth. In other words, we need to build programs with "scope and sequence." Such thinking will not come easily to librarians, who have historically lacked the institutional mandate to develop programs in this way. While *information literacy* gets increasing attention from administrators both inside and outside the library, very few curriculum committees seem willing to transform libraries into teaching departments.

## WRITING PROGRAMS

One answer to this problem can be found in our relationship with writing programs. Like library instruction, writing programs began as part of the student-centered approach to instruction that grew and matured during the 1970s and 1980s. Unlike writing programs, library instruction has never found a suitable departmental niche in which to grow and mature. Writing programs began as English department subdepartments. While the senior members of the English department studied and taught Shakespeare, Milton, or Hemingway, the junior members—often teaching assistants and adjuncts—carried the major load for undergraduate "service courses." Teaching these writing classes was often seen as a way to pay dues in the department. Along the way, however, many English instructors found that they liked teaching writing, and a growing group of talented teachers began to choose to teach writing classes over literature classes, further lending legitimacy to the teaching of composition. Today, a huge body of literature exists under the general heading of "writing theory."[1] On some campuses, writing programs have risen to higher profiles than their literary colleagues.

In a listserv post to the *Alliance for Computers in Writing* discussion list (ACW-L) during the fall of 1998, one composition instructor posited a model for determining how "mature" the writing programs on any given campus have become.[2] While the model suggests linear development, programs usually develop in nonlinear ways. This writer suggested that, minimally and first of all, a program needed to have made a philosophical commitment to teaching its freshman composition classes by emphasizing "writing process" over product. This commitment provides the foundation for the overall development of the program and is the first indicator of progress toward program maturity. The next phase of evolution in writing programs is staffing the Writing Center with student tutors. Writing Across the Curriculum (WAC) represents the next stage of growth in the writing program. Finally, Portfolio Assessment, as part of the WAC program, indicates that programs have matured and become integrated into the general education mission of the university. This useful "maturity model" gives writing programs a chance to measure their own evolution, and it also gives them goals to meet to move to the next level.

## RESEARCH PROCESS MODEL

The writing process model is one that librarians would do well to study and understand. As with writing programs, library instruction has often been the province of the young and energetic, a way for those new to the profession to cut their teeth with public service on the way toward more senior positions. As in writing programs, many talented librarians over the years have found instruction such an important and satisfying library role that they have chosen to build their careers around teaching. For these librarians, the writing program model is a powerful one. We can learn valuable lessons from writing programs about establishing institutional identity and about building scope and sequence into our programs. The constructivist pedagogy that has given rise to writing programs is eminently suited to our purposes in library instruction, and, as luck would have it, most libraries already have at least fledgling relationships with writing programs on our campuses. Unfortunately, very few libraries even begin to tap the potential inherent in those relationships.

Before about 1975, English composition was taught by asking students to read "good compositions" and imitate them. In contrast to this model, current writing theory is built from the observation that each student is unique and must construct his or her own knowledge and voice. Rather than imitating others, students must discover their voice and vision by moving through four observable stages—brainstorming, drafting, revising, and editing. Taken together, these four steps comprise the *writing process*. At the most basic level, the writing program movement has been built around this single, simple observation: Writing is a process and must be taught that way. While the four steps in the process are not exactly linear (the process is recursive with all four modes present in all four stages), there is general movement from brainstorming through drafting and revising toward editing. We need to recognize that in academic situations, where the end product of research is almost always a piece of writing, the *writing process* model is a *research process* model. This point bears emphasizing. The writing process and the research process are not merely similar for college students: They are *one and the same process*.

During the brainstorming phase, students have a specific kind of need from the library. They need to use databases, the library catalog, and the subject classification system to help them generate ideas about themes, perspectives, and controversies that exist within the published discussions of their topic. Their electronic searches will likely be "keyword" searches since they will be using the databases as brainstorming tools. As they begin to draft their papers, their demands on the library shift. Their needs become more focused, and their argument begins to take shape. Their electronic searches should become more focused at this time, and perhaps the narrowing strategies offered by Boolean connectors and subject searching will be more appropriate. In the revision phase, their argument sharpens further. Often, during revision, students will rediscover sources they first found while brainstorming. These sources assume importance once the direction of the paper has taken shape. Finally, during the editing process, students need to work with specific bibliographic information. They need details and facts. When looked at through the lens of the writing process, students' engagement with the library becomes more coherent and "teachable."

Consequently, in order to work with composition classes, librarians need to learn to teach research *as a process*. We need to teach from the point of view of the students' research process, and we need to use our instructional sessions to help students discover a research method that works for them. Personally, I prefer to teach students in the brainstorming phase. I want the session to be exploratory and open because I think library instruction works best at this stage of the process. If the students are well into their research, however, I have to adjust my class to match the more focused efforts that should be under way at that time. The basic, minimal goal of a librarian should be to engage the research process and address the students with content appropriate to their stage of development with the topic. Certain strategies work better than others. Students learn by doing, not by listening, so hands-on workshop sessions tend to more effective than lecture. Librarians need to avoid the temptation to cover "everything" during such sessions. Lecture is rarely effective in helping researchers develop, and focusing on coverage is nearly always a bad idea. Students will only absorb what is useful to them today, and trying to give them "everything" they will need in the research process is almost as ineffective as giving them nothing. Negotiating with the instructor is the only useful way to know where to aim the class.

## THE WRITING CENTER MODEL

Once our library instruction programs have matured to the point that we have made a philosophical commitment to teaching on the process model, our next stage of growth is the Writing Center model. In a Writing Center, trained student tutors work with other students to improve their writing. The Writing Center model is powerful for several reasons, most notably because it provides a "just in time" resource for writers. As at the Reference Desk, writing tutors are available when students need writing consultation. Writing Centers differ from the Reference Desk in at least one major way. They are staffed by student tutors rather than degreed professionals. These students typically enjoy very satisfying work as mentors to other students while getting the intellectual satisfaction of sharing a collegial relationship with their professional colleagues. If the college has a Writing Center, it very likely will welcome library instruction as part of the training of the tutors. Indeed, some Writing Centers have been willing to go so far as to rename themselves as Writing and Research Centers with the added value of database searching and information literacy incorporated into their mission.

When librarians join writing teachers in the context of the Writing Center, interesting and exciting things can happen. Writing Centers are collaborative by nature, and librarians invigorate the staff by bringing new skills and perspectives to the mix. Like librarians, writing teachers have seen a revolution in their work because of the rapid rise of information technology. The Writing Center can help librarians cope with the stress of the new technology by giving us new colleagues and new venues for our teaching. Students no longer produce just "papers," but in some disciplines may be asked to produce Web pages, PowerPoint presentations, or even digital portfolios. Librarians, with their historical mandate to collect all kinds of media, can make tremendous contributions to the redefining of communication and the way it is taught in the electronic age. In technology-rich Writing Centers, the line between writing and research tends to blur, making the collaboration between librarians and the Writing Center almost imperative. One common extension of the Writing Center is the On-Line Writing Lab (OWL), which provides a logical place for new media and new forms of communication to converge. In the OWL, the integration of databases and on-line instruction can be seamlessly incorporated to invigorate and energize both the writing instruction and the research instruction.

## WRITING ACROSS THE CURRICULUM

With a Writing Center in place, the next logical step in developing a relationship with writing programs is Writing Across the Curriculum. WAC is built around the notion that once students enter into an academic major, they become part of the discourse community of that major. Engineering majors learn to talk, think, and write like engineers. Their model is quite different from the talking, thinking, and writing of social scientists. Writing Across the Curriculum programs acknowledge that difference, and rather than privilege the conventions of the English department, the writing instructors focus on the conventions of the disciplines. At this point, students have moved past the basic survival stage that marks freshman writers. They need advanced information from advanced databases, and they need to make fine distinctions and evaluations in order to succeed in their majors.

At this level, librarians can make major contributions to the learning process by helping students identify appropriate resources and teaching them to evaluate and classify what they encounter. This higher-order teaching, while not productive with freshmen, fits quite nicely with the kind of *Writing in the Major* courses that evolve in a WAC program. One recent innovation in WAC theory is ECAC (Electronic Communication Across the Curriculum). In moving from WAC to ECAC (i.e., from *writing* to *electronic communication)*, the writing program signals an awareness of the shifting paradigm from pen and ink to computers. ECAC embraces composition in new media—such as E-mail, Web page production, and computer-mediated learning—and explores the rhetorical implications of composing in the evolving media. ECAC, as such, is a logical place to begin to work with *information literacy* concepts. Both WAC and ECAC are driven by the same central assumptions as the freshman writing course. In other words, to be effective, librarians must remember that writing and research are one and the same process that must be engaged through workshops, peer review, and exploration from the student's point of view.


## ASSESSMENT

Every library instruction program faces the challenge of assessment. Traditionally, libraries have done quantitative assessment, counting sessions and students and measuring success by numbers. Such measurement might always be necessary, but librarians should never be deceived into thinking that quantity equals quality. In order to know whether a student has successfully incorporated appropriate research materials into his or her research, an expert needs to evaluate the use of those resources in the context of the written work. In other words, we need to grade the bibliography and the use of sources in the same way we grade the writing. Currently, many colleges use a portfolio assessment program to measure student progress toward writing competency. While the task of evaluating every student's portfolio may seem overwhelming, very large research universities commonly undertake the task for all their students. Portfolio assessment usually depends on a standardized rubric. We can and should include as part of that rubric the appropriate identification and use of library resources. While we might need to train assessors how to identify appropriate use, this training process is valuable in its own right as part of our mission to educate the entire academic community.


## SIX TRAITS MODEL

What would such a rubric look like? We might choose to adopt a system such as Six Traits Scoring, used by writing instructors across the country. The exciting thing about the Six Traits model is that writing teachers often incorporate it into the way they teach writing. In this way, Six Traits becomes both an assessment tool and a teaching tool. Teaching students to assess each others' work based on the Six Traits gives them a better idea what they, as writers, should be doing. The Six Traits are

1. Ideas
2. Organization
3. Voice
4. Word choice
5. Sentence fluency
6. Conventions

Students are encourage to recognize these traits in their own writing and to understand that their writing will be evaluated based on these traits.

In order to integrate themselves into the portfolio process, librarians need to develop something like a Six Traits for bibliographic purposes. The rubric might include

1. Appropriateness of the sources for academic level
2. Relevance of sources for the purpose of the paper
3. Coherence of sources taken as a group (the whole bibliography)
4. Awareness of inherent biases in sources

Each of these traits would be scored one through five, resulting in a holistic score. As with Six Traits, the rubric should be taught to the students as part of the research process so they know and understand what evaluators are looking for. Then, this evaluation should be incorporated into the assessment of the writing portfolio as one more step in the process, rather than as an overwhelming new program of evaluation for faculty or librarians.

Some campuses have fully evolved writing programs. They have freshman composition courses committed to writing process pedagogy, they have Writing Centers with an OWL component, they have Writing Across the Curriculum, and they have portfolio assessment as a component of the General Education Program. Librarians fortunate enough to work in this kind of educational climate should find boundless opportunities to work with the writing programs because with such highly evolved writing programs comes a highly collaborative academic culture. People and programs that can make a significant contribution to the writing programs (as librarians definitely can) are valued and embraced. Very few campuses, however, have all these components of the highly evolved program in place. Most campuses have one or all pieces in some degree of evolution. In such cases, it is in our own self-interest as librarians to help writing programs evolve.

## COLLABORATION STRATEGIES

Together, libraries and writing programs are powerful allies with a compelling mission. Librarians can and should participate in articulating that mission for the rest of the academy. By collaborating, librarians and writing instructors together can make the case that writing and research share the same literacy mandate and deserve to be supported in their mission. First of all, librarians should aggressively pursue truly collaborative partnerships with writing teachers. If writing teachers in the institution lack the academic status to grow and initiate change, librarians can use the push for information literacy to advocate the strengthening of the writing program. If the freshman composition program has been solidly established, but the writing faculty has been unable to take the next step to the establishment of a Writing Center, then librarians can join with writing programs to help the campus move to the next level. If finding a location for the Writing Center is an issue (as it often is), librarians can make the case that the best location for a Writing Center is in the library. The step toward WAC is perhaps the hardest to take on campuses, but that step is crucial for making advanced information literacy a part of the curriculum. As accrediting agencies demand that we be accountable for information literacy, we must develop meaningful assessment tools such as portfolio assessment. These programs will be much more effective (and easy to implement) in the context of a writing portfolio. In short, as libraries are charged with developing programs to address information literacy issues, we can use the writing programs to help us develop scope and sequence, and writing programs can use libraries to further argue for the evolution of their own agenda. By understanding and allying ourselves with the progressive mission of writing programs, librarians can help solidify existing programs and also be advocates for the expansion and growing coherence of those yet to be established.

While collaboration between librarians and writing instructors may seem natural, in fact, such partnerships often fail to reach their potential because of major differences between the ways that librarians and writing instructors approach their jobs. To help make the relationship work, librarians need to examine four major issues. Writing program culture is different from library culture. Writing instructors are highly theoretical and much less task-driven than librarians. Librarians need to work to appreciate this perspective and what it brings to the relationship. Specifically, librarians need to avoid becoming impatient with the brainstorming and mental drafting that writing teachers do as part of the creative, program-building process. Second, librarians need to learn to talk about pedagogy. Too often, our library instruction literature seems to suggest that knowing the right "tips and tricks" to manage a classroom constitutes good teaching. We need to be willing to explore on a meaningful level the philosophies behind our teaching. We need to get away from the "tips and tricks" mentality toward a more substantial theory of teaching and learning. Writing programs have developed a strong and coherent pedagogy we can adapt to our uses if we make the effort to do so. Third, we need to become entirely comfortable with collaboration. We need to avoid a sense that by collaborating with writing programs, we lose our identities or lose control over the dissemination of information. Some loss of control will occur in the process, but in general, libraries have a mission quite distinct from writing programs, and our sharing of instructional goals will not confuse our larger mission with theirs. In terms of teaching and learning, our missions are quite compatible, and what we stand to gain from working as allies with writing programs far outweighs any uncomfortable loss of control we may experience as we learn to work together.

## NOTES

1. The overwhelming body of literature dealing with the theory and practice of writing instruction makes it difficult to begin reading without guidance. The following texts are widely used in the training of writing teachers in colleges and universities, and they provide a suitable starting point for librarians who want to know more about the major ideas that have transformed composition programs: Victor Villanueva Jr., ed., *Cross-Talk in Comp Theory: A Reader* (Urbana, Ill.: National Council of Teachers of English, 1997); Sondra Perl, ed., *Landmark Essays on the Writing Process* (Mahwah, N.J.: Hermagoras Press, 1994); Christina Murphy and Joe Law, eds., *Landmark Essays on Writing Centers* (Mahwah, N.J.: Hermagoras Press, 1995); Charles Bazerman and David R. Russell, eds., *Landmark Essays on Writing Across the Curriculum* (Mahwah, N.J.: Hermagoras Press, 1994); Richard E. Young and Yameng Liu, eds., *Landmark Essays on Rhetorical Invention in Writing* (Mahwah, N.J.: Hermagoras Press, 1994); Peter Elbow, ed., *Landmark Essays on Voice and Writing* (Mahwah, N.J.: Hermagoras Press, 1994).

2. My efforts to identify the originator of this ACW-L post have been unsuccessful. I have searched the list's archives and sent a general query to the list in attempts to locate the writer. It is with regret that I must report the author as anonymous.

# 19

# Mass Instruction That Works: Teaching 900 First-Year Biology Students in Five Days

*Randy Reichardt and Sandy Campbell*

The Science and Technology Library of the University of Alberta was approached by the Department of Biological Sciences in 1995 to assist in implementing a basic library research assignment into a new course, *Biology 108: Organisms in Their Environment.* Between 800 and 900 students register for this course each term. This chapter details the history and current status of the award-winning Biology 108 Library Instruction Program at the University of Alberta.

## 1995–1997

In 1995, the departments of botany, entomology, genetics, zoology, and microbiology merged into the Department of Biological Sciences, forming the largest department at the University of Alberta. The newly formed department approached the Science and Technology Library, requesting that a basic library research assignment be incorporated into its new course, *Biology 108: Organisms in Their Environment.* Each term, 800 to 900 students register for this course, 90 percent of whom are first-year students. Students attend one large lecture per week in three sections, and then split up into forty to forty-five three-hour labs, held from Monday afternoon until Friday morning. Many of these labs occur simultaneously, up to five at a time. To instruct the students in forty-five labs in one week in September and in January appeared at the time to be a logistical nightmare for the librarians of the SciTech Library. It was felt that the best solution at that time was to make slight revisions and incorporate an existing basic research assignment used in similar classes taught to first-year engineering and agriculture students, with a video called "Finding Frankenstein," which was developed to introduce new users to the University of Alberta Libraries.[1]

The biological sciences liaison librarian worked with the Biology 108 lab coordinator to refine the assignment. The assignment made use of the paper copy of the Wilson index, *Biological and Agricultural Index* (*BAI*). Students in each lab would be shown the video, followed by a short series of overheads to explain how to locate relevant references in a subject-specific index. The assignment was then explained in detail, and students were given individual superceded monthly copies of *BAI* or *General Science Index*.

Each Biology 108 lab section is taught by a graduate teaching assistant (TA). Once each term before the assignment, the teaching assistants met with the biological sciences librarian, who reviewed the video and assignment with them. The TAs would then present the assignment to each of their lab sections. Students would work on the first half of the assignment in their labs, and then complete the assignment in the library.

Each student was assigned a topic in the life sciences. The student would search *BAI* to find a relevant article and record the subject heading and complete bibliographic citation of choice. The student would then use the library's on-line catalogue to locate the journal in the library, and once found, locate and photocopy the article.

While students were able to complete the assignments, there were some inconsistencies in the delivery of the assignment by the TAs. This was through no fault of their own, but rather a result of using twenty-five to thirty different instructors to present the same assignment. It was unrealistic to expect the teaching assistants, some of them new to campus each term, to be able to explain the intricacies and details of searching a subject index, and to field questions about the library itself. Students experienced varying degrees of frustration with the assignment and were often left with a less-than-positive first impression of the library system at the University of Alberta. There was also a dramatic increase in the number of questions at the Reference Desk during these assignments.

## 1997–2000

In the summer of 1997, the Science and Technology Library developed a Bibliographic Instruction (BI) Team to cope with large instruction projects. This allowed more staff members to be involved in the management of the Biology 108 library instruction project. At the same time, on-line versions of *Biological and Agricultural Index* and *General Science Abstracts* were now available. Team members decided to deliver the instruction themselves, with the cooperation of the TAs of each lab section. With seven or eight instructors available, each instructor would deliver five to six sessions in five days, and the TAs, valuable collaborators in this project, could concentrate on preparing for and marking the assignments. The BI Team hoped this method would ensure a consistent delivery of instruction, increase students' information literacy skills, reduce the load at the Reference Desk, and provide greater visibility of library staff to a large student group. The biological sciences librarian worked closely with the Biology 108 lab coordinator, revising the assignment to meet the department's needs and introduced information skills in a practical, step-by-step manner. Two assignments resulted from this: (1) students search for the title of a book and record its call number and location, and (2) search for an article on an assigned topic in an on-line subject-specific database, record the citation information, locate the journal and the article, and summarize the article. The BI Team developed a common presentation, designed to teach the information skills required for completion of the assignments that were now embedded in the Biology 108 laboratory manual. The presentation was scripted, rehearsed, and revised by the BI Team. The TAs assigned book titles from a list prepared by the team and assigned subject headings based on an assigned letter per lab section. The TAs ensured that each topic had at least ten to fifteen citations, and that some of these were accessible to first-year students.

During the first week of laboratory classes in September and January, the BI Team went to the labs and delivered the presentation. Normally five instructors taught simultaneously. The presentation required about forty-five minutes and incorporated a number of different teaching methods, including

- an introductory questionnaire that allowed the students to test their own knowledge of the information covered in the session and gave them the chance to focus on the content of the session
- a PowerPoint presentation of the core material that they required
- live demonstrations of on-line catalog and subject database searching using examples, which paralleled each of the two library-based lab assignments

After the laboratory presentations, students went to the library, completed the assignments within a two-week period, and returned them to their TAs for marking. Library staff was available for consultation during this time. The library's in-class presentation remained accessible via the Web, allowing students to review it at any time. As well, all documentation embedded in the Biology 108 lab manual was also made available on the Web, including copies of the assignments.

During its developmental stages in 1997 and early 1998, the program was thoroughly evaluated. The instructors and the assignments were reviewed by the students using questionnaires. Professional literature assisted in the development of the questionnaires.[2] Approximately 85 percent of the students felt that the program was a benefit to their understanding of and confidence in using the library, understanding of an on-line subject-specific database, and the application of knowledge to other assignments and projects. Evaluations are now conducted when substantial changes are made to the instructional program and when new instructors join the teaching team.

## WHY THIS PROGRAM IS A SUCCESS

1. It is embedded into a course and is a marked exercise, which causes the students to take it seriously.
2. It is delivered consistently to all students in the course.
3. It is delivered to the students just before they need to use the skills in other assignments, making it highly relevant.
4. It involves and has the support of all the stakeholders.
5. It is delivered at a level appropriate to the students' knowledge levels.
6. It is practical and hands-on, allowing the students to learn by *doing*.
7. It takes the student through a progression of library skills.
8. It tries to take into account several learning styles.
9. It allows the student the flexibility to work at his or her own pace.
10. It does not require a large commitment from any one staff member.

Evaluations as well as informal discussion and feedback from students and teaching assistants suggested that the revised Biology 108 Library Instruction Program has been successful from the outset. In addition, the BI Team learned that it is capable of undertaking mass instruction in a short period of time and managing it successfully.

## CONTRIBUTIONS TO LIBRARY OPERATIONS

Attempting to instruct a large number of students in a short period of time has always been a difficult task for instruction librarians. By including a program within the structure of the lab sessions and working with a team of instructors, the Science and Technology Library has been able to deliver effective instruction, build good public relations for the library, and develop a strong relationship with the Department of Biological Sciences.

## Benefits to the Students

1. Student stress is lowered.
2. Students receive a positive library experience.
3. Students learn the core information skills.
4. Students are better prepared to work on any subsequent research assignments.

## Benefits to the Department of Biological Sciences

1. The department is now assured that this part of its curriculum is taught professionally.
2. The department receives fewer complaints from its students.
3. The Biology 108 TAs can focus on preparing for and marking the assignments rather than delivering the presentations as well.
4. Students are better prepared to work on subsequent research assignments for this course.

## Benefits to the Library

1. The library and librarians receive very positive public relations through this project.
   - the students get to know a library staff member in the context of their laboratory
   - the students see library staff as competent users of technology
   - the library is associated with success at finding information rather than frustration
2. The volume of Biology 108 questions at the Information Desk is dramatically reduced.
3. Stress on the reference staff is reduced.
4. The BI Team has increased its team effectiveness.
5. Individual team members have improved their teaching skills through sessions delivered and through coaching other team members.

In April 1999, the Library Association of Alberta awarded the Biology 108 Library Instruction Program its Award of Excellence in Library Service. Further information is available at the following Web site: <http://www.library.ualberta.ca/library_html/help/lib_instruct/bio108.html>. This site includes the PowerPoint presentation given in the lab, introductory questionnaire, assignments, and assignment instructions.

## NOTES

1. *Finding Frankenstein: An Introduction to the University of Alberta Library System* (Edmonton, Alberta: Vicom, 1993), video recording.

2. Diane Shonrock, ed., "Evaluating Library Instruction: Sample Questions, Forms, and Strategies for Practical Use," Library Instruction Roundtable, American Library Association Research Committee (Chicago: American Library Association, 1996).

# 20

# Improving World Civilizations Teaching and Learning through Educational Technology: A Continuing Program in Faculty–Librarian Collaboration

*Carole Ann Fabian*

Advancements in computer technologies and increased access to Web-based resources provide educators not only with an innovative information delivery system for course content but also with a rich array of supplementary instructional and bibliographic resources. The application of multiple technologies to the presentation of course materials can enhance both teaching and student learning. A major initiative, *Access99*, is being implemented at the University of Buffalo (UB) to help faculty integrate these technologies into their teaching.[1] High enrollment freshmen courses are being given primary attention and support in this effort; among them is "UGC111 and 112: World Civilizations." The University Libraries, the College of Arts and Science, the Educational Technology Center (ETC), Computing and Information Technology (CIT), and the senior vice provost for educational technology are providing ongoing support for this project. The goals of the *Access99* program together with the world civilizations faculty commitment to effective teaching and improved student learning provided the basis for the creation of faculty–librarian partnerships to explore educational technologies and teaching effectiveness strategies.

## BACKGROUND

World Civilizations (World Civ) is a two-semester required general education course offered every fall and spring semester. There are twelve to fifteen sections of 200 students, each meeting for two lectures per week and once weekly in twenty-person recitation groups led by instructors and TAs. Faculty (approximately fifty) are self-nominated to teach World Civ from a broad disciplinary base, including history, political science, architecture, urban planning, geography, comparative literatures, art history, and philosophy, among others. Each faculty member develops a unique syllabus within departmental guidelines and with a global, cross-cultural emphasis. This diversity of curricula allows students to choose among sections with different subject emphasis. Faculty select one of seven authorized texts, and many also require directed readings in primary texts. Librarians have historically partnered with these faculty members to provide resource materials and cooperative instruction.

## THE WORLD CIVILIZATIONS COMMITTEE

The World Civilizations Committee meets monthly to discuss course management and scholarly topics as they pertain to the teaching of World Civ. For faculty, it is an opportunity to share resources, research, and reviews of current literature, and to discuss the challenges of teaching large-enrollment courses. Librarians are integral members of the World Civ committee. For us, the meetings provide an invaluable window into the teaching experience and an opportunity to address some faculty teaching concerns, to market library resources and services, and to advance the information literacy goals of the University Libraries. The librarians have taken a lead role in initiating and planning many team projects.

The large-enrollment teaching experience presents certain teaching and learning challenges; these coupled with a perceived "disconnect" between faculty teaching styles and student learning styles suggest a need to reexamine pedagogical approaches and to consider educational technologies that could potentially ameliorate some of the teaching and learning problems. An Educational Technology Planning Team was created as a subgroup of the World Civilizations Committee.[2] The planning team was charged with reviewing the needs of the World Civ faculty and students, evaluating available technologies, and designing a strategic plan and implementation program for the integration of multiple technologies into the World Civilizations program to comply with the *Access99* initiative. During a three-month study period, the team explored a variety of pedagogical approaches and technology resources, and identified several specific goals and strategies to address them:

***Goal 1: Initiate incremental course redesign.***    Strategy: Present seminars, workshops, and individualized faculty consultations to assess teaching effectiveness; suggest alternate teaching methods and introduce educational technologies.

***Goal 2: Promote an active, learner-centered model of instruction.***   Strategy: Suggest teaching strategies for use in both lecture and recitation settings that provide opportunities for students to take responsibility for their knowledge acquisition, empower students to peer-instruct, and create collaborative learning opportunities.

***Goal 3: Provide integrated on-line access to enhanced course materials.***   Strategy: Facilitate the construction of course Web sites and central resource Web pages; instruct faculty and TAs in Web site development and maintenance skills.

***Goal 4: Instruct in information literacy skills.***   Strategy: Contextualize research methods instruction. Integrate research skill building into a series of preliminary assignments that culminate in the final research report. Collaborate with faculty to provide on-line guides, worksheets, and in-class contextual instruction in which each assignment incrementally introduces students to both the process and the content needed to successfully complete research projects.

***Goal 5: Engage students in course content.***   Strategy: Create course Web pages for each section with links to relevant resources that integrate a variety of Web-based resources for enrichment and primary course content. Suggest assignments that use these resources as points of departure for evaluation, discussion, and comparison with required readings.

***Goal 6: Accommodate diverse learning styles.***   Strategy: Suggest a variety of student-performance options that allow all learners to express themselves successfully. For example, research results can be presented in a variety of optional modes: poster sessions, Web pages, written reports, PowerPoint presentations, or debates. Students will still need to go through all the research phases and provide bibliographic documentation, but the material will be presented in a mode that will yield more interest and satisfaction and potentially contribute to a student work portfolio that will serve the student beyond the confines of the course.

***Goal 7: Improve student satisfaction with the course.***   Strategy: Increase the frequency and kinds of interactions available between faculty and students. The use of a variety of communication modes including course listservs, on-line office hours, and discussion boards provide opportunities for all students to express themselves and to engage with course material.

## WORLD CIVILIZATIONS PLANNING TEAM PROJECTS

To achieve these common goals, the planning team conceived of several Web resources and an intensive instructor training program. All team projects have been designed as prototypes for continual implementation and as ongoing support for all World Civ instructors. Six specific projects have been undertaken to date:

1. World Civilizations Faculty Resource Site <http://www.world-civ. buffalo.edu> is an electronic "resource room" for the faculty technology development that includes an extensive guide to Internet resources in World Civ, pedagogy resources, a copyright primer, a link to UB's centrally supported course management tool (CMT), a course page template, links to World Civ course homepages, an HTML toolbox, and links to various "HELP" personnel associated with the project.[3] Librarians designed the site to guide faculty through the various content-based resources, technology resources, and instructional opportunities available for developing a technology integrated course. It is supplemental to the individualized consultation and technology and resource support provided through the Educational Technology Center and the University Libraries.

2. World Civilizations Student Resource Site <http://www.world-civ. buffalo.edu/students> provides a gateway to World Civilizations course Web sites and related resources including links to the Undergraduate Library World Civ research guide, selected Internet resources, UB resource pages, and faculty/TA E-mail. Used as an asynchronous resource for the seated classroom, students can access course information, materials, and supplemental resources through one centralized Web resource as needed and at their convenience.

3. Individual Faculty Ed Tech mentoring. Faculty members are invited to schedule individual consultations in the Educational Technology Center, where they work with librarians to identify pedagogical goals, and explore, select, and integrate educational technologies into their World Civ teaching (most often through the development of a course Web site). We have promoted incremental technology development for most professors, initially concentrating on content delivery and adding interactive enhancements as their technology proficiency, interest, and time allow. By defining achievable technology goals, faculty are more satisfied with their results and are more encouraged to continue development and to gradually redesign their course to accommodate new pedagogical approaches.

4. World Civilizations Faculty–TA Special Seminar: Improving World Civilizations Teaching and Learning through Educational Technology (May 17–21, 1999) was a five-day intensive program during which faculty examined and reacted to educational technology opportunities available at UB. Twenty peer instructors (librarians and faculty) presented and led discussion in five areas: pedagogy,

information literacy, Web-based educational technologies, interactivity with students, and copyright and intellectual property in
the digital environment. Time for hands-on activities and group
discussion was provided each day. The seminar was well attended
and resulted in each of the fifteen World Civ sections implementing some technology integration for fall '99.

5. The fall '99 mini camp targeted instructors for the spring 2000 semester. We used a roundtable discussion format for these sessions
and they proved to be our most successful program for initiating
pedagogical reform. Librarians and ETC staff met with small
groups of faculty and TAs for group discussions focused on specific teaching problems and suggested strategies for addressing
them. Among the topics discussed were: ice-breaker activities for
large lecture and recitation meetings, how to encourage student
participation in class, communicating with students using technology, and developing skill-building assignments for information literacy and improved writing. Follow-up meetings were
scheduled with each instructor to plan and implement specific
technology products, instructional sessions, course assignments,
and resource selection for spring semester courses.

6. Information Literacy integration. Librarians provided information
literacy instruction at the World Civ spring and fall workshops and
in individual faculty consultations. At World Civilizations Committee meetings, faculty are regularly informed of the instructional support offered through the libraries for in-class group instruction, on-line research guides, and traditional Reference Desk
services. We actively promote several on-line research guides developed by the Oscar A. Silverman Undergraduate Library specifically for undergraduate students including

  • UGL Research Assistant <http://ublib.buffalo.edu/libraries/
    units/ugl/tutorials/research.html>
  • World Civilizations: Prehistory to 1500 <http://ublib.buffalo.
    edu/libraries/units/ugl/center/wciv.html>
  • World Civilizations: 1500 to the Present <http://ublib.buffalo.
    edu/libraries/units/ugl/center/wciv.html>

Each of these resources can be accessed from individual course pages,
the World Civilizations Student Resource Site <http://www.world-civ.
buffalo.edu>, as well as from the undergraduate library homepage
<http://ublib.buffalo.edu/libraries/units/ugl/>. Additionally, librarians
regularly meet with individual faculty members to plan instruction sessions and to assist in creating assignments that effectively integrate
skill-building activities and course content. Both faculty and librarians
acknowledge the effectiveness of this contextual teaching and learning
experience.

## CONCLUSION

The World Civilizations faculty and university librarians continue to work together toward more innovative teaching methods and greater integration of educational technologies. One of the greatest successes of our programs to date has been relationship building in an atmosphere of continual change. Changes in technologies, institutional initiatives, and support bases have all affected the direction we take. But our focus, our mission, has remained constant: improve teaching and student learning. Additionally, we have learned to implement technologies effectively and, when appropriate, to faculty instructional goals. Our collaborations have shaped our goals and have provided a catalyst for creativity. The process of working closely with faculty in both planning and implementing various projects has led us to the following conclusions:

- Model successful strategies; the experiences of peers are often the best marketing tool for our initiatives.
- Small-group interactions and individual outreach efforts seem to be the most effective means of engaging each new semester's faculty in our programs.
- Provide a high degree of individualized services and support; reassure faculty that we share and are stakeholders in their goals of improved teaching and learning.
- Advocate incremental adoption of new teaching methods and technologies to create more adaptable, flexible, and achievable projects.
- Maximize outreach opportunities by attending faculty meetings, new faculty orientations, and TA training seminars. Each venue presents opportunities for marketing library programs, resources, and services.
- Be a partnership "broker." The most successful projects happen because of the cumulative efforts and talents of project teams. Identify knowledge bases across campus that may have shared goals and facilitate their interaction on course teams.

## NOTES

1. The *Access99* <http://www.access99.buffalo.edu/> initiative requires that incoming students have access to a personal computer beyond those provided in the public computing sites and that they must develop proficiency in computer use including productivity software, E-mail, and the use of Web-based resources. To ensure that students have ample opportunity to learn and practice these skills, UB faculty are being encouraged to develop computer-intensive courses and class assignments. A major effort is under way to help

faculty redesign their courses using interactive computing technologies; high-enrollment, entry-level individual courses are being given primary attention and support. These include Psychology 101, Chemistry 101, Computer Science 101, World Civilizations, Biology 200, and English Composition. Course support for World Civ came in the form of advocacy for faculty desktop computer upgrades, technology training opportunities, and library and technology staff dedicated to the *Access99* goals.

2. The World Civilizations Educational Technology Planning Team included Dr. Claude Welch (Political Science), Dr. James Bono (History), Donald McGuire (Classics), Carole Ann Fabian (Educational Technology Center Librarian), and Leslie McCain (College of Arts and Sciences Technology Node). Additional team support was provided by Glendora Johnson-Cooper (Oscar A. Silverman Undergraduate Library, collection development coordinator), Susana Tejada (Lockwood Memorial Library, art/art history librarian), Michelle LaVoie (graduate assistant), and the staff of the Educational Technology Center.

3. During the fall 1999 semester, UB centrally supported the TopClass course management tool. The university will adopt Blackboard's CourseInfo CMT for fall 2000. World Civilizations instructors will be given training and support for its use throughout the upcoming semesters. Faculty will be encouraged to use this CMT as a more efficient and flexible alternative to individually designed and created course Web pages.

# 21

# New Learners, New Models: Cultivating an Information Literacy Program

*Andrée J. Rathemacher, Mary C. MacDonald, and Joanna M. Burkhardt*

The beginnings of a comprehensive plan for information literacy at the University of Rhode Island (URI) date to March 1998, when a group of interested reference librarians met with the vice provost for Information Services/Dean of Libraries to address information literacy goals and to investigate how they could best be integrated into the curriculum. A number of reference librarians had been informally discussing ways to improve the library's instruction program, and the interest of our new vice provost/dean in developing an information literacy program and offering credit-generating courses in the library provided the avenue and support we needed for these thoughts to come together into a plan.

## CURRENT LIBRARY INSTRUCTION PROGRAM

The starting point for the development of a program to teach information literacy at the University of Rhode Island was an examination of the current state of library instruction. The University Library has a very active bibliographic instruction program. In academic year 1998–99, eight reference librarians, assisted by three graduate students of library science, taught 325 library instruction sessions that reached 7,323 students out of a student population of approximately 14,000. These numbers have been growing steadily over the past three years, and reflect a 1 percent increase in number of classes taught and a 37 percent increase in number of students reached from 1995–96.

Of the total sessions taught in 1998–99, 46 percent were for students in two introductory freshman courses. Every semester, librarians teach two "bibliographic instruction (BI) blitzes," one for URI 101, a one-credit course familiarizing freshmen with college life, and one for Writing 101, a beginning introductory writing course. In URI 101, librarians introduce students to the on-line catalog, and in Writing 101, students are introduced to the library's core, interdisciplinary periodical database.

In addition to the freshmen "blitzes," individual reference librarians teach "one-shot" bibliographic instruction classes in their areas of expertise. In 1998–99, librarians taught 160 of these subject-specific classes, accounting for 49 percent of all classes taught. These classes are typically requested by individual faculty members who contact the appropriate librarian to arrange a session in the library. The instruction is usually geared to introducing students to a particular set of information resources that they will need to complete a specific assignment in the course.

While this system is a sincere attempt to provide students with an understanding of the library and specific research tools, it is haphazard and not subject to an overall plan or strategy. "One-shot" instruction depends solely on the initiative of individual faculty members to request a library session, which is then subject to the ability to find a mutually acceptable time and location for instruction to take place. Furthermore, since these sessions tend to be planned around the practical library skills needed to complete a specific assignment, a conceptual understanding of how information is structured, overall research strategies, and how to critically evaluate information once it is found are deemphasized.

Furthermore, the "one-shot" system misses many students. Some students receive similar instruction multiple times throughout their undergraduate studies, while others receive only minimal instruction, if any at all. Whether or not a student receives instruction varies by discipline and also by course within an area of study. For example, business students tend to receive more library instruction than engineering students do, and within the College of Business, marketing students receive more library instruction than do finance students. Part of this discrepancy is due to the varying research requirements of different programs, and part is simply the result of varying levels of individual initiative exhibited by instructional faculty members and librarians.

In contrast to the "one-shot" instruction just described, the URI 101 and Writing 101 programs are more methodical and thought-out, in that a standardized set of basic concepts and tools are covered and all students in these classes are reached. However, these programs too have shortcomings. Each class receives only fifty minutes or at most one hour and fifteen minutes of instruction, which only scratches the surface of what students need to learn. Furthermore, in our experience, students do not appear to retain much of what is covered in these sessions.

Both modes of instruction, "one-shot" BIs and URI 101/Writing 101 "blitzes," are very time- and resource-intensive. For "one-shot" classes, librarians must prepare customized presentations and lessons geared to the particular assignment at hand. The content of URI 101/Writing 101 sessions is standardized, but covering the large number of sections each semester at current staffing levels is a strain.

## WHY CHANGE?

In order to develop an effective information literacy program, we not only needed to identify what we thought should change, but how to change it. We needed to create a vision that would allow us to work toward what it was that we wanted to accomplish.

As a starting point, we examined the 1989 American Library Association (ALA) President's Report on information literacy. The report recommends a "learning process [that] would actively involve students in the process of knowing when they have a need for information, identifying information needed to address a given problem, finding needed information, evaluating the information, organizing the information, and using the information effectively to address the issue at hand."[1] In addition to the information literacy competencies outlined in the ALA report, there were two additional ideas we wanted to address in the development of our program. One was the need to incorporate information concepts, as opposed to just "skills," into our instruction. Second, we were excited about the extended opportunities we were creating for increased student/library interaction, for example, through credit-generating courses in information literacy. To enhance the learning, we would need to use an instructional method that allows students a sense of discovery and empowerment in their research that would remain with them long after their university experience.

We drew on the research of Patricia Senn Breivik who, in *Student Learning in an Information Age*, reports on the limits of the lecture system in the classroom. She argues that "classroom business-as-usual cannot be tolerated on campuses that place a high value on student learning."[2] She refers to the 1994 Association for the Study of Higher Education–Educational Resources Information Center Higher Education Report, *Redesigning Higher Education: Producing Dramatic Gains in Student Learning*, which documents research on the limitations of lecture as a method of instruction.[3] "If higher-order thinking skills are 'retained and used long after the individual has forgotten the detailed specifics of the subject matter taught in schools"[4] and if, as the old adage suggests, education is what remains after the facts are forgotten, what does the accumulated research reviewed [in this report] imply for the quality of our graduates? Would it not be wiser to focus less on facts and more on developing higher-order skills?"[5]

We also referred to the Carnegie Foundation's 1998 Boyer Commission Report, *Reinventing Undergraduate Education: A Blueprint for America's Research Universities.*[6] The commission provides ten suggestions for improving undergraduate education with recommendations for each. Number one on its list is "Make Research-Based Learning the Standard." Research-based learning, action research, inquiry learning, and authentic learning are all models involved in producing learning from within, learning that will remain with the students long after they have completed the task at hand. "Resource based learning is a commonsense approach to learning. If students are to continue learning throughout their lives, they must be able to access, evaluate, organize, and present information from all the real-world sources existing in today's information society."[7]

Finally, we developed a working definition of information literacy at the University of Rhode Island Libraries. Christine Bruce, in *The Seven Faces of Information Literacy,* discusses several definitions of "information literacy."[8] The most popular definition in use currently was developed by Christine Doyle using the Delphi technique: "Information literacy is the ability to access, evaluate and use information from a variety of sources." Recognizing Shapiro and Hughes's contribution suggesting that academe should conceive of information literacy as a new liberal art, we formulated our own definition: "Information literacy is the ability to understand the concepts and values of information in the context of data, information, and knowledge. Further, it is the ability to understand where information comes from, where it goes, and what the relationship is between the learner and the information world. It also means being able to effectively gather, analyze, and use information in a meaningful way."[9]

## DRAFT PLAN

In October 1999, we released our "Draft Plan #2 for Information Literacy at the University of Rhode Island." The plan includes the following objectives:

- Develop a definition of information literacy for the University of Rhode Island.
- Develop and introduce an incremental, four-year-plus program for student mastery of information literacy concepts and skills.

- Implement the program by working with teaching faculty outside the libraries.
- Provide more teaching labs, locations, and facilities.
- Develop a core group of library faculty specifically for teaching.

For each objective we developed action items, time frames, and responsible parties. While these are still in a fluid state, we have made considerable progress in envisioning new models for the information literacy framework.

Students at the freshman, sophomore, and junior levels would have the option of achieving information literacy competency by fulfilling a series of instructional modules or by taking the three-credit course Library 120: Introduction to Information Literacy or the one-credit course Library 140: Special Topics in Information Literacy at the appropriate times. The senior year of the information literacy program would require completing a capstone portfolio project, in conjunction with the capstone course required for graduation in the student's major.

The draft plan also addresses information literacy needs of graduate students and faculty by calling for seminars and workshops in those areas. Also suggested are annual meetings to introduce new information products to faculty. Finally, the draft plan calls for the creation of a learning laboratory dedicated to the support of librarian–faculty collaboration in the design of courses and assignments.

## THE COURSES

While the "Draft Plan #2 for Information Literacy at the University of Rhode Island" is a comprehensive document that addresses working toward information literacy on a number of levels, in our view, the credit courses are truly the heart of the program. They are also the source of our experience and accomplishments in information literacy instruction thus far.

### Library 140: Special Topics in Information Literacy

Library 140: Special Topics in Information Literacy was the first credit-generating course developed and taught under the library's fledgling information literacy program. It was the result of discussions among a working group of librarians and supportive teaching faculty who determined that the most promising way of successfully integrating information literacy into the curriculum was to develop partnerships with faculty teaching core courses in major disciplines. The discipline on which the group decided to focus first was business.

Library 140 is a one-credit course that covers the information resources in a particular subject area and is designed to run concurrently with a course in that discipline. In spring semester 1999, reference librarians Andrée Rathemacher and Mary MacDonald team taught two sections of the course with a focus on business information. Students who enrolled in Professor Clay Sink's sections of Management 110: Introduction to Business were required to also register for Library 140. Both sections of Library 140 were fully enrolled, with twenty-five students each.

Taught in a workshop style, the course covered general information concepts as well as business information. Each class began with a short introduction to the day's topic. Students then gathered into groups to work on an in-class worksheet. There was no final exam for the course. Instead, each student wrote a "Memo-to-Your-Manager" on one of a number of current issues in business. The memo served as an assessment tool by which students demonstrated how well they had mastered the learning objectives of articulating their information needs, developing search strategies, and finding, critically evaluating, and communicating information.

Student evaluations of the course were positive overall. Some students seemed to resent being "forced" to enroll in a course they had not planned on taking. However, the majority found the class very helpful. The results of a survey of the students in the class conducted by the university's Instructional Development Program revealed that 94 percent of the students surveyed thought they learned "a great deal" or "a fair amount," and 73 percent rated the course "excellent" or "good." While a number of students complained that the course was too much work for one credit, most had positive comments, such as: "It was not as bad as I first assumed! Some of the lessons actually helped me in my other classes!"; "I found it very helpful for my business classes and many other classes. Many students don't know how to do research. This class teaches that!"; and "I learned a lot in this course, and I know what I learned will help me a lot in my university and more future life [sic]. In my opinion, everybody has to learn what we studied in this course."

Students seemed to appreciate the "hands-on" nature of the class. However, students complained if there was too much presentation by the instructors or if they couldn't see the immediate relevance of the material covered. It was interesting to note that many students seemed to resist our attempts to provide them with a more conceptual framework through discussing, for example, the principles behind subject headings and descriptors, or why companies are required to disclose financial information, or how to evaluate sources of information. This led us to question whether or not freshmen are ready to engage with information-related concepts at a more abstract level.

In retrospect, the level of student engagement with the course might have been higher had it been more closely integrated with the content of Management 110, as students did not always see the relevance of what was covered in Library 140 to what they were learning in management. This would have required working more closely with the instructor of Management 110 to coordinate the content of both classes as well as a more flexible approach on our part regarding what we wanted to cover. These issues will be reconsidered as we reinvent Library 140.

Unfortunately, the future of Library 140 in its current form is in question. Two more sections of the course with a focus on business information were scheduled for fall 1999—one that would again run concurrent with a section of Management 110, and one that would be open to anyone who wanted to enroll. However, during the summer, the university administration decided that concurrent registration could not be required of students. With Library 140 no longer required, only a few students registered for the section connected to Management 110, and only a handful registered for the "stand-alone" section. Both sections were canceled. We plan to revisit Library 140 in the future, but for now we are focusing our energies on Library 120: Introduction to Information Literacy.

## Library 120: Introduction to Information Literacy

Library 120: Introduction to Information Literacy was the second credit-generating course developed and taught in the library's information literacy program. It was developed by library faculty in consultation with instructional faculty as a natural precursor to Library 140. Library 120 was born out of the faculty's perceived need for a broader and deeper understanding of information, information retrieval, and evaluation and analysis of information.

The course goal is to create lifelong learners, problem solvers, and independent and critical thinkers. The course is based on active learning in the evolving world of information. We felt that students taking this course in its present form would be both interested and motivated, as it is not a requirement for any program. We also felt that a three-credit course would be "taken seriously" by most students.

Library 120 is a three-credit elective that focuses on the basic conceptual understanding of what information is, where it comes from, and how it is used. Active, hands-on learning is central in this course. The course begins with a short introduction to information in everyday life. Classes lead students from the organization of information, the uses for information, and the audiences for which information is provided, to academic information tools. We address questions such as what is a catalog, what is an index, what are subject headings, what are descriptors, what is a keyword, and why are all these things useful. The Internet is explored as a separate unit, with concepts from other units reemphasized for this specialized medium. Critical thinking skills and resource evaluation techniques are stressed throughout the course. Weekly in-class and take-home exercises and worksheets provide reinforcement and practice for both skills and concepts.

The final project for the course is to provide a "paper trail" for research leading to a research paper, which could be one assigned for another class or just a topic of interest. We ask for a topic thesis statement, a list of search terms used, and a notation of which ones "worked" and which ones did not. We ask what research tools were used, what information was found in each, what resources were used, and which of those provided material actually pertinent to the topic. We require a detailed outline of the paper or the paper itself, and a complete bibliography.

The first section of Library 120 was taught by Mary MacDonald and Joanna Burkhardt in fall semester 1999. The course was taught at the Providence campus of the university, which caters to older, nontraditional students. The average Providence campus student is forty years old, works full-time, and has a family. These students are very focused, very motivated, and very enthusiastic. We felt that Library 120 would get a fair trial and an honest evaluation from this population. We also felt that this group would better tolerate the vagaries and glitches associated with a new course.

As expected, students were excited about the course and its content. They were eager and appreciative participants in class discussions and assignments and took the subject and the work seriously. The only complaint we heard was "Why wasn't this course offered before?" Students have volunteered to write letters to various deans and directors in support of the course. While we have yet to see the final results of this first semester, we expect our evaluations to be good.

We have scheduled two sections of Library 120 for the spring semester 2000, one in Kingston at the main campus and one in Providence. We are doing our own marketing of the course, which includes word of mouth, posters, and written recommendations from our first class.

With an eye to the future of our program, we have begun the process of petitioning for this course to fill a general education requirement for the university in the area of communications. Making Library 120 a general education option has subsequently received the support of the library faculty, the administration at the Providence campus, and the faculty senate's General Education Committee. If approved as a general education course, it would be one of only six that students can take to satisfy the communications requirement.

## INFORMATION LITERACY MODULES

While credit-generating courses are at the center of our draft plan for information literacy at the university, we envision these courses being supplemented by instructional "modules." We conceive of modules as tutorials, some of which are Web based, covering general topics such as the library catalog, periodical databases, and research strategies, as well as subject-specific topics such as company information or drug information. Web-based modules could be used either as stand-alone units for students to work through on their own or as teaching aids for librarians in a classroom setting.

Developing Web-based modules to teach information literacy competencies would enable us to reach more students than we can through credit courses or traditional bibliographic instruction alone. Furthermore, they would be readily adaptable to the distance learning environment. Modules would also eliminate redundancies in instruction that now exist.

Going forward with this plan will require a tremendous amount of collaboration and cooperation with teaching faculty in different departments and colleges, because without their willingness to integrate modules into the curriculum, modules will at best be nothing but substitutes for "one-shot" instruction sessions and won't reach all the students for whom they were intended.

To move forward in this direction we have plans to develop a Web-based module on the library catalog. We hope to test it on selected URI 101 classes in the coming semesters.

## CONCLUSION

With our plan still in draft form, and having taught each of our credit-generating courses just once, we are still in the early stages of a full-grown information literacy program. What we are doing is a work in progress, and many of our recommendations will take time, collaboration, and effort to accomplish. Yet we now have the beginnings of what we hope will be a thriving four-year program at the University of Rhode Island. As we move forward and implement additional pieces of the plan, we hope to gather additional support, suggestions, assistance, and impetus from our constituents. We expect our plan to evolve as we gain experience. In the final analysis, we hope to incorporate a new and much needed understanding of information and information literacy into the URI college experience. This, in turn, will provide powerful skills and analytical expertise that students will use in all of their postcollege pursuits.

## NOTES

1. American Library Association, Presidential Committee on Information Literacy, "Final Report" (Chicago: American Library Association, 1989). <http://www.ala.org/acrl/nili/ilit1st.html> [accessed 3 November 1999].

2. Patricia Senn Breivik, *Student Learning in the Information Age*, American Council on Education/Oryx Press Series on Higher Education (Phoenix, Ariz.: Oryx Press, 1998), 23.

3. Breivik, *Student Learning in the Information Age*, 23–24.

4. B. S. Bloom, "The Search for Methods of Group Intervention as Effective One-to-One Tutoring," *Educational Leadership* 41 (1984): 14; quoted in Breivik, *Student Learning in the Information Age*, 24.

5. Lion Gardiner, *Redesigning Higher Education: Producing Dramatic Gains in Student Learning*, ASHE-ERIC Higher Education Report, No. 7 (Washington, D.C.: Graduate School of Education and Human Development, George Washington University, 1994), 46–47; quoted in Breivik, *Student Learning in the Information Age*, 24.

6. Boyer Commission on Educating Undergraduates in the Research University, "Reinventing Undergraduate Education: A Blueprint for America's Research Universities," (Albany, N.Y.: SUNY Press, 1998). <http://notes.cc.sunysb.edu/Pres/boyer.nsf> [accessed 4 November 1999].

7. Breivik, *Student Learning in the Information Age*, 25.

8. Christine Bruce, *The Seven Faces of Information Literacy* (Adelaide, Australia: Auslib Press, 1997), 26.

9. Jeremy J. Shapiro and Shelly K. Hughes, "Information Literacy as a Liberal Art: Enlightenment Proposals for a New Curriculum," *Educom Review* 31, no. 2 (March–April 1996). <http://www.educause.edu/pub/er/review/Articles/31231.html> (accessed 21 October 1999].

# 22

# A Grass-Roots Approach to Integrating Information Literacy into the Curriculum

*Marybeth McCartin*

The 1990s were an unprecedented time of change for libraries. The emergence of the Internet and other major advancements in information technology challenged librarians to seriously reexamine a number of long-standing assumptions about the nature of libraries and information services. For their part, instruction librarians saw a need to adapt bibliographic instruction approaches to the conditions of a transforming information environment.

## INFORMATION LITERACY MOVEMENT

The information literacy movement evolved in the 1990s in response to changing ideas about library instruction. Until then, library instruction tended to focus on how to use specific tools.[1] But in this past decade, librarians began to realize that—in a constantly changing information universe—a more conceptual, process-oriented approach to instruction is imperative.[2] It became clear that to function in a dynamic information environment, students need skills and strategies that can be applied to a variety of information needs and scenarios.

In the latter half of the decade, instruction librarians engaged in intense dialogue about what information literacy really means. These discussions, fueled by organizations such as the Information Literacy Institute and the National Forum on Information Literacy, recently resulted in a common understanding and representation of information literacy, including a shared notion of the information literacy competencies students need for success in academics and beyond.

By now, many academic libraries have developed their own official information literacy policy and information literacy competencies statements. While the language may differ to some degree from institution to institution, the basis of these documents is very much the same.

## INFORMATION LITERACY COMPETENCIES

New York University (NYU) Libraries has had a working information literacy competencies statement, drafted by the Instructional Services Team, since early 1998. The competencies statement—a concrete, pragmatic instrument—gives us an important foundation on which to base information literacy programming. The statement reflects our philosophical position on information literacy, but it is also meant to be a practical source for librarians to consult when preparing bibliographic instruction sessions and discussing information literacy issues with teaching faculty.[3]

## IMPLEMENTATION STRATEGIES

With a working competencies statement in place, our Instructional Services Team began in spring 1998 to plan a strategy for introducing information literacy to the university community. A few critical concerns surfaced during our early discussions: How would we get our information literacy message across to all of NYU—a diverse community of over 50,000 students and more than 2,300 faculty? How could we compete with other prevailing educational issues for faculty and administrator attention? Would an information literacy campaign only increase demand for bibliographic instruction beyond our ability to respond?

These concerns led the team to make two immediate decisions. Realizing it was futile to try to reach the whole university at once, our first decision was to choose a manageable population on which to focus an initial information literacy effort. Believing that information literacy is best achieved when it is addressed *throughout* higher education and that it is important to start early, we chose first-year students as our target group. We further narrowed this population to freshmen involved in the Morse Academic Plan (MAP), a general education core curriculum—consisting of courses in writing, societies and cultures, and scientific inquiry—in which 62 percent of all full-time freshmen (approximately 3,300 students) are required to participate.[4] In an effort to curtail a possible deluge of requests for bibliographic instruction, our second decision was to try to persuade MAP faculty to collaborate with us at the course development level to determine alternative ways of interjecting an information literacy component into their classes.

One member of the Instructional Services Team was well connected with a respected, influential faculty member associated with MAP and invited her to one of our meetings. Professor Nancy Regalado, director of medieval and Renaissance studies, was preparing to teach her first MAP course in the fall and was interested in hearing our ideas. At the meeting, the team talked about our ambition to make information literacy part of the academic experience at NYU and introduced the libraries' competencies statement. Professor Regalado, inspired by our views, suggested that we jointly pitch a MAP-wide information literacy proposal to the assistant director of MAP.

She arranged a meeting with the assistant director, at which we emphasized how closely our information literacy competencies correspond to the objectives of MAP:

**MAP Meets Information Literacy**

| Map Objective* | Corresponding Info. Lit. Competency** |
|---|---|
| Help students become independent and creative thinkers . . . to thrive in dynamic circumstance | *Comp. 9a:* Posses a conceptual framework for information seeking that can be applied to a variety of research questions and environments |
| Encourage students to develop the habits of lifelong learning and inquiry | *Comp. 8b:* Appreciate the relationship between information literacy and lifelong learning |
| Introduce students to methods by which societies may be studied, analyzed, and explored | *Comp. 5a:* Understand and apply essential information-seeking concepts and practices |
| Develop students' abilities to read critically, think rigorously, and write effectively | *Comp. 6b:* Consistently analyze information for relevance and quality |

\* Extracted from *The Morse Academic Plan* brochure
\*\* Extracted from the *NYU Libraries Information Literacy Competencies Statement*

The libraries' emphasis was that no education is complete without addressing information literacy and we advocated that an information literacy component be added to MAP. The assistant director agreed that information literacy deserves a place in MAP, but pointed out that the NYU faculty tend to actively resist curriculum mandates. He stressed that, given the NYU culture, the success of our initiative depends on the faculty coming to their own conclusion that information literacy be an official part of MAP. He encouraged us to win the faculty over from the ground up by initiating collaborative pilot projects. Successful pilot projects could then be presented to other MAP faculty to elicit further projects. Once a series of successful pilot projects—involving an increasing number of faculty—was completed and acknowledged as worthwhile, we would be in a better position to make information literacy a confirmed part of MAP.

## PILOT PROJECT

Professor Regalado was interested in collaborating on the first pilot project as she prepared to teach a MAP course called Conversations of the West: Antiquity and the Middle Ages. Conversations of the West is a requirement for all MAP freshmen, and they can choose from four possible tracks: Antiquity and the Middle Ages, Antiquity and the Renaissance, Antiquity and the Enlightenment, and Antiquity and the Nineteenth Century. Conversations of the West is not a survey course; it involves reading and discussing classic texts, examining how they influence a culture's thinking, traditions, and ideals. All Conversations tracks have the same general objectives: to provide a context for the study of the liberal arts, to foster an understanding of how cultures develop and change, and to introduce methods of sociological study.

Within this framework, Professor Regalado's track focuses on how the medievals interpreted themes and stories in selected texts to fit their belief systems and worldview. Assigned texts include the *Bible*, Plato's *Symposium*, Petrarch's *Secretum*, *Oedipus the King*, Augustine's *Confessions*, and *The Canterbury Tales*.

Preparations for the Library-Conversations of the West pilot project began in June 1998. On the library side, the project involved the head of Instructional Services, a library associate from the General and Humanities Reference Unit, and a student worker. On the Conversations side, participants included Professor Regalado and her two preceptors. The group met several times over the summer to talk about Conversations objectives versus library/information literacy objectives, and to work out how to weave them together. We brainstormed about library assignments and ways to convey an information literacy thread throughout the course.

The pilot ran in fall 1998. It encompassed both sections of Professor Regalado's Conversations class for a total enrollment of sixty students. The library assignments we designed for the project are probably the clearest illustration of how we integrated information literacy objectives into the course. At first we were uncertain about which kinds of assignments would be most appropriate. We wanted any library assignments to blend inconspicuously with the existing syllabus and yet be in keeping with the nature of the class—which is not about research, but about reading, thinking, and exchanging ideas.

The fact that students would not be doing research forced us to think creatively about library assignments and helped reinforce the idea that information literacy skill acquisition is gradual. Given the nature and level of the class, we decided it was quite acceptable to focus on very basic library and information literacy objectives. We reasoned that, after being introduced to the basics in this first semester course, students would be in a good position to tackle the more rigorous library assignments they would encounter in later semesters.

In developing our assignments, we asked ourselves what students absolutely need to know in order to succeed in this course. We decided that, since a high number of Conversations readings are on reserve at the library, students need to immediately locate the Reserve Desk, understand how to search for materials using the on-line catalog's Reserve menu, and become familiar with Reserve Desk procedures. Students also need to locate photocopiers and get comfortable operating them, since all Reserve materials are noncirculating. (Not to mention that copiers, in general, play such an important role in students' day-to-day work.) In addition, students need to be able to use the catalog's main menu to search for materials in the regular collection as well as locate items in the stacks. Finally, because we created a Web site as a home base for this class, students need to understand the basics of the Web.

## ASSIGNMENT DESIGN

To address all these objectives, we designed one required assignment and one extra credit assignment. The required "Library Quest" instructed students to borrow Petrarch's *Secretum* from the Reserve Collection in Bobst Library (NYU's main library) and copy the text in three different ways: (1) photocopy the entire reading, (2) hand copy one page, and (3) with a partner, transcribe two paragraphs from dictation. Students were requested to write a one-page essay on their impression of each technique, commenting on which method most enabled them to "connect with" and retain the message of the text. On the library side, the purpose of the assignment was to introduce students to the library environment, the Reserve Collection, and the mechanics of using copy cards and photocopiers—mundane but essential basics can be obstacles even to more advanced researchers. On the Conversations side, the purpose of the assignment was to help students explore ways in which people relate to the printed word and to reflect on the methods used over time to record and hand down texts.

The students' essays were interesting, with remarks ranging from the pragmatic to the philosophical. One student wrote, "Each way I use to copy the text has a different impact on my impressions and understanding of it. . . . I believe that copying from dictation is the best way to get a feeling of the text one is copying because you [sic] have to listen to it carefully as you write it down." Another student noted, "Photocopying is worthless when it comes to getting acquainted with the material."

Some students offered more profound insights. One wrote, "Technology in my opinion has the ability to distance people from the subject and others. Even in everyday life, one no longer has to venture outside to meet people but instead can go into a chat room. In college one can copy an article, place it somewhere and then forget it exists." Along the same line, another remarked, "I have concluded from this assignment that as technology advances, society slacks. Once men and women worked diligently and strenuously to copy books, today we only push a button." But another student made an opposing point: "The creation of modern technology has changed our relationship with the written word. Although it does remove us from the publication process, it also preserves the work with less possibility for human error and makes literature available to more people."

The second part of the Library Quest had the students find a copy of Petrarch's *Secretum* in the stacks and write a paragraph describing the books shelved near this title. The purpose of this exercise was to convey that books are organized by subject and that browsing the shelves can be a part of library research.

The students who chose to tackle the extra credit assignment were asked to use a search engine to find one scholarly and one nonscholarly Web site related to any topic covered in the Conversations class and provide a written evaluation of each. We provided the students with a set of criteria on which to base their evaluations. The scholarly sites chosen by the students were posted to the class Web site.

The Web had a presence throughout the course since we created a class Web site that pulled together the components of the course and gave structure to our pilot project.[5] Designing the Web site proved to be the most labor-intensive part of the pilot project. Professor Regalado had never before used the Web in her classes, and neither she nor her preceptors knew the first thing about Web site design and maintenance. Therefore, responsibility for creating the site fell on the Library side of the project. Most of the work was delegated to the pilot project's student assistant, who was experienced in Web site design. The student assistant also taught the Conversations preceptors basic HTML so that they could maintain the site during the semester.

Included on the Web site were an on-line discussion group, the class syllabus, and links to outside Web sources. The site also contained a page of "Library Links" from which students could get to the Library's home page, the on-line catalog, the virtual tour of the Library, and several library instruction tutorials. This page included a link to a "Web Links" page that listed on-line tutorials covering Web basics such as how to use search engines. The "Library Links" and "Web Links" sections were the library's way of connecting with Conversations students, since a bibliographic instruction session was not part of the project. Another way we connected with the students was through the class discussion group, which was monitored by the project's library associate.

## PROJECT EVALUATION

A survey was administered at the end of the project to collect data about the students and determine their attitudes toward the information literacy component of the course. Ninety-five percent of the surveys were returned. In the completed surveys, 12 percent of the students identified themselves as having had no prior experience using libraries, while another 30 percent said they had only a little experience. By contrast, only 4 percent of the students said they never used the Web before, while 53 percent reported using the Web often and 25 percent identified themselves as "Net Heads." Fifty-two percent said the Library Quest assignment was the first time they had used Bobst Library and 70 percent said they used Bobst again after the Library Quest (8 percent to access other Conversations Reserve readings, 12 percent to search for additional Reserve readings, 31 percent to access Reserve readings for other classes, and 49 percent to search for additional readings for other classes). Eighty-eight percent of students reported using the class Web site at least once during the semester, although a disappointing 24 percent reported that they used the Library Links on the class Web page. (On the more positive side, of the 24 percent, 92 percent said they found the Library Links useful.) Finally, 65 percent of the students reported that they now feel well prepared to use Bobst Library.

## CONCLUSION

Having analyzed the results of the pilot project, Library–Conversations project participants would urge anyone planning a similar information literacy effort to consider these points:

- Library and information literacy skills can not be acquired instantly in one bibliographic instruction session or course-integrated effort. They are developed over time.
- Concrete documents, such as an information literacy competency statement and a pilot project report, clarify the library's position and are easier to sell to faculty and administrators than abstractions.
- Understanding your institution's particular culture is critical.

- Starting small and gradually building support may be the best approach.
- Partnering with an influential, well-respected faculty member can be a great asset.
- Courses that do not require research can still be candidates for information literacy projects—it just takes some creative thinking.
- Information literacy objectives can be threaded into courses in ways that do not require bibliographic instruction sessions.
- Collaboration projects teach faculty about information literacy skills along with their students.
- Completing a successful pilot project does not mean the work is done; it is important to keep up the momentum.

With this project under our belt, the Instructional Services Team now has a sound model for further information literacy projects. Our next step is to target a few more MAP faculty to work with on collaborative efforts. Professor Regalado, who is pleased with the results of her project and continues to use the Conversations model, has been helpful in this regard, advocating participation in information literacy projects among her colleagues. The Instructional Services Team plans to continue the process of collaborating with teaching faculty on individual pilot projects for several more semesters. At that point, we hope to have sufficient faculty support to make information literacy an official component of MAP.

## NOTES

1. Maureen Kilcullen, "Teaching Librarians to Teach: Recommendations on What We Need to Know," *Reference Services Review* 26 (Summer 1998): 9.
2. Loanne Snavely and Natasha Cooper, "Competing Agendas in Higher Education: Finding a Place for Information Literacy," *Reference and User Services Quarterly* 37 (Fall 1997): 53.
3. The NYU Libraries Information Literacy Competencies Statement was officially adopted at a libraries-wide forum in February 1999.
4. Of the seven undergraduate schools that enroll freshmen, four have elected to participate in MAP. They include the College of Arts and Science (which also administers MAP), the School of Education, the School of Business, and the School of Social Work.
5. The Web site URL is <http://www.nyu.edu/classes/regalado/index.htm>.

# 23

# Making Sense of Science: The University of Iowa Science Information Literacy Initiative

*Barbara I. Dewey and Karen Zimmerman*

## WHY SCIENCE INFORMATION LITERACY?

The ability to locate, critically analyze, organize, and apply scientific information is an important skill for University of Iowa science and technology graduates. On a daily basis students preparing for professional and academic careers in science and technology will need to correctly locate, evaluate, and apply science information from the constantly growing and rapidly changing universe of print, electronic, multimedia, and Web-based sources.

Advancing information literacy in science and technology is of major importance at the highest levels of national policy. Albert Henderson writes that "an ideal vision of science requires goals and strategies to deal directly with the growth of new information. 'Information Age' science policy fails to do this. By ignoring the study of science communications, it fosters a policy vacuum on information."[1] Although the more general concept of "science literacy" has been recognized as a concern and challenge in the United States, particularly since the post-Sputnik era, proponents have focused primarily on recruiting students into the sciences and heightening the public's understanding of science issues rather than on addressing effective scientific information seeking.[2] Academic libraries have not developed comprehensive science-based literacy programs although many science librarians have been successful in promoting certain information-seeking skills such as specific database manipulation and Web searching. For example, a widely cited *College & Research Libraries* article reviewing the advances of information literacy efforts by librarians made no mention of specific applications in science or technology.[3] The University of Iowa Science Information Literacy Initiative seeks to address this void for the campus and as a potential model for other institutions.

## THE UNIVERSITY OF
## IOWA INFORMATION LITERACY INITIATIVE

The University of Iowa Libraries is considered a leader in library user education and was cited recently in a major research library journal as one of six institutions demonstrating the best practices and models for information literacy in the United States.[4] The Science Information Literacy Initiative is an outgrowth of the University of Iowa Information Literacy Initiative (UIII), an emerging program developed in cooperation with the College of Liberal Arts to integrate key information literacy components directly into courses in a discipline-based, customized way.[5] These information literacy initiatives constitute a major advance in the libraries' user education program that emphasizes collaborative work with faculty, creative application of information technology and teaching methods, and aggressive efforts to make information resources in all formats understandable and accessible. Iowa's strong reputation is based on its success in integrating library instruction in the university's curriculum through a variety of innovative methods. For example, Library Explorer, a Web-based library instruction program, is used by rhetoric faculty to provide the basics of library use and search strategies for new students.[6] In 1998–99 librarians conducted 318 in-class library instruction sessions supporting a wide variety of subject areas reaching more than 5,000 undergraduate students.

The TWIST (Teaching with Innovative Style and Technology) project, funded by the Roy J. Carver Charitable Trust, has created a model program for training librarians and faculty to integrate networked information technology into the teaching and learning process.[7] For example, during the fall semester 1999, more than sixty-four faculty were partnered with sixteen librarians in eighty-three courses to develop new Web-based methods of instruction and information delivery. TWIST also provides classes and self-paced tutorials for faculty in a variety of departments on applying new learning technologies and linking course content to information resources. TWIST's impact is most accurately captured by an English professor, who said that "for me and my department, TWIST has made a profound, transformative, and enduring difference." The TWIST program was one of three finalists for the prestigious University of Iowa 1998 President's Award for Technology Innovation. Faculty enthusiasm for TWIST is an important ingredient for willingness to participate in the information literacy initiatives.

Launching of UIII was based on several opportune factors, including the appointment of a new dean of the College of Liberal Arts who was supportive, the fact that the college curriculum was beginning to include more active learning and problem-solving models, that the University of Iowa Office of the Provost's new strategic plan is emphasizing "comprehensive writing excellence" and "revitalizing the University Libraries" as priority initiatives, and heightened faculty interest on the programs noted above.[8]

## THE ROY J. CARVER CHARITABLE TRUST

A major factor in the development of the Science Information Literacy initiative was the interest and subsequent funding of the project by the Roy J. Carver Charitable Trust. The Carver Trust had funded the successful Information Arcade, the Information Commons, TWIST, and a new Biological Sciences Library, a total of $2.13 million in awards. Senior library staff members developed a prospectus and presentation for Carver and were then encouraged to submit a formal grant proposal. Funding of $270,000 was recently received for the two-year project. Funding supports a coordinator, an instructional designer, and two graduate assistants.

## SCALING INFORMATION LITERACY

Both the UIII and the Science Information Literacy Initiative are based on the University of Iowa Libraries' philosophy that integrated curriculum-based user education is the most effective and has the greatest ability to scale for developing students' portfolio of information literacy skills. The University of Iowa's student population is large, consisting of about 20,000 undergraduates and 8,000 graduate students. Currently, the Libraries reach only about half of the undergraduates through some type of user education program and only in a scattered way. An important outgrowth of the information literacy programs will be development of alternative methods for faculty to incorporate into their courses for each component, including Web-based methods, in-class presentations, use of existing library Web tutorials, and other means since librarians are not numerous enough to appear in every introductory class at a university of Iowa's size.

## STUDENT LEARNING OBJECTIVES

Development of relevant student learning objectives in partnership with faculty is an essential part of the Science Information Literacy

Initiative. Below are examples of objectives likely to be included in the program:

- Identify problems that require solutions based on scientific information.
- Identify appropriate scientific information sources and execute effective search strategies.
- Interpret and analyze search results.
- Critically evaluate scientific information retrieved.
- Organize, synthesize, and apply scientific information.
- Understand the structure of the information environment and the process by which scholarly and other information in the science and technology fields are produced and disseminated.
- Understand the ethical issues related to access and use of scientific information.

Flexibility will be the hallmark of the Science Information Literacy Initiative because individual fields in science and technology are structured differently. For example, physics students require the use of digital "preprints" or articles found on the Web that have not yet been published, while astronomy students require the ability to locate photographs. Experimental psychology students must be able to locate appropriate research articles in the literature of psychology as well as in bioscience and medical indexes. Mechanical engineering students must locate all relevant design and safety standards for a particular product using a wide variety of print and electronic sources for industry and governmental regulations. Chemistry students need to be able to plan and execute experiments based on chemical research literature such as searching for chemical and physical properties of substances. Faculty and librarians will select the most appropriate "assignment" delivery and evaluation methods to meet the learning objectives determined to be most critical.

## METHODOLOGY AND PROJECT EVALUATION

Science Information Literacy project staff and science librarians are working directly with select faculty in each science discipline to customize curriculum components that meet the student learning objectives. Faculty and librarians will test these curriculum components in actual courses and may present them as Web-based instruction, in-class instruction, or some other format depending on course requirements, needs, and structure. Evaluation of the project will be accomplished using appropriate tools to measure students' acquisition of the learning objectives. Information literacy components deemed successful on the basis of student outcomes will be developed into an easily adaptable program for widespread use throughout the science and technology curriculum.

## INITIAL PROJECTS

Building on information literacy components already under way seemed the best way to begin structuring components of the Science Information Literacy Initiative for fall semester 1999. Starting out slowly also allowed the librarians to plan on expansion and incorporation of project components over the duration of the grant period.

One example project initiated in the fall semester exemplifies a simple expansion of a learning assignment already in place for a course in the science education division of the School of Education. For several semesters, students in the course "Methods of Elementary School Science" had been given an assignment to browse the Web to locate science education resources that would be useful in their future K–12 teaching. In this assignment, each student would locate several useful Web sites, making a one-page annotated bibliography of four Web sites to share with fellow classmates. Students were given URLs for two educational sites and were to find others using a search engine of their choice. They were also given a list of several common search engines.

The librarian liaison for the School of Education met with the faculty member responsible for the assignment and offered to provide a summary of criteria for the students to use when choosing Web sites for their bibliographies. It was actually rather surprising to the librarian that the assignment had been given to students without any discussion of evaluation of Web sites. The fact that the faculty member had not considered the students' need for guidance was an indication that there is a need for a literacy program. Once the concept was suggested, the faculty member agreed that this would be a helpful addition to the assignment and could be implemented without any major restructuring of the course.

After discussion with the faculty member, the librarian and the project coordinator developed a simple Web page that could be added to the course Web page or handed out as a printed guide. The page included a very brief summary of questions to consider when reviewing a Web page, a short description of using the domain address as an evaluative tool, and some sample course-related Web sites on which to practice.

One value of this simple add-on to an existing course assignment was that it provided a very nonthreatening way to begin discussing information literacy skills with the faculty member. He could easily see that with little effort on his part, his assignment would be made more useful for the students. There was no time taken from an already full course schedule.

From the viewpoint of the librarian, this initial assignment can become the basis for a more extensive plan to gradually expand the information literacy component of the course. For instance, with enough prior planning with the faculty member, she could meet with the class and go over the criteria for evaluating information for the course and broaden the scope of the assignment to include other literacy components.

A second focus during the initial semester of the Science Information Literacy Initiative was to build upon work already being done in the School of Engineering. One basic learning outcome for engineering students is the ability to gather and critically evaluate and synthesize print and electronic information.

Engineers designing a product in industry must not only be able to find all the relevant technical design information but must also be able to search the patent and standards literature. Students in the senior-level mechanical engineering design class were given an assignment in which they selected a product and then searched for all relevant design and safety standards that apply to that product. The students were to write a report and deliver a class presentation on the standardization issues involved with the product. To complete the assignment, students had to be able to successfully search a variety of print and electronic sources for industry, national, international, and government standards and regulations that apply.

Students in Engineering 1 were given a "Writing, Information Acquisition, and Assessment" assignment in which they were to write a report on a device, invention, or engineering topic of their choice. The goals of the assignment were to help the student learn more about an area of engineering that interests them, to use print and electronic resources in the library or on the Internet, and to improve writing skills. Among requirements for the paper was the following statement: "You must document the report with at least six references, at least three of which must be technical references obtained from the engineering library or engineering journals. At least two of your references should come from information that you obtained on the Internet."

To enhance the information literacy component of the assignment, a second part of the assignment required the students to select the best Web resource used in Part 1 and explain why the Web site was a good site. The engineering librarian developed a handout based on Esther Grassian's *Thinking Critically about World Wide Web Resources* for the students to use in completing this part of the assignment and met with the class to discuss resources and evaluating information.[9]

Again, this addition to an existing assignment was a very simple way to begin building on an already developed collaborative process between the engineering librarian and a faculty member without causing a major restructuring of a course. Over the two-year grant period, continued collaboration will gradually incorporate other assignments into the engineering curriculum that will increase the information literacy skills of students in the University of Iowa's engineering program.

## BUILDING AN INTERFACE TO
## SCIENTIFIC INFORMATION RESOURCES

Besides enhancing course assignments, the University of Iowa plans to develop an easier interface for beginning-level students in the sciences who need to access various science information databases. This part of the project is currently in the initial development stage, but will include examination of various basic science databases to determine how beginners might best choose which database to use in response to particular needs.

One full-time instructional technologist has been hired to assist in developing this interface as well as any other instructional materials for the librarian–faculty partners to use in creating assignments. Two half-time graduate assistants will also work on development of learning materials.

## CONCLUSION

Prior project development such as UIII and TWIST has taught project librarians that gradually integrating new initiatives into the existing framework is sometimes a slower process than we might like, but patience developing the collaborative process often pays off in the final outcome. We have at this point laid the groundwork for successful implementation of our project goals and hope to report on our further progress at a later date.

## NOTES

1. Albert Henderson, "Science in the Twilight Zone; Or, Are Science Libraries Related to Science?" *Issues in Science and Technology Librarianship* (Fall 1998): 1. <http://www.ucsb.edu/istl/98-fall/article1.html> [accessed 29 August 2000].

2. William J. Paisley, "Scientific Literacy and the Competition for Public Attention and Understanding," *Science Communication* 20, no. 1 (September 1998): 70–80.

3. Shirley J. Behrens, "A Conceptual Analysis and Historical Overview of Information Literacy," *College & Research Libraries* 55, no. 4 (July 1994): 309–22.

4. Cerise Oberman, Bonnie Gratch Lindauer, and Betsy Wilson, "Integrating Information Literacy into the Curriculum: How Is Your Library Measuring Up?" *C & R L News* 59, no. 5 (May 1998): 347–52.

5. UIII, University of Iowa Information Literacy Initiative <http://www.lib.uiowa.edu/ref/trio/uiiindex.html> [accessed 29 August 2000].

6. Library Explorer, University of Iowa Libraries <http://explorer.lib.uiowa.edu/> [accessed 29 August 2000].

7. TWIST (Teaching with Style and Innovative Technology), University of Iowa Libraries <http://twist.lib.uiowa.edu> [accessed 29 August 2000].

8. University of Iowa, Office of the Provost Strategic Plan, 2000–2005 <http://www.uiowa.edu/~provost/plan/plan2000.htm> [accessed 29 August 2000].

9. Esther Grassian, "Thinking Critically about World Wide Web Resources." <http://www.library.ucla.edu/libraries/college/instruct/web/critical.htm> [accessed 29 August 2000].

# 24

# Information Literacy
# and Psychological Science:
# A Case Study of Collaboration

*Elizabeth O. Hutchins and Bonnie S. Sherman*

The dynamic information environment and a nationwide interest in information literacy are having a significant impact on pedagogy—the way professors teach and the way students learn. In colleges and universities around the country, faculties are exploring ways to ensure that their graduates are proficient in library research and information literacy skills. At St. Olaf College, collaboration between faculty in the library and other academic departments has enabled students to acquire this expertise within the disciplinary framework of their academic courses and to respond to the continual challenge of changing information resources.

For experienced researchers, a constant adaptation to change in technology and information resources is a challenge. For novice researchers, it can be truly daunting. Wherever students may be in terms of computer expertise, one of the key issues at St. Olaf College is not whether students are or can become skilled at accessing information in its most expedient form, but whether they can discriminate between the types of information they have found: basic or advanced, objective or biased, popular or scholarly. Additionally, students need to be adept in developing hypotheses, creating search strategies, and critically evaluating scholarly research. They also need to understand the distinction between information and knowledge and to be able to conduct research within the theoretical framework of a particular discipline. The ultimate goal is for students proficient in information literacy skills to be able to participate in scholarly discourse with sufficient ownership of the research they have conducted to contribute to the knowledge of that discipline.[1]

The Departments of Psychology and the College Libraries have worked collaboratively for more than fifteen years to teach undergraduates to do research. This partnership's evolution virtually parallels that of the Association of College and Research Libraries' Bibliographic Instruction Section (now the Instruction Section) and St. Olaf College's bibliographic instruction program, both of which were established in 1977. At that time, supported by a National Endowment for the Humanities grant, St. Olaf committed itself to course-related and course-integrated library instruction modeled after Earlham College's program.[2] Since then, bibliographic instruction at the college has been linked to specific courses and assignments, with the program growing incrementally.

The collaboration between the Department of Psychology and the library is not surprising. Both faculties are committed to open-ended resource-based learning. In addition, both support an active, hands-on, investigative approach that recognizes that science finds its research base as easily in the library as in the laboratory or field.[3]

An introductory psychology course at St. Olaf provides a case study of faculty collaboration in integrating information literacy and psychological science, as well as an example of a shared vision and commitment to inquiry-based learning. The significant features of this course include team teaching; a three-hour, hands-on information literacy laboratory; cooperative learning groups; and a student preceptor program.

## DESCRIPTIVE OVERVIEW OF THE INTRODUCTORY PSYCHOLOGY COURSE

Library research instruction is taught most effectively when it is (1) linked to or integrated into specific courses; (2) responding to a student's need to know, which is frequently connected to a specific course assignment; and (3) developed and taught collaboratively by faculty in a discipline and faculty in the library working in partnership. St. Olaf College faculty have found this to be true both from their experience working collaboratively for over fifteen years and also from the scholarly literature on the subject.[4]

Therefore, when the Department of Psychology began to redesign its curriculum at the introductory level under a National Science Foundation Course Development Grant, the design was made collaboratively with library faculty. As a result, the proposed research-laboratory component of the course included a three-hour library laboratory. A library instruction session for an academic course is not a new idea. What was new about this library research component was (1) its integration into the introductory psychology course content/syllabus, (2) its integration into specific laboratory assignments, and (3) its totally collaborative nature.

## INTEGRATION OF INFORMATION LITERACY
## INTO PSYCHOLOGY COURSE CONTENT

Integrating information literacy into an introductory psychology course began as the Department of Psychology developed a new approach that included a three-hour laboratory session each week. Class meetings were designed to complement and support laboratories. One of these laboratory sessions was specifically constructed to be held in the library, to familiarize students with resources relevant to psychological research, to provide them with the opportunity to develop skills in information literacy, and to facilitate the research they would be designing and presenting in the course.

In addition, each of the other laboratory sessions was designed with an information literacy component. Students were assigned a journal article to read as background preparation for the investigative work they would be undertaking in psychology laboratories that week. They read articles, learned new vocabulary, familiarized themselves with experimental methods, searched for more information about authors' professional work, and critiqued the research they read. Students wrote summaries of their findings and analyses, and brought this work to the laboratory session; their reports were their entrance tickets to the laboratory session, ensuring that they were prepared for the upcoming laboratory work. Scholarly review of relevant literature is an important component of all research. These students began to discover this in their very first course in psychology.

## INTEGRATION INTO SPECIFIC LABORATORY ASSIGNMENTS

For each laboratory, students were given a number of specific investigative questions as well as a long-term project, to investigate play in children, researching either age or gender differences. The play project was the topic for an in-depth literature search and the focus of the information literacy lab; it gave the students a need to know which was related to a specific course. During the first laboratory meeting, students viewed videotapes of the behavior of children, of snow monkeys, and other animals at the Minnesota zoo. They learned something about observing and recording observations. They also learned that they needed to define terms, to give them operational definitions, and to be specific about what question they might ask and how they might develop a hypothesis. Understanding each of these proved essential for the information literacy lab that would follow.

Then, within the initial laboratory and while subsequently working in teams, students began to (1) compose a question they could research in the field, (2) define the relevant terms and components, and (3) select a place to observe the chosen behavior. Using their question, they created a written hypothesis and shared it with other students and the instructors, who gave written suggestions and comments.

The next laboratory session was conducted in the library. Here, using their hypotheses, students sought to discover resources that would answer the question or contribute to an answer of it. By the end of the information literacy laboratory, most students had changed, refined, or redirected the hypothesis they had proposed initially. They had, for example, narrowed it, broadened it, or made it more specific or more informative. They also had found resources that supported the method or approach they had proposed for their own study, thus situating their research in previously published literature.

Over the next few weeks, the student teams gathered relevant data needed for their investigation. They then met in another laboratory session designed to help them complete basic statistics and understand the data they had collected. Subsequently, students and faculty discussed together how one might interpret each of the findings.

At the last laboratory session, students presented their research in poster format. They presented, for each group study, an introduction, their hypothesis, method, results and discussion, and the references they had used. These students viewed other student posters, discovering more about play, about research, and about talking about their research. In addition, some of these introductory students later presented these posters at regional meetings.[5]

These field and library laboratory sessions were interwoven with other laboratory sessions that were more traditionally oriented: a laboratory session in neuropsychology, in psychophysiology, and in operant psychology, for example.

## COLLABORATIVE NATURE OF THE COURSE

First, this course was developed collaboratively. Faculty from the library and faculty from the Department of Psychology worked together from the very beginning of the idea, over a summer, through an outside review, and throughout the following two years. Collaboration in the first summer was among four faculty members from the Department of Psychology, two faculty members from the library, and four senior students in psychology, all of whom worked together. These four senior students taught the laboratories with faculty in the initial semester. They became student preceptors.

At this writing, the course has been taught five times in this collaborative pattern. Within each laboratory session of fifteen students, there are five teams of three students each. These student teams work collaboratively in developing a question, examining resources in the library, finding a way to observe and collect data, completing statistics, and in preparing and presenting a poster. Thus the course is collaborative in its development, in its implementation, and in its teaching. It is collaborative among two different student groups (introductory students and senior student preceptors), and two different faculty groups in the Department of Psychology and the library. The focus is on investigative research, and everyone seeks to foster this.

## INFORMATION LITERACY LABORATORY

The development, implementation, and evaluation of the information literacy laboratory have been closely connected to that of the course. They continually illustrate the priority placed on ongoing collaboration at all levels and on the consistent integration of information literacy into course material. With the goal of this hands-on laboratory being to prepare students for and support them in their field research on children's play behavior, such integration is a natural outcome of the students' resource-based investigations.

## DESCRIPTIVE OVERVIEW OF THE INFORMATION LITERACY LABORATORY

Designed in the same format as the eight other laboratories in the course, the information literacy laboratory includes sections on objectives, introduction and background, terms, methods with materials and procedure, laboratory exercises, and discussion questions. Students record their discoveries in a laboratory notebook, which the student preceptor examines and comments on after each laboratory.

As previously noted, a class of sixty students is divided into four laboratory sessions. Each of these is taught—in the case of the information literacy laboratory—by a librarian and a student preceptor. To prepare the four preceptors for this teaching role, the librarian offers a workshop guiding them through the laboratory's philosophy, goals, strategy, and resources so that they, in turn, can be mentors to the students.

During the laboratory itself, the librarian offers about twenty-five minutes of instruction on the research strategies and resources to be used in the laboratory. Using a student hypothesis as a lens, this instruction reviews much of the introductory material included in their laboratory notebook for this class: search terms and controlled vocabulary, Boolean logic, the use of the *Thesaurus of Psychological Index Terms*, keyword and subject searching, popular and scholarly works, ways to search *PsycINFO* effectively, and the importance of allowing the literature search to inform the hypothesis. The focus is on research as a problem-solving process, with the students' hypotheses at the heart of it. The rest of the laboratory is a hands-on exploration of the students' hypotheses, during which the librarian and preceptor are available for advice and coaching.

## PARADIGM SHIFT

Over the past two years, this laboratory has gone through a paradigm shift from a focus on teaching to a focus on learning.[6] Specifically, it has changed in three significant ways, which have allowed increased attention to critical thinking skills and student-centered learning within the framework of psychology.

1. While retaining a focus on research strategies, the laboratory now gives primary attention to the students' hypotheses. Why? Because the hypothesis is the jumping off place for the students' need to know. It is from this that students derive their search terms. And it is through this disciplinary lens that students can critique resources to see if they may be useful for their field research and their final poster presentation. If the hypothesis is too broad or too narrow, the literature search will help them discover this. This is exceedingly important, for if the hypothesis is too broad or too narrow, students will be unable to undertake their field research successfully.

2. The number of resources and databases to be examined has been diminished, a move that has allowed more in-depth investigation of selected resources, particularly within *PsycINFO*. While maintaining a focus on the research process, which answers students' questions of "How do I *do* this?" the number of tasks to be completed has been cut, so that students have more time to concentrate on the content of their hypothesis and resources, which answers "How do I *think* about this?" Shifting the laboratory away from the faculty's desire to have students explore all types of psychological resources to the students' desire to find relevant resources directly linked to their needs has increased their engagement in the laboratory.

3. The laboratory has been revised to include open-ended divergent thinking questions, a feature of the other eight labs in the course.

As a result of these revisions, which were in direct response to student feedback, the most fruitful student work is now seen in the ways in which they identify variables, select related keywords and descriptors, and define and redefine a hypothesis.

**Figure 1    Sample Student Hypothesis**

*Original Hypothesis:*

We believe that the ratio between boys' contact with boys and girls' contact with girls will be relatively even. We also believe that the ratio between same-sex touch and coed touch will differ, with coed touching being significantly lower.

*Selected keywords & subject headings:*

| Contact Touch Interaction | Boy* Child* Human males | Girl* Child* Human females |
|---|---|---|

*Revised Hypothesis:*

Boys and girls will equally demonstrate physical touch with members of their same sex in the course of childhood play behavior.

*Comment by the students:*

We consolidated our two hypotheses, deleting the coed part. We also replaced the word "contact" with "touch," because contact is a very broad term in psychology.

It is extraordinarily rewarding to see students use a literature search to hone their hypothesis, as well as to hear them have that "ah-ha" experience when they find an article that connects with it.

## ASSESSMENT OF THE
## INTRODUCTORY PSYCHOLOGY COURSE

This course was subject to both internal and external review and assessment procedures. St. Olaf College's Office of Educational Research continues to assist in evaluation of the student-preceptor teaching each semester as well as with the evaluation of faculty in the classroom component of the course.

An independent evaluation specialist who had extensive experience in program evaluation in educational settings worked cooperatively with us from the beginning of the project. He conducted interviews with students and with focus groups comprising faculty and student preceptors. The specialist also prepared an end-of-course evaluation summary that was presented to the preceptor–faculty team before the beginning of the following semester.

## EVALUATION OF THE COURSE AS A WHOLE

In a final interview with thirty-seven students, selected at random from one of the courses in May of 1998, the following conclusions were drawn: (1) Participation in the laboratory investigations helped students to understand the discipline of psychology. The response was 65 percent "definitely yes," 35 percent "generally yes," and 0 responding "generally no." (2) To a large extent, the collaborative, student-research groups added to the value of the laboratory: 62 percent of the students responded "definitely yes," 24 percent, "generally yes," and 13 percent, "generally no." Those who said "generally no" commented that it was sometimes difficult for groups to agree, that sometimes group members did not work equally, that it was difficult to schedule off-campus work for the group project. (3) One hundred percent of the students said that the student preceptors facilitated the investigative process.

All the components of the course (readings, psychology laboratories, information literacy laboratory, and lecture) fit together "most definitely" for 35 percent of the students; for 51 percent, these "generally" fit together, and for 14 percent, they did not fit. In general, those students who found that the pieces did not seem to fit together for them reported in interviews that it was the lecture component that did not fit. They commented, for example, that laboratory and lecture should be more parallel, that the laboratory work should be discussed more in class, or that the class sessions should be used to relate the textbook to the laboratory. The assessment here is helpful in continuing to place the laboratory first, structuring the class sessions to complement and extend this research.

It was surprising and a bit disappointing to find that only 16 percent of the students who took the course wanted to continue in either psychology or other investigative sciences. Nonetheless, it was encouraging to discover that 95 percent of the students were satisfied with what they learned in the course. The course evaluation concluded, "The laboratories were effective . . . in helping students understand how to investigate questions in psychology."

## EVALUATION OF THE
## INFORMATION LITERACY LABORATORY

Constant revision of the information literacy laboratory reflects both the importance of ongoing course and laboratory evaluation, and the significant impact of continual changes in electronic resources and database searching. In particular, the student laboratory notebooks provided immediate feedback on the information literacy laboratory.

Figure 2   Summary of Feedback on Labs: 1997–1999

| STRENGTHS | SUGGESTIONS |
|---|---|
| • Identifying key terms<br>• Keyword vs. subject searches<br>• Learning how to use the thesaurus<br>• Broadening and narrowing search with AND, OR, & *<br>• Hands-on practice<br>• Variety of search strategies and resources<br>• Revising observational definition/hypothesis<br>• Understanding research process<br>• Helpful in investigation | • Cut down the number of sources to be searched to allow for more in-depth exploration<br>• Eliminate Web site searches Hard-to-find material on specific hypothesis<br>• Integrate research skills throughout the rest of the course<br>• Make it less task-oriented<br>• Somewhat basic for upper-class students |

They documented the resources found, responses to divergent thinking questions, and the students' final appraisals, which resulted in the three revisions noted above.

One interesting assessment outcome we discovered was the direct link between student appreciation of the laboratory and the demographic distribution of the class. Whether students were first-year or upper-class students, majors or nonmajors, bore a direct correlation to their evaluation of the course. This laboratory was deemed to be very useful to first-year students but less so to upper-level students who might be taking it for distribution purposes and who thought they already knew the material. Also, prospective psychology majors were considerably more motivated than others who may not have been prepared for such a rigorous laboratory course.

## SPIN OFF OF LIBRARY–PSYCHOLOGY DEPARTMENT COLLABORATION

The collaboration between the library and psychology department in the development of this course has had direct spin-offs within the psychology curriculum. As a result of the collaboration, a biopsychology course was revised to incorporate a highly accountable, team-taught research process in place of a laboratory. The course placed scholarly research as one of its primary goals, counting 40 percent of a student's grade. Developmental research skills were woven throughout the course including preliminary bibliographies, annotated bibliographies, several drafts of the final project, the maintenance of a research journal, and a final essay documenting the research process. The psychology professor and librarian shared the instruction and assessment of this part of the course and graded different aspects of it. Students consulted either or both of them depending on the particular aspect of research in which a student was involved.

In addition, there have been renewed discussions between faculty in the library and the Department of Psychology to discuss the core research competencies considered essential for psychology students to have in accessing and using information resources. The Department of Psychology is including information literacy concerns in the revision of its major.

## CONCLUSION

In summary, we affirm that quality library research and instruction and the acquisition of information literacy skills are most effective when they are integrated into a disciplinary framework, woven into the structure of a course, and supported by collaboration between faculty in that discipline and the library.

## NOTES

1. For a discussion of the distinction between information and knowledge, see Karen Price, "Information Processing and the Making of Meaning," in *Gateways to Knowledge: The Role of Academic Libraries in Teaching, Learning, and Research*, ed. Lawrence Dowler (Cambridge, Mass.: MIT Press, 1997), 169–79.

2. For a description of Earlham's program, see Evan Farber, "Bibliographic Instruction at Earlham College," in *Bibliographic Instruction in Practice: A Tribute to the Legacy of Evan Ira Farber*, ed. Larry Hardesty, Jamie Hastreiter, and David Henderson (Ann Arbor, Mich.: Pierian Press, 1993), 1–25.

3. For other examples of collaboration between faculty in the library and psychology departments, see Elizabeth W. Carter and Timothy K. Daugherty, "Library Instruction and Psychology—A Cooperative Effort," *Technical Services Quarterly* 16, no. 1 (1998): 33–41; and Kris Huber and Bonnie Sherman, "Scholarly Networking in Action," *Research Strategies* 10 (Winter 1992): 40–43.

4. For a historical overview of course-related library instruction, see Evan Farber, "Faculty–Librarian Cooperation: A Personal Retrospective," *Reference Services Review* 27, no. 3 (1999): 229–34; and Thomas G. Kirk Jr., "Course-Related Bibliographic Instruction in the 1990s," *Reference Services Review* 27, no. 3 (1999): 235–41. For further discussion of collaboration, see Sonia Bodi, "Collaborating with Faculty in Teaching Critical Thinking: The Role of Librarian," *Research Strategies* 10, no. 2 (1992): 69–76; Larry Hardesty, "Faculty Culture and Bibliographic Instruction: An Exploratory Analysis," *Library Trends* 44, no. 2 (Fall 1995): 339–67; Evelyn B. Haynes, "Librarian–Faculty Partnerships

in Instruction," *Advances in Librarianship* 20 (1996): 191–222; and Gloria J. Leckie and Anne Fullerton, "The Roles of Academic Librarians in Fostering a Pedagogy for Information Literacy," in *Racing Toward Tomorrow*, Association of College and Research Libraries 1999 National Conference Papers 1999, <http://www.ala.org/acrl/leckie.pdf> [accessed 16 January 2000].

5. For other uses of poster sessions, see Evan Farber and Sara Penhale, "Using Poster Sessions in Introductory Science Courses: An Example at Earlham," *Research Strategies* 13, no. 1 (Winter 1995): 55–59.

6. For a discussion of these paradigms, see Robert B. Barr and John Tagg, "From Teaching to Learning: A New Paradigm for Undergraduate Education," *Change* 27 (November–December 1995): 13–25. For additional readings on student-centered learning, see Joan M. Bechtel, "Conversation, a New Paradigm for Librarianship?" *College & Research Libraries* 47, no. 3 (May 1986): 219–24; Peter Fensham, Richard Gunstone, and Richard White, eds., *The Content of Science: A Constructivist Approach to its Teaching and Learning* (London: Falmer Press, 1994); Barbara Fister, "The Research Processes of Undergraduate Students," *Journal of Academic Librarianship* 18, no. 3 (July 1992): 163–69; Taylor E. Hubbard, "Bibliographic Instruction and Postmodern Pedagogy," *Library Trends* 44, no. 2 (Fall 1995): 439–52; and Marjorie M. Warmkessel and Joseph M. McCade, "Integrating Information Literacy into the Curriculum," *Research Strategies* 15, no. 2 (Spring 1997): 80–88.

# 25

# Faculty–Librarian Team Teach Information Literacy Survival Skills

*Shelley Cudiner and Oskar R. Harmon*

## OUR COURSE OUTLINE

Our course is divided into three sections: Fundamental Web Browser Concepts, Search Engines, and Applications of Literacy Survival Skills. The fundamental browser concepts introduced are explanation of a URL, examples of Web portals and their functions, explanation of hyperlinks and bookmarks, and hands-on use of Netscape Composer to write a Web page with hyperlinks. The search engine concepts discussed are the difference between surfing and searching, Boolean logic and Venn diagrams, and how to design Boolean searches in Alta Vista. We conclude this section with a discussion of several library database search engines including the on-line catalog of the University Library, InfoTrac, Dow Jones, and ABI Global Inform. The literacy survival skill applications consist of several projects including creating a personal Web portal, maintaining a file of bookmarks on diskette, converting a MSWord hyperlinked manuscript to a PDF file using Adobe Acrobat Writer 4.0, and conducting a comparison/evaluation between an academic Web site and a nonacademic Web site. We administer an entry and exit survey, and surveys at the conclusion of each section of material. This chapter represents a status report at the point of completing the first of the three sections of the course.

## THE SURVEY ASSESSMENT TOOL

Throughout the course we administer short on-line assessment surveys. Their purpose is to measure improvement of information literacy skills over the course of the semester. We administer four surveys, including an entry and exit survey. The surveys have ten to thirty questions, and require approximately fifteen to thirty minutes to complete. The first assessment (the entry survey) has two types of questions. One type relates to background and the other to skill level. An example background question is "I am taking this course to improve my overall computer skills." There are four response options ranging from "strongly agree" to "disagree." Another background question is "Do you have Web access at home?" In our data analysis we are interested in discovering the correlation of student backgrounds with skill level and with learning outcomes. The other type of question relates to initial skill level. We ask approximately fifteen questions on specific skills that are to be covered in the course. In the follow-up assessments these questions are rephrased. In our data analysis these questions are used to measure and analyze learning outcomes.

## FIRST "ENTRY" ASSESSMENT RESULTS

The first assessment survey, administered on the first day of class, has twenty-five questions: eight questions that relate to student background and motivation for taking the class, and seventeen that are skill evaluation.

### Background Questions

Five of the background questions are multiple choice, three are short answer. We analyze the former responses. Three of the multiple choice background questions relate to motivation for taking the course; motivations such as: improve computer skills, learn computer research skills, and learn to write Web pages. The remaining multiple choice questions relate to whether or not the student has Web access at home, and a preferred Web search engine. To summarize the results: two-thirds of the respondents "strongly agree" they are taking the class to improve their computer skills, and two-thirds of the respondents have Web access at home.

### Skill Evaluation Questions

Seventeen of the remaining questions on Assessment One are skill evaluation questions that have right or wrong answers, and the response "don't know." A summary of test scores is shown in figure 2, and figure 3 reports the questions and the tabulated responses. The average correct score is 35 percent, and the range of scores is 5.8 percent to 65 percent correct. These questions are about knowledge of the

196     *Shelley Cudiner and Oskar R. Harmon*

skills to be taught in the course. Approximately 30 percent generally select the response "don't know." Of the seventeen skill evaluation questions there are only four questions for which respondents select the correct answer 50 percent or more of the time (questions 10, 11, 14, and 19). Those questions are about where a Web page is posted, what is an example of a Web browser, what is an example of a URL, and what is the function of the Interlibrary Loan Department. The questions with a low percentage correct are about strategies for conducting database searches. Because the majority of the questions relate to skills not yet taught, the low mean score implies that the class is entering with the appropriate level of beginner skills. The significant percentage (30 percent) of "don't know" responses is a strong signal that class members recognize that they do not yet know the skills the course is designed to teach them.

## CROSS TABULATION OF BACKGROUND AND SKILL LEVEL

Of fourteen respondents that completed all test questions, the average percent correct is 35 percent. Figure 1 shows the cross tabulation between responses to the question Desire to Improve Computer Skill with the outcome: Percent Correct on First Assessment Survey. The table shows that of the eight respondents strongly motivated to improve their

Figure 1    Cross Tabulation of Motivation and First Assessment Score

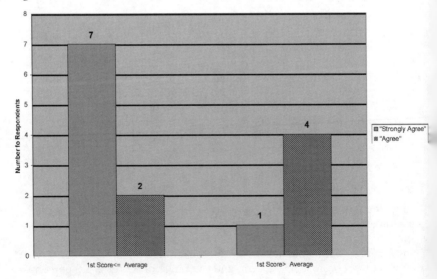

computer skills, 87 percent (seven) have scores below the average score. Also, of the six respondents that were less strongly motivated to improve their computer skills, 67 percent (four) have scores above the average score. These results suggest a close correlation between the respondents' desire for improvement and a measured need for skill improvement. Thus, most of the respondents that feel a relatively strong desire to improve their skills scored relatively low on the skills evaluation questions, and most with a relatively less strong desire scored relatively high on the skills evaluation questions.

## SECOND ASSESSMENT RESULTS

There are ten questions; all have right or wrong answers. The average score is 75 percent and the range is 50 percent to 100 percent.

### Whose Test Scores Improved?

Figure 2 compares the test scores for the group responding "strongly agree" and the group responding "agree" to the question "Taking the

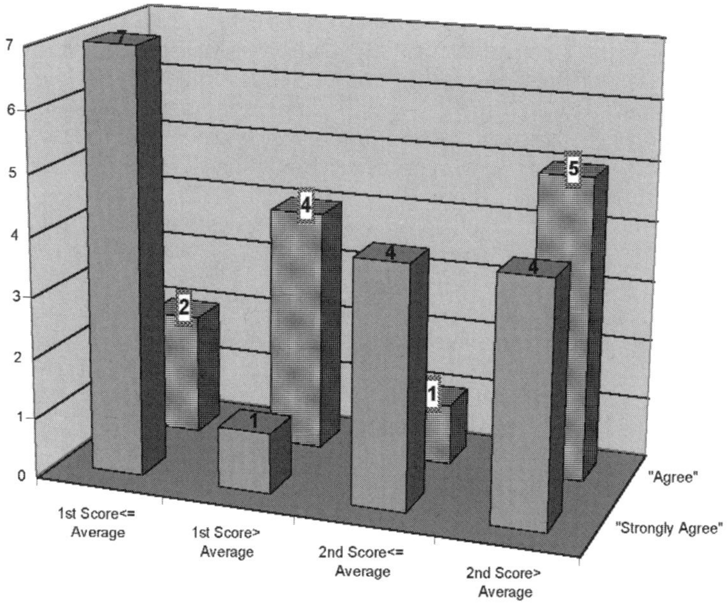

Figure 2    Test Scores and Response to Question about Motivation

class to improve my overall computer skills?" The comparison shows that the "strongly agree" group has significant improvement. On the first test, one of eight scored above the average; on the second test, four of eight scored above the average. For the "agree" group, there is no change in outcomes. On the first test, four of six scored above the average; on the second test, five of six scored above the average.

In summary, the students whose scores improved most significantly were the students who responded "strongly agree" to the motivational question, and who scored below the average on the first test. However, it is also the case that the students whose scores did not improve significantly were either in the group of "strongly agree" and low first test scores, or scored above average on both tests. Hence, the motivation question does not explain the differences in test score improvement.

## WHAT EXPLAINS THE IMPROVEMENT IN TEST SCORES?

The questions on the second test may be divided into two groups.

The relatively easy questions are the seven questions (1 to 4, 8, and 9) to which generally 90 percent of the class responded correctly, and relatively difficult questions, of which generally 50 percent or less of the students selected the correct answer. Question number five asks for the file extension of Adobe Acrobat files; 57 percent responded correctly. Question number six asks about the function of hyperlinked text; 36 percent responded correctly. Question number ten asks about the functionality of right and left mouse clicks in a Web browser; 57 percent responded correctly. A cross tabulation show that uniformly almost all of the students responding correctly to the trio of relatively difficult questions have Web access at home, and that of the four students without Web access (and responding to all the questions), only one scored correct answers. A cross tabulation of Web access at home, motivation, and scores on first and second tests shows a similar effect of having Web access at home. As shown in figure 3, the four students responding "no Web access at home" (and completing both tests) scored at or below the average score on both tests.

## CONCLUSION

In our course, we use a series of assessment surveys to analyze learning outcomes. At the time this chapter was written, we have completed the first third of the course. Our first assessment survey shows that in a class of sixteen students, ten have Web access at home, and the sixteen are evenly divided between those that have a relatively strong desire to improve their computer skills and those that feel relatively less strongly.

Figure 3    Web Access, Test Scores, and Response to Question about Motivation

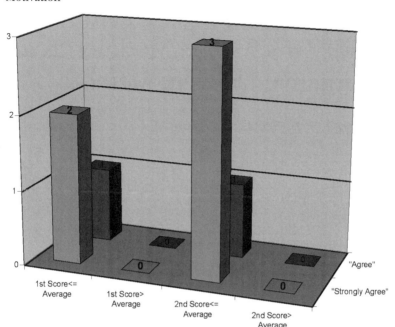

The results of the second survey assessment show that those with the relatively strong desire to improve their computer skills have a measured need for improvement. Whereas those that have a relatively less strong desire to improve scored relatively higher on the assessment. The second assessment shows that most of the group that scored well on the first test continued to with high scores. Of the group with low first test scores, half (four) recorded above average scores on the second assessment. Another apparent explanatory factor of test improvement is having Web access at home. Because we teach at a regional campus of a state university system, and there is no on-campus student housing, this is a potentially interesting result, bearing on the importance of providing accessible Web access on campus.

# 26

# On-Line Course Integrated Library Instruction Modules as an Alternative Delivery Method

*Melissa Koenig and Eric Novotny*

Since spring semester 1993, the main library at the University of Illinois at Chicago (UIC) has provided workshops for students enrolled in the Communication 100 course taught on campus. Historically, students received three extra-credit points for attending one fifty-minute library instruction session. These sessions were system-specific and covered either UICCAT (the university's card catalog), IBIS (a collection of periodical indexes), or ILLINET (the statewide card catalog).

While these sessions were well attended—there were extra credit points at stake—there was concern that the workshops were not meaningful to students. The workshops were given outside of the course context and often students got the same presentation in other classes such as LAS100 (a freshman seminar class) and English 161 (an English composition class). Not only was there concern about the value to the students, the number of sessions each semester—usually between twenty-five and forty—was straining the already stretched resources of the library instruction staff.

With the cooperation and support of the Communication 100 instructor, the library decided in the spring of 1999 to create a series of computer-assisted instruction (CAI) modules that would introduce students to the library.[1] These modules would also introduce students to library tools (such as the catalog, indexes, and the Internet), library terminology, and other library concepts. While it was generally believed that these modules would be an effective alternative to doing in-person library workshops, no one was ultimately sure what effect this type of instruction would have on students' learning.

There are few studies that directly compare different library bibliographic instruction (BI) teaching methods to assess learning outcomes.
Marsha Markman and Gordon Leighton polled college freshmen in a
1987 study to assess student attitudes toward and preferences for instruction delivered as a lecture/discussion or as a workbook. They
found that most students preferred the lecture/discussion technique.[2] In
1989, V. Lonnie Lawson compared the overall effectiveness of patrons
who completed CAI and those who went on a library tour. This study
found that CAI was an effective alternative to tours based on pretest and
posttest results.[3] A study in 1994 by Joan M. Cherry and her colleagues
compared learning outcomes of those who completed an on-line tutorial and those who had no instruction. They found that there were no
significant performance differences between these two groups.[4]

A study conducted during the fall of 1998 by Carol Anne Germain,
Trudi E. Jacobson, and Sue Kaczor compared the effectiveness of Web-
based instruction to in-class instruction. They found that the learning
outcomes, as measured by performance on pretest and posttest questions, were about equal for both groups. They also found that instruction, regardless of type, made a significant difference in the students'
test performance.[5] While these four studies used some form of pretest
and posttest to measure the results, still others based their conclusions
on qualitative feedback.[6]

Because of the small body of research and the inconsistent results, the
librarians at UIC decided to assess the effectiveness of CAI as an alternative delivery method before putting a lot of time and energy into it. For
this reason, it was decided to do a pilot research test on a small class. Not
only would starting with a smaller group make the testing of the module
technology easier, it would also allow the librarians to test the pretest
and posttest instruments. These test instruments will later be used on a
larger sample size to get meaningful data about learning outcomes.

## DESIGN CONSIDERATIONS

In the spring of 1999, the library instruction coordinator and the Communication 100 instructor began talking about using CAI to conduct
some of the Communication workshops. It was decided that these CAI
modules would be loosely integrated into the Communication 100 curriculum. They would also contain a quizzing/review feature to help
with retention and ensure some accountability.

Each module was developed to cover a single specific skill or
concept. The first module is intended to be a basic orientation to the
library and its services. It also covers the concept of basic library
tools—catalogs, indexes, encyclopedias, dictionaries, and librarians.

The second module covers the catalog, while the third module covers the parts of a database and how to read citations in library catalogs and periodical indexes. The fourth module talks about Internet resources, and the fifth covers periodical indexes. Before being made available to students, each module was reviewed by library faculty for clarity, content, and technical soundness.

Once the curriculum was defined, the library instruction coordinator explored a variety of software options. Microsoft PowerPoint was chosen for a number of reasons, not least of which was its ease of use. Since this was a pilot, it was decided that it would be better to start simple and small with the understanding that once the modules were created, they could always be migrated to more sophisticated software options. PowerPoint also had the advantage of being readily available and compatible with multiple computer platforms.

Each of the five modules was developed to take approximately ten minutes to complete. The ten-minute time limit was chosen by design because research has shown that a person's attention tends to diminish over time.[7] In order to maximize learning, it was decided that the lessons would be given in ten-minute segments instead of in one fifty-minute session. This design also allowed the CAI lessons to be delivered over time, making the initial development easier since they didn't all have to be completed at once.

The use of PowerPoint reinforced the design decision to simplify the content. The limited slide space required the content to be basic, straightforward, and short. The addition of graphics and screen shots added to the readability of the modules while also limiting the amount of text on the screen. On-line documentation design guides most frequently suggest the following basic guidelines: simplify the display, replace text with graphics, and use blank space actively.[8]

Research has shown that if you engage students in lively activities, the learning experience is more meaningful.[9] Action buttons were used to add some interactivity into the static PowerPoint presentation. These buttons, a standard option for PowerPoint presentations, allowed users to "choose" different paths within each CAI module. Depending on the choices made, students receive feedback. Although clumsy at times, this option allows for a more sophisticated feel without the need to learn higher-end software or advanced Web programming languages.

The review section added to the end of each module is another interactive feature. Not only was it hoped that these review sections would reinforce the lessons taught, it was also a necessary addition to ensure accountability. Because the students were getting extra credit from their course instructor, the library had to have some way of ensuring that each student had completed each module. Upon completion of the review section, and only upon completion, the students are prompted for their ID number. These ID numbers are manually recorded and reported to the Communication 100 instructor. The reviews for the first four modules were created using a combination of Macromedia's DreamWeaver Attain and CGI Scripting. The final review section was created using only CGI scripting.

## RESEARCH METHODOLOGY

To test the effectiveness of the modules, the library staff decided to compare pretest/posttest performance of those who had completed the CAI modules with those who attended a traditional in-class library workshop. With the cooperation of the Communication 100 instructor, the library staff randomly assigned the students registered in the summer 1999 session of Communication 100 to one of two groups—on-line instruction or library workshop. All students were given a pretest that asked some general demographic (class standing) information and questions about their current familiarity with and confidence using specific library systems. Each pretest also included a twenty-question skills test.[10] This test was developed by library staff based on similar questionnaires found in the literature.[11]

The pretest was administered during a regular class session. At this time, the librarians explained the pilot to the students and informed them that they would receive their at-random group assignments via E-mail. Students were also asked for their preferences for workshop times. A series of workshops were scheduled based on these preferences to ensure that at least one day/time would be convenient to all workshop participants.

The pretest was administered in the second week of the semester. Workshops were held in the latter half of the semester, and on-line participants were given access to the CAI modules from the third week through the day before the last class. In the last class meeting, all students attending were administered one of three posttests. The posttest that a student received depended on the type of instruction he or she had completed: library workshop, on-line module, or no instruction. The latter was a self-selected group.

Each posttest had the same questions about familiarity with and confidence using different library systems and the same twenty-question library skills test. Additionally, each posttest had a series of evaluative questions about the type of instruction received. Those who chose to not participate were asked questions about why they declined instruction.

## PRETEST/POSTTEST RESULTS

The completed pretests and posttests were collected and analyzed using Statistical Package for Social Sciences. In cases where students completed only one of the skills tests, the scores were not tabulated or analyzed in any way. Only cases in which both the pretest and posttest were completed were examined. There were thirty-seven such cases. The breakdown by BI type was as follows: eighteen traditional in-library workshops, thirteen on-line CAI tutorials, and six self-selected participants who opted for no library instruction. The small sample size (thirty-seven useable tests) limits the generalizations that can be made from the data obtained, but some of the differences found between groups were large enough to indicate statistical significance. While other performance differences were not statistically reliable, they do suggest areas for further inquiry.

The library skills test contained twenty questions with scores for each question ranging from zero for an incorrect answer, to four for a complex question requiring ranking of multiple resources. Partial credit was given for questions having more than one acceptable response. A perfect score on the test was thirty points. The highest individual score recorded was twenty-eight on the pretest while the highest posttest score was twenty-seven.

As a group, the class's library knowledge improved as measured by pretest and posttest performance on the library skills test. The mean scores improved from 15.7 on the pretest to 17.19 on the posttest. This difference was found to be statistically significant (p = .039) indicating that the differences were not likely to be caused by random change. It seems clear that the class as a whole improved during the course of the semester. It does not, however, prove anything about the effectiveness of library instruction.

It may be argued that student performance naturally increases over the course of a semester due to a variety of factors that may be completely independent of library instruction. Such factors may include increased familiarity with the campus in general, discussions with friends, other course assignments requiring use of the library, interaction with a librarian at the Reference Desk, and a general increase in confidence. The difference between the pretest and posttest mean scores for the no instruction group show just this type of increase.

While the rise in mean scores is statistically significant and noteworthy, it does not tell us anything about which BI delivery method was the most effective. To assess effectiveness, the mean scores were also analyzed by type of BI (table 1). The group with the highest mean score prior to instruction were the workshop participants (16.56), while those assigned to the CAI tutorial had the lowest mean scores (14.54). The posttest scores show that the on-line tutorial participants went from having the lowest mean score to the highest mean score (14.54 to 18.08). The workshop attendees showed virtually no improvement in performance (16.56 to 16.61), and perhaps more alarming is that those who received no instruction at all actually

**Table 1    Mean Scores for Library Skills Test**

| Instruction Type | Pretest | Posttest | % Change |
|---|---|---|---|
| No Instruction (6 cases) | 15.67 | 17.00 | +8 |
| In-library Workshop (18 cases) | 16.56 | 16.61 | +0 |
| CAI Tutorial (13 cases) | 14.54 | 18.08 | +24 |

(Maximum score = 30)

performed better on the posttest than those who participated in the traditional in-library workshops (15.67 to 17.00).

The differences between the three groups detailed above did not prove to be statistically significant, most likely because of the small numbers in each group. The differences are, however, highly suggestive and indicate the need for additional studies involving a larger student population. Such research could uncover valuable information about the relative impact of different forms of library instruction on student performance.

Of course, performance on a test is only one possible measure of the effectiveness of library instruction. Several questions also asked students about their perceived success levels at performing various library tasks (e.g., using the on-line catalog, locating articles, etc.). Students rated their success on a scale from one (unlikely to be successful) to five (very likely to be successful). These questions were combined to form an overall confidence ranking for students taking the class. Table 2 presents the results of these measures.

The participants who received some form of library instruction (CAI tutorial or library workshop) showed large increases in their perceived ability to locate information. The workshop attendees finished the semester with the highest confidence rating (26.67), although as can be seen in the posttest results, their scores did not necessarily justify such

**Table 2    Mean Scores for Library Skills Confidence Test**

| Instruction Type | Pretest | Posttest | % Change |
|---|---|---|---|
| No Instruction (6 cases) | 20.4 | 21.8 | 7 |
| In-library Workshop (18 cases) | 22.28 | 26.67 | 20 |
| CAI Tutorial (13 cases) | 20.69 | 24.46 | 18 |

(Maximum score = 29)

optimism. The CAI tutorial participants and those who did not receive instruction began with similar confidence ratings (20.4 for the no instruction group, and 20.69 for the CAI group), but by the end of the semester, those taking the CAI tutorial showed a marked improvement in their perceived level of success at using the library (24.46 for the CAI group versus 21.80 for the no instruction group).

Despite the small sample sizes, these changes between pretest and posttest confidence rankings between groups was significant. The increase in posttest confidence rating for those participants who received some form of library instruction (either the CAI tutorial or library workshop) was significantly higher than those who did not receive instruction. The difference between those receiving no BI and the workshop participants is more pronounced ($p = .001$) than between the no BI group and the CAI tutorial participants ($p = .069$). Not surprisingly, the increase in confidence ratings for the group as a whole between the pretest and posttest was also significant ($p = .007$).

## CONCLUSION

While still preliminary, the results appear to be an endorsement of library instruction while providing evidence supporting the hypothesis that on-line instruction can be as effective as traditional instructional methods. In fact, this study showed that the on-line delivery method proved most effective at delivering content as measured by student's performance on the library skills test. While at a minimum the goal was to "do no harm" to students by introducing on-line instruction, the results go much further, hinting that some students might learn certain basic library skills most productively via computer. This has obvious implications for a library such as UIC with its large undergraduate population in need of introductory library instruction.

The data also suggests that the human touch is still necessary. As shown in the results, the in-library workshop attendees showed the highest confidence ratings of any group. It can be theorized that this is due to the personal attention they received. This theory is bolstered by written comments received from workshop attendees, who listed the librarians' attention to their needs and the ability to ask questions as reasons why they preferred in-library instruction. A future approach to on-line tutorials might be to better emulate the immediate feedback that made library workshops a preferred option for many.

Since this data is only preliminary, the pilot test is being repeated on a much larger scale in fall semester 2000. It is hoped that the larger class size (typical enrollment exceeds 700 students) will produce results that are more statistically reliable. This should allow for more meaningful comparisons across groups.

Other aspects of the study are also being revised based on feedback from participants. Most specifically, several questions on the library skills test have been modified based on responses in the pilot project, which indicated that students may have been confused by or did not interpret the questions correctly. The revised instrument also contains more straightforward measures focusing on the aspects of librarianship we expect the students to know by the end of the course.

While this group of librarians hopes to continue these studies to get a better picture of learning outcomes, it is hoped that other librarians will engage in similar research, allowing for a greater body of data for analysis. More research needs to be conducted to ensure that library instructional resources are employed in the most constructive and beneficial fashion.

## NOTES

1. CAI modules are available at <http://www.uic.edu/depts/lib/libclasses/comm100/63md3.html>.
2. Marsha C. Markman and Gordon B. Leighton, "Exploring Freshman Composition Student Attitudes About Library Instruction Sessions and Workbooks: Two Studies," *Research Strategies* 5 (Summer 1987): 126–34.
3. V. Lonnie Lawson, "Using a Computer-Assisted Instruction Program to Replace the Traditional Library Tour: An Experimental Study, *RQ* 29, no. 1 (Fall 1989): 71–79.
4. Joan M. Cherry, Weijing Yuan, and Marshall Clinton, "Evaluating the Effectiveness of a Concept-Based Computer Tutorial for OPAC Users (at the University of Toronto)," *College & Research Libraries* 55, no. 4 (July 1994): 355–64.
5. Carol Anne Germain, Trudi E. Jacobson, and Sue Kaczor, "A Comparison of the Effectiveness of Presentation Formats for Instruction: Teaching First Year Students," *College & Research Libraries* 61, no. 1 (January 2000): 65–72.
6. Lana Dixon, Marie Garrett, Rita Smith, and Alan Wallace, "Building Library Skills: Computer-Assisted Instruction for Undergraduates," *Research Strategies* 13, no. 4 (Fall 1995): 196–208.
7. William Horton, *Designing and Writing On-Line Documentation: Hypermedia for Self-Supporting Products* (New York: Wiley, 1994), 11; and Gregg Richardson, "Computer-Assisted Library Instruction? Consider Your Resource, Commitment, and Needs," *Research Strategies* 12, no. 1 (Winter 1994): 45–55.
8. Horton, *Designing and Writing On-Line Documentation*, 236–38; and Richardson, "Computer-Assisted Library Instruction," 45–55.
9. Patrick Ragains, "Four Variations of Drueke's Active Learning Paradigm," *Research Strategies* 13, no. 1 (Winter 1995): 40–50; and Jeanetta Drueke, "Active Learning in the University Library Instruction Classroom," *Research Strategies* 10, no. 2 (Spring 1992): 77–83.
10. For a copy of the skills test used, please contact the authors directly at mkoenig@uic.edu or novotny@uic.edu.
11. We looked at a number of skills tests when designing the one we used. Some of the examples included Shelley Phipps and Ruth Dickstein,

"Library Knowledge Questionnaire," and Larry Hardesty et al., "Library-Use Instruction Evaluation," both available in *Reference Assessment Manual* (Ann Arbor, Mich.: Pierian Press, 1995). The disk accompanying the book contains the survey instruments. Also, "Library Science 102 Assessment" from Tacoma Community College. This assignment was posted to the Bibliographic Instruction Listserve (BI-L).

# 27

## Hype, High Hopes, and Damage Control: Facilitating End-User Learning During a System Migration

*Lynne Rudasill, Lori A. DuBois, and Susan E. Searing*

On August 18, 1998, the University of Illinois at Urbana-Champaign (UIUC) launched a new integrated library system to replace its twenty-year-old ILLINET On-line software. In preparing for our conversion to a new system, we discovered several other institutions were either planning for or recovering from their own system migration. Our purpose here is to provide some insight into the process and problems of system migration from the frontlines of library use instruction. The following account will describe the background for our system migration, the planning that occurred, the instructional strategies we used, and the results of our efforts. We hope that this experience highlights some of the universal problems and solutions for those who are about to embark upon a similar project.

### A BRIEF HISTORY OF ILLINET ON-LINE

The genesis and development of ILLINET On-Line is not unlike that of many other systems. Hugh Atkinson, university librarian from 1976 to 1986, was instrumental in bringing the first automated circulation system to the Urbana-Champaign campus. The circulation system was soon coupled with an electronic database of bibliographic records, and ILLINET On-Line began to take shape. The catalog was expanded to include the records of some forty-five libraries in the state of Illinois. By 1991, a new interface allowed patrons to search the records for citations and circulation purposes in a fairly seamless manner. The catalog was managed by the Illinois Library Computer Systems Office (ILCSO). In the mid-1990s, the possibilities of using a Web interface, Z39.50 connectivity, Y2K problems, and an archaic computer language set the process in motion to provide new, integrated software for the catalog, which now contained approximately eleven million records. The library hoped to leapfrog from the old system into a truly integrated, object-oriented system from Data Research Associates (DRA) called TAOS. Implementation was planned for the fall of 1996, but because of problems with software development, including difficulties in the conversion of records for use under the new system, the start date eventually moved to August 18, 1998. Compounding the problem was the fact that TAOS still did not fully exist. ILCSO announced that when the migration occurred, the change would not be to the long-awaited Web interface, but to a new and different telnet interface. The Web interface for the union catalog would be labeled "experimental" and remain in "beta test" stage for an unknown period of time.

## PRELIMINARY PLANNING—UIUC AND ILCSO

The planning process was initiated along two fronts. ILCSO's consortium-wide efforts proceeded using the assets of several of the institutional members. At the same time, we began to work through the process at the University of Illinois.

It might be said that ILCSO visualized the process as one of concentric rings of training. Twenty-five individuals attended a weeklong workshop in St. Louis in June 1997 titled "Training the Trainers." This group then traveled throughout Illinois presenting sessions discussing resistance to change, learning styles, and other aspects of adult learning to individuals who had been selected to do training at their own institutions. Finally, ILCSO provided the opportunity for trainers from DRA to come in and work with this same audience to teach the particulars of the new software. ILCSO also provided a general Web site for training tips, scripts, and other shared information.

On the home front, rather than expanding concentric circles, we were working on a model that better reflected the spiraling down of information to our users. We approached the problems in several ways—through the Invisible College, the Task Force on User Education, and Environment Scans.

### The Invisible College

We began by contacting our peers through the Bibliographic Instruction Listserv, or BI-L, and through personal channels. Overwhelmingly, responses indicated that the key to the process of change would be to have highly trained staff, from the student assistants to the university librarian, able to answer questions concerning the new system. Our first reality check occurred in this area of internal training. We would not be able to work with anything other than a test database until the very day of migration. The test database was predicated upon public library use and lacked the complexity of a large research collection's catalog; therefore, any scripts we developed would probably not be very effective when migration finally occurred.

## The Task Force on User Education

In late fall 1997, approximately nine months before the new system rolled out, the Task Force on User Education began to organize itself and take stock of its resources. The task force consisted of eighteen members representing the various subject and functional divisions of the University Library. Although the task force had no designated budget, we were assured that money would be available when it was needed.

The library user education program at the undergraduate level that had worked so well for us at an earlier date had fallen victim to several budget cuts until it consisted of only one librarian on a temporary appointment. The departmentalization of the library, nearly forty units in all, compounded the difficulty in offering a well-coordinated and effective instruction program at all levels.

## Environmental Scan

In addition to the problems in coordination of instruction, facilities provided another area of difficulty for us. An environmental scan identified the resources available to us, as well as a number of barriers with which we would have to deal. The Undergraduate Library computer lab, under the control of the campus computing services, has a classroom with twenty-five workstations, and Grainger Engineering Library Information Center has a smaller electronic classroom with fifteen workstations. Computer center-controlled classroom resources would have to be scheduled well in advance, no easy task with an uncertain implementation schedule. We identified a number of wired classrooms controlled by schools and departments, but their owners were reluctant to let us use them for open workshops.

To compound matters, the system rollout was slated for summer, when many faculty and students would not be in residence. News of the new library system would be just one more drop in the flood of information to hit users upon their return to campus in the fall.

## IMPLEMENTING INSTRUCTIONAL STRATEGIES

### Developing Priorities

The task force discussed many ideas for promoting and teaching the new system. In choosing which ideas to put into action, we were guided by the results of a general library user survey conducted in spring 1998. Two survey questions were relevant to our mission.

One question read, "What is the best way for you to learn about using the library?" Here we had instruction in mind. Respondents selected any number of the following choices:

- Small group demonstrations with a librarian or library staff member
- One-on-one demonstrations with a librarian or library staff member
- Library Web pages or other on-line guides
- Printed guides distributed by the library
- Library research class for credit
- As a class session in my university courses
- On my own

The responses showed a clear preference for unmediated learning. "On my own" and "Library Web pages or other on-line guides" scored highest (see fig. 1).

Another survey question asked, "How do you find out about *new* materials and services offered by the library?" Here we were thinking of outreach and awareness rather than instruction per se. The choices for respondents were:

- Library Web pages
- Library newsletters
- Library signs or posters
- Departmental Web pages
- Departmental newsletters
- Librarians or library staff members
- Friends or colleagues
- News media

Again, respondents strongly favored methods that did not involve interacting with library staff. "Friends or colleagues" scored highest. The next most popular choices were unmediated Web pages and signs (see fig. 2).

Approximately eight months before the switchover, we launched a Web site dubbed "Books & Bytes." On it we posted samples of the new OPAC (On-Line Public Access Catalog) screens, made links to ILCSO and DRA sites, and explained the reasons for switching systems and the choice of DRA. We intended "Books & Bytes" to grow as imple-

Figure 1   Top Ways to Learn to Use the Library

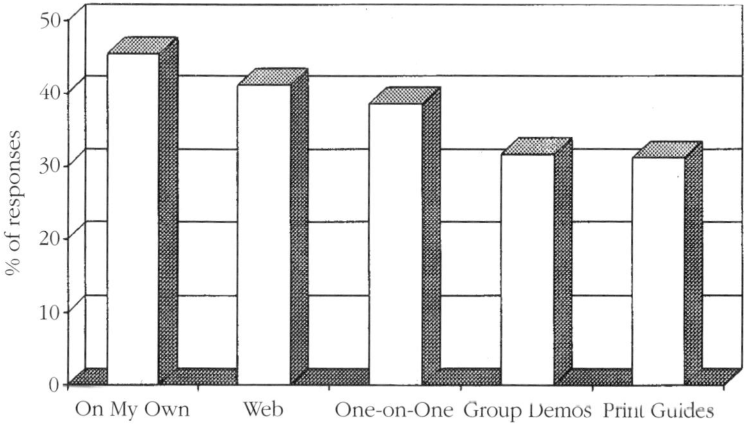

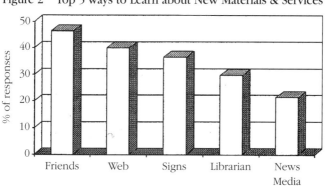

mentation neared, and to be a postimplementation gateway to tutorials and electronic handouts. "Books & Bytes" on the Web was the foundation on which our other efforts were built. But the survey had also confirmed that our users have a variety of learning preferences. A significant minority chose mediated methods such as demonstrations and classes. To reach the entire campus with information about the new system, we needed to employ multiple strategies.

## Electronic Strategies

We committed ourselves to provide as much information as possible on the Web, linked so that users could easily discover it for themselves. "Books & Bytes" was linked from the main campus news and calendar

Figure 2   Top 5 Ways to Learn about New Materials & Services

page, from the main library home page, and from the individual home pages of departmental libraries. We also pledged that every paper handout would have a Web-based counterpart.

The library is not the only source of Web-based information about library resources. The campus academic computing service maintains an extensive handbook on its Web site, including chapters on the on-line catalog and other networked library resources. Members of the task force rewrote these chapters and submitted them for electronic publication.

The Undergraduate Library's instruction librarian created an on-line, self-paced tutorial. The tutorial is accessed from the Web and features a live telnet connection to the OPAC. The content is essentially the same as our hands-on workshops. To track use by classes and reinforce learning, it incorporates an interactive quiz. Within the library, the tutorial became a popular tool for training student workers, since they can access it during slow times at service desks. Subsections, such as the instructions for configuring a Web browser to launch a telnet session, do double duty as help screens. The tutorial is linked from numerous places within the library's Web space.

The problem with these Web-based approaches is that they are passive. Users must go looking for them or be nudged toward them; we couldn't be certain that the people who most needed to know about the new on-line catalog were reached via our Web pages. Therefore we turned to another familiar technology, E-mail, to get the message out.

Until quite recently, our campus E-mail service did not support broadcast messages to a wide audience, so we devised a system of "trickle down E-mail." The task force crafted messages and relied on departmental librarians to forward them to users in the departments they serve. We used this method sparingly: for instance, to announce a delay in the switchover date and to provide instructions on confusing routines. Communication via E-mail proved critical for dealing with unforeseen glitches that threatened to harm the library's relationship with its users.

It's tempting to overemphasize the damage control aspects of the migration, since problems with the new system created a great deal of stress both for library staff and for users. Therefore, since every new software installation creates unique and unpredictable crises, one example should suffice. Because the OCLC loader program did not work as expected, we experienced a delay of several months in adding new titles to the catalog. This situation was a potential public relations nightmare. Faculty began complaining that not only had we mounted a new system that they couldn't get the hang of, we had stopped buying new books! In response to this crisis, the acquisitions department developed the Web-based "Gap Shelflist," which we publicized to users through trickle-down E-mail and highly visible links on library Web pages.

Listening and responding to user complaints was vitally important, not just to uphold the library's image as responsive and service oriented, but also to gather feedback that drove the development of help screens and handouts. A suggestion box feature within the OPAC itself and E-mail links on Web pages encouraged users to air their gripes and share invaluable information about their interactions with the system.

## Print Strategies

The Web and E-mail were the backbone of our efforts, but other, more traditional strategies were also important. Reaching all users meant using print as well as electronic means. Again, we took a combination of active and passive approaches. We produced a small searching guide—known to us as "the pocket guide"—that was distributed to all faculty members and graduate students via their departments and to undergraduate students via dormitory mail boxes. It was accompanied by a letter from the university librarian.

Printed handouts were another facet of our instructional effort. We had a quick guide to the two interfaces ready on day one. Other handouts were prepared over the following weeks, after improvements to the interface and functionality were made and the system was stabilized. For the telnet interface, we wrote step-by-step guides for a number of processes, such as viewing the borrower's account, searching for journals, and accessing the system remotely. Every printed handout was also converted to an HTML document and posted on the library's Web site.

## Workshops

The print handouts doubled as documentation for workshops. Given our huge campus population and our decentralized library structure, most user education inevitably takes place in the departmental libraries. Some libraries conducted workshops or demonstrations for target audiences, but most of the smaller libraries simply provided one-on-one teaching in the reference context. The task force sponsored centralized workshops during the fall 1998 term, more or less as a safety net for users who would not receive instruction otherwise or who preferred a classroom environment. Students in some freshman classes were required to attend a workshop; thus the participants were a mix of experienced and naïve library users.

We made a crucial decision at the outset: to teach the new system without reference to the old system. For the freshmen and other newcomers who attended, a side-by-side comparison would have been baffling. Another important choice was to teach in a hands-on mode. At the conclusion of each fifty-minute session, we asked participants to fill out a Web-based workshop evaluation form while they were still seated at the workstations. The following semester, we repeated the basic on-line catalog open workshops and added workshops on advanced searching techniques. Workshop attendance was modest but the impact was positive, as we discuss below.

## Publicity Strategies

The task force realized early on that our instructional efforts had to be supported by active marketing. We set out to generate some positive buzz about the new system. Since the survey showed that more than 20 percent of our users find out about new library services through campus news media, we worked with the library's Office of Development and Public Affairs to place feature stories and ads in the daily student newspaper and other local outlets. On day one, we decorated the public workstations with balloons, and staff wore large "Ask Me" buttons. Then, one balmy afternoon shortly after the start of fall term, we gave out free lemonade and cookies at the entrance to the Undergraduate Library—all to signal that a big change had come to the library.

Midway through the fall term, when problems with the new system had become painfully apparent and user dissatisfaction was growing, we turned to the campus news media again to help with damage control. The university librarian issued an open letter to the UIUC community, outlining the measures being taken to improve the system. The reverse side of the letter listed sources of help, including our Web-based handouts, the on-line tutorial, the workshops, and the library's Information Desk and Telephone Center.

## One-On-One Strategies

Finally, we also tried to facilitate one-on-one learning, because nearly 40 percent of the 1998 library survey respondents indicated that they preferred individual instruction from a library staff member. The balloons and "Ask Me" buttons also signaled the readiness of library staff to introduce users to the new system. In addition, the task force prepared a ten-minute "miniscript" for use in one-on-one teaching situations.

These diverse methods—electronic and print, group and individual, internal and external—added up to a full instructional and promotional initiative, many pieces of which have been absorbed into our ongoing user education programs. Our teaching experience was also a powerful learning experience.

## RESULTS OF THE INSTRUCTIONAL STRATEGIES

### Assessing Our Efforts through the Spring 1999 User Survey

To assess the success of the various methods of introducing the new system to users and their reactions to the new system, we included questions about the catalog on the general library user survey conducted in spring 1999. One survey question read: The library launched a new on-line catalog system last August. How did you learn about it? (Check all that apply.)

- Library Web page
- Brochure picked up in a library
- Brochure received through campus mail
- E-mail
- Print news media (*Daily Illini, Inside Illinois, News-Gazette*, etc.)
- Broadcast news media (local radio, TV)
- Workshop
- Presentation in class
- On-line tutorial
- From a library staff member
- From a friend or colleague
- Discovered it on my own
- Other

The top five responses to this survey question appear in figure 3. Nearly half of the respondents indicated that they had learned about the new system through the library Web page. While it is not clear whether they discovered the new system through the "Books & Bytes" Web site that the Task Force on User Education had prepared, or other announcements on the library's Web site, it is clear that using the Web was a successful strategy.

The 1999 survey results also reinforced what users had told us in the 1998 survey about preferring to learn about the library on their own. Nearly 30 percent of the respondents to the 1999 survey indicated that they had discovered the new system on their own. Again, it is not clear

**Figure 3    Top 5 Ways People Learned about the New System**

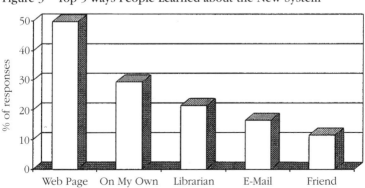

what "discovered on my own" means. Unlike the 1998 survey, the 1999 survey asked about the users' actual experience, not their ideal way of learning. It cannot be determined from this data if users were unhappy that the library did not offer enough support to help them or were proud of having figured out the system on their own.

Survey results also supported the role of public service staff in user education. From the beginning, the task force assumed that the bulk of instruction would not take place in a workshop or through the tutorial, but on an as-needed basis in the many departmental libraries. Nearly 22 percent of the respondents indicated that they had learned about the new system from a staff member. This finding stresses the critical importance of well-trained library staff who are able to cope not only with the changes and pressures that implementing a new system has on its own day-to-day work but also with teaching patrons and dealing with their emotional responses to the new system.

## SUCCESS OF "BOOKS & BYTES"

The transaction logs for the "Books & Bytes" site are also illuminating. The main page received more than 11,000 hits during both summer 1998 and fall 1998, with nearly 5,000 hits occurring in August when the transition took place. After the main page, the News and Links page received the most hits, with more than 3,000 hits during summer 1998. This result shows users' interest in learning about the changes that would be occurring with the system transition. By spring 1999, usage of the "Books & Bytes" page dropped dramatically. Since the site had met its objectives, it was delinked from the many visible places on the library's Web site, and a more encompassing user education Web site was created.

## WORKSHOP ATTENDANCE AND TUTORIAL USAGE

Although the workshop and the tutorial did not make the list of the top five ways people learned about the new on-line catalog system, a comparison of these two methods is interesting. Attendance at the workshops totaled 312 during fall and spring semesters, and approximately 349 people completed the on-line tutorial during the same time period. The similarity in these numbers validates the task force's assumption that instruction should be offered in a variety of ways to match the learning styles of our users. Despite the fact that attendance at library workshops has always been low, it was important to offer hands-on workshops for those people who prefer face-to-face group instruction. Workshop participants viewed the workshops as an effective

Figure 4   Workshop Attendance and Tutorial Usage

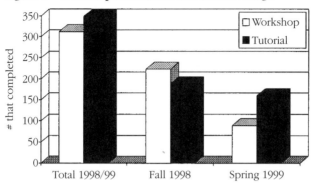

instructional method, with more than 92 percent of the people who submitted the on-line evaluation form indicating that they felt more confident using the library after taking the workshop, and 89 percent indicating that they would be more self-sufficient in using the library. While attending a workshop can help users become familiar with using the new system, fitting a workshop into a person's busy schedule can be difficult. The tutorial helped to reach both the busy people and the independent learners. The breakdown of usage by semester (as shown in figure 4) shows that more people opted to use the tutorial second semester after the system had been up for awhile.

## DEALING WITH NEGATIVE REACTIONS TO THE NEW SYSTEM

Despite the various methods of promoting the new system, the task force never really considered how to deal with frustrated and angry patrons in the implementation plan. To help deal with these patrons, some training was given to library staff after it became apparent that the system's deficiencies were making users hostile. While this training was helpful, it occurred too late. Training the staff to deal with frustration also doesn't help users who toil (and boil) away in their offices and never interact with a sympathetic library worker who can set them on the right track.

To help remote users, the library used the on-line suggestion box feature built into the catalog as well as an E-mail link for comments on our Web pages. The library received more than 200 questions and comments through these channels from fall 1998 through summer 1999. Based on this feedback, the task force was able to improve existing handouts and help pages as well as provide individual instruction to frustrated users.

Feedback on user frustration was also collected in an open-ended question about the catalog on the 1999 user survey. Many people took the opportunity to express their displeasure with the new system. The most common comments described the new system as "not user friendly," "confusing," and "a major disappointment." It is important to deal with these types of negative reactions because they create a great barrier to user education. Users who are not emotionally able to overlook the deficiencies of a system are not in a position to learn how to use it effectively.

## CONCLUSION

Certainly some of the problems experienced at the University of Illinois are unique to the installation of this particular software. Likewise, the campus culture and library organization shaped the instructional strategies used. However, some truths may be derived from this experience that may benefit other libraries facing system migrations.

1. Train public service staff well. The best teachers are librarians and staff who know the system well. The migration to a new system was hampered at the University of Illinois Library by an inadequate training database, last-minute changes to the system, and a summer implementation that meant staff had to juggle vacations and training sessions. Allow as much time for internal training and practice as possible.
2. Use all possible avenues of communication and instruction. Many users prefer to learn on their own or from friends, so maximize the opportunities for that kind of learning to take place.
3. Be honest with users. If the system will have drawbacks, don't gloss over them. The user will discover them right away.
4. Provide means for problem solving and venting, and respond to user input promptly.
5. Work with technology specialists on campus to foresee and prevent technical problems that will taint users' experiences with the new system. For many UIUC users, complications with the telnet software on their home or office PC soured them on the system before they could give it a fair trial.
6. Don't be discouraged. Count the successes, not the failures. A frequent library user on the University of Illinois faculty declared immediately after the switch that the library had cut him off forever from the resources he needs because the new system was utterly unusable. A few months later, he grudgingly admitted that the library had not, in fact, destroyed his career as a scholar. He still

doesn't like the new on-line catalog, but thanks to patient teaching and coaching, he's learned to use it effectively.

7. Finally, be patient. Understand how hard it can be for the user to make the transition, and be aware that, even though the system may change overnight, the education of users will continue as an issue of increasing importance in the long term as well as the short term.

Although each institution faces unique problems in the attempt to migrate technologies, the concepts of planning, execution, and assessment of results are universal. This discussion of the experience at the University of Illinois Library will, we hope, offer some insight and assistance to those who will execute similar changes in years to come.

# 28

# Designing Effective Instructional and Outreach Programs for Underrepresented Undergraduate Students: The Iowa Approach

*Janice Simmons-Welburn*

Since the early 1990s, academic libraries have turned their attention toward creating effective responses to trends in cultural diversity on college and university campuses. In addition to seeking diversity among staff and developing programs to increase staff awareness and understanding of cultural differences, the issue of providing services to underrepresented and culturally diverse undergraduate student populations through effective and sustained outreach initiatives has also become a focus in public services.

This chapter uses the University of Iowa as a reference point to foster dialogue over the importance of creating and enhancing opportunities for and developing partnerships between the University Libraries and offices and organizations throughout the campus that have responsibility for programs aimed at student populations traditionally underrepresented at colleges and universities for cultural or socioeconomic reasons. Among the examples are partnerships with campus programs from the Regents' Institutions On-line (TRIO) such as Upward Bound, and programs focused on underrepresented students sponsored by the office of the provost and the Graduate College.

## RATIONALE

It is commonly understood that the face of American higher education has changed dramatically over the course of the twentieth century. Following the end of World War II, it can be argued that higher education—which had once been regarded as the domain of the elite—was redefined in a spirit of democratic renewal. The nation experienced an opening of higher education, because of the synergy between federal educational initiatives such as the GI Bill, a succession of higher education acts, the expansion of federal guaranteed student aid programs, and the actions of the Civil Rights movement that turned—to paraphrase NAACP Chairman Julian Bond—*protest* into *policy*. As a consequence, colleges and universities have experienced a transformation in the demographics of their students. Today there are many more students on our campuses who are low income/ first generation or are from populations that are culturally underrepresented among baccalaureate and advanced degree holders. Colleges and universities acknowledge that students come with greater risk factors than before, and that it is necessary if not vital to the health and well-being of our educational aims to effect an institutional response to avoid academic failure. As a consequence, we have adopted numerous program initiatives through a reallocation of resources, new appropriations, and external funding designed not only to encourage greater participation in higher education, but also to ensure success. As institutions, we have adopted program initiatives by developing an array of academic support services. As libraries, we seek opportunities to partner with these initiatives to reduce risk factors by promoting information literacy as a core academic skill.

Before elaborating on this last point, I want to spend more time on distinguishing characteristics of our student populations. Here I wish to focus on students from populations that the College Board once called "the forgotten half."[1] According to Lawrence E. Gladieux and Watson Scott Swail:

> The good news of the past decade is that more people are attaining higher levels of education and filling millions of skilled, high-paying jobs generated by a booming, globally competitive economy. The bad news is that opportunities for education beyond high school remain unequal across society, wage and wealth disparities have reached unprecedented extremes, and the least educated and skilled are getting a smaller and smaller piece of the pie. In a "winner-take-all society," the stakes get bigger. More of The Forgotten Half may be finding upward mobility through postsecondary education than a decade ago, but those who are left behind today have less pay and less protection in an increasingly volatile job market.

Study after study produced by the College Board, the National Center for Educational Statistics, and by ACT reach the same conclusions. Despite significant strides in the past three decades, there continues to be a lag in degree attainment and overall college and graduate school success between African American, Latino, and Native American students, and students from low-income backgrounds, and other students enrolled in higher education. However, it is also important to distinguish between cultural and socioeconomic factors differentiating students when we consider appropriate interventions. Let us first consider low-income students.

## LOW-INCOME STUDENTS AND EDUCATIONAL ACHIEVEMENT

The National Center for Education Statistics reports that low-income high school graduates are half as likely to enroll in college immediately as higher income students, due in part to the difficulties they experience in navigating their way through high school to college.[2] Low-income students are also likely to enter college with higher academic risk factors than other students. While some of this has been attributed to economic, family, and personal characteristics, the disparity in access to the resources that prepare students for the rigors of college cannot be underestimated as factors contributing to college success or failure.

It is widely accepted that educational achievement in high school is one of the strongest predictors of college success.[3] National studies repeatedly report that academic preparation through educational and education-enhancement activities combined with aspiration and motivation for college are crucial to earning college degrees. In addition, reports from the community of school librarians and media specialists also indicate that strategies intended to implement concerted efforts in information literacy at level K through twelfth grade greatly enhance students' educational experiences by teaching methods of dealing with rich information environments. In a volume of essays exploring the Information-Age school library, Carol Collier Kuhlthau wrote:

> My studies demonstrate the importance of teaching the information search process rather than assuming that students will acquire an understanding of the process on their own. The information-age school must create an environment in which students can experience the information search process and provide situations where they can reflect and become aware of their own process. Through reflection on their own experiences, students internalize the process for transference to other situations.

What Kuhlthau argues is quite necessary to prepare college-bound students for academic success in higher education and, ultimately, to graduate students who are information literate. Yet it also raises other questions about the underserved in education. How well does the human and financial resource commitment to teaching the information search process and information literacy in general translate across America's complex system of public education, a system marked by what Jonathan Kozol accurately depicted as "savage inequalities"? What of the students who enter college having graduated from schools with one-room libraries; inadequate collections, periodicals, and books; and nonexistent computing resources?

There are also concerns about the nation's non-Asian minorities who continue to be underrepresented among college and university undergraduates. A recent College Board report "Reaching the Top" found both signs of progress and trouble.[4] The National Task Force on Minority High Achievement, the report's authors, found that:

> During the past 35 years, concerted efforts to promote the educational progress of underrepresented minority groups has reaped some important benefits—African-American students now graduate from high school or earn equivalency diplomas at the same rate as whites, 87 percent,

that:

> data from the National Assessment of Educational Progress (NAEP) show that some progress has been made in narrowing the overall performance gap between minority and white students. In the mid-1990s, for example, the gap in average math scores for 17-year-olds was about one-third smaller than it was in the early 1970s,

and that:

> The Task Force identified several interventions that reverse some of the academic under-productivity of minority students.

Yet troubling signs in performance persist, as measured by standardized test scores and academic performance in college among black, Latino, and Native American students at virtually all socioeconomic levels. Both the College Board report and a recent National Center for Education Statistics working paper note that underrepresented minority students continue to experience higher attrition from college even when well qualified for college admission.[5]

None of this suggests a lack of intelligence or lack of ability to perform at an acceptable level of academic ability. Rather, the evidence suggests—as do the conclusions of the College Board report—that as with low-income students, there are risk factors (perhaps nonacademic) associated with the college experience that requires institutional intervention. What follows are descriptions of such programs at Iowa and how the University Libraries has positioned itself to be an integral part of the planning and implementation of these programs.

## THE MEANING OF INFORMATION LITERACY
## IN THE PRESENT CONTEXT

Admittedly, academic libraries begin at a deficit when attempting to convince the directors of academic support programs of the role of information literacy, and we must be aware that many of these programs exist to improve math and writing skills and to increase degree aspirations. Our efforts must demonstrate added value, and the meaning of what we mean by information literacy must be clear.

In *Student Learning in the Information Age: The Move Toward a New Literacy*, Patricia Breivik wrote, "In this next century, an 'educated graduate' will no longer be defined as one who has absorbed a certain body of factual information, but as one who knows how to find, evaluate, and apply needed information."[6] Locating, evaluating, organizing, and using information are key elements to information literacy, according to Breivik. The elements of becoming information literate include

- Understanding the process for acquiring information
- Evaluating the effectiveness of resources available to obtain information
- Mastering skills needed to acquire and store information
- Awareness of trends in policy development regarding information[7]

Breivik goes on to argue for the need to develop effective campus strategies to garner the financial support and human resources to ensure information literacy for all students. However, we must be cautious about crafting strategy with such a broad stroke, especially given the size, complexity, and diversity of an institution such as Iowa, with nearly 20,000 undergraduates hailing from urban, suburban, and rural communities. Our respective institutions have recognized this through an array of initiatives, such as enhancing honors programs, creating projects around cultural diversity, and developing efforts to respond to the needs of first-generation and low-income students.

## UPWARD BOUND

The U.S. Department of Education reported in a survey of colleges and universities that "roughly one-third of all institutions offered at least one program for precollegiate students in 1993–94. Programs were especially common at large institutions (71 percent) and at public institutions (45 percent)."[8] Upward Bound is probably one of the largest and best known programs, serving low-income students within geographic regions that are close to the host university. It is one of six Special Programs for Disadvantaged Students (TRIO) programs administered by the U.S. Department of Education that stem from the 1964 Civil Rights Act. At Iowa, low-income first-generation high school students are invited to the university for an eight-week program that combines intensive instruction in college preparatory courses (rhetoric and mathematics) with an orientation to college life in an effort to build a bridge into higher education.

Upward Bound staff and librarians at the university have recognized that an essential part of student preparation for the demands of college should entail the development of strategies and skills in locating and using information in support of course-related assignments. Accordingly, the pathway to better support for the Upward Bound summer program's curriculum occurred in two stages of development.

First, under the direction of then Diversity/Special Services Librarian William Welburn in cooperation with Janice Simmons-Welburn and Marsha Forys, the libraries developed a series of skill-building experiences designed to expose students to appropriate use of the libraries' print and electronic information resources. Second, with the involvement of Susan Vega-Garcia (then the libraries' minority research resident), the library sessions were integrated more closely into other curriculum in the Upward Bound summer program. Typically, the libraries' program lasted for one to two weeks of the eight-week summer program.

The initiative has resulted in closer association with the Upward Bound program and its staff. The libraries have written in support of the university's program in their effort to seek renewal for their grant from the U.S. Department of Education Office of TRIO Programs. The libraries' letter of support described the successful collaboration between both entities in heightening the awareness of student participants in the importance of libraries not only in their success as students but as lifelong learners.

## SUMMER RESEARCH OPPORTUNITIES PROGRAM

The second example illustrates the libraries' role in working with a program designed to increase the number of high achieving minority students in Ph.D. programs, especially in areas where students are critically underrepresented. In this context, "at risk" involves encouraging persistence among students who are often scarcely visible in some disciplines and, subsequently, succumb to the pressures of isolation and frustration and eventually abandon their educational goals. In *Life After College*, a National Center for Education Statistics (NCES) report from the Baccalaureate and Beyond Longitudinal Study, it was found that the advanced degree expectations of black and Latino 1992–93 bachelor's degree recipients did not diminish by 1997 as quickly as other students surveyed.[9] However, such aspirations can fade rapidly, especially for students facing six or more years of doctoral study.

Many research universities have created summer undergraduate research programs. At the University of Iowa, the Summer Research

Opportunities Program (SROP) administered by the Graduate College was created more than ten years ago to encourage more undergraduate students from backgrounds that are underrepresented in
doctoral programs to continue their education without interruption.
Approximately 75 percent of the university's SROP alumni have enrolled in graduate school, and many have earned Ph.D. degrees.

SROP students are expected to devote eight weeks of their summer—normally between their junior and senior years—to research
conducted under the direction of a faculty mentor. For some, this involves intensive work in the laboratory, while others spend many
hours researching information in the University Libraries. Library staff
has worked with SROP to create a heightened awareness of library and
Internet resources that are useful if not essential for graduate-level research. Sandra Ballasch and Lissa Lord created a Web page they've presented to the students in a ninety-minute workshop that familiarizes
the students with library and Internet resources. The SROP Web page
remains available for the students well beyond the eight-week program. SROP students, many of whom are from other colleges, continue
to make use of the page from their home institutions. In addition, SROP
students are introduced to the Libraries' Research Consultation services, which they use independently.

## CONCLUSION

When Carol Kuhlthau concluded her recapitulation of the Information
Search Process model as it relates to the mission of school libraries and
media centers, she wrote, "The information-age school library prepares
children for productive living in an information-rich environment. Library media programs need to be reconstructed to serve the information-age school. Our mission is for every child to have the opportunity
to become information literate."[10]

Given the persistence of inequality in our nation's system of educating our youth, this may be a goal achievable only in the distant future.
It is higher education's more immediate responsibility to embrace this
mission for those students who walk through our institutions' doors. It
is also incumbent upon libraries in higher education to seek opportunities for collaboration across campus to design effective programs that
link students to information as educated graduates meeting the challenges of the next century.

## NOTES

1. Lawrence E. Gladieux and Watson Scott Swail, *Postsecondary Education:
Student Success Not Just Access* (New York: College Board, 1998).

2. *The Condition of Education 1998* (Washington, D.C.: U.S. Department of Education, 1998), Supplemental Table 7–1.

3. "What Helps or Hinders Students' Educational Achievement?" *ACT Information Brief*, 99–102.

4. National Task Force on Minority High Achievement, *Reaching the Top* (New York: College Board, October 1999).

5. National Task Force on Minority High Achievement, *Reaching the Top.* See also, *Projected Postsecondary Outcomes of 1992 High School Graduates*, U.S. Department of Education, National Center for Education Statistics (NCES), Working Paper No. 1999–15 (June 1999).

6. Patricia Breivik, *Student Learning in the Information Age* (Washington, D.C.: American Council on Education, 1998), 2.

7. Breivik, *Student Learning in the Information Age*, 5.

8. *Statistical Analysis Report: Programs at Higher Education Institutions for Disadvantaged Precollege Students* (Washington, D.C.: NCES, 1995).

9. *Life after College: A Descriptive Summary of 1992–93 Bachelor's Degree Recipients in 1997* (Washington, D.C.: NCES, 1999).

10. Carol Collier Kuhlthau, "The Process of Learning from Information," in *The Virtual School Library: Gateway to the Information Superhighway*, ed. Carol Collier Kuhlthau (Englewood, Colo.: Libraries Unlimited, 1996), 103.

# 29

# Tale of Two Collaborations

*Diane Dallis and Emily Okada*

The Indiana University Bloomington Undergraduate Library has worked with two summer undergraduate programs for several years: the Groups program and the Intensive Freshman Seminars program. Although there is a difference in how they expect the libraries to participate in their programs, the administrators and instructors of both programs value information literacy skills and the role of librarians in teaching these skills.

Over the years, librarians have seen a convergence in the needs and interests of the students participating in these seemingly very different programs. The trust that program administrators have in the abilities and motives of librarians allowed us to pursue some new approaches to meeting student information needs.

## SETTING THE STAGE:
## THE STUDENTS, THE CAMPUS, THE LIBRARIES

Indiana University Bloomington (IUB) is located in southern Indiana. Bloomington has a population of about 61,000. The number of undergraduate students enrolled at IUB in the fall of 1999 was 27,461. Most of these students are state residents; some come from large cities such as Indianapolis, others from small towns such as Monon (population 1,500). The majority of new IUB undergraduates are "traditional" students who are eighteen to nineteen years of age and living away from their parents' home for the first time. Regardless of their background, these students all have some level of adjustment to make to university life. Most freshmen attend a two-day summer orientation program with

230

their parents where they register for fall classes, work out financial aid procedures, and learn about campus services, including library services.

The collections of the IUB Libraries, totaling more than 5 million books and 40,000 journals, magazines, and newspapers, are distributed across campus through a system of libraries including our Main Library, 15 subject-specific campus libraries, and 12 Halls of Residence (dormitory) libraries. The Main Library holds the Research Collections, Government Publications Department, and the Undergraduate Library and constitutes more than half of the IUB system collections. In addition, students can access more than 140 databases from the libraries' Web site. Needless to say, students are often overwhelmed by the size and number of decisions they need to make when using the libraries.

## PROGRAM PARTNERS

Librarians from IUB Libraries' Undergraduate Library Services Department have worked with the Groups program and the Intensive Freshman Seminars for years. Both programs are designed to help new college students make a successful transition from high school to university life.

The Groups program has been in existence for more than thirty years. The six-week summer program admits 200 to 250 students and is designed to support, retain, and increase the graduation rates of first-generation, low-income, and disabled students. Students are admitted based on their high school academic performance and financial need. Students receive full scholarships to take part in the program. The summer residency includes a critical thinking course, English composition, and math, all taught by graduate student instructors.

The director of the Groups program is a staunch library advocate and we receive a lot of moral support from her and all the other Groups administrative staff. Over the years, library tours have been offered as part of campus orientation for the students during the first week of the program. These tours are never well attended, and our efforts to develop general class-unrelated introduction and orientation activities to information sources (including using the World Wide Web) and library services have met with only marginal success.

Although we have yet to devise successful and meaningful extracurricular information literacy/library orientation activities for the Groups program, we have been very successful with one specific class: X152, or Critical Reading and Reasoning for the New College Student. The course is coordinated by a faculty member from the School of Education who also serves as the director of the Student Academic Center, a learning support service center, and it is taught by assistant instructors (AIs), most of whom are graduate students in the School of Education. The coordinator and instructors are almost as zealous about information literacy as the librarians involved. Planning meetings with librarians and instructors have always involved discussions that ultimately lead to concrete, practical ways to build library research skills into course projects.

The Intensive Freshman Seminars (IFS) program admits about 300 students at a total cost of about $800. There are no special academic requirements for admission; however, students must be enrolled at IUB for the following academic year. The seminar is three credits in three weeks. Students learn in small groups with faculty while they are becoming familiar with campus and services. The seminar topics are unique with titles such as "Mind, Values, and Our World," "Funk and Pharaohs: Communicating Culture through Dress," and "Sacred Places: The Architecture of Faith."

The libraries were involved in the initial planning for the IFS program. The result of this very early involvement are some built-in extracurricular library activities. Library orientation takes place on the second day of the program (a Sunday), before the seminars meet, and is an official, required IFS activity. A one-hour database searching and on-line catalog workshop is scheduled by the IFS office for each seminar group. These hands-on workshops are conducted during the first week of the three-week program. For some IFS students, these two activities are the extent of their library contact during the program. The first IFS director and subsequent directors have all expressed the belief that it is important for the students to learn to use library and information resources effectively, and although they cannot control actual content and activities for each seminar, their commitment to these extracurricular activities has been strong and consistent.

A librarian liaison is assigned to each IFS faculty member. These volunteers are often subject specialists/bibliographers. These pairings are made early in the year when IFS faculty are in the early stages of developing a syllabus. Incorporating information literacy skills/library research instruction into the actual seminar varies greatly from seminar to seminar. Many do not require any kind of library research. Others incorporate quite a bit, and faculty may work closely with the librarian to incorporate information literacy activities into seminar requirements. IFS librarian liaisons may visit a seminar as a guest lecturer, lead a hands-on session related to the seminar topic, write pathfinders (print or electronic), compile bibliographies, or provide individual or group consultation. Some students have quite a bit of contact with "their librarian."

## PROGRAM AND STUDENT CHARACTERISTICS

The differences between the Groups and the IFS programs are obvious. Groups classes (including X152) are coordinated and funded by the Groups program, and content and activities are controlled by the department (English, Math, Student Academic Center/Education) and the course coordinator (teaching faculty). Instructors are usually graduate students hired as assistant instructors. Students have been identified as having potential, but being "at risk," and the courses could be characterized as "remedial."

Intensive Freshman Seminars are coordinated and funded by the Office of Summer Sessions and Special Programs. Professors submit a proposal for a seminar and the topics are expected to be unique. Once a seminar is accepted, content and activities related to that seminar are controlled by the professor. Students are accepted on a first-come-first served basis; any student who will be a first semester freshman in the fall and who pays the registration fee may participate. The courses could be characterized as "enrichment."

How do these characteristics affect the library orientation and information literacy activities developed for the programs? Not as profoundly as you might expect.

In planning for summer 1999, we identified traits the students had in common. In both programs, the majority of the students are excited about being in the program, they are motivated to succeed, overwhelmed by the size of the campus and the size of the library facilities and collections, are not sure where they "fit in," and are afraid to look uncool or uninformed in front of their peers. They are all taking a big step: making the transition from high school student to college student and many have trouble making the right choices that their new-found independence requires. Most of them do not understand basic database-searching techniques, and most of them need a review of basic library research skills. Levels of computer competence varies in both groups, but even those students who are least comfortable with computers are beguiled by the "power" of the Internet.

## A SLIGHT SHIFT IN ATTITUDE

While observing a trio of students doing some research in the Undergraduate Library, a librarian commented on the fact that they seemed comfortable and that it was nice to see that they obviously felt that this was "their" library. "Wouldn't it be nice if all students had positive feelings about this place?" was the wistful observation.

This was the beginning of a shift in our attitude toward what we ought to accomplish when working with the Groups and IFS students. Our goal would be to create a sense of belonging and to encourage a sense of competence. We would focus on the students' feelings about the library and their ability to successfully use the resources and services available. We would not abandon our objectives of teaching database-searching basics, or providing a physical orientation to the building, or attempting to guide them along in evaluating data or information. But we would use the old tried-and-true methods to focus on concepts and process rather than on details and procedure. Not profound. But easier said than done!

Our commitment and courage to make some changes to both programs were bolstered not only by the positive reaction from the administrators, staff, and instructors in both programs, but also by three important factors: (1) the existence of two hands-on computer instruction clusters in the Undergraduate Library—one with twelve terminals and the other with fourteen, (2) an extremely energetic, dependable, and competent graduate student intern from the School of Library and Information Science (SLIS), and (3) the World Wide Web. We were also realistic. We considered the following:

**Timing.**    The Groups students would be on campus for approximately eight weeks in July and August. The X152 coordinator guaranteed two library visits, one for an hour and the other for two hours. The Intensive Freshman Seminar program ran for three weeks, just before the fall semester. There would be the usual orientation tours on the first Sunday and the one-hour database-searching workshop the first week.

**Planning.**    For Groups/X152, although not involved in determining course objectives, librarians were involved with planning very early on, before actual exercises or the syllabus was set, in mid-March. For IFS, we would proceed as in years past and have complete control over content and format of the orientation tours and database workshops.

**Staffing.**    We would depend heavily on our AIs (graduate students from SLIS who participate in our bibliographic instruction program as instructors for the 100-level "one-shots," specifically those done for the English Composition classes) and on the student intern.

**Training.**    Training needs were minimal, Librarians were familiar with the programs, and the AIs all had experience. The main challenge would be to keep everyone informed and advised as planning was carried out. We arranged to do some training for Groups/X152 instructors to familiarize them with the resources their students would be learning to use. We also made a presentation at an IFS faculty orientation session about the goals and objectives of the library activities.

**Access to Technology.**    Indiana University Bloomington has been identified as one of the "most wired" campuses. Students in both programs would have adequate access to the World Wide Web. Library staff would also have access to the technology and had developed the skills needed to take advantage of the World Wide Web to deliver instruction.

**Relevancy.**    The Groups/X152 coordinator and instructors were committed to integrating the library activities/exercises into the course requirements. IFS administrators were firmly committed to providing a "library experience" for all IFS students regardless of whether or not library research was required in the actual seminar a student was taking.

***Avoiding Information Overload.*** We resolved to encourage the students to explore all possibilities for learning through the libraries without overwhelming them with those same possibilities. A fine line to tread.

***Budget.*** We received no extra funding so would have to "make do" with what we had.

## LIBRARIES' RESPONSE

We created a self-guided library tour for both IFS and Groups/X152 that combined elements of a worksheet, a hands-on session, and a contest. This tour required the students to venture into the stacks, which made the program coordinators happy, and the students enjoyed themselves as they learned about the library building and the system.

Students worked in teams of two or three to answer all the questions on a worksheet. Class teams began the tour/worksheet at staggered times throughout the day to ease the potential shock to other library users. The worksheet takes students through the library and requires them to go into the library stacks and locate books using call numbers, look at bound periodicals and recognize volume numbers and dates, use the Web-based Reserve Reading Catalog, find the hours a specific library is open, and so on. Students who are the first to complete the worksheet within a given time slot win a small prize and everyone who completes the worksheet is entered in a drawing for a gift certificate to the university bookstore. The individual program administrators pay for the prizes.

## GROUPS/X152

In addition to the library orientation, Groups/X152 students were introduced to library concepts through Web-based tutorials; a two-hour, hands-on working session; and library-focused course assignments. We worked closely with the X152 course coordinator to develop a section of the student workbook. Completion of many of the workbook assignments required students to read Web-based tutorials and use an interactive database user guide that we created. The integration of the traditional assignment on paper with the Web-based instructional tools revealed two benefits. (1) The students learned basic database searching concepts on their own, and (2) they could work on the assignments at any time of day and could refer to the tutorials as much as they needed.

The Web-based tutorials and the interactive user guide were originally developed to supplement traditional "one-shot" library instruction sessions. The interactive user guide is a Web page that divides the computer screen into two sections through the use of HTML frames. One side allows the user to interact with the database and the other side gives directions and information, for example, "Getting Started," "Creating a Basic Search," and "Printing Records."

The "Guide to Library Research," the Web-based tutorial, is made up of several components, for example, "Library Terms and Research Concepts," "Defining and Focusing a Research Topic," and "Evaluating Information." Ideally, the entire tutorial or parts can be given as an assignment that students complete before a hands-on instruction session.

Each module has an on-line test or a printable worksheet at the end. The results of the test can be submitted via E-mail to an instructor and all the components of the tutorial have a "printable notes" feature that summarizes the tutorials for the students' future reference.

The purpose of the two-hour library session was to collect journal and magazine articles for a term paper and for class discussion. A library instructor started the class with a demonstration that lasted about thirty minutes, then allowed the students to work on their own and provided individual assistance as needed. Because most of the students had read the tutorials and completed the worksheets, they understood the basics of database searching and the concepts of library research and were able to focus on their information search. Some referred to the printable notes from the tutorial during the session, others continued to search the database using the interactive user guide. We believe that the freedom to approach the information search on their own terms, as well as the support of the librarian and course instructor allowed the students to feel comfortable and "in control" of this learning experience.

## INTENSIVE FRESHMAN SEMINAR

In addition to the orientation tour, each seminar has a hands-on library instruction session that introduces the students to the library catalog. Most of the classes do not have an assignment that requires library research but the session is tailored to the seminar topic. The library experience varies with each IFS group. Some faculty worked with the librarian liaison in advance of the session, which made it a more meaningful experience, while other faculty considered the library instruction session optional. However, a few IFS faculty arranged for additional instruction or for the creation of course-specific library Web pages. For example, one IFS faculty instructor worked with a librarian to create a Web page of library resources and guides that were specific to that seminar topic. In addition to course-specific resources, the page also included some parts of the Web-based tutorial. All IFS students share the orientation experience and learn the basics of searching the catalog, which seems to have a positive impact on their attitudes about the library.

## GIVING UP ON (THE MYTH OF) CONTROL

While developing the instruction and orientation for both student groups, we often paused and asked ourselves questions such as "How will we know if they actually read that tutorial?" or "What if they don't really complete the self-guided tour worksheet and just get the answers from another team?" Ultimately, we decided that most people only learn a subject or a process when it is meaningful and relevant to their needs. After thinking about these questions and reflecting on experiences with giving guided tours and providing instruction to student groups and classes, we realized that we don't control the learning in these situations either. What we then focused on was creating a low-stress library experience for all the students that would result in a positive attitude about libraries. We hoped that we would accomplish this by allowing the *learners* to control the experience within set parameters of the self-guided orientation tours and self-paced, Web-based tutorials.

## WHAT WORKED, WHAT COULD WORK BETTER

The self-guided orientation worked. It was low stress and involved minimal "adult supervision." Some instructors objected to the contest-like atmosphere or to the fact that not everyone won a prize. We felt that engaging the students in this way created a much more positive attitude than the traditional guided tour. Students actually took less time doing the self-guided tour. The tour included a trip into the stacks and into some "quiet study" areas, which would have been impossible with a group of twenty to forty people on a guided tour. The most common comment we heard was "This wasn't so bad." The second most common comment was "Did you see that book, magazine, 'thing' on [fill in the blank with any number of subjects] up there on the fourth/sixth/tenth floor?" The third most common comment overheard by librarians was "Hey, they have Pizza Hut down in the Food Court!"

The first introduction to the library Web page immediately followed the self-guided orientation tour. This hands-on experience did not include "instruction." Students were shown where the Web page was and what was on it. Groups/X152 students were shown the library Web page designed specifically for their use that included a link to an article that assured them that the Indiana University Main Library is not sinking (a common student myth). Students had the most fun using the resources on the Internet Quick Reference page that is maintained by the Library Reference Department. Again, low stress, minimal "adult supervision."

Library commitment of staff and time was minimal compared to that of previous years. Advance preparation was the key to success as was communication with all Main Library departments.

The Groups/X152 information literacy component was especially successful. Informal feedback indicates that much of the success can be attributed to the fact that although all the exercises were developed by librarians, the students and the instructors controlled when the exercises were done and how they were graded. The modular approach also enabled instructors to identify and assist those students who were having trouble with the concepts or skills before they gave up trying.

It turns out that our biggest challenge lies not with the students but with their instructors. We worked (collaborated?) early and in great depth with program coordinators and administrators, but our contact and communication with instructors, the people working most directly with the students, could have come much earlier in the planning process. We need more time to be sure that all the instructors understand what our goals are. We also need to provide enough information well in advance so that the instructors are able to do what they'll be asking their students to do!

We need to develop more opportunities for students to practice critical thinking and evaluation skills.


## EVALUATION AND ASSESSMENT

To determine if this new approach is working, we are developing assessment and evaluation tools to use with these programs in the future. In addition, it is equally important that we justify the resources and the time spent on this relatively small number of students (about 500 to 550). We plan to solicit student evaluations and feedback on their library experience and to get faculty and instructor evaluations of the library component.

We hope to work closely with an instructor or faculty member in a truly collaborative environment so that we might be able to exert more influence on the student outcomes in order to evaluate and assess within the context of the course. This would allow us to learn how this approach affects the overall learning experience.


## OBSERVATIONS AND RECOMMENDATIONS

When we wrote our proposal for the presentation given at the Iowa Powerful Learning, Powerful Partnerships Symposium, we used the word "collaboration." As we prepared the presentation, we realized that "collaboration" was a little premature. When we're at our most optimistic, we convince ourselves that we are "partners." When we're being realistic, we say that we have great "relationships" with the Groups and with the IFS programs.

This isn't bad. It's just not collaboration! It is, however, the first step in the relationship–partnership–collaboration continuum. As we work our way along this continuum, there are "truths" that guide us.

In relationships with program administrators, sometimes you get moral support only, and that's okay. Sometimes you get active support, financially or programmatically, and that's great! The support of program administrators, even just moral support, is crucial and lends credibility to all your efforts. It's important to identify and respect the administrator's goals and objectives for the program.

In relationships with instructors, it's important to realize that they are often not included in preliminary (program) planning. New instructors especially may need our support and assistance in updating their library research skills and familiarity with electronic resources so that they can confidently work with their students. This may not be the case with full-time faculty, but don't make assumptions. Although reference and instruction librarians are required to keep up with the "latest" in in formation and library resources and research techniques, teaching faculty often don't have the time to learn about these resources or techniques in enough depth to teach them to their students.

In relationships with students, you may need to determine what your role will be: partner, helper, or teacher in the learning enterprise. Is it important for you to be recognized as an information expert or to be considered a respected authority? Whatever you decide, it's important to give students the opportunity to take responsibility for learning. Listen to their concerns but remember that it may be difficult for them to know what they need because they are not aware of the possibilities.

We don't deny that how we are perceived by others (colleague or support service? teacher or helper?) affects the development of a relationship. However, we recommend a minimum amount of analysis and hand wringing about what our role in a particular relationship–partnership–collaboration means about us as librarians or as individuals. Our recommendations are to

Communicate.
Act with creativity and competence.
Recognize and respect the goals and objectives of others.
Have a clear agenda.
Make YOUR goals and objectives obvious.
Make sure your reasons are understood.
Take every opportunity to raise awareness about what librarians can do.
Get feedback from all involved.
Discuss problems immediately.
Celebrate your successes, every one of them.

# 30

# Designed to Serve from a Distance: Developing Library Web Pages to Support Distance Education

*Stephen H. Dew*

The Internet has revolutionized the way that all academic libraries provide services, but it has been especially revolutionary for academic libraries serving distance education programs. Prior to the Internet, students and faculty who were located far from campus had only one way to access their library's catalog, subject indexes, and other resources—they had to drive to the campus. Now, however, through the Internet, students and faculty can instantly access on-line catalogs, subject databases, full-text documents, and other electronic resources and services from their homes or offices, no matter how far they are located from campus. Certainly during the last decade, the Internet has had the most profound influence on how libraries provide resources and services. No doubt that during the next decade, the Internet will continue this profound influence, and those libraries that best serve their distance-education students will most likely be those libraries that best use the power of the Internet to provide access to electronic resources and services.

Importantly, large and ever-increasing numbers of distance-education students are relying on the Internet for their information needs. Last year, in a survey of our distance-education students at the University of Iowa, we discovered that a vast majority of our students (more than 80 percent) have convenient access to the Internet, and clearly, in the foreseeable future, this number is only going to increase. How successful those students are in using library services and resources has been and will be determined in large measure by how well the library has developed its Web pages.

Although as librarians we try to come in contact with as many students as we can, it is not always possible to come into personal contact with every student, and in the case of distance-education students who are frequently far from campus, circumstances for direct contact can be even more difficult. For a significant number of the distance-education students, the interface that they have with the library's Web pages may be the only direct contact that they have with the library during their entire student careers. How the library presents its services and resources on the Web clearly affects how well students are able to utilize its potential. Developing successful Web pages is clearly a challenge.

I have been employed as coordinator of Library Services for Distance Education at the University of Iowa Libraries since September 1998. Probably the most important project that I have worked on during that time was developing a Web site to support distance-education library services. During the last year, I read a good deal of material about Web page development, and I learned to work with Claris Homepage (a Web-editing tool). Eventually, I created a distance-education home page and a Web site supported by about two dozen additional Web pages. The site can be located at the following URL: <http://www.lib.uiowa.edu/disted/index>.

As I developed these pages, I think that I made many right decisions, but I am also aware that I made several wrong decisions. One of the wonderful things about Web page development, however, is that if you have erred in some particular aspect of the Web-page presentation, you usually can correct the problem without a great deal of trouble. From my readings, I was able to recognize some things that needed attention, and I have prepared a bibliography of the works that I found most useful in my preparation for Web-page development. The most useful work on the list, for me anyway, was the book by Metz and Junion-Metz. In addition to recognizing some mistakes from my readings, I was also most fortunate to receive feedback from colleagues who reviewed my pages during the development stage. This chapter is based upon my experience in developing library Web pages to support the unique needs of distance-education students. It will emphasize the special nature of library services that support distance-education programs, and it will highlight the importance of Web-page design and development in serving students and faculty from a distance.

First of all, from my readings and discussions with colleagues, I have come to the conclusion that the best philosophy of Web page design must begin with the admonition, "Keep it simple, logical, and consistent." Adding complexity to a Web page through the use of graphics and large numbers of links can be self-defeating. Complexity adds to the loading time for Web pages, and for many distance-education students with lower-level computers and Web browsers, this can cause a significant hassle. In addition, complexity can confuse and frustrate the user looking for a specific resource or service. Complexity of graphics and links may make the page look pretty, but it usually hinders the usability of the page. The key concepts for design and organization of a Web page are simplicity, logic, and consistency.

In order to increase the usability of all library Web pages for all users, the distance-education home page should follow library policy and be consistent with all other library Web pages. For larger libraries, which may have several branch libraries, many Web pages, and a large number of resources (such as the University of Iowa), this is especially true—consistency of appearance and organization between Web pages is key to increasing usability.

In my case, I followed library policy by including the "Library Logo" at the top with the "Header title." The title should be made as descriptive as possible for the content and the audience, and in this case it is titled "Distance-Education Library Services." The title should not only be added to the header at the top of the Web page, but it also should be added as a browser title. The browser title is visible in a corner of most Web browsers, and when the page is printed, the title shows up in the top left-hand corner. The URL for the page should be brief and consistent with the title—"disted" being the key identifier in this case. The term "index" appearing at the end of the URL indicates that this is the home page for "disted." Following library policy, at the top, links are provided to the library home page and the university home page, and in addition, the page is divided into two sides.

On the left side of my home page is a list of links to "Information and Services." On the right side is a list of links to "On-Line Resources." These two divisions are logical, and since they are consistent for the home page of the library system and the home pages for all of the branch libraries, the usability of the site should be enhanced.

The text on the page is black. The links are blue. The background is white, and importantly, there is ample white space between the various blocks of information. Although there is no hard rule on what colors to use in Web page development, in this case, these color combinations follow library policy and are actually standard practices for most libraries. For clarity and usability, the contrast must be strong between the background color and the colors of the text and the links. Most authors writing about Web page development recommend a light background with dark text and links, with white or light gray being the backgrounds most used. In many of the Web-editing tools, blue is a default color for links, and therefore, blue has become the standard color. A recent study found that blue was the color of more than 80 percent of the links on the library Web pages reviewed. Whatever colors one chooses for the background, text, and links, those colors should be maintained consistently throughout the Web site. Changing colors or

font styles and sizes will only confuse the user and decrease the usability of the site. In addition to the blue color for links, the titles of the
links should clearly indicate their purpose. When necessary, however,
that purpose can be clarified by adding a brief annotation.

Another library logo appears at the bottom of my home page, containing links to a searching tool, an index, a glossary, and help information. Following this logo is a copyright statement, an E-mail link to
me (the creator of the home page), the URL for the page, and a note on
when the page was last updated. The type of information appearing
after this logo is not only consistent with library policy, it is also standard recommended practice for all Web page development. It fully
identifies who is responsible for the creation and maintenance of the
page; it informs you when the page was last revised; and it provides an
immediate E-mail link to contact the page's creator.

Although the "look" and "feel" of the distance-education home page
is very important for its usability, the real value of the page can be
measured in large part by its "content." The home page should provide
clear links to all of the major services and resources provided to support distance-education students. In developing my home page, I recognized six major categories that should be represented in the content
of the page. A brief discussion of each category follows.

The home page should provide a link to information about who is
eligible for library services and how they can register. In my case, I
have linked to a page that informs the reader that library services are
limited to students enrolled in one of the degree-granting programs
sponsored by the Center for Credit Programs or the School of Management at the University of Iowa. The Web page provides the addresses, toll-free telephone numbers, and E-mail links to the center
and the school.

In addition to informing users about who is eligible, the home page
should provide links to the most relevant electronic resources for
distance-education students, and if there are several degree-granting
programs, subject divisions should be made. The University of Iowa
has several thousand students in distance-education programs, but
these programs can be divided into eight broad subject categories—
business, computer science, electrical engineering, education, liberal
studies, library science, nursing and health sciences, and social work.
Some of the subjects (business, nursing, and engineering, for example)
are covered so well by branch library home pages that I essentially
have just linked to the branch libraries. For other subjects, however
(liberal studies, library science, and social work, for instance), I have
developed lists of the most relevant resources. For these lists, which
run several pages in length, I have eased user access by providing a
table of contents at the top of each list, with anchors providing quick
access to the relevant subdivisions of the list.

How a library provides access to many of these electronic resources can be tricky, however. In most cases, contracts for Web-based databases require that access be limited to the students, faculty, and staff at each institution. In some cases, access can be limited by requiring an ID number and a password. This method allows for both on-campus and off-campus users, but informing all students of the proper password can be difficult. Changing it and then trying to reinform all students of the correct password can be even more difficult. For security reasons, however, the password probably should be changed regularly each semester or each year.

Another method of controlling access to individuals at a particular institution involves the use of computer Internet Protocol (IP) addresses. In their contracts with universities and other institutions, many database vendors restrict users by their computer IP addresses, thus limiting all users to those with on-campus or on-site IP addresses only. Such a situation can cause a serious problem for students located off-campus. Many schools get around the problem, however, by developing something called a "proxy server." This is what the University of Iowa has done. When an off-campus student connects his or her computer with our proxy server, the student can access any of the library's restricted databases, because in the database connection, the proxy server provides á false IP address, masking the fact that the student is accessing the file from off-campus. Essentially, for the database vendor, it appears as if the student's computer is actually located on-campus. On all of the "shortcut" links from my home page, I have included a note about the proxy server with a link to instructions on how to configure one's Web-browser to work with it.

A category of content that should be represented on the distance-education home page is information regarding document delivery services, including, if possible, Web-based submission forms. A growing number of libraries are offering direct document delivery services to their distance-education students. At the University of Iowa, we began offering a document delivery service to all distance-education students during the fall of 1999. For a charge of three dollars, a student can have an article faxed to any telephone number or mailed to any address, and he or she can have a book delivered by UPS to any address. The materials are usually sent out within twenty-four to forty-eight hours, and the cost is charged to the student's university bill. The Web pages that I have developed under this link provide information on the service as well as Web-based forms for submitting requests.

Another category of content that should be represented on the home page is information on reference services, including a Web-based submission form, if possible. In this case, my link goes directly to an E-mail reference request form, and it also informs the user about my toll-free telephone number in case the student would prefer to talk to me. In addition, for students needing more in-depth assistance with a research project, I have included a link to a Web-based consultation form.

A category of content that should be represented on the home page is access to Web-based tutorials and other methods of user education. In my case, I have linked to the library's computer-assisted instruction module entitled "Library Explorer." This tutorial is primarily designed to help undergraduates, such as those enrolled in our off-campus Bachelor of Liberal Studies program. In addition, links to on-line help are provided in several locations, and the Frequently Asked Questions Web page also serves an educational purpose.

Another category of content that should be represented on the distance-education home page is access to some form of evaluation and feedback, preferably offering a Web-based submission form. In this case, the E-mail link that appears at the bottom of each of my Web pages is a standard practice for providing one method for feedback and evaluation, and most regular Internet users would recognize this link as a method for asking questions or providing feedback. In addition, however, in order to provide a more obvious method for evaluation, I have provided a link to a Web-based "Suggestion" form, highlighting my desire for student feedback. In the near future, I hope to develop an on-line evaluation form, addressing specific questions and concerns, in order to get additional feedback.

The Internet has profoundly influenced the manner in which libraries serve distance-education students. Now, students far from campus can access most of the electronic resources and services that are available to on-campus students. In order to ease the access and usability of the library's resources and services, Web pages must be designed with remote, off-campus users in mind. These users will, of course, have a wide variety of Internet experiences and skills, and the design should take that truth to heart. In order to increase the usability of the Web site, the creator would be wise to develop a philosophy that emphasizes consistency, simplicity, and logic in the presentation, as well as the relevancy of the content. For distance-education librarians, the Internet represents the most powerful tool available for reaching our primary clientele. We should seize the opportunity to use this tool to serve our students. By developing Web sites to support off-campus students, distance-education librarians can succeed in overcoming the challenge of location and remoteness. Through hard work and a commonsense philosophy, librarians can develop strong Web sites that are designed to serve from a distance.

# 31

# Supporting and Educating Students at a Distance: The Open University (U.K.) Library's Experience of Developing Learner Support

*Alison Bremner*

The Open University (OU) is the largest distance-learning university in the United Kingdom and has approximately 175,000 students. The library's remittal since 1995 has been to provide services to these students, particularly via electronic means. This is a phased development and it is anticipated that in the early stages, the services will be offered to mainly postgraduate and project-based courses. However, all students can access the library's Web pages and are able to use the information there to assist their studies <http://www.open.ac.uk/library/>.

Students may wish to use traditional library resources, and so the library has produced a database entitled Access to U.K. Higher Education Libraries, which gives details of borrowing rights and opening times at other U.K. academic libraries. All the information is verified by the institution on a six-month basis.

Learner support staff register students to enable them to use on-line databases and electronic journals, and 7,500 students registered to use the resources in 1999. Guides to the resources available are produced in electronic and paper format.

The library has a service entitled ROUTES (Resources for Open University Teachers and Students), which is building a collection of Internet resources selected to support OU courses. A key feature of the service is that subject-specialist librarians, academic staff, and OU students are all involved in the selection procedure. ROUTES describes and classifies these resources following strict cataloging and evaluation criteria to ensure that the information is both accurate and reliable <http://routes.open.ac.uk/>.

In keeping with other libraries, the OU Library is trying to balance the provision of electronic and nonelectronic resources. Library staff are working with academic colleagues within faculties to produce a Collection Management Policy that should give guidelines for the development of paper and electronic collections over the next ten years.

# 32

# Information Competency Continuum: A University, K–12 Collaboration

*Eleanor Mitchell and Stephanie Sterling Brasley*

We have been asked (and have had occasion to remind ourselves) why a college library would launch an instructional initiative that focuses on a K–12 population at UCLA. We provide a host of reference, research, and instructional services for more than 16,000 undergraduates. We are also involved with the community beyond our own campus through an ambitious schedule of exhibits, performances, and programs aimed at advanced placement high school and community college students from Los Angeles. Like many academic librarians, we sometimes recoil from the added workload of school-aged visitors (particularly in large unruly numbers, particularly during peak study times for our own students). Our area of expertise is at the farther end of the information-seeking spectrum.

One factor that drove our involvement with a K–12 initiative was self-interest. While the primary focus of the College Library is on the undergraduate student at UCLA, increasingly librarians work with high school students—both those enrolled in the advanced placement courses and those who find their way here because of our visibility and central location. Interactions with our own incoming freshmen and these high school and community college students have suggested that there is much that could be done to better prepare them, and sooner, for the kinds of information experiences that they encounter in college. Such preparation would serve them at every level of their schooling, and would both reinforce and expand upon skills learned at each level. Such preparation would, in a sense, make our jobs easier.

Another motivation to extend our instructional initiatives was a desire to support the university's commitment to community outreach.

In 1995, the University of California's (UC) Regents Outreach Task Force was charged with developing new directions for UC outreach to increase the number of disadvantaged students eligible to enroll at the university. Under the rubric of "community outreach to create opportunities," it was hoped that partnering with the K–14 community would both improve existing school environments and begin building the competencies for future success.

An existing initiative on our own campus provided another way to connect our programmatic ambitions to those of our environment and to demonstrate the library's interest in aligning its efforts with and supporting those of the UCLA administration. The UCLA K–16 Collaborative was established in 1996 as a model for university involvement in the community. The intent was to focus on a single geographic area and make a replicable difference. The collaborative focused on the Venice–Westchester Cluster of the Los Angeles Unified School District (LAUSD), with 25,000 students, notable for its ethnic and socioeconomic diversity. Using multiple strategies and approaches, from teacher development to curricular reform to family outreach, and partnering with other academic, corporate, public, and community entities, the aim was to create a replicable model for high academic achievement. With these two university and school district programs providing a framework, College Library developed a pilot program to explore the extension of information literacy efforts into a local public school environment.

## THE INFORMATION LITERACY
## INSTRUCTIONAL PIPELINE PARTNERSHIP

The Information Literacy Instructional Pipeline Partnership (ILIPP) grew from College Library's efforts to interact with the community, in a meaningful way, at an appropriate level, lending expertise and a coordinating presence. The "pipeline" speaks to the sense that the kind of literacy that we would like to see in our own students can begin early on in the educational experience, as children learn to incorporate quality information into their school assignments.

The seeds for this project were planted in meetings with Vice Chancellor Raymond Paredes from the Office of Academic Development at UCLA, who directed us to the existing Venice–Westchester relationship and the possibility of incorporating support and technology of the UC Nexus project. With this geographic focus, we were able to identify working partners, other stakeholders in the community, and schools with whom we could explore needs and develop the programmatic parameters. At a planning retreat held at the Los Angeles Public Library's Venice Branch in December of 1998, we started from a stated interest in literacy programs and moved co-operatively to a focus on information literacy rather than reading literacy. This was an area of similar need but one that had greater immediate relevance to those of us in higher education. The planning participants developed program criteria against which we continue to measure our plans: realistic goals, concrete evaluation tools, teacher training component, replicability, and so forth. After presenting the retreat outcomes to district elementary school principals in January, we drafted grant proposals and waited.

In August 1999, we received notification that our first proposal had been funded by a University of California initiative called UC Nexus. We were able to garner additional monetary support from the UCLA/Venice–Westchester Collaborative. In sum, we received approximately $28,000 from grants. While a modest amount, this provided basic support to implement the project. In addition, the UCLA Library contributed substantive in-kind contributions in the form of overhead costs for office equipment and supplies, release time for the librarian project coordinator, and UCLA librarian trainers and instructors.

## PARTNERS

When formulating the plan for an information literacy pilot, we identified partners who shared our vision and offered elements necessary to its success. We discovered that frequently, when we introduced the phrase "information literacy" in discussions, people automatically thought we were speaking of either computer literacy or educational technology. So, at times, we had to clarify the concept so that all project partners were starting from the same point of reference.

The primary partners (and participants) in this project were the Venice–Westchester teachers and librarians. The project aimed to recruit twenty teachers from elementary, middle, and secondary schools, and representatives from public and school libraries. When drafting criteria for teacher selection, we hoped to have a balance of teachers across grade levels and subject areas. We were looking for teachers interested in learning or improving their own information literacy and instructional technology skills. We hoped to attract individuals who had influence among colleagues and who might be opinion leaders. Thus, the best participant would be someone whose enthusiasm would be contagious, and who would be able to effect a change in the culture and instructional practices of his or her school. Recruitment efforts stressed advantages to the school and to the individual teacher. One of the program's major benefits included an enhancement of the teacher participants' knowledge and skills base in the area of information literacy, and instructional technology and design. Concomitant advantages for teachers included built-in incentives—continuing education credits and stipends. In addition, schools were compensated with funds to pay substitute teachers during the weekday institute sessions.

## PARTICIPANTS

Our initial participants were seven high school teachers, six elementary school teachers, and one middle school teacher. We endeavored to form cadres of teachers at each school to provide a support infrastructure for them in addition to the support provided by the program coordinator and steering committee members. Public library, middle school, and high school librarians rounded out the pilot group.

## FUNDING SOURCE

The pilot's primary funding source and a major partner was UC Nexus, a project of the University of California Office of the President. According to its Web site, "UC Nexus uses Internet technologies to connect University of California faculty, staff and students with K–12 teachers, students, and their schools and communities" <http://nexus-44a-2.berkeley.edu/Home/index.asp>. UC Nexus offers an on-line interactive learning space that has a number of features, the core one for our project being "My Communities." "My Communities" enabled formal and informal collaborative groups to engage in synchronous and asynchronous discussions, post messages to a bulletin board, and so on. This feature supported our focus on communication and feedback among participants.

UC Nexus required that those given grants build in strong university faculty collaborations as part of any K–12 activities. Although, as librarians, we were accustomed to interacting with faculty to meet mutual instruction objectives for students, the requirement allowed us to communicate and collaborate with faculty in a meaningful way. We partnered with faculty members from UCLA's Graduate School of Education and Information Studies (GSE and IS) and from the Library Information Science program at San Jose State University, who acted as presenters, discussion leaders, and evaluators. The UCLA Graduate School of Education and Information Studies brought to the project both information science faculty who were thoroughly versed in the information literacy subject matter and research, and education faculty with expertise in school, administrative, and curricular matters. In addition to these critical groups, community colleges in the area were another important link in the information literacy partnership continuum.

Other partners were librarian and teacher practitioners who lead some of the institute segments.

A successful information literacy program requires a strong link between the school library media center librarian and teachers. However, the LAUSD, the largest school district in the country, does not provide library media teachers in its elementary schools, relying instead, like many California public elementary school libraries, on volunteers and part-time paraprofessional staff. While we were fortunate to have the involvement from the beginning of the LAUSD Media Services Office, we needed librarians to actively partner with the classroom teachers when there was no school librarian. We sought to form partnerships with public library systems, in particular, the Los Angeles Public Library (LAPL), which serves the schools in this cluster. Such relationships between Venice–Westchester Cluster elementary school teachers and LAPL librarians supported key approaches of our pilot program.

## THE ILIPP PROGRAM

The key objectives of ILIPP were to introduce teachers to the concept of information competencies, to promote the development of lesson plans and class activities that integrate these competencies, to teach K–12 students information skills, and to introduce new technologies and use them to enhance teacher collaboration and communication. The program concept emerged from a community of practitioners— librarians and educators—rather than from top to down from an administrative entity, and was based upon some shared, core notions. Librarians and classroom teachers were to share expertise and collaborate on curricular design. There would be a sequence of grade- and discipline-based curricular modules. There would be mechanisms for sharing results and evaluating outcomes. Also, the project would be replicable and ongoing.

There are many definitions and models of information literacy from education, information science, and related fields, such as psychology and history. The ILIPP planning committee was challenged to find among all of these perspectives a balanced approach to teaching information literacy skills. The American Association of School Librarians (AASL) and the Association for Educational Communications Technology (AECT) developed nine information standards for student learning that are described in *Information Power: Building Partnerships for Learning*. Their standards were divided into three broad categories, the first pertaining to information literacy, the second to independent learning, and the third to social responsibility. For the pilot, we focused on the standards in the information literacy category that state: "The student who is information literate: accesses information efficiently and effectively; evaluates information critically and competently; and uses information accurately and creatively." Indicators, "standards in action," and content-area standards examples were spelled out in the companion volume to *Information Power,* titled *Information Literacy Standards for Student Learning.*

The California School Library Association (CSLA) recently published the second edition of *From Library Skills to Information Literacy: A Handbook for the Twenty-First Century.* Its information literacy model closely mirrored that of AASL/AECT in that the primary goal was to teach students to access, evaluate, and use information. The CSLA work, which was written for teachers and library media teachers, was adopted as the primary text for the ILIPP institute, along with *Information Literacy Standards for Student Learning.* Key chapters from *Information Literacy: A Review of the Research: A Guide for Practitioners and Researchers* by David Loertscher and Blanche Woolls, as well as articles and Web site URLs, were disseminated to teachers in resources notebooks.

As in many other school districts involved in ongoing curricular reform, statewide and district standards are the underpinnings to what teachers teach students in Venice–Westchester. Our primary tactic for galvanizing school administrators was to acknowledge the importance of the standards and to highlight those standards that spoke to information literacy issues. The institute's curriculum, then, was a melding of the national, state, and professional standards mentioned above with those articulated by the district in which Venice–Westchester operated.

## INFORMATION LITERACY INSTITUTE

The ILIPP Information Literacy Institute consisted of five all-day, nonconsecutive sessions during a six-month period beginning in January 2000. The UC Nexus on-line learning environment, a distance education component, complemented and supplemented the in-class sessions. The goal of the first two days was to lay the theoretical foundation for information literacy concepts. A faculty member from the GSE and IS Department of Information Studies led a session on the universe of information. Information literacy definitions and models were presented, with teacher and librarian participants creating a working definition that fit their school community. A portion of the second day and the entire third day focused on teaching participants how to use specific sources, primarily those available electronically. Instructors emphasized the rich resources of the Los Angeles Public Library, the University of California's California Digital Library, and sources available from LAUSDNet (LAUSD's Web site).

On the fourth day, teachers and librarians worked in groups according to grade areas to develop lesson plans. An instructional technology teacher led a segment on how to incorporate technology into the curriculum so that teachers would be able to devise both traditional lesson plans as well as Web-based activities. An education advocate from PacBell taught teachers how to use Filamentality, a software product that helps teachers create Web-based activities, such as Web quests. Teachers presented lesson plans formally to the group on the fifth day. An overarching goal for our instructors was to have them model the teaching techniques we hoped teachers would use in their classrooms. Thus, we planned instructional sessions that incorporated active learning, collaborative learning, resource-based learning, the Socratic method, and so on, for the in-person and virtual sessions.

The on-line sessions provided participants the means to follow up and respond to material presented at the in-person sessions, to engage in discussions with faculty on information-related topics, and to communicate and collaborate with colleagues. While planning these sessions, we recognized that we had to be cognizant of the underlying principles and issues related to distance education. Fortunately, the UC Nexus principal investigator, Laura (Beth) Wellman, was very experienced in hosting in-person and on-line institutes and furnished us with feedback on our on-line assignments.

## ASSESSMENT

Evaluation of both the overall program and the institute was a key element of our design. One approach to assessment was the first day assignment, where participants completed an information literacy pretest and a questionnaire on their computer-related skills. At the end of the program, they completed a posttest, posted journal entries to the UC Nexus Web site, and participated in focus groups. We looked at the program's process and infrastructure for the institute and made recommendations for improvements the following year. We will incorporate these suggestions into a dissemination plan for the program. Due to the short time frame this year, teachers did not have the opportunity to teach any of the lessons they developed. We hope to have teachers present their lessons and assess student performance in another phase of the project.

## CONCLUSION

It has been a challenge to find information in the literature on similar collaborative models centered on information literacy partnerships involving K–12. Presentations at conferences have been the primary vehicle by which we have found out about comparable ventures. These characteristics form the heart of our program:

- Standards-based approach
- Melding of national and local standards to make the pilot relevant to that community
- Teacher-mentor model
- Sequenced approach
- Teacher participant representation from K–12
- Actual and virtual learning environments
- Traditional and Web-based lesson plans
- Cadres of teachers from same site form internal learning community
- Melding of theory and practice

The pilot partnership has been a departure from the College Library's traditional outreach efforts. However, we made fruitful contacts in other departments, introduced a replicable model to teachers, and brought heightened visibility to the library both on campus and in the surrounding community. The College Library has laid a foundation for similar meaningful collaborations.

# 33

# Teaching Evidence-Based Health Care: A Model for Developing Faculty–Librarian Partnerships

*Clarissa C. Fisher and Rick W. Wilson*

Evidence-based health care requires practitioners to develop decision-making skills based on analysis of research data. It requires a knowledge of information sources: how to locate, to evaluate, and apply the results found in those sources. Therefore, instruction using evidence-based health care lends itself to collaboration and partnership between teaching faculty and librarians who teach these information-seeking skills.

The authors, a physical therapist and a librarian, devised a project to introduce physical therapy students to evidence-based health care. The authors believed that this introduction would enhance the students' ability to function in evidence-based health care by improving their information-seeking skills, their critical thinking skills, and their professional judgment.

Professional judgment is the keystone of medical practice. In 1990, the American Philosophical Association defined professional judgment as "A goal oriented decision making or problem solving process carried out in the interest of a client wherein one gives reasoned consideration to relevant information, criteria, methods, content, principles, policies, and resources."[1] This definition depicts the close relationship between professional judgment and the goals of evidence-based health care.

Each of the authors had specific contributions to make in the development of the evidence-based class based upon their expertise of teaching in their specialties. This collaborative effort resulted in the following decisions. Though there are entire programs based on evidence-based health care, it was decided to offer the experience in a single course. The graduate level course, Scientific Inquiry in the Physical

Therapy curriculum, was chosen. The authors decided to rely heavily on information technology because the depth and breadth of research information needed could be easily and rapidly identified by its use. It was decided that the assignment should be one that would develop critical thinking and decision-making skills as well as lifelong learning skills. Database selection, instruction in information-seeking skills, and instruction in the criteria for evaluating information were included, since locating information that supports patient care decisions is integral to this method of teaching. Evaluation of the results of using this paradigm would be necessary for future decision making concerning the appropriateness of this teaching methodology.

## METHODOLOGY

The Scientific Inquiry class was composed of thirty-one graduate students and was divided into seven groups of four each and one group of three. Each group was assigned a common musculoskeletal problem normally seen in practice, that is, thoracic outlet syndrome, subacromial impingement, lateral epicondylitis, carpal tunnel syndrome, trochanteric bursitis, retropatellar pain syndrome, ankle inversion sprains, and plantar fasciitis. Each student in the group investigated the efficacy of a particular aspect of therapeutic intervention such as the use of physical agents, therapeutic exercise, manual therapy, and patient/family education. The outcome of the group assignment was for each group to develop a clinical guideline for its problem by locating research studies to support the best treatment recommended and the identification and exclusion of other possibilities. A clinical guideline provides access to authoritative sources grounded in solid clinical research for the making of patient care decisions and are the standard treatment used by practitioners.

The details of the assignment were included in an educational prescription: "that patient care situations would be used by the students to decide what needed to be learned and the class presentations would include: what information they located, how they located the information, the validity and usefulness of the information and how the information would influence their clinical judgment."[2] Note that the emphasis is on how, what, and the application of clinical judgment.

To assist the students in identifying research materials, it was decided that the following information sources would be used: current library CD databases, print materials, on-line databases, and a class Web page containing links to full-text materials. The class Web page contained four very broad subject areas identified as physical therapy, evidence-based practice, biomechanics, and miscellaneous.

These subject areas included links to class assignments, association Web pages, full-text textbooks, clinical guidelines, and links to other libraries. Students could also interact with the instructor via E-mail.

The on-line databases to be taught included MEDLINE via PubMed, and the NCLIVE databases including Cumulative Index to Nursing and Allied Health Literature, Academic Search Elite, Health Sources Plus, ERIC, and Clinical Reference Systems. PubMed, the free Web version of MEDLINE supported by the National Library of Medicine, was chosen as the main database for searching. This choice was based on the premise that PubMed will be the database students will use when out in practice and on research that indicates that MEDLINE indexes 95 percent to 100 percent of the articles in the top twenty-five journals cited by physical therapists.[3] The other databases do not consistently rank this high in the percentage of material covered.

The Cumulative Index to Nursing and Allied Health Literature (CINAHL) was also chosen for use as it indexes the literature of the allied health professions. It places great emphasis on patient education techniques and information, one of the four areas students were to research.

The NCLIVE databases were included because of the availability of full-text articles in these databases. Several major journals in each subject are indexed and are provided with full text. In addition, some of the peripheral literature for physical therapy is also available in full text. Using these databases augmented the number of journals available to students locally.

## INFORMATION SEEKING SESSION I

The first information-seeking skills session was an introduction to the mechanics of using the Basic Search feature in PubMed, which is keyword based, and keyword searching in the other databases. Indexing and database construction were also introduced, as the understanding of these features are crucial in the construction of subject-specific searches. Next was the identification of the separate search concepts that compose each search question. Proper coverage of all search question concepts is accomplished by using Boolean operators to combine concepts to form the search strategy.

The basic search feature of PubMed was introduced so the students could perform a keyword search and to give the students the "feel" for searching. The basic search screen in PubMed maps keyword searches to MeSH browser subject headings and transparently explodes them. Using this feature allowed the students to perform broad searches without understanding exactly how the results were achieved. A fuller explanation of these features was included in the second session after the students had experimented with the database.

At the end of the first session, the students were given an assignment to search their topic using the basic search feature in PubMed and keyword searches in the other databases that were introduced. In the second session, students were to present their search strategies and the number of articles located. Before the second class meeting, the librarian performed a benchmark search on each topic to determine the amount of information available and to determine different strategies needed to identify the material available in each area.

## INFORMATION SEEKING SESSION II

When the students returned for the second information seeking session, they were excited about their searches even though they had been somewhat frustrated with the results. They had located either too much information, too little information, or had been unable to locate any research data on their topic. The patient education aspect of the topic gave students the most difficulty, as little research has been performed in this area. Each student's search problems were discussed and alternative search strategies suggested by the class.

After their initial attempts at searching, the students were eager and ready for more complex strategies. To increase the quality and specificity of student searches, new skills including limiting, advanced Boolean searching, use of specific-subject heading/subheading combinations, and the meaning and use of "explode" were taught. In addition, tips on the use of specific subject headings for locating research and treatment outcomes were introduced using the MeSH Browser. The choice of which databases to search was considered, as each database has a particular strength. Recommendations concerning the kind of topics that run best in a particular database were given. Class time was then allocated for students to work on their searches with assistance from the professor and the librarian. At the end of the class, they were encouraged to contact the librarian if they continued to have difficulties.

## ARTICLE EVALUATION

Evaluation of informational articles is an essential step in identifying the best research to be applied to patient care. Students were responsible for reading, discussing, and applying the information in the following articles that would help them to evaluate the literature. These articles were in a series titled "User's Guides to Medical Literature" authored by faculty at McMaster University. They were published in the *Journal of the American Medical Association* in 1993–94. The articles include "how to get started, how to use an article about therapy or prevention (were the results valid and applicable?), how to use and article about a diagnostic test (were the results valid and applicable?), how to use an article about harm, how to use an article about prognosis and how to use an overview."[4]

## EVALUATION OF TEACHING EVIDENCE-BASED HEALTH CARE

To evaluate the success or failure of this attempt at teaching evidence-based health care, the California Critical Thinking Dispositions Inventory (CCTDI) and the California Critical Thinking Skills Test (CCTST) were administered to the students. The students were tested twice, once at the beginning of the semester and once at the end of the semester to measure the amount of change in critical thinking and decision making during the semester. In addition to these tests, an analysis of the citations from each paper was performed. Instructor anecdotal comments were also considered part of the evaluation.

**Responsiveness of CCTDI Scores. Longitudinal Data From First Year Physical Therapy Students (N = 31)**

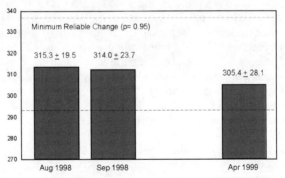

**Responsiveness of CCTST Scores. Longitudinal Data From First Year Physical Therapy Students (N = 31)**

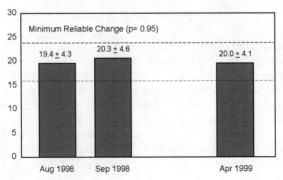

# RESULTS

The charts indicate that there was no meaningful change in scores produced by the CCTDI or the CCTST over the course of the academic year. The dotted line represents the minimum reliable change. Data from the present study produced critical values ($p > 0.95$) for meaningful gain scores of 19 points for the CCTDI and 4 points for the CCTST. Though student scores fluctuated slightly between the pretest and the posttest, neither test reached the threshold of meaningful change. This finding of no significant change in critical thinking scores supports previous studies conducted with other health professions students.[5] Most of our physical therapy students' scores were clustered in the upper end of the scale on the pretest. This phenomenon would have the effect of limiting the available range of improvement for our physical therapy students, leading to systematic underestimation of critical thinking gains for the group. Other published studies demonstrated a meaningful gain in critical thinking skills.[6] The pretest scores of subjects in these studies were considerably lower than in the previously mentioned studies, including our study.

Possible explanations for not observing any change in the critical thinking scores are (1) undesirable measurement properties of the critical thinking tests, particularly the ceiling-effects that may have limited the available range of improvement scores for our students, leading to systematic underestimation of critical thinking gains for the group; (2) students successfully demonstrated their ability to identify, locate, retrieve, interpret, and apply evidence from the literature to clinical problems; and (3) the skills required to identify, locate, retrieve, interpret, and apply evidence from the literature to clinical problems are not represented in critical thinking tests designed for use with a general population of college-educated people.

The analysis of the student papers produced the following results. The 31 papers contained 244 citations to journal articles with an average of 8 journal citations per paper. The 244 citations were located in 60 professional journals. Of those 60 journals cited, 70 percent were refereed journals. That is, between five and six journals per paper were from refereed journals. The authors believe that the high use of peer-reviewed journals speaks to the quality of the students' information retrieval efforts. Patient education was the aspect of each problem that was the most difficult for the students to document and may account for some of the nonrefereed journals.

It may also be possible, based on the above test scores, that the students did not improve their critical thinking skills. However, the authors believe that the quality of the finished projects argues against this conclusion.

# CONCLUSION

Using class assignments to locate research materials for decision making is within the purview of physical therapists. Teaching searching skills for identifying and locating research materials is within the purview of librarians. Students receive quality instruction by combining the expertise of the faculty member and the librarian.

Patient education is an important aspect of the treatment for any condition. It will be retained as an aspect of each topic. A better explanation will be given concerning the lack of research data in this area and care plans indicating patient education will be accepted as support documents for decision making. Patient education is definitely an area needing additional research.

# NOTES

1. American Philosophical Association, "Critical Thinking: A Statement of Expert Consensus for Purposes of Educational Assessment and Instruction," (1990). ERIC document # ED315–423.

2. D. L. Sackett, W. S. Richardson, W. Rosenberg, and R. B. Haynes, *Evidence-Based Medicine: How to Practice and Teach EBM* (London: Churchill Livingston, 1998).

3. E. M. Wakiji, "Mapping the Literature of Physical Therapy," *Bulletin of the Medical Library Association* 85, no. 3 (July 1997): 284–88.

4. A. D. Oxman, D. L. Sackett, and G. H. Guyatt, "How to Get Started," *JAMA, the Journal of the American Medical Association* 270, no. 17 (November 2, 1933): 2093–5; G. H. Guyatt, D. L. Sackett, and D. J. Cook, "Users' Guides to the Medical Literature. II. How to Use an Article about Therapy or Prevention. A. Are the Results of the Study Valid?" *JAMA, the Journal of the American Medical Association* 270, no. 21 (December 1, 1993): 2598–601; Guyatt, Sackett, and Cook, "Users' Guides to the Medical Literature. II. How to Use an Article about Therapy or Prevention. B. What Were the Results and Will They Help Me in Caring for My Patients?" *JAMA, the Journal of the American Medical Association*; R. Jaeschke, G. H. Guyatt, and D. L. Sackett, "Users' Guides to the Medical Literature. III. How to Use an Article about a Diagnostic Test. A. Are the Results of the Study Valid?" *JAMA, the Journal of the American Medical Association* 271, no. 5 (February 2, 1994): 389–91; Jaeschke, Guyatt, and Sackett, "Users' Guides to the Medical Literature. III. How to Use an Article about a Diagnostic Test. B. What Are the Results and Will They Help Me in Caring for My Patients?" *JAMA, the Journal of the American Medical Association* 271, no. 9 (March 2, 1994): 703–7; M. S. Levine, Walter H. Lee, T. Haines, A. Holbrook, and V. Moyer, "Users' Guides to the Medical Literature. IV. How to Use an Article about Harm," *JAMA, the Journal of the American Medical Association* 271, no. 20 (May 25, 1994): 1615-9; and A. Laupacis, G. Wells, W. S. Richardson, and P. Tugwell, "Users' Guides to the Medical Literature. V. How to Use an Article

about Prognosis," *JAMA, the Journal of the American Medical Association* 272, no. 3 (July 20, 1994): 234–7.

5. A. D. Oxman, D. J. Cook, and G. H. Guyatt, "Users' Guides to the Medical Literature. VI. How to Use an Overview," *JAMA, the Journal of the American Medical Association* 272, no. 17 (November 2, 1994): 1367–71; C. A. Pepa, J. M. Brown, and E. M. Alverson, "A Comparison of Critical Thinking Abilities between Accelerated and Traditional Baccalaureate Students," *Journal of Nursing Education* 36, no. 1 (January 1997): 46–48; E. Sullivan, "Critical Thinking, Creativity, Clinical Performance, and Achievement in RN Students," *Nurse Educator* 12, no. 2 (February 1987): 12–16; and M. H. Adams, L. M. Stover, and J. F. Whitlow, "A Longitudinal Evaluation of Baccalaureate Nursing Students' Critical Thinking Abilities," *Journal of Nursing Education* 38, no. 3 (March 1999): 139–41.

6. M. Berger, "Critical Thinking Ability and Nursing Students," *Journal of Nursing Education* 23 (1984): 306–8; and M. S. Gross, E. S. Takazawa, and C. L. Rose, "Critical Thinking and Nursing Education," *Journal of Nursing Education* 26, no. 8 (August 1987): 317–23.

# 34

# Web Technology and Evidence-Based Medicine: Usability Testing an EBM Web Site

*Robert Vander Hart and Margaret Spinner*

Evidence-based medicine (EBM) has been defined as "the conscientious, explicit, and judicious use of current best evidence in making decisions about the care of individual patients. The practice of evidence-based medicine means integrating individual clinical expertise with the best available external clinical evidence from systematic research."[1] As this definition implies, the nature of EBM necessitates the efficient retrieval of quality clinical information. Web sites that aim to provide instruction in EBM search methods must address the severe time constraints that exist for their primary audience—clinicians and medical students. For Web designers truly interested in producing an effective learning resource, usability testing is becoming the most reliable and often the easiest assessment technique available. Web site usability tests offer much more accurate and honest feedback about users' experiences than surveys or focus groups.

In 1998, two librarians at the University of Massachusetts Medical School teamed with a faculty member from the Department of Family Medicine and Community Health on a Web-based initiative to facilitate instruction in evidence-based practice. This partnership culminated in the award of an Innovations in Medical Education Grant (IMEG) from the University's Office of Medical Education. Project goals were to provide a vehicle for communication and collaboration on EBM-based programs and education; to facilitate the integration of EBM practice into the undergraduate medical curriculum, third-year clerkships, and faculty development programs; and to introduce a distance-learning option for the study of EBM.

The project Web site <http://library.umassmed.edu/EBM/index.html> is organized into several sections. Team members developed the content of three of these sections, which provide information on the definition and components of EBM and also include tutorials accessible to the public. The remaining sections link to database resources and other sites devoted to EBM education and practice.

## TUTORIAL EXERCISE

The heart of the EBM Web site as a learning tool is the tutorial exercise. This three-part exercise guides individual users through the process of defining a clinical question, deciding on the best type of study to address the question, and performing a literature search. Second-year medical students in the Patient, Physician, and Society (PPS) class completed this tutorial in the spring of 1999. Rather than having to complete this assignment as a group in a computer lab, students were free to complete the Web-based tutorial at their convenience either at home or in the library.

### Part 1: Defining the Clinical Question

Part 1 begins with a case study written by the project team's faculty member. This hypothetical scenario presents a clinical problem pertaining to the prognosis of a sixty-four-year-old woman diagnosed with congestive heart failure (CHF). The student is instructed to formulate a clinical question that addresses all the relevant factors of the case. General tips are provided to assist the student in this task. After entering their question, their name, and E-mail address in Web form boxes, students submit their work. Perl scripts are used to send this information to members of the development team.

The student is then taken to a page generated by Perl scripts. This page reprints the question and asks, "Is Your Question Complete?" After reading case-specific help, the student has the opportunity to review and revise the question. The help text addresses these issues: type of treatment provided to the patient, type and severity of CHF, cause of CHF, relevant demographic factors, time of onset of CHF, and specific measure of future risk.

After submitting a revised question, the student is taken by Perl scripts to a new screen and presented with a sample question written by the team's faculty member. The sample question links to the relevant case-specific help text, and for comparative purposes the student's revised question is also printed on the screen. After reviewing their question in light of the sample question, the students proceed to Part 2.

**Part 2: Deciding on the Best Type of Study to Address the Question**

The purpose of this part of the tutorial is to help students identify the most useful type of study for various types of clinical questions (etiology, diagnosis, prognosis, and therapy). For reference purposes the sample question from Part 1 is reprinted on the screen. Help is available to the student in the form of a chart that matches the type of clinical question with the most appropriate type of study. Students submit their answer, name, and E-mail address in a manner similar to Part 1. They are then presented with the correct answer and a brief statement about ideal study conditions.

**Part 3: Performing a Literature Search**

Part 3 includes the literature search assignment in which the student must query the MEDLINE database to locate relevant studies that answer the clinical question and qualify as *best* evidence. The actual search interface utilizes frames technology with search help provided on the left and the Ovid Technologies' Web gateway log-in screen in the center frame. Navigational buttons along the top of the screen link to the assignment statement, the case study, and the sample clinical question. Students decide on the two best articles from their search results and submit the MEDLINE records plus their search strategy via E-mail to members of the project team.

## TUTORIAL EVALUATION

At the completion of the Web-based tutorial exercise, students filled out a paper evaluation form in which they rated the effectiveness of the tutorial's design and help screens. They were given space on the form to describe strengths and weaknesses of the exercise and to make suggestions for improving the tutorial. The results were analyzed and the exercise received generally positive remarks. For example, in response to the statement, "Providing directions for searching on the left side of the screen with the Ovid window on the right was helpful," nearly 44 percent of the respondents agreed strongly, and almost 38 percent moderately agreed. These percentages would seem to indicate that the design of the literature search interface was effective.

Some of the students' remarks, however, were inconsistent. For example, when students were asked on the evaluation form how the tutorial could be improved, one student responded "Delete it!" while others wrote that no changes were necessary. Many students fill out evaluation forms in a hurried manner and do not always give a great deal of thought to their comments if any are made at all. Considering these factors, the project team realized that the evaluations were unreliable as a true measure of the tutorial's success or failure.

## USABILITY TESTING

The team investigated a feasible alternative to survey methods of assessing a Web site's success. Usability testing was identified as an effective tool. Usability studies have increasingly become a necessary step in effective ongoing Web site design and improvement. Web sites devoted to advocating usability techniques have increased designers' awareness of the need to test their own sites.[2]

Usability studies can be easy and inexpensive to perform and are usually effective with as few as five or six volunteers.[3] Test administrators observe volunteers completing several tasks on a Web site and record the volunteers' comments and behaviors. Volunteers' browsing paths and the amounts of time they require to complete each task are also noted. Most tests need not take much longer than thirty minutes. To avoid reducing the value of test results, observers should resist the temptation to provide help or suggestions while the volunteer is performing the tasks. Most Web site usability problems become readily apparent to designers within the first two or three administrations of a test.

## EBM TESTING AND REPORTING

A usability study of the EBM Web site was undertaken. The main goal for the study was to test the accuracy of the spring 1999 evaluations. For example, were the help screens provided on the tutorial really useful, as 74 percent of the responses on the evaluation forms indicated? The team also hoped to reexamine initial assumptions about the overall organization of the site and how intuitive it was for users to navigate.

The test consisted of six timed tasks. The first five were relatively simple and direct, while the last task for the volunteer was the completion of the entire tutorial exercise. Total duration of the test was about forty-five minutes. The team also developed and used an observer form that allowed test administrators to record demographic information about the volunteer and the location of the test site. For each task, the form provided space to note the elapsed time, the browsing path, and each volunteer's comments and actions.

The team conducted the test with five volunteers. The group was composed of four medical students and one librarian. Only one volunteer indicated having used the EBM site before. Most tasks were successfully completed within the allotted time. Detailed test data were recorded on a spreadsheet program to facilitate interpretation.

## RESULTS

During administration of the tests, several issues became apparent to the observers. Volunteers found navigation in the tutorial difficult because of its unidirectional design. For example, the case study statement only appears on the initial page of Part 1, but the observers found that users needed to refer back to it on later screens. Also, the help frame in the literature search section of Part 3 was used incorrectly and in a haphazard fashion. One volunteer actually minimized the frame so that it was completely hidden. The test administrators concluded that this reluctance to use the help frame was due to the excessive amount of text combined with a small font size.

## NEXT PHASE OF THE EBM SITE

Future improvement of the EBM Web site will be impacted by the results gathered from the usability testing. The team will provide access to the case study from each part of the tutorial. The help frame in Part 3 of the existing tutorial will be revised by reducing the volume of text and by developing a more readable format.

There are plans to expand the site to include several more tutorials, which will address all four types of clinical questions. A glossary database of EBM-related terms will be available at various points of need within the tutorial. This glossary feature will be facilitated by the upcoming implementation of the ColdFusion Web development system on the library's server. Finally, the development team has learned that any future changes made to the EBM Web site must be tested by additional usability studies prior to releasing the revisions to users of the Web site.

## NOTES

1. David L. Sackett et al., *Evidence-based Medicine: How to Practice & Teach EBM* (New York: Churchill Livingstone, 1997), 2.

2. See for example, Jakob Nielsen, *useit.com: Jakob Nielsen's site (Usable Information Technology)* <http://www.useit.com> [accessed 19 January 2000].

3. Alison J. Head, "Web Redemption and the Promise of Usability," *Online* 23, no. 6 (November–December 1999): 26.

# 35

# Integrating Library and Information Competencies into the Nursing Curriculum through Faculty–Librarian Collaboration

*Karla J. Block*

Health Information Access for Rural Nurse Practitioners is a three-year (1997–2000) collaborative project funded by an Information Systems grant from the National Library of Medicine. The project focuses upon the needs of rural students enrolled in the six graduate nurse practitioner (NP) programs in Minnesota, and unites the efforts of project staff and librarians from each of the six participating institutions. These diverse institutions include the College of St. Catherine (St. Paul), the College of St. Scholastica (Duluth), Metropolitan State University (St. Paul), Minnesota State University-Mankato (Mankato), University of Minnesota (Minneapolis), and Winona State University-Rochester Center (Rochester).

## PROJECT BACKGROUND

Two other collaborative projects in the state of Minnesota set the stage for Health Information Access for Rural Nurse Practitioners. In the early 1990s, the Minnesota legislature developed a grant initiative to improve access for the education of rural NP students, develop rural clinical education sites, and develop opportunities for NPs to practice in rural areas of the state. In response to this initiative, the graduate NP programs in the state submitted a joint grant proposal outlining a collaborative strategy. Their proposal was accepted and has been funded continuously since 1994. Each school identified a faculty coordinator for the project and together the schools embarked on activities such as recruiting students, developing rural clinical education sites, recruiting rural clinical preceptors, coordinating rural student placement for clinical education, and releasing public information about NPs. Another collaborative project is Minnesota Partnerships for Training, funded by a five-year (1997–2001) grant from the Robert Wood Johnson Foundation. The purpose of this project is to meet the primary health care needs in rural and urban underserved areas of Minnesota through community-based education programs for NPs, certified nurse midwives (CNMs), and physician assistants (PAs). Some key activities of this project have been developing distance learning courses, recruiting students, establishing interdisciplinary clinical education sites, and releasing public information about NPs, CNMs, and PAs. Health Information Access for Rural Nurse Practitioners grew out of the collaborative groundwork that had been laid by these other two innovative and collaborative projects.

Health Information Access for Rural Nurse Practitioners targets students who are currently enrolled in a graduate NP program in Minnesota and live in a rural area fifty miles or more from the institution they attend. Since 1997, the project has served more than one hundred students from Minnesota, North Dakota, South Dakota, Iowa, Wisconsin, and Canada. Most of the students have worked in the nursing field for many years and live in a rural area that does not provide easy access to educational opportunities in advanced practice nursing. Most of the students are bound to their rural homes by jobs and families, making relocation to an urban area unlikely or impossible. While some of the students take advantage of distance education courses offered online or via interactive television, most travel long distances at least once per week to attend classes. Health Information Access for Rural Nurse Practitioners was designed with an eye to the special challenges faced by rural students who live a long distance from the schools they attend.

## SUPPORT AND SERVICE AREAS

The project is headquartered at the Biomedical Library at the University of Minnesota. Project staff include two principal investigators (Ellen Nagle from the Biomedical Library and Christine Mueller from the School of Nursing), a project manager/training coordinator (Karla Block), and a computer technician (Steve Irons). A librarian from each of the collaborating institutions acts as a library liaison (Cindy Stromgren, St. Catherine; Kevin McGrew, St. Scholastica; Diane Richards, Minnesota State University-Mankato; Mary Ito Dennison, Winona State University-Rochester; and Dawn Littleton, University of Minnesota).

In order to facilitate access to electronic health sciences information and library resources, the project provides support and services in five main areas: document delivery, library instruction, technology support, evaluation, and faculty development. Document delivery services allow rural students and their clinical preceptors to obtain photocopies or faxes of health sciences documents for a subsidized rate (usually free), while library instruction services introduce nursing students to useful databases or library resources in a group or individual setting. Technology support includes the loan of laptop computers and portable printers to selected students and clinical preceptors, financial assistance to obtain local Internet service for selected students, and technical support for students via a toll-free phone line, E-mail address, or in-person consultations with the project's computer technician. Rural NP students, rural clinical preceptors, and nursing faculty are asked to participate in an extensive evaluation process that is being conducted by the Minnesota Center for Survey Research. The project also emphasizes faculty development efforts aimed at encouraging nursing faculty to incorporate electronic health sciences information and library resources into their coursework, especially for rural students.

The project's emphasis on library instruction for students and professional development opportunities for faculty gave rise to several questions. What skills do nursing students need to access and use electronic health sciences resources in their educational programs and clinical practice? How can faculty incorporate into their courses and curriculum the opportunities for students to develop and use these skills? What role can librarians play in assisting faculty to develop teaching and learning strategies to promote these skills? Through their involvement with Health Information Access for Rural Nurse Practitioners, faculty members and librarians from the six NP programs in Minnesota collaborated to develop practical solutions to these important questions.

## LIBRARY AND INFORMATION-SEEKING COMPETENCIES

The first question to be answered was, "What skills do nursing students need to access and utilize electronic health sciences resources in their educational programs and clinical practice? To address this question, the library liaisons and project staff collaborated to develop a set of library and information-seeking competencies. The individuals involved wanted to develop a list of practical skills and knowledge that could be recommended for all NP students. This set of competencies would focus on the library and information-seeking skills that would help NP students become information literate and successful lifelong professional learners. The competencies were divided into ten categories: basic technical skills, basic searching skills, library services, library online catalog, bibliographic databases, print resources, Internet and Web, electronic journals and texts, evaluating resources, and citing resources. As one example, the category of evaluating resources includes the following competencies: understand that information differs in level of quality, understand basic criteria for evaluating resources, evaluate resources to determine which information fits the identified need, apply evaluation criteria to print and electronic resources, contrast scholarly and popular materials, and differentiate high quality resources from poor quality resources. The complete list of competencies is available on the Web at <http://www.biomed.lib.umn.edu/nursgrant/student/complist.html>.

Individuals involved in this project conceived of several potential uses for the competencies. NP students could use the competencies as a self-assessment tool, allowing them to identify strengths and weaknesses and link to resources aimed at building their skills. Long-term goals included transforming the competencies into a formal assessment tool, complete with skills tests or activities and on-line or in-person tutorials. The competencies could also be used by librarians as a way to tailor library instruction sessions for both groups and individuals. The competencies might be useful not only for undergraduate and graduate nursing education, but for continuing education of current practitioners as well. Some of the faculty from the six NP programs involved in the project discussed using the competencies as course prerequisites or entrance requirements, and there was considerable interest in working to integrate the competencies into the nursing curriculum.

Once the competencies had been developed, librarians and faculty members from each institution were ready to collaborate to address the two remaining questions, "How can faculty incorporate into their courses and the curriculum the opportunities for students to develop and utilize these skills?" and "What role can librarians play in assisting faculty to develop teaching and learning strategies to promote these skills?" The faculty coordinators from the Collaborative Rural Nurse Practitioner Project, or another faculty designee, were paired with the library liaisons from their respective institutions. The faculty–librarian teams were charged with producing a curriculum exemplar for a nursing course at their institution.

A curriculum exemplar was defined as a teaching or learning strategy that has been developed for a course (a module or unit, a class session, or an assignment), involves the use of electronic health sciences resources, builds upon the library and information-seeking competencies, and includes a measurable outcome. The process of creating the curriculum exemplars was intentionally left fairly unstructured, with the hopes that each team would find the flexibility and creativity needed to produce an exemplar well suited for each unique circumstance. In most cases, the faculty member was encouraged to select the course for which the exemplar would be used. Some chose an introductory course that was required of all students, while others chose a course focused on the institution's mission. The faculty member was also encouraged to suggest a content area for the exemplar. Some chose an especially challenging, controversial, or important topic, or one that addressed a previous lack of formal content. Some topics addressed a common area of care that would be faced by students in rural practice, while others hoped to remedy difficulties in finding information on a particular topic. In most cases, the faculty member and librarian collaborated to narrow a content area or focus on a specific aspect of a topic. The final content areas were quite diverse, and included advance directives in geriatrics, botanicals in alternative and complementary care, female genital mutilation, cultural issues in hormone replacement therapy, a geriatric case study on chronic pain, and ethics in nursing care.

## CURRICULUM EXEMPLARS

A summary of each curriculum exemplar can be found on-line at <http://www.biomed.lib.umn.edu/nursgrant/student/currexem.html>, and two of the exemplars will be highlighted here. A common theme in the exemplars was asking students to locate and evaluate health sciences resources (often Web-based resources). The exemplar on ethics in nursing care was developed for a course at the College of St. Catherine. In the past, students had often found it difficult to locate appropriate ethics-related information. To solve this problem, the curriculum exemplar focused on the development and use of a Web page to make finding information easier. The page was developed to be useful for both undergraduate and graduate nursing students, although student feedback suggests that the page needs to be further refined for graduate student use. The URL for the page <http://www.stkate.edu/library/guides/ethics.html> has been included in the syllabus for several courses. In addition, students in this particular course are asked to use the page when completing an ethics project that asks them to analyze ethical issues in advanced practice nursing through application of ethical principles and development of an ethical decision-making framework. While the students are asked to use the page, the library liaison and faculty member are working to make the outcome more measurable (perhaps by requiring students to critique and evaluate the Web page as part of their assignment).

The exemplar on advance directives in geriatrics was developed for a beginning, required course at Metropolitan State University. The topic of advance directives was chosen because of the importance of addressing ethical content throughout the curriculum; a graduation competence for NP students at this institution is competence in the analysis of current ethical issues. The exemplar involves two assignments, each of which lays the foundation for other activities later in the course. One assignment requires the students to successfully complete two Cumulative Index to Nursing and Allied Health Literature searches. From their search results, students are asked to select and locate three articles for critique and class discussion later in the course. The second assignment asks students to use a checklist of quality for Web-based resources to evaluate an on-line continuing education module <http://www.springnet.com/ce/p704a.html> about advance directives. The knowledge gained in this assignment will be used later in the course to role play a family case conference.

## CHALLENGES AND SUCCESSES

The process of collaboration between faculty members and librarians to develop these curriculum exemplars was marked both by challenges and successes. In most cases, this project involved collaboration between two individuals who had never before worked together. The teams had to establish mutually agreeable work schedules and deadlines, while remaining flexible about when and how to meet. One of the challenges faced revolved around the issue of time. A general lack of time and the need to devote time to other commitments was sometimes an issue. A related challenge was simply overcoming the perception that this project would be extremely time consuming or involve too many in-person meetings. Most of the teams found that they could meet by phone, E-mail, or in person, and that the project did not require as much time as they initially had feared. Another challenge was the act of establishing a working relationship given different styles and the need to work as partners. Roles also had to be clarified, as the teams sometimes struggled to determine who should or would take the lead. Because the collaboration involved six institutions and many individuals, it was not always easy to make progress. Having project staff from Health Information Access for Rural Nurse Practitioners available to coordinate the effort was quite useful. Another challenge revolved around choosing appropriate topics for the exemplars. The original topics suggested by faculty members were often quite broad, so the faculty members and librarians had to work together to choose a manageable and well-defined topic. Staff turnover was a challenge in some instances. A final challenge was conducting ongoing evaluation of the process and the products, and each team was encouraged to solicit feedback from the students, as well as the faculty members and librarians working on a particular exemplar.

Despite the challenges, the curriculum exemplar collaboration was a success. Each of the six schools produced a successful exemplar, thereby addressing important content areas for NP students. Through development of the exemplars, faculty members and librarians found one valuable way in which library and information-seeking competencies can be incorporated into the curriculum. The project placed an emphasis on promoting lifelong professional learning for nurse practitioners, something that faculty and librarians alike appreciated. Strong working relationships evolved, and the project served as a catalyst for other collaborative ventures. In one instance, work on this project encouraged collaboration with systems staff to introduce a proxy server for remote database access. In another instance, this project motivated collaboration between the school's writing center and the library. The curriculum exemplars also served as a model for similar projects in other courses, and it wasn't unusual for faculty members to request Web pages or library instruction sessions for other classes. Overall, the curriculum exemplar collaboration was successful and can serve as a model for other collaborative ventures between librarians and faculty.

# 36

# Improving Nurses' Access to and Use of Professionally Relevant Information in a BSN Completion Program

*Mary L. Kinnaman, Susan Sykes Berry, and Kathy Ballou*

The health care delivery system is undergoing rapid and massive change. This change is primarily being driven by public demand for accessible and affordable health care that meets its expectations for quality of care and service. The response to this demand is increased competition among health care providers and financiers of health care to demonstrate control of cost along with provision of quality care. An aging population, rapidity of technological advances in health care, and changes in reimbursement for government-financed health care adds to the challenge health professionals face in attempting to meet public expectations.

## NURSING ROLE DEVELOPMENT
## IN THE MIDST OF HEALTH CARE CHANGE

Over the past five to seven years there has been an increasing appeal by health care providers, employers, and the public to evaluate and revise the educational process of all the health professions to better meet the challenges presented by the rapidly changing health care delivery system. Landmark reports by the Pew Health Professions Commission clearly highlighted the importance of health professionals knowing how to access and use health care information and research results in their practice.

In 1998, the American Association of Colleges of Nursing (AACN) Task Force on the Essentials of Baccalaureate Education for Professional Nursing Practice published a document (*The Essentials of Baccalaureate Education*) providing a "framework for developing, defining, and revising baccalaureate nursing curricula" (cover letter) for the twenty-first century. These revised standards now form the basis of the accreditation process for nursing schools choosing the Commission on Collegiate Nursing Education (CCNE) as their accrediting organization. As of January 4, 2000, the CCNE Web site lists 64 nursing schools as fully accredited and 299 preliminarily accredited by its organization. The *Essentials* document emphasizes the necessity for professional nurses to be able to access and use health care information and research related to their professional practice as a role responsibility, as a core competency, as part of core nursing knowledge required, and as part of ongoing professional role development.

## RESPONDING TO THE CHALLENGE OF CHANGE

The University of Missouri-Kansas City (UMKC) is an urban university in a large midwestern city located on the Missouri side of the Kansas/Missouri line. UMKC is the only public institution with a school of nursing in the Kansas City, Missouri area. Nursing programs currently offered by the UMKC School of Nursing include a baccalaureate or master's degree for returning registered nurses, master's, and an inter-campus, cooperative doctoral program.

The mission of the baccalaureate in nursing program at UMKC is to meet the needs of a rapidly changing health care system and the needs of adult professionals. Working closely with community advisors, responding to students' program recommendations as working health professionals, and responding to the challenges of the Pew Health Professions Commission and newly drafted standards by AACN, the nursing baccalaureate program was revised.

The new, innovative baccalaureate program was implemented in 1998. The program, as structured, is designed to allow employed registered nurses to complete a baccalaureate degree in only eighteen months. The program structure is developmental and progression is sequential. The framework for the program is based on Steven Covey's Principle-Centered Leadership Model. The premise provided by this framework is that professionals must be able to manage themselves before they can effectively manage others. Nine program goals overarch four didactic courses and one clinical application course. Each didactic course has six or seven objectives and represents five or six credit hours. The names of the didactic courses demonstrate the developmental and sequential progression of the program:

***Block I.***    Tools for Personal Effectiveness
***Block II.***    Tools for Interpersonal Effectiveness
***Block III.***    Effectiveness in Human Health Outcomes
***Block IV.***    Effectiveness in Complex Health Systems

In addition to program goals and course objectives, eleven competencies form measures for assessment of program outcomes. Two of the eleven competencies—provision of knowledge-based care and technology utilization—specifically require graduates to be able to access and use information for professional practice.

## CHARACTERISTICS OF BACCALAUREATE STUDENTS AT UMKC SCHOOL OF NURSING

Registered nurses returning to UMKC for their first professional degree range widely in age and experience. Some nurses have just graduated from a two-year associate degree program or a diploma program, while others have been in nursing ten, twenty, thirty, or more years. The majority who have been out of school for a number of years find the use of computer technology and access to information by computers an incredible challenge. More than 90 percent of these students remain in full-time nursing positions and have significant family obligations while they are simultaneously enrolled in the full-time course of study necessary to complete the program in eighteen months.

Success in school, as in today's nursing environment, is dependent on the students' ability to learn how to navigate efficiently and effectively through the information maze in their school, home, or clinical setting. Empowering students with necessary skills and resources to access useful health care information is one way the BSN program fosters student success both as students and as health care professionals.

## HELPING STUDENTS CONQUER THE INFORMATION MAZE

In 1998, the UMKC Health Sciences Library hired an instructional reference librarian who is also a registered nurse. One of this individual's responsibilities is to assist the School of Nursing faculty and students with accessing and using bibliographic databases. In discussing how to maximize use of this resource and best meet the students' identified need to understand more about how to use bibliographic databases, a decision was reached to use class time to facilitate skill development using the computer learning center at the UMKC School of Nursing.

Early in the first nursing core course, Tools for Personal Effectiveness, the instructional reference librarian facilitates a three-hour experiential class on the use of bibliographic databases. Together with the course instructor, objectives established for this learning activity were developed.

## LEARNING UNIT OBJECTIVES

By the end of this class the student will be able to:

1. Explain the types of information covered in a bibliographic database
2. Differentiate when to use specific medical and nursing databases
3. Differentiate between a popular and scholarly journal
4. Perform a simple search on the CINAHL database from Ovid
5. Perform a simple search on Internet Grateful Med from the National Library of Medicine
6. Search the Health Sciences Library catalog to determine if a particular journal is available, and if not, explain how to procure a particular article from that journal
7. Obtain a remote access account from the university or the Health Sciences Library

## STRUCTURED APPROACH USED FOR LEARNING UNIT

### Remote Access

Because the majority of students in the program work full time, work a variety of shifts, and have many family responsibilities, actual visits to the library are seen as onerous. Remote access, available to all enrolled UMKC students, provides an excellent alternative for accessing information. If a specific journal article is available on-line or can be ordered through Loansome Doc, it is particularly beneficial to the student.

To use the remote access available to them, students must first apply for an account, which previously required a trip to the library. Now, students fill out the necessary paperwork for remote access during the class and learn how to use the remote account from home. Once the remote account is established, the student is able to access UMKC licensed proprietary bibliographic databases from his or her home computer.

### Basics of Bibliographic Databases

For many of the students enrolled in the baccalaureate program, their last experience finding journal articles involved using books in the library such as *Index Medicus* and the *Cumulative Nursing Indexes*. If they were unable to find what they needed, a librarian could assist them by running a computer search. There were no computers in the library, at least none that were accessible by the students. For these students, the databases are mysterious and confusing, so time is spent helping the student mentally make the transition from these books to a computerized database. The basics of what a database is and what it does is reviewed and discussed. The acronyms used by the databases are also "decoded" to demystify them.

### Differentiating the Library Catalog from a Bibliographic Database

Once a student accesses the library's Internet site, either remotely or at the library, he or she is confronted with a decision. To proceed, the student must choose between accessing one of the bibliographic databases or using the library catalog to search for library holdings. Differences between the library catalog and bibliographic databases such as CINAHL are discussed. Discussion is supported by the use of on-line demonstrations with overhead screen displays for the class as well as by individual hands-on experience. Then, to ensure that the students will leave understanding the difference between the library catalog and CINAHL, several brief experiential exercises are used so the student can practice making the correct choice with different scenarios.

### Remote Access and the Use and Availability of Specific Bibliographic Databases

Once students are comfortable with accessing UMKC's library Web site and correctly choosing between the library catalog and a bibliographic database, the instructional reference librarian facilitates a discussion regarding the bibliographic databases available. The relevance of several databases to nursing is discussed, with multiple examples used to promote accurate choice of databases for specific clinical scenarios. The acronyms for the databases are also discussed and decoded to assure the student understands the differences between the various databases.

As all bibliographic databases are not available remotely, the instructional reference librarian also reviews with students those databases available and not available from their computers at home or work. Written information is also provided for the student's future reference regarding the availability of bibliographic databases. While all bibliographic databases licensed by Ovid are available remotely, others are restricted to access from a UMKC computer.

### Using the Library Catalog

After students use the bibliographic databases to search and obtain a list of references, the next step is to determine if articles of interest identified from the search are available in the university's holdings. In order to understand this process, the students identify several journal titles and are instructed in how to search the library catalog for the journal. Also explained are how to determine if issues of the journal are or are not available. Students then perform additional exercises to practice determining a journal's availability at UMKC.

## Differentiating Scholarly Journals from Popular (or Trade) Journals

When nursing students return to school, they typically are most familiar with the nursing "trade" journals rather than the more "scholarly" journals. Frequently, faculty require students to use the more scholarly works as references for assignments. Many of the students are unclear on how to know if a journal is considered scholarly. To help students learn to make this differentiation, a number and a variety of journals are pulled for review. Students then rate each journal on a sliding scale based on written criteria that is provided and reviewed prior to the exercise. This exercise initiates a great deal of discussion and seems to be of particular interest to students.

## The Search Strategy

With the basics now covered, search strategy is discussed. Written material along with demonstrations using overhead screen displays are used to explain how to get the best results from a search. Boolean operators, descriptors, and subject headings in MeSH are explained. Students again are asked to complete a number of simple exercises as a way to assess their ability to employ these search strategies.

## The Search

To make the search relevant to the students' needs, the instructional reference librarian completes a search using CINAHL by Ovid on a topic provided by the students. The relevance of the results to the topic is discussed and the search is then repeated using MEDLINE, which is accessed using Internet Grateful Med from the National Library of Medicine. This further demonstrates how each database works, and also provides access to a database that will be available to them once the students have graduated from the program.

Finally, students complete an independent search for information on a paper assigned in the course. This final experiential exercise accomplishes several goals at once. The instructional reference librarian and course instructor are able to validate student understanding of the material presented by having students construct a search, choose a database, use the database, and find out if the library has the journals. Any areas where students remain unclear are then addressed immediately.

## EVALUATION AND RECOMMENDATIONS

This experiential approach is well received by the students and is highly recommended in student evaluations as a necessary component of the program. In addition, the activity assists working students to identify with and develop a positive relationship with the library and library personnel and will hopefully encourage more and better future use of the instructional reference librarian.

One enhancement planned for next year is to run several sessions of the unit, limiting the number of students to four or five per session. This will better ensure that every student meets all of the objectives and has ample opportunity to complete the exercises and receive personal feedback from the instructional reference librarian.

## CONCLUSION

The availability of computerized bibliographic databases makes professional information readily available to the nurse. Skill in using these tools is imperative for nurses to fulfill their professional role responsibilities and supports their becoming lifelong learners. This learning module offers one way to ensure that nurses begin a journey that will hopefully continue through their career.

# 37

# Web-Based Instruction for Undergraduate Nurses

*Richard Eimas and Hope Barton*

The nursing profession continues to mature, grow stronger, and take a greater role in American health care. Nevertheless, as the profession evolves, it faces numerous challenges including those of image, differing philosophies of educational preparation, recruitment and retention, and changing expectations for on-the-job performance. Students aspiring to enter the profession deserve every opportunity to obtain the information literacy skills that will help them deal effectively with these challenges. To meet professional role expectations, nursing students must understand how to obtain and evaluate information effectively in order to stay current and take a leadership role in their profession. The key is to provide them with literacy skills that can be used in lifelong learning. E. Gordon Gee, former president of the University of Colorado, expressed this very well when he commented:

> In an era when today's truths become tomorrow's outdated concepts, individuals who are unable to gather pertinent information are equally as illiterate as those who are unable to read or write.[1]

## INCREASES IN NURSING LITERATURE

Within the last decade, the new focus on research, evidence-based health care, the development of new specialty areas, and advanced practice roles have resulted in great strides in nursing research and a dramatic increase in the amount of publishing. Although this literature is diversifying and expanding rapidly, it is of little value unless its practitioners read and apply it.

Because nursing practice needs to be based on state-of-the-art knowledge, an important goal of nursing education is to encourage and assist students in accessing this rich body of knowledge. Many nursing faculty members recognize that a well-developed information base is essential for effective clinical care as well as for planning and problem solving. They realize that information resources are constantly changing and the half-life of information keeps shrinking. So it is vitally important for students to master information-seeking skills rather than facts during their undergraduate years.

A study at the University of Northern Colorado showed that information literacy programs resulted in a 35 percent increase in the research and scholarly activities of nursing students after graduation.[2] The nature of their scholarly activities also expanded from writing nursing care standards and proposals for job classifications to writing journal articles, presenting papers at conferences, and participating in major research projects. Another study has shown that nursing students' interest in the use of the library is chiefly determined by the value attached to library research by the faculty member.[3] The study found that the kind of direction given by faculty can mean the difference between a superficial use of materials or an in-depth use of the vast information network available in most health sciences libraries. It also found that one of the biggest problems faculty face when assigning a library research project is how to help students begin the research process.

## PARTNERSHIPS WITH THE COLLEGE OF NURSING

Librarians have traditionally been involved in providing basic library skills. But advances in technology and the explosion of biomedical literature have brought librarians and faculty together in new partnerships that combine the skills of both professions. Faculty at the University of Iowa College of Nursing has placed a high value on information literacy skills. They have involved the library in instructing students very early in the nursing curriculum to lay the groundwork for effective information retrieval, usage, and understanding of the research process. The library's first large-scale user education program began in 1992 when a faculty member approached library staff with a set of library and information skills she wanted her students to develop in their required introductory course Professional Nursing: An Overview. Working with the instructor, library staff designed a program to introduce students to the physical layout of the library, provide an understanding of library services and policies, teach them how to search citation databases available in the library, and locate articles found in their searches. These skills were all needed for the students to complete their course project, which included performing a literature search of the MEDLINE or CINAHL (Cumulative Index to Nursing and Allied Health Literature) databases, downloading the strategy and results to disk, and writing a research paper based on the results of their database search. The students were graded not only for their research paper but also on their search strategy and its results.

The library component of *Professional Nursing: An Overview* was to be given during the fall and spring semesters to classes of from 130 to 200 students. To work effectively with a large class, students were divided into groups of twenty-five for the library sessions that were given outside the regular class period. In order not to interfere with the students' busy schedules, the library scheduled from six to eight sessions either first thing in the morning or late in the afternoon during a two- to three-week period early in the semester. Attendance at a library session was mandatory and students were asked to sign up for the date and time of their choice. Attendance sheets were returned to the instructor and absentees were required to sign up for another session. Students who did not attend a session received a final semester grade reduced by five points.

The initial library program included an "armchair" tour of the library using the library map handout, an explanation of basic library policies and hours, the elementary skills needed to search and use OASIS (the libraries' On-Line Public Access Catalog [OPAC]), and an introduction to searching CINAHL, which was only available on CD-ROM at that time. The librarians used printed handouts and transparencies of both the building and search screens as teaching aids. The last five to seven minutes of each class were devoted to a tour of the library's third level, where the major service points are located.

## APPLICATION OF TECHNOLOGY TO LEARNING

The years from 1993 through 1996 were largely a transitional period during which it was possible to improve the teaching methodology because of technological advances that were implemented by the library. The first major advance occurred when the library partnered with the health sciences colleges to develop the Healthnet system for delivery of health-related citation databases such as MEDLINE. As more computer terminals were acquired and networking was introduced, it became possible to provide live demonstrations of OASIS and CINAHL using a laptop computer and an LCD projector. This was an important improvement because earlier student evaluations had indicated the students' desire for live demonstrations. In 1995, a one-hour lecture titled Research Strategies: Utilizing Information Effectively was added to the course. This presentation was given to the entire class by a library staff member during a regularly scheduled class period in one of the College of Nursing's large lecture rooms.

In the fall of 1996, only one month after the Information Commons (a state-of-the-art electronic classroom facility) was opened, the first classes were held in its electronic classroom. Although moving to the Information Commons was a significant step forward, it was necessary to eliminate the walking tour of the library in order to take full advantage of the opportunities provided by individual workstations for each student. The library staff was able to begin to take advantage of its technological capabilities and, most importantly, give the students hands-on capability so they could follow the instructor at their workstations and do the demonstration searches themselves. The library overview, which included the "armchair" tour of the library, an explanation of basic library policies and hours, as well as information on OASIS and Healthnet, was converted to PowerPoint for the lecture portion of the class. Following the library overview, the entire class was able to join the instructor in doing the demonstration searches at its workstations. However, all of this was not without difficulties and we learned that for some students, the temptations of E-mail and Internet surfing were too overpowering during the lecture segment of the class. As a result, when it came time for the demonstration searches, valuable class time frequently had to be spent resetting one or more workstations so the students could join the rest of the class.

In 1997, the PowerPoint presentation was moved to a Web site and students are now asked to follow the instructor through the presentation by clicking on each slide when prompted.[4] The Web site includes the PowerPoint library overview, links to OASIS and Healthnet, OASIS search examples, the PowerPoint presentation on Research Strategies: Utilizing Information Effectively, and an E-mail link to the session presenters for follow-up questions.

The Web site proved to be highly successful and has kept the students fully engaged for the entire class session and greatly decreased their interest in E-mail and Internet surfing. Available to students at any hour of the day or night, the Web site has also been used in orientation activities for staff, visiting faculty, and researchers. It has been adapted for use in several other courses and was also used as a starting point for creation of a Web site for the library system's distance education program. In addition, the two to four librarians who have been involved in presenting these sessions each semester find that there is now greater consistency in presentation but still room for individual teaching preferences.

The library's reference staff has reported that with the addition of live and then hands-on demonstrations, students have been able to search more independently and have asked far fewer questions when working on their database searches. At the same time, nursing faculty have noted significant improvements in the quality of the students' work and attribute it to better search skills resulting from hands-on instruction and availability of the Web site.

## A NEW CURRICULUM

The undergraduate curriculum is currently under revision and Professional Nursing: An Overview was last taught in the spring of 1999. We are presently working with the College of Nursing faculty to help them integrate information literacy instruction into the new curriculum. Although substantial progress has been made, future enhancements would include an Internet searching component, a page containing links to Internet nursing resources, and perhaps a video tour of the building. We are confident that the partnership that has been established between the College of Nursing faculty in teaching information literacy skills will continue as the new curriculum is implemented.

## NOTES

1. E. Gordon Gee and Patricia S. Breivik, "Libraries and Learning," in *Libraries and the Search for Academic Excellence*, ed. Patricia S. Breivik and Robert Wedgeworth (Lanham, Md: Scarecrow Press, 1988), 27.

2. Lynne M. Fox et al., "A Multidimensional Evaluation of a Nursing Information-Literacy Program," *Bulletin of the Medical Library Association* 84, no. 2 (April 1996): 182–90.

3. Susan M. Weaver, "Information Literacy: Educating for Lifelong Learning," *Nurse Educator* 18, no. 4 (July–August 1993): 30–32.

4. See <http://www.lib.uiowa.edu/hardin-www/classes/profnurs/index-main.htm>.

# 38

# Partnering with Occupational Therapy: The Evolution of an Information Literacy Program

*Rebecca S. Graves*

An information literacy program requires a collaborative effort. In our case, it is the result of both the librarians' as well as the Department of Occupational Therapy chair's belief that knowing how to find information is more than simply knowing where the books are in the campus library. The following is a look at how our workshops for occupational therapy students are evolving toward an information literacy program.

The program was developed at the University of Missouri-Columbia with a partnership between the Department of Occupational Therapy and the J. Otto Lottes Health Sciences Library. Established in 1839, the University of Missouri-Columbia is the largest research university in Missouri. It is the main campus of the four-campus state system and supports 250 undergraduate and 90 graduate degrees.

## BACKGROUND

The Department of Occupational Therapy is an accredited four and one-half year program that includes two summers of study. Thirty to 36 students are accepted each year out of approximately 70 to 100 applicants. Students must have at minimum a 3.0 GPA and one hundred hours or more of relevant volunteer service. For those accepted in the program, there is a 100 percent placement rate. The department supports 4.75 faculty positions.

The J. Otto Lottes Health Sciences Library supports the schools of medicine, nursing, and health-related professions, as well as the University Hospital and Clinics. The library offers more than 200,000 total volumes and 1,496 print and more than 500 electronic journal titles. Staffing consists of eight librarians and thirteen staff members. Of the eight librarians, the four Information Services librarians share in teaching the workshops. In partnership with Information Technology Services (ITS), the library houses a computer lab containing ten networked PC workstations that can comfortably hold up to sixteen students. This lab and additional computers on the first floor of the library are managed by ITS. The computer lab is open to student use when not reserved for hands-on workshops.

## LIBRARY WORKSHOPS

Established in the early '90s, the library workshops for the occupational therapy students consisted of meeting with the students in the fall of their junior and senior years to instruct them in how to use the library's on-line catalog and databases, such as the Cumulative Index to Nursing and Allied Health Literature (CINAHL), through the Ovid interface. They also received instruction in the use of electronic textbooks such as Harrison's Plus. In the winter semester of 1996, an Internet searching workshop was added.

While the content of these workshops was relevant and necessary, it was felt that the workshops could be improved. Over the summer of 1997, the program was evaluated by the Educational Services librarian. Of particular interest was the idea of information literacy in contrast to library orientation. A working definition was developed that library orientation consisted primarily of "one shot" workshops that may or may not be integrated with coursework. Library orientation workshops also are much more specific to the actual library building and collection or a specific database. The objective of library orientation is short term in that its purpose is to make students familiar with resources that they will use for that semester or at most until they graduate.

Information literacy, on the other hand, consists of multiple sessions that are typically integrated with coursework. The objective of information literacy is long term. Even though it might acquaint students with local resources, ultimately its goal is to build their ability to find and use a variety of information sources both before and after graduation. Within this context, library orientation may be a part of information literacy.

Concurrently, the Department of Occupational Therapy chair was reviewing campus resources available to the students in regard to research, computing, and writing. The Department of Occupational Therapy was able to fund a part-time student position to assist in this review by collecting and organizing the information on the various resources including the health sciences library. The Educational Services librarian met with the student and discussed how these resources could be harnessed for an information literacy program.

After reviewing the program, the basic structure of holding workshops for both juniors and seniors at the beginning of their fall and winter semesters was retained. Some topics, such as the library's catalog, were dropped from the program, while others such as electronic texts were combined with other topics into one workshop. The current program is as follows.

## AN INFORMATION LITERACY FOCUS

The librarians first meet with the students the fall of their junior year for an hour and a half. During this session, the students are given a hands-on introduction to searching CINAHL on Ovid and OT BibSys through the Web, and to specific Web sites relevant to their studies. They are also instructed in how to evaluate information found on the Web. They are given an assignment of completing a Web tutorial of OT BibSys and must submit a printout of their search results to their instructor. As one of their assignments for the semester is a paper on an occupational therapist, the students are given information about historical and biographical sources.

At the beginning of the juniors' winter semester, they meet for a one and one-half hour, hands-on workshop on searching the Internet for occupational therapy sources. This workshop covers various search engines and directories, particularly ones specific to health information such as the Hardin Medical Directory and Medical World Search. During this semester, the students take an on-line course, create their own Web page, and use Internet sources for a paper and poster session.

The seniors meet with the librarians at the beginning of their fall semester for a one and one-half hour, hands-on workshop that reviews searching CINAHL on Ovid and searching OT BibSys as well as evaluating information sources on the Web. At this point, more advanced searching techniques, such as exploding on subject headings and using subheadings, are introduced. As the students will be working on case studies of patients with specific disorders or diseases, they are introduced to searching electronic texts such as STAT!-Ref and Harrison's Plus.

During winter semester of their senior year, the students, in groups of three, accomplish a meta-analysis as their main assignment. Their last library workshop builds on the assignment by giving a broad-brush coverage of the research process, including how to find examples of meta-analysis and its process. They are guided in identifying resources such as colleagues, databases, and the Internet as well as the advantages and disadvantages of each. The difficulty of searching for articles in the occupational therapy literature, as it covers multiple disciplines and occupational therapy terms that are often only accessible through text word searching, is covered. Students are given printouts of the same article retrieved from several databases—CINAHL, PsycINFO, MEDLINE, Eric, and Rehabdata—and review the differences among them.

In the past, this workshop was given as a two-hour lecture/demonstration. In 1999, it was given in an hour and a half, and time was allowed for the students to work in their groups to begin their research. They were also given a handout on how to access databases and other resources during the summer and fall semester, when they will be doing fieldwork, as well as how to access databases and resources once they graduate in December.

## EVALUATION OF THE PROGRAM

To judge the impact of this program, we devised a pre- and posttest given in the fall workshops. The juniors are given a posttest after the section on searching CINAHL. They are asked to find articles on shoulder pain after stroke and to print out their search strategy. This allows the instructors to see if the students are using subject headings, and if they are using the combine-set and limit-set features.

The seniors are given both a pretest and a posttest. At the beginning of the workshop, the seniors are asked to find articles on educating patients on assisted technology devices and to print out their search strategy. They are then taken through a review of searching CINAHL. When finished, they are again asked to find articles on the same question stated above. Their two strategies are compared to see what they have mastered over the previous year and what they have learned from the workshop. The pretests showed a wide variation in skill, while the results of the posttest were much more uniform. In the posttest, most of the students were using subject headings and the combine-set and limit-set features. Some used the explode option to access more subject headings and few used subheadings.

Other sources of information on the program come from the Department of Occupational Therapy. Each year, they survey the incoming juniors on their computer and searching skills. A focus group is planned for winter 2000. This information is used not only to assess the level of the students' skill, but also to evaluate what information should continue to be covered in the workshops, what should be added, and how it should be taught.

## CHALLENGES

When librarians meet with one group of students four times over two years, challenges arise that do not in a traditional library orientation.

One main challenge is relevancy. On one hand, students need more than one workshop on searching skills; yet, the students themselves need to buy into the need for repetition and practice. This is one of the purposes of the pre- and posttests for the seniors. It shows where their knowledge is weak and allows them to see quick improvement in their searching skills.

Relevancy is also an issue in regard to the students' general skills and comfort on computers, specifically in regard to using the Internet. The level of computer skill overall is increasing with each new class of students. However, many students mistake their comfort for competence and are content to stay with the few searching tools that they know. Pointing out the specialized search engines and higher-level searching is not sufficient. The students must also understand why they need to know this.

Meeting with the students four times over two years allows the librarians to cover searching and research sources at a deeper level. In turn, this requires that the librarians are current with the print and online resources available in occupational therapy and related disciplines. It also demands a deep knowledge of these sources in order to be able to teach as well as to convince the students of the importance of the subject. If the librarian does not buy in to the necessity of in-depth understanding, the students certainly will not.

An additional challenge is time. There is a wealth of information to cover and even a four-part program does not allow for total content coverage and the practice necessary to master it. Time is required for keeping current with occupational therapy resources, various databases, and searching skills. Finally, there is the time required to reevaluate and revise the workshops each semester.

## CONCLUSION

As the subtitle states, this program is still evolving. It has moved closer to being an information literacy program; yet, there is still more growth to come. There is a good relationship between the Educational Services librarian and the Department of Occupational Therapy chair; however, there is little contact with the three other full-time faculty members. Building relationships with these three individuals would in turn assist in increasing the integration of coursework into the workshops, making them more obviously relevant to the students. Overlying all of this is the need for continued assessment, both of the skills that the students arrive with and those that they learn through the program. Having data on the program will help in keeping the program relevant and useful to the students and productive for both the Department of Occupational Therapy and the health sciences library.

# 39

# Information Literacy and International Health Topics

*Richard Eimas, John Schacht, Afeworki Paulos, and Sandy Ballasch*

The University of Iowa Libraries has long had a User Education Program designed to instruct students, faculty, and staff through such means as lectures, seminars, workshops, handouts, and Web-based tutorials. Although these methods have frequently been successful, experience has shown that these strategies are not sufficient or comprehensive enough to develop fully effective information skills. The best way for students to become truly information literate is for information skills to be integrated into the university's curriculum.

The information environment is too complex and changing too rapidly for us to expect students to acquire information literacy skills without a planned, systematic, cumulative instructional program. The University Libraries, in partnership with the College of Liberal Arts, has invited all faculty and teaching staff to consider implementing a University of Iowa Information Literacy Initiative (UIII) component in their courses to improve student learning through the development of information literacy skills.

## UIII

The Information Literacy Initiative is, then, a program in partnership with faculty to achieve greater information literacy for University of Iowa students. The project has been developed based on the following assumptions:

- Students need an introduction to critical thinking and research skills to prepare them for a lifetime of changing information needs.

- Collaborative relationships between the academic departments and the University Libraries are one of the most effective ways to reach students.
- Effective learning is frequently tied to a particular information need—class or discipline specific.
- Students and teachers have different learning and teaching styles and acquire information in different ways. Any information literacy program must accommodate these differences by using a variety of approaches that provide practice in these skills.

## INFORMATION LITERACY SKILLS

The program is intended to teach seven information literacy skills:

1. Articulation of a problem statement—students learn strategies for refining an assignment into a well-formulated research question.
2. Development of a search strategy—students construct search statements using Boolean operators, limiters, and keywords.
3. Identification of appropriate information sources—students practice retrieving information from libraries' on-line public access catalogs, World Wide Web resources, and citation databases.
4. Evaluation of information retrieved—students apply criteria to evaluate the accuracy, authenticity, and value of the information they have retrieved as it relates to their research topic.
5. Organization and application of information to the problem—students learn to organize their information and draw conclusions based on various points of view.
6. Understand the scholarly communication system—students are taught to distinguish between scholarly and popular sources and understand the peer review process.
7. Understand the ethical use of information—students are introduced to the principles of academic freedom, exercise both responsibilities and rights in their use of copyrighted information, and avoid plagiarism.

Each of these skills is broad in scope and is composed of a number of elements that the student must master. The University Libraries has organized its program so that information gathering and basic evaluative techniques are taught during the freshman and sophomore years. These skills include

- Knowing how to develop and use an effective search strategy
- Understanding how to search print and electronic sources
- Learning to apply evaluative criteria to print or electronic information

The responsible use of information and greater sophistication in information gathering is taught during the junior and senior years. These skills include

- Understanding the principles of copyright and fair use
- Being able to use information ethically and avoid plagiarism
- Knowing how to use interlibrary loan and other research services

## UIII AND PARTNERSHIPS

The program has been implemented by having librarians meet with faculty to discuss course goals and the skills that faculty would like emphasized in their courses. They then collaboratively design the approach that best suits the goals of the course.

Ideally, students need to practice and immediately apply information skills to their coursework if they are to improve and develop their competencies. For instance, librarians and faculty can work together when a term paper is assigned to develop exercises that require practice in the development of a search strategy appropriate to the problem statement, the evaluation of bias in sources, and the use of accepted citation practices. Librarians can present a class session on critical assessment of the quality of Web-based information resources complete with an evaluation of various search engines that might be used to locate the sites. Or librarians can collaborate in the development of assignments that require the use of complex data sets and the synthesis of information from multiple sources.

During the spring of 1999, John Schacht, a reference librarian from Information, Research, and Instructional Services, was contacted by Professor Paul Greenough of the history department to assist him in developing his course on the history of international health within the framework of the libraries' information literacy initiative. Sandra Ballasch, a reference librarian from Information, Research, and Instructional Services and Central Processing Services; Afeworki Paulos, International Studies bibliographer; and Richard Eimas from the Hardin Library for the Health Sciences were invited to join the team in order to provide the needed expertise for the course.

In conjunction with Dr. Greenough, it was determined that the process would include class sessions with presentations, demonstrations, and assignments as well as the creation of a Web page to provide continued access to the resources demonstrated during the class sessions. All presentations were in the libraries' Information Arcade so that the class would have an opportunity to have first-hand experience in visiting Web sites and doing Internet searching with experienced library staff available to provide assistance.

During the initial electronic resources session, key concepts were outlined; fundamentals of how to evaluate information resources were presented; and health, anthropological, and general periodical databases were demonstrated. In the follow-up session, specific databases such as MEDLINE, Anthropology Literature, and SearchBank were demonstrated.[1] A number of primary sources, such as the U.S. Agency for International Development, the Census of India, World Health Organization, and the Global Health Council were also demonstrated.

## WEB EVALUATION

An important element of the initial session was to emphasize the need to evaluate Web resources. Schacht had experienced a rather startling confirmation of that need when working with an undergraduate history class on American slavery. Student evaluations following a voluntary workshop on Web searching and evaluation indicated that while most students liked the searching experience, many didn't like the evaluation segment because they felt it was "pretty obvious" or they "already knew it." But the course professor, after reviewing the results of an assignment given to the entire class, noted that those who attended the workshop brought a clear set of evaluative criteria to the Web sites, while those who didn't attend mostly described the site graphics.

In addition to students' resistance and lack of interest in learning how to evaluate Web sites, a second problem was the fact that most site evaluation criteria currently on the Web do not meet the needs of college- or university-level history courses.

This is because, generally speaking, historians don't like easy answers when it comes to evaluation. In a sense, the very core of scholarship in the field is the weighing and evaluation of sources. Objectivity, which is a prime consideration in some evaluation schemes, is often derided in history as being impossible to achieve. Whether or not a Web site is up to date is often unimportant because, in history, there is no real onus attached to an opinion's being at odds with mainstream opinion.

But there are steps that can be taken to overcome these difficulties, some of which are also present to some degree in a number of other fields. First, draw a contrast between the lack of selection and filtering with respect to Web content on the one hand with the large amount of selection and filtering that does go on with respect to other kinds of sources. This is particularly true of the books and journal articles that undergraduates are likely to find when using library research tools. Many undergraduates are not aware that most of the specialized books and journal articles they encounter have been subject to peer review before they are published. A brief explanation of peer review in those formats helps point out the great difference between those sources and the many Web pages that have not been screened or evaluated.

Second, clearly delineating the unique challenges of source evaluation in a discipline—such as the ones mentioned in history—can help convince students that evaluation may be a little more complicated than they thought.

Third, if there is time, the points one wishes to make can be done with interactive learning and can heighten interest and break down resistance. Nancy Young and Diane Prorak of the University of Idaho presented some good ideas related to enhancing student interest in a general Web site evaluation session that could be adapted and employed in the context of a particular course to help solve the problems that have been outlined.[2] One idea they emphasized was that the lesson doesn't really sink in unless there is active hands-on learning. But of course it is vitally important to balance these considerations with all of the course objectives so that the best use is made of the available time.

Fourth and finally, point the students toward a good set of evaluative criteria, always with the caveat that even those criteria have to be used carefully in a field such as history. A very workable set of criteria is that by Elizabeth Kirk, a librarian at Johns Hopkins, and another by Robert Harris, professor of English at Vanguard University of Southern California.[3] Neither set is specifically aimed at history as a discipline, but each does have the merit of appreciating some of the complexities and difficulties about evaluation that have been mentioned.

## A FOCUS ON RESOURCES

Among the resources covered during the presentations and demonstrations was OASIS, the Libraries' On-Line Public Access Catalog (OPAC). OASIS includes not only the Libraries' OPAC but also specialized subject databases such as AFRI (Africana Database) and HSAT (History of Science and Technology), as well as other catalogs such as RLIN (a union catalog of more than 63 million items held in comprehensive research libraries, archival repositories, museums, and academic, public, law, technical, and corporate libraries) and CRLC (Center for Research Libraries in Chicago). Resources from the Libraries-Wide Information System (LWIS) Web site and the Internet included the CIC-VEL (providing access to the catalogs of all Big Ten Universities and the University of Chicago) and Eureka (Research Libraries' Group On-Line World Wide Web Catalog), as well as selected Internet search engines such as those available through the LWIS Gateway to the Internet and Yahoo. In addition, specialized databases available through the Hardin Library's Healthnet system and the National Library of Medicine were included.

Before focusing on the specific resources that were relevant to international health topics, it was important to present some of the key concepts and factors influencing international health. The World Health Organization defines health as "a state of complete physical, mental and social well-being and not merely the absence of disease or infirmity."[4] The international dimension or globalization refers "to a world in which societies, cultures, polities and economies have in some sense, come closer together."[5] The two most important elements of globalization are economics and technology. The economic aspect involves closer cooperation and linkage among world economies and faster and easier global communication and transportation inherent among the advances being made in new technological achievements.

Globalization may have both positive and negative effects on international health. Among the positive aspects is the ability of the world community to respond quickly to serious worldwide health threats, such as the Ebola crisis in Zaire (now the Democratic Republic of Congo) a few years ago. Among the negative effects is the fact that increased cultural contacts and exchanges have the potential of allowing diseases to spread quickly if adequate preventive measures are not taken. An excellent example of this is the movement of refugees across borders, which happens regularly and can easily transmit diseases between peoples.

Economic inequality between and within nations along with the nature of their governmental administrations have implications on health policy. In order to understand the evolution of governments and their health policies, it is necessary to understand the history of specific countries. Accordingly, it is important to understand the local and national cultures of the different countries.

International politics is another important factor. Many Third World countries that receive aid from other countries use a portion of that aid to improve the health of their people. But aid also comes with conditions; for example, the Structural Adjustment Programs in many African countries meant reduced government subsidies for health and social services. Another factor to be considered is whether or not international health policy in the industrialized countries is perceived to be part of their national interest or is simply policy based on humanitarian considerations.

## SEARCHING TECHNIQUES

During the demonstration sessions, searches were done in MEDLINE along with the Anthropological Literature and SearchBank databases.[6]

General keyword searches using "globalization and health" as well as "culture and health" were demonstrated. The Search Bank database concentrates on social, cultural, economic, political, and historical aspects and provides simple bibliographic citations and sometimes full text in the retrieval. A variety of keyword searches, such as "India colonial history" and "health," "health women" and "Middle East," "global health" and "national interest," and "global health" and "inequalities" were demonstrated. Subject searches such as medical history and India, traditional medicine and Ghana, and traditional medicine and Africa were demonstrated.

In order to locate primary sources on the Internet, it is helpful to search government and international organization Web sites for likely possibilities. There are many of these resources on the Internet, and the demonstration concentrated on how some of these could be located through a major university library site such as the University of Iowa's. The Web sites of the U.S. Agency for International Development and Center for Disease Control and Prevention were demonstrated.

The Web sites of foreign countries are very important for doing research on international health topics, and many countries now have Web sites or are in the process of developing them. The 1991 census of India is a good example. Students were shown how to explore that site and locate useful information.

A number of international organizations have developed Web sites, and many of these can be located through the Global Health Council Web site or the World Health Organization site.

Here are several of the pages developed by Sandra Ballasch for the course including the introductory page, general resources, health sciences resources, and selected Internet search engines.

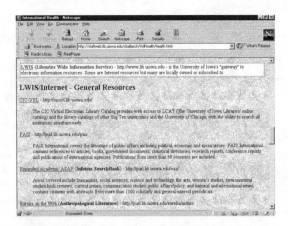

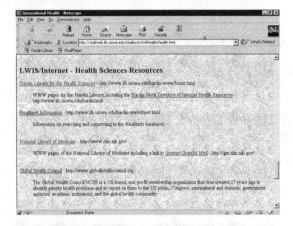

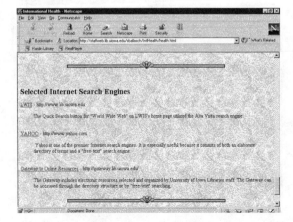

## NOTES

1. Effective November 1, 1999, all SearchBank customers were upgraded to InfoTrac Web—the Gale Group's Web-based search engine.

2. Nancy Young and Diane Prorak, "Using the Web to Evaluate the Web: Teaching Web Site Evaluation at the University of Idaho Library." Poster session presented at Educating the University Community in a Dynamic Information Environment, November 11–12, 1999, at the University of Iowa, Iowa City.

3. Elizabeth E. Kirk, "Evaluating Information Found on the Internet," <http://milton.mse.jhu.edu:8001/research/education/net.html> [accessed 1 May 2000]; and Robert Harris, "Evaluating Internet Research Sources," <http://www.sccu.edu/faculty/R_Harris/evalu8it.htm> [accessed 1 May 2000].

4. Ginger L. Gist, "Learning from Experience," *Journal of Environmental Health* 61, no. 4 (November 1998): 4.

5. Ray Kiely, *Globalisation and the Third World* (London: Routledge, 1998), 3.

6. Describes articles and essays on anthropology and archaeology, including art history, demography, economics, psychology, and religious studies.

# 40

# Preassessment of Library Skills: Why Bother?

*Marsha Miller*

To some, the title of this chapter may seem rhetorical, redundant, self-serving, or even self-defeating. *Everyone* agrees that developing library search strategies is important, don't they? But which library skills? For what students? And when? Teaching faculty and students alike are used to a variety of assessment tools, within their disciplines, upon entering college, and so on. Therefore, some level of preassessment would seem to be an integral and obvious component of any library instruction program, especially one well integrated into its campus environment. Librarians and teaching faculty ideally work together to prepare students to receive and process the information presented so that students see the big picture (i.e., the value of library and information-seeking skills as a part of the academic experience, going past the specific assignment and course, through their academic career, and beyond). In planning library instruction, librarians ideally (there's that word again) work with concrete information (sometimes from past contact) about the course and/or professor, as well as from assumptions about the course, level, professor, or student group. The audience members, both teacher and student, arrive with varying levels of knowledge and their own assumptions about the library and the imminent library session.

Realistically, the librarian may receive very little help from the teaching faculty in advance of the session, especially if the instruction program is new, small, or undersupported by the academic community. Experienced instruction librarians have learned to be very proactive in working with teaching faculty, including the gathering of information before an instructional session. Initially, the simple request to receive a copy of the syllabus or library assignment can create an atmosphere of

puzzlement, wariness, or both. Asking for more preplanning by requesting a preassessment *process* could simply overwhelm the professor, especially if there's any feeling that the library session is a necessary evil, taking class time away from more important matters, or if the
professor feels that the librarian may be encroaching on her/his academic freedom (the *in my classroom I am God* syndrome). If, however, the professor is truly committed to the same goals and objectives
of the library instruction program, she/he may actually initiate a planning conference. From that starting point, the program has the potential of becoming a successful example of academic collaboration with
the needs of the student learner at the center.

While little formal preassessment has taken place at Indiana State
University (ISU), several initiatives, including a growing Freshman Year
Experience (twenty-three Learning Communities during fall 1999 with
a projection of fifty for fall 2000), and a general education Information
Technology Literacy course planned for pilot implementation in fall
2000, mean that more (nonlibrarian) university personnel than ever before are in a position to need to explore (collaboratively) what preassessment can do to help prepare students for their library experience. Librarians at ISU have been exploring the library literature, as
well as higher education literature generally, to further their role in
such initiatives. Terminology, between the *insiders* (librarians) and
everyone else (classroom teachers, administrators of the various initiatives) can be a problem. The instruction librarian is all too familiar with
the professor who calls to schedule the library tour, when he/she
means (or should mean) an instructional session. Too often *they* say,
we want our students to know *how to use the library*, we want the *library tour*, show the students the library resources they'll need, just do
what you do every year. Librarians talk about *information handling
skills, information seeking skills, the information search process*, and
*search strategies*. Communication continues to improve, and initiatives
such as those mentioned above can only help the process. Assessment
needs to be built in from the beginning, or as soon as possible.

## PREASSESS: WHY?

If teaching faculty agree to preassess their students prior to a library instruction experience, it lends legitimacy to that experience, especially
if the students meet only once with a librarian. It can reinforce to the
students that the knowledge base needed to prepare for library research at the college/university level is going to be markedly different
than their public school's requirements and expectations. Preassessment can give the clearest possible picture, both to the librarian and
the teaching faculty member, of the spectrum of library experience (or

lack of) for each unique class. Librarians will be able to adapt their basic presentation to each group. Preassessment can allay preconceived notions on the part of both faculty and students that include

- Knowledge of computers does not equal knowledge of library research strategies, or Internet research strategies.
- Basic knowledge of the library catalog does not mean students are proficient with on-line search strategies (e.g., controlled vocabulary, keyword, and keyword/Boolean search techniques).
- Students arrive for library sessions with an *I already know this*, or *Why do I need to know this?* or *I had this in freshman comp so why am I here again?* attitudes.
- Students don't ask questions during the session(s) but later need basic assistance they may or may not be able to get, or will not seek out.

## PREASSESS: WHAT?

While the literature dedicated to assessing pre- and/or postlibrary skills is adequate (it could be better), there is almost no end to the different criteria applied to extant formal or informal assessments. On-line assessments at individual library Web sites provide some excellent examples of current practice. Assessment tools viewed on-line and in the literature include

- Library and technical skills: those needed by students, based on information from faculty, course syllabi, and so on
- Library and technical skills: those students already have, discovered by asking the students
- Navigational skills: have the students found the library? Found the resources, departments, and so on?
- Attitudes: Do students read? Like to read? Use libraries? Like libraries? (implying that a better attitude or a fondness for reading make a better library researcher)
- Comfort and/or anxiety levels in using libraries, trying to find information
- Research skills: did students, prior to their university library experience, have an opportunity to develop specific skills?
- Demographics: are students first-year students from rural areas with few library opportunities? graduate students who, theoretically, already developed some form of basic library survival skills at their previous institution (on their own or through a formal program)? nontraditional-age students with fears of college, computers, libraries, plus many time constraints?

Examples of all of these have been observed, but it often seems that the assessments try to do to much, or too little, without a systematic framework that answers the basic question: what do we intend to do with the information thus gathered? An example of this "catch-all" format is the St. Olaf survey (Geffert and Christensen 1998). Part of the reason may be that librarians are not generally experienced in the development of assessment tools. Partnering with research faculty or the university's Center for Teaching and Learning would work toward developing better instruments. Too often, librarians have limited opportunities for assessment and, therefore, have to take what they can get (i.e., is the all-encompassing assessment instrument better than none?).

## THE CLASSROOM TEACHER'S ROLE

The classroom teacher can assess the need for library skills instruction by examining course assignments, how topics will be assigned or chosen, parameters for acceptable types of resources, and desired content of the library session. Teachers do not do students any favors by blithely saying that any topic will do. Some freshman composition teachers expect students to be able to rationally choose topics within their majors, but students may not be prepared to do this. Resources such as *10,000 Ideas for Term Papers, Projects, Reports, and Speeches* would help if in the hands of every freshman composition teacher. Often specific criteria that used to function in the all-print environment do not adapt well today. When students had the card catalog, the *Reader's Guide to Periodical Literature*, and the *Social Sciences Index*, it was easy to specify: three books, one magazine article, and three (professional, scholarly) journal articles. The student new to academic library research is now confronted by multitype databases such as ProQuest that make it difficult for the student to distinguish the magazine from the journal article. This is another example where teachers may need to readjust their project criteria to better fit today's on-line research environment.

The self-assessment tool illustrated here (table 1) is one way of providing the teaching faculty an opportunity to self-assess their classroom's research component.

Designed as a think piece (there is no rating scale), this table was developed by the author to accompany a 1998 mailing to academic department heads that detailed library instruction contacts for a five-year period. Department heads were encouraged to share this with their faculty.

The classroom teacher must agree that the library component is an integral part of the assignment, that time is not being *given up* to come to a library session. Assignments must be continually updated to take into consideration technological advances, or changes in vendors that

**Table 1   Does My Course Need Library Instruction**

| A self-assessment tool | | |
|---|---|---|
| I should help my students develop the ability to use the literature of my discipline available in the library. | ❏ Yes | ❏ No |
| My students should have specific instructions on how to use the library in each course in which I require its use. | ❏ Yes | ❏ No |
| It should take considerable time for students to master the skills needed to use the library for my courses. | ❏ Yes | ❏ No |
| I should be familiar with the range of library resources useful in teaching my students. | ❏ Yes | ❏ No |
| For students in my courses, the library should be considered primarily as a place to study textbooks, lecture notes, and similar materials. | ❏ Yes | ❏ No |
| I stay aware of new reference/library sources (print and electronic) that I might add to my reading assignments; course bibliographies, regular reserve/electronic reserve, etc. | ❏ Yes | ❏ No |
| I should develop an interesting problem to introduce my students to the library. | ❏ Yes | ❏ No |
| I should have the main responsibility for ensuring that my students make good use of the library. | ❏ Yes | ❏ No |
| My students should use the library to learn how scholars examine major works and ideas in my discipline. | ❏ Yes | ❏ No |
| I should be better prepared to teach students how to make good use of the library. | ❏ Yes | ❏ No |
| I should evaluate the library assignments of my students on the same basis as any other assignments for my courses. | ❏ Yes | ❏ No |
| It should reflect poorly on my department if the library is not heavily used by students in our courses. | ❏ Yes | ❏ No |
| My students must use specific library resources; e.g., a reference book/series; an electronic index; an Internet-based full-text resource. | ❏ Yes | ❏ No |
| I am using the same library assignment I've always used; it still works well and accomplishes its goals. | ❏ Yes | ❏ No |
| I would like to develop a library assignment that accomplishes goals that have recently been redesigned. | ❏ Yes | ❏ No |
| Student frustration in using the library should be considered a normal part of learning how to use the library. | ❏ Yes | ❏ No |
| Librarians should help me by teaching my students how to use the library. | ❏ Yes | ❏ No |
| I need to incorporate Internet-based resources and Web sites but am unsure how to accomplish this. | ❏ Yes | ❏ No |
| Students should be able to learn needed library skills in my discipline quickly and independently. | ❏ Yes | ❏ No |

change the title of a database (e.g., PsycLit or PsycInfo). The librarian is consulted as an equal partner as the teacher prepares for the instructional session. The Learning Community Initiative at Indiana State University is an excellent example of this partnership. During fall 1999, one freshman year experience course (Univ 101, Learning in the Academic Community) was paired with a discipline-based course. Faculty for each course formed a team before the semester started; the team included one Information Services liaison (usually a librarian), and one Learning Community peer instructor (undergraduate student). While participation varied, often the librarian interacted with the students throughout the semester, on-line and/or in-person, and conducted the library sessions for one or both classes. In addition, sessions were planned to complement each other.

The classroom faculty is in a position to assess the current level of library skills for each student, and can design, or help design, an assessment specific to the subject area. Her/his own library use methods can also be assessed: can those methods be a model for student use, or are they the antithesis of library skills needed by the average undergraduate student? Do his/her own skills/methods need to be updated?

The results of the assessment may be reported back to the teacher before the session or shared with the students as the session begins. This has proven very successful with graduate students who may overestimate their skills; not only do they have a chance to assess their skills, they can prioritize resources listed on the survey. Their answers can be used to tailor the session to their specific needs. Given time, librarians can develop special handouts or on-line support materials for the course. As a result, students are more focused on the session. They feel they have a stake in the learning process. Librarians and teachers have worked collaboratively to make the instruction more valuable for everyone.

## PREASSESS: WHEN?

Preassessment can take place prior to the scheduled class session. The librarian supplies the assessment tool, the teacher administers the survey, returning it to the librarian. The librarian may visit the classroom to administer and collect the survey. If there is no formal assessment prior to the instructional session, librarians can begin by informally surveying the students. Students could respond to questions such as

- How many have had an instructional session before?
- What library skills do students think are important?
- What problems have they experienced? what has frustrated them about using any library/this library? what have they liked about libraries?

308         *Marsha Miller*

For courses such as Univ 101, students can be asked to look at all of their course syllabi, identifying library assignments and projects, looking for specific criteria (if any), and assisting the librarian to identify skills sets upon which to concentrate.

## CONCLUSION

Assessment is a well-established pedagogical tool. As librarians continue to build partnerships with teaching faculty, to build instructional programs that integrate library skills throughout the entire curriculum, preassessment of library and information-seeking skills should become a natural part of the package.

# 41

# Implementing an Assessment Program for Student Information Competency at Appalachian State University

*Dr. W. Bede Mitchell and Dr. Ann Viles*

What is the impetus for the use of assessment methods in libraries and for library instruction/bibliographic instruction/information literacy librarians? The answer is to find out whether or not what is taught is useful and has carryover from the initial session to at least the end of the student's studies. Mechanisms of assessment must be implemented that demonstrate that the requisite cognitive concepts and skills are being learned. If instruction librarians want to continue instructional programs, those programs must be shown to be necessary to other learning experiences. This must be done in order to garner support from library administrators, campus administration, faculty, and students.[1]

On September 9, 1999, three weeks after beginning its fall semester, Appalachian State University did not hold classes in order that the campus could conduct formal assessments of student learning. At Appalachian, student learning assessment is coordinated by the University Assessment Committee and consists of cohort-based testing so that each entering class contributes unique information to the university's understanding of learning outcomes created by the curriculum, policies, and extracurricular experiences. Students are tested as freshmen, second semester sophomores, and seniors with focus on a selected core curriculum element.[2]

The 1999 cohort of ninety-four randomly selected Appalachian freshmen completed a hands-on assessment of computing skills, including word processing, E-mail, spreadsheet, and Web navigation. The remainder of the freshman class, 1,951 students, completed a self-assessment survey of computing experiences and an information literacy test. The purpose of the information literacy test was to establish a benchmark for entering freshmen, which will be used to determine changes in their skills when they are tested again as second semester sophomores and as seniors.

Appalachian's investment in cohort-based testing enabled the institution's librarians to implement an information literacy assessment program that follows the counsel of the Association of College and Research Libraries:

> Formal evaluation tools may include the following: General library knowledge surveys (or "pre-tests") offered to incoming first-year students, re-offered at a midpoint in the students' careers and again near graduation, to assess whether the library's program of curricular instruction is producing more information-literate students.[3]

This chapter will recount the results of the first test and summarize some lessons to be applied to future cohort assessments.

## OTHER PROGRAMS MEASURING STUDENTS' INFORMATION LITERACY SKILLS

The 1999 information literacy tests were the culmination of several years of discussions about how best to measure the effectiveness of the Appalachian State University Library's bibliographic instruction programs. As part of those discussions, we reviewed the professional literature for reports of information literacy skills assessment at other postsecondary institutions so we could benefit from the experiences of our colleagues. One of the first things we noticed was that while there are some variations in the ways various academic libraries define information literacy, there are also notable overlaps and similarities. For example, the California State University Dominguez Hills-University Library assessment instrument tests five information competencies:

1. Student knows the range of sources including their limits and potential
2. Student knows how to use a range of information tools, from the contents of a book to a database
3. Student knows how to judge the quality of information
4. Student formulates appropriate research questions
5. Student has the ability to organize, synthesize, and apply information in a logical form[4]

Compare these competencies to the information literacy skills of seniors that the University of Wisconsin-Stevens Point tested during 1995–96, the ability to:

1. access information from a range of sources (Internet, journals, books)
2. organize the information accessed
3. evaluate the quality of the information found
4. synthesize and present a report on the information collected[5]

We also found that some assessment programs relied heavily on student self-assessment. This was the approach used by Cornell University in surveying more than three hundred graduates of Cornell's business and finance programs.[6] Similarly, the University of California at Berkeley administered self-assessment surveys of library user skill levels, but also conducted tests of actual skill levels to graduating seniors in political science and sociology during spring semester 1994. "Overall, 93 percent of students surveyed perceived their library skills as fair, pretty good, or excellent. . . . [However,] "63 percent of the graduates received poor to failing scores on the survey questions. Only 1.2 percent of the students scored 90 percent or higher in correctly answering the survey questions."[7]

Another program that tested actual skills, in this case by analyzing student research papers, was conducted by the library and the Division of Information Studies of Nanyang Technological University (NTU) in Singapore. Like the Berkeley researchers, they also concluded that many students have limited information literacy and skills. The NTU researchers found that the students spent little time defining problems and placing questions in context. Rather, they interpreted questions literally and looked for material that mentioned those words listed in the question. The students in this study demonstrated little familiarity with the framework of knowledge and ways to locate information. They searched for articles in the library's on-line catalog instead of subject databases and were unaware of the relative value of refereed and non-refereed sources. On the positive side, the NTU students were "found to be capable in the areas of extracting information, note taking, synthesizing the information and then developing impressive presentations."[8]

Finally, we found instances where scholars were attempting to measure the effectiveness of methods for teaching information literacy. In one representative study, Janelle Wertzberger at Gettysburg College completed a "Quantitative Assessment of Student's Library Skills and Attitudes" during fall semester 1998. The objective was to evaluate the relative effectiveness of group library instruction and individual library instruction. Over a two-month period, 405 students completed tests before and after library group instruction or individual consultation sessions. The tests contained a number of questions about student attitudes and six multiple-choice questions about library research. The multiple-choice questions tested knowledge about the on-line catalog, periodical databases, article citations, and evaluation of search tools and search results. Overall, the Gettysburg students' answers were correct about 60 percent of the time, and those who had not had prior library instruction improved their scores by an average of 4 percent after the library instruction was completed.[9]

The lessons that we took from our literature review included the importance of carefully defining the information literacy skills and abilities we wanted to test, the advantages of performance-based tests over purely self-assessment approaches, and the desirability of pre- and posttesting.

## METHODOLOGY FOR APPALACHIAN STATE UNIVERSITY'S ASSESSMENT PROGRAM

The actual designing, testing, and refining of Appalachian's information literacy assessment instrument was a collaborative effort involving librarians, faculty, and students. We were able to take advantage of several university committees in order to include all of these constituencies in our planning process. We began with the Learning Communities Council, which serves as an advisory board for the Freshman Interest Group (FIG) program and promotes communication and collaboration among learning communities across the campus. The library is represented on the Learning Communities Council, and a librarian serves as a full team member in each FIG. Preliminary work on the assessment instrument began during the week of May 17, 1999, when one session of the training for the 1999–2000 FIG faculty and staff teams was devoted to group exercises that brainstormed ways to assess students' information competency. In addition, faculty members from a number of different academic departments and the university's Assessment Office consulted and collaborated with library faculty throughout the summer to design the assessment instrument.

At the heart of the brainstorming and planning for the assessment instrument was the key question of how to measure the information literacy competencies we as a university expect from our graduates. These competencies were defined in the policy titled "Information Literacy Goals for Appalachian State University Students," which had been adopted in 1997. In that document, we stated that the principal information literacy goals for an Appalachian graduate should be (a) understands library and information organization and how to find needed information, (b) knows how to evaluate and use information, and (c) knows the primary body of literature in his/her discipline. For the purposes of our benchmarking, it appeared to be clearly inappropriate to test first-year college students for knowledge of the primary body of literature in particular disciplines. We decided instead to focus on measuring basic information skills and knowledge implied by the performance outcomes specified in the first two literacy goals. As evidence of understanding library and information organization and how to find needed information, the desired performance outcomes are

A1. Uses services that are available to assist in locating information
A2. Identifies potential sources of information
A3. Understands the basic structure of print and electronic resources and strategies used to access information from them
A4. Understands standard terms such as bibliographic citation, periodical index, abstract, and so on
A5. Writes correct bibliographic citations following discipline guidelines

The desired performance outcomes for knowing how to evaluate and use information are

B1. Distinguishes scholarly from popular or biased treatments of a subject
B2. Determines the quality and usefulness of information based on relevant criteria
B3. Integrates new information into existing knowledge to enhance critical thinking and problem solving
B4. Recognizes the ethics of scholarly research, such as providing bibliographic citations for cited material, and respecting intellectual property rights

A draft of the first test was posted to the ACRL Information Literacy Immersion listserv in early August for critique and suggestions from a group of librarians who are particularly interested in information literacy. Many of the suggestions were incorporated in the test that was administered on September 9.

A pilot test of the survey instrument was conducted with a small group of twenty-two library student assistants in early August. The results of this test along with the students' comments and suggestions were used to make the final revisions to the instrument. The test administered on September 9 consisted of a series of multiple-choice questions. Only one question dealt with the use of available services for assistance in locating information (A1). Two questions involved some critical thinking and problem solving (B3), and one pertained to copyright as an aspect of the ethics of scholarly research (B4), although there was no expectation that selected-response questions would give significant information about the skills and concepts in either B3 or B4. Four questions each addressed knowledge of terminology (A4), identification of potential information sources (A2), and distinguishing scholarly sources from popular or biased sources (B1). Six dealt with bibliographic citations (A5), although not in specific disciplines. Seven addressed the evaluation of information (B2). Nine questions pertained to understanding the basic structure of information resources and strategies used to access information from them (A3).

As noted earlier, ninety-four randomly selected Appalachian freshmen completed a hands-on assessment of computing skills, including word processing, E-mail, spreadsheet, and Web navigation. The remainder of the freshman class, 1,951 students, completed both a self-assessment survey of computing experiences and an information literacy test. Both of these instruments contained elements relevant to information literacy. The survey asked the students to rate their own skills in searching the Web and to answer the information literacy questions designed by the librarians, while the hands-on test had students retrieve and cite information from the Web.

## RESULTS OF THE INFORMATION LITERACY TESTS

Overall, the students answered 72.7 percent of the information literacy questions correctly. Ninety-five percent indicated that a librarian should be consulted for help with finding, choosing, and using information sources. The highest and lowest percentage of correct answers occurred in a group of questions about an excerpt from the *Readers Guide to Periodical Literature*. Ninety-nine percent could recognize a publication date, 97 percent could identify an author, 97 percent knew the volume number of the article cited, but only 38 percent recognized that the title of the periodical in the citation was the italicized *Time*. There is some speculation that the ease of obtaining full-text articles in on-line databases is blurring the concept of articles in distinct periodicals, and this could possibly support that hypothesis. Eighty percent could arrange books in Dewey call number order (prevalently used in high school libraries), but only 44 percent could arrange books in the Library of Congress classification order (usually employed in college and university libraries). It will be interesting to find out if the Library of Congress order scores improve in later tests after the students are supposedly more familiar with the university library. Seventy-five percent believed that most components of a Web page are protected by copyright.

Of the four questions related to the identification of potential information sources (A2), only 64 percent of the students recognized several ways to choose the best articles from a long list of citations, 71 percent knew that encyclopedias were good sources for finding introductory materials about a topic, 82 percent knew how to identify the information contained in a book, and 93 percent knew that periodicals were more likely to have current information than books, encyclopedias, or bibliographies. Scores for questions related to A3 ranged irregularly from 44 percent to 82 percent correct. Looking separately at those pertaining to the structure of information sources and those pertaining to search strategies still gave disparate results, so it appeared likely that some of the questions in this set were not valid. Scores for questions related to the evaluation of information (B2) were also quite mixed, leading again to the suspicion that, in spite of our best efforts, the questions were not validly measuring what they were intended to test. These groups of questions need to be improved in the next version of the instrument. The students generally scored high on the questions involving terminology (A4), although many librarians would be disappointed to know that 34 percent would look for books in biographical dictionaries, periodical indexes, or gazetteers rather than in library catalogs. With regard to bibliographic citations, only 38 percent of the students, as mentioned above, could identify a periodical title in a citation, and 54 percent had difficulty identifying information about the author and/or producer of a Web page. The percentage of correct answers for questions related to scholarly versus popular and biased sources were generally low—ranging from 57 percent to 73 percent.

## RESULTS OF THE COMPUTING TESTS

Randy Swing has summarized the results of the hands-on assessment of computing skills and the self-assessment survey of computing experiences.[10] More than "two-thirds of Appalachian students considered themselves to be expert or above average in searching the Web." Of the students taking the hands-on test, 90 percent successfully located information about a past president, and nearly 75 percent could cite the URL for the source of the information. One indicator from the hands-on test showed misunderstanding about Web-based materials.

Sixty percent of students incorrectly reported that the federal government required Web sites to identify the authors, dates created, and host institutions. This finding suggested that students believed Web information was "controlled" by federal law and highlights the gap between abilities to access information and abilities to critically evaluate Web information. Faculty cannot assume that freshmen understand the variance in quality across the Web sources. Thirty-three percent of the students in the hands-on test indicated that they had received instruction in searching electronic library resources in the classroom, and 25 percent reported seeking help outside the classroom for finding information on the Web.

A difference between faculty and student investment in information search strategies was recorded. Faculty focused on teaching students to use electronic library resources while students sought help for conducting searches on the Web. These data may indicate different levels of trust of Web materials and comfort differences in using the two kinds of resources. Clearly faculty and students approach information searches differently.

## WHAT WE LEARNED ABOUT CONSTRUCTING INFORMATION LITERACY TESTS

First, if the assessment is a selected-response or fill-in-the-blank test that will be used to diagnose basic skills, it should contain at least ten questions—preferably more—for each skill area. The questions pertaining to each skill area should be considered a subtest, and these subtests should yield separate scores on the various elements needed for mastery of the skill.[11] Ergo, our test should have been longer.

Second, avoid using *all of the above* or *none of the above*, particularly when the question calls for students to choose "the best answer." This type of question can hurt students who are too quick (but know their stuff), and may read the first answer choice, recognize it as correct, and mark it, then move on to the next question without reading the other answer choices.[12] Here is an example of this problem:

22. Which of the following statements best describes the information provided about the author and/or producer of the Web site?
    A. The author of the article is named
    B. The producer is identified
    C. There is a link to information about the producer
    D. All of the above

Confirming McBride's analysis, 47 percent of the Appalachian students answered letter A, and 46 percent more correctly answered letter D. As a result, the question was wasted since we have no way of knowing how many of the 47 percent really thought only A was correct and how many just didn't read all of the options.

Third, make every question count. Have specific purposes in mind for every question: expected results, significance of results, null hypotheses, relationships to other questions. If you cannot define these for a particular question, don't use it.

Fourth, connect to other assessments. We did this to some extent but could have taken greater advantage of other concurrent tests and already completed tests at Appalachian and other institutions. Outcomes assessment of information literacy is too complex for any single effort to be significant as a stand-alone measurement.

Last, be ambitious. Multiple-choice tests are easier to score, but many aspects of information literacy can be measured better with hands-on tests, short assignments, and open-ended questions. We need to recruit all the collaborators we possibly can and expand the scope of this test before we meet these same students in a couple of years.

## FUTURE ACTIONS

How can the results be applied to improve student learning of information skills? The faculty and librarians who contributed to the development of the assessment instrument must take the lead in sharing the test results with their colleagues and considering the implications for the content being taught and the pedagogical methodologies being employed at Appalachian. From the time the freshmen have taken the first information literacy test until the time they graduate, there is ample time for strong information literacy skills to be inculcated, but it will only be done after careful curricular planning and preparation.

## A FINAL WORD

It might be asked: What aspects of the students' university experience does this assessment really address? Is the university able to take full responsibility for all that students learn during their college careers, even that which is learned purely through student self-instruction? How will we be able to guarantee that gains in the ability to find and evaluate information can be credited to the university rather than to students' independent efforts? Perhaps there is no answer to these questions that will convince skeptics, but such concerns about student assessment can and are extended to all aspects of college education. For any field, what is the guarantee that many individual students already had mastered certain skills and abilities before coming to the university, or that many students may have developed their mastery outside of formal instruction? The fact that we cannot offer such guarantees for any specific individual case is, after all, why we test the aggregated student body when we attempt to measure institutional performance. There are no adequate data to create a presumption that most changes in students' academic skills and abilities are due to extracurricular experiences rather than the targeted efforts of the university, so it satisfies common sense to assume that trends in aggregated scores are due to the university's influence.

## NOTES

1. Lois M. Pausch and Mary Pagliero Popp, Assessment of Information Literacy: Lessons from the Higher Education Assessment Movement 1997 <http://www.ala.org/acrl/paperhtm/d30.html> [accessed 4 October 1999].

2. Randy Swing, Hands-On Computing Assessment—Overview 1999 <http://www.appstate.edu/www_docs/depart/irp/assessment/compoverview999.html> [accessed 13 October 1999].

3. "Standards for College Libraries: A Draft," *College & Research Libraries News* 60 (May 1999): 376.

4. California State University, Dominguez Hills-University Library, "Summary List of Information Competencies to Recommend to California State University," *Information Competency Project* 1999 <http://library.csudh.edu/infocomp/list.htm> [accessed 18 October 1999].

5. University of Wisconsin-Stevens Point, "Information Literacy Assessment, UW-Stevens Point, Spring 1996." Campus Assessment Committee, University of Wisconsin-Stevens Point, 1996, photocopy, 1.

6. Mary Ochs et al., *Assessing the Value of an Information Literacy Program,* ERIC, ED 340385 (Ithaca, N.Y.: Cornell University Albert R. Mann Library, 1991).

7. Pat Davitt Maughan, *The Teaching Library: Information Literacy Survey* 1995 <http://www.lib.berkeley.edu/TeachingLib/Survey.html> [accessed 18 October 1999].

8. Mark Hepworth, "A Study of Undergraduate Information Literacy and Skills: The Inclusion of Information Literacy and Skills in the Undergraduate Curriculum." Paper presented at the annual meeting of the International Federation of Library Associations and Institutions, Bangkok, Thailand, August 1999 <http://www.ifla.org/IV/ifla65/papers/107-124e.htm> [accessed 29 October 1999].

9. Janelle Wertzberger, "Quantitative Assessment of Students' Library Skills and Attitudes." Poster session presented at the biannual meeting of the Association of College and Research Libraries, Detroit, Michigan, April 1999 <http://www.gettysburg.edu/~jwertzbe/poster/> [accessed 15 Octber 1999].

10. All quotes in this section are taken from Randy Swing, *Appalachian State University: Freshman Computing Skills and Experiences* 1999 <http://www1.appstate.edu/dept/irp/assessment/compute/compute99.doc> [accessed 29 October 1999].

11. Amanda McBride, "Letting Students Shine: Assessment to Promote Student Learning," *Focus* 31 (1999): 9.

12. McBride, "Letting Students Shine," 19.

# 42

## Situated Learning at the Georgia Tech Library: Moving from an Instructivist to a Constructivist Model of Undergraduate User Education

*Julie Wood*

> The challenge for educators is to develop strategies that teach content in ways that also teach thinking and problem-solving skills.
>
> —R. Scott Grabinger (1996, 665)

Recently, librarians have begun incorporating "active learning" techniques into their instruction programs. The most common example of this is the inclusion of hands-on practice time during classes. While this is a step in the right direction, little research has been done, or literature written, about the value of active learning in library instruction. In addition to discussing the benefits of active learning and "situated learning," the literature of cognitive science and educational technology also discuss constructivism as a learning paradigm. This is a shift from the instructivist model of education to the constructivist model. The Georgia Tech Library and Information Center's Instruction Program has begun this paradigm shift.

Until a few years ago, the Georgia Tech Library and Information Center had no formal instructional program. Emphasis was placed on homogenous fifty-minute "chalk 'n' talk" lectures. Orientation sessions and tours were also offered for specific courses. Sessions were conducted in a traditional lecture-style environment and only the instructor had access to a computer. Today, the Georgia Tech Library has successfully initiated an instructional program that has increased the number of classes by 77 percent and the attendance rate by 66 percent (1997–98 statistics). The library's program focuses on information competencies and user-centered instruction and employs a framework of situated learning culled from the educational theories of cognitive science.

The library has two state-of-the-art classrooms that enable every student in attendance to have access to a computer. Students are active participants in the sessions, completing hands-on exercises or working on research questions as a group and then presenting their findings to the class. Another new initiative, the Internet and Library Research Clinic, is a drop-in environment where information consultants offer in-depth research assistance to students. In addition, an information competency working paper was drafted in September 1998. It undergirds the program and supports the decision-making process.

By moving from an "instructivist" model of teaching to a "constructivist" model, we have moved into the paradigm of active learning. Cognitive science calls this "situated learning" or "constructivist" training and it offers us a new epistemology for learning—one that emphasizes active perception over concepts and representation. "Situated learning" is built on two principles, (1) learning is an active process wherein the learner constructs knowledge rather than merely acquires it, and (2) instruction is a process of supporting that construction rather than communicating knowledge (Duffy and Cunningham 1996, 171).

This theory of learning is not vastly different from other approaches commonly used in library education programs. However, it does constitute a different way of looking at learning and talking about learning that our faculty members understand. This approach works at Georgia Tech because of our technical/scientific culture and our strong cognitive science program.

## WHY IS THIS PARADIGM RELEVANT?

"Instructivist" and "constructivist" are terms that come from the fields of cognitive science and educational theory. Introducing these concepts provides the profession with new epistemology for learning—one that emphasizes active perception over concepts and representation. Having a new, up-to-date language for what we do also keeps us relevant. The academic world is giving attention to situated learning and constructivist thinking, especially in relation to instructional design.

Research has proven this paradigm works. Cognitive scientists have studied this paradigm for at least a dozen years now. Their research literature is filled with complementary and opposing viewpoints on the theory and practice of constructivist learning. Their conclusion is that this paradigm works.

As an audience for learning, today's undergraduate students are the "MTV generation." Their experience of life is one that expects stimulation. They cannot relate to the lecture setting where they are expected to sit and listen to a "sage on the stage" for hours. If they are not "doing," they are apt to tune out the session altogether.

Finally, this paradigm is relevant because its implementation fosters relationships with faculty members. Effective implementation of these theories requires librarians to work closely with faculty members to develop classes specifically for their courses. Librarians and faculty members must work together to design a meaningful learning experience.

## THE INSTRUCTIVIST APPROACH

The instructivist approach assumes the following (Fardouly 1998):

- Learning is a result of instruction and therefore students should be instructed in what to learn. The instructor knows best what material students need to learn. Students are not part of the process.
- Learning is a stimulus-response association that shapes desirable behaviors. Students receive a stimulus and are taught or shown how to respond. This does not include any explanation or experimentation.
- *Teaching* strategies include feedback, reinforcement, review, and practice. These are not *learning* strategies. Teachers give students feedback (communication is primarily one way), lesson points are reinforced with examples, material is reviewed, and students are expected to practice the tasks.
- Learning is goal oriented. Goals, perhaps "finding books in the library," are identified but not explained.
- Learning tasks are reduced into individual components. This is a step-by-step approach to any task being learned.
- Tasks must be mastered independently, then assembled.

## THE CONSTRUCTIVIST APPROACH

Contrasted with the instructivist approach, the constructivist approach has its own assumptions (Fardouly 1998):

- Students construct for themselves meaningful knowledge as a result of their own activities and interaction with others. Students have a hand in the process and make their own connections between the various learning activities.
- *Learning* strategies include library research, problem- and case-based learning, doing assignments and projects, group work, discussions, and fieldwork. The process is very learning-focused. Students are not simply learning by rote or repetition but by a variety of strategies.

- Classroom teaching is a stimulus to the student's real learning that mostly takes place outside formal classes. The teacher assumes that each student brings something valuable to the classroom— his or her own experiences. Meaningful learning does not take place in a vacuum.
- Classes are unstructured with individualized activities and much discussion. The lecture format is discarded or minimized. Classes include variety and communication is a two-way interchange.
- Students engage actively with the subject matter and transform new information into a form that makes personal sense to them and connects with prior knowledge. When knowledge becomes personalized, it has true meaning to the individual rather than being a simple memorization of rules, steps, or facts.
- Students are placed immediately into a realistic context with specific coaching provided as needed. Just as knowledge cannot be separated from the context in which it exists, learning is also contextual.

## SITUATED LEARNING AND ACTIVE LEARNING

Situated learning occurs when students work on "authentic tasks" whose execution takes place in a "real-world" setting. It does not occur when students are taught decontextualized knowledge and skills.

—William Winn (1993, 16)

Situated learning bridges the gap between learning and using. In this context, "how" something is learned is just as important as "what" is learned. Learning how to use a tool involves far more than an enumeration of explicit rules. One must also know and understand the environment in which that tool is used. Situated learning gives a real-world context to knowledge. Students are given tasks to which they can relate. Tasks, and indeed learning itself, are "situated" in a real-world setting. They are authentic to the learner's environment. In this case, college is the environment and the college culture also plays a part in this discussion. A traditional example of situated learning is the apprenticeship.

As a complement to situated learning, active learning involves activity on the part of the learner. "To be actively involved, students must engage in such higher-order thinking tasks as analysis, synthesis, and evaluation" (Bonwell and Eison 1991, 1). This does not imply a student *actively* listening to a lecture. Students must do more than just listen. They must read, write, discuss, or be engaged in solving problems.

Duffy and Cunningham describe this as a "framework of learning as situated in activity" (1996, 174).

## CHANGING THE LEARNING ENVIRONMENT

### REALs

The concept of Rich Environments for Active Learning (REALs) is based on constructivist theories. Among others, these include active learning and situated learning. A REAL is the environment in which these theories can be brought together. In *Rich Environments for Active Learning*, Grabinger defines REALs as environments that "provide activities that, instead of transferring knowledge to students, engage students in a continuous process of building and reshaping understanding as a natural consequence of their experiences and interactions with the world in authentic ways" (1996, 665). Grabinger also asserts that REALs are comprehensive or holistic instructional systems that promote study and investigation in authentic contexts, promote cooperative learning among students and teachers, promote high-level thinking processes, and assess student progress through realistic tasks and performance (1996, 668).

## RESHAPING INSTRUCTION

Instruction has come to a point where it must be "reshaped" to remain relevant and accessible by students. The information age demands it. No longer is it acceptable to provide instruction in "the same old way." Instruction programs must become learning programs. Learning environments must be more responsive than ever and innovation is key.

In addition to introducing situated learning and active learning into the classroom, there are other features that can be added to build a REAL. These include modeling and explaining, coaching, articulation, reflection, exploration, and sequence (Wilson and Cole 1996, 606).

By *modeling and explaining,* the instructor shows how the research process unfolds and explains why it happens that way. It is important that the demonstration and explanation be integrated to allow for recognition of the connection. An example of a model would be a demonstration of false starts to an on-line search. This would require explanations of "dead ends" (especially in relation to search terms), how to build and refine a search strategy, and the differences between keywords and subject terms.

*Coaching* requires that the instructor observe students as they work through a research problem, providing hints and help as necessary. This is a good way to determine progress in completing the exercise and assessment of effective learning. Verbal interaction with students is important in coaching. Students can be asked what they are thinking as they search and how they are making their decisions. This is an excellent way to integrate problem-based learning into an instruction program.

*Articulation* requires students to verbally articulate their research process. This is effective when students are required to come up to the instructor's PC and explain their decision-making process. Thinking aloud is another form of articulation. Verbalizing helps tacit knowledge become explicit.

*Reflection* allows students to look back over their effort and ana-lyze how well they accomplished the task. This often influences goal-setting and leads to intentional learning. *Exploration* allows students to try different strategies and examine the results. An example of this is to have a group of students each take a different resource and re-search the same topic, then regroup and discuss how well each of the resources addressed the topic.

*Sequence* relates to the development of the learning material. Plan the material so that it flows in order of increasing complexity with in-creasing diversity, variety, examples, or concepts. A good example of this is "scaffolding." The instructor provides the needed structure, out-line, or framework for the research and gradually removes it.

When integrating the concept of a REAL into an instruction program, it is important to understand the underlying holistic philosophy. This learning environment is a powerful tool. But it cannot realize its full potential unless the instructor takes steps to understand what the learn-ers bring with them—their experiences, knowledge, and the environ-ment from which they are coming. With this insight, the instructor can provide authentic, relevant learning activities that build on the learners' existing knowledge and experience.

## AT GEORGIA TECH

With the continual development of our information competency pro-gram, we move to further embrace this new constructivist paradigm. In addition to the two state-of-the-art classrooms, a growing roster of classes, and the Internet and Library Research Clinic, hands-on seg-ments are included in all classes and the development of a truly inter-active Web-based tutorial is in progress.

The Georgia Tech Library and Information Center has an informa-tion consulting program in place. Each librarian functions as a con-sultant to one or more specific colleges, schools, or departments (e.g., College of Management, School of Biomedical Engineering, De-partment of Modern Languages). This program provides faculty, staff, and students with a main "point of contact" who is also an informa-tion professional and who has specialized subject knowledge and focus. Information consultants have formed active partnerships with faculty members. These partnerships are crucial for the long-term growth and development of the information competency program and they serve to increase the credibility and visibility of the library on campus. The rapport built in to these partnerships also enables the information consultants to informally integrate information competency into the curriculum of many courses.

This new focus on collaborative and active learning obligates us to develop our own teaching skills. In order to facilitate this, we participate in the Teaching Fellows program sponsored by the Georgia Tech Center for the Enhancement of Teaching and Learning. This program gives Tech faculty the opportunity to enroll in a series of weekly seminars on instruction as well as take practical tests for improving their own teaching skills.

We want our students to have a powerful learning experience, but moving to the truly constructivist paradigm requires curriculum reform on a broad basis. It requires that information competency be an integral part of every course of study on campus. It is a political activity and may take a considerable amount of time to accomplish. A "working document" helps in negotiation. Our document, "Information Competencies: Students, Scholars, and Librarians," provides us with a basis for what we are doing and with a touchstone by which to test our activities and programs. This document must be regularly updated in order to remain current and viable.

These activities have exhilarated us, and as we continue to explore the constructivist model of learning, we identify dynamic opportunities to further undergraduate user education and add value to the learning experience.

> We can start with the commonsense recognition that real life is messy, that the problems we confront in everyday life are what earlier cognitivists labeled *ill-structured*—that is, they are open-ended, multifaceted problems in which solutions are equivocal.
>
> —Joseph Petraglia (1998, 13)

# Bibliography

## Chapter 8: Development of a Faculty Web Training Program at George Washington University

*Backspace*. "Download I/O/D4: The Web Stalker." *Web Stalker*. <http://bak. spc.org/iod/iod4.html> [accessed 29 December 1999].

Blackboard. 1999. "Blackboard Products and Services." *Course Info*. <http:// company.blackboard.com/CourseInfo/index.html> [accessed 29 December 1999].

Brown, Kim. "An In-Depth Interview with Jennifer Fleming." *Webreview.com*. <http://webreview.com/pub/web98east/21/flemingiview.html> [accessed 21 August 1999].

Clark, Barbara I., Nancy N. Knupfer, Judy E. Mahoney, Kevin M. Kramer, Hamed Ghazali, and Nabel Al-Ani. "Creating Web pages: Is Anyone Considering Visual Literacy?" Paper presented at the annual conference of the International Visual Literacy Association, Cheyenne, Wyoming, October 1996, ERIC, ED 408990, 1997.

Fleming, Jennifer. 1997. "In Defense of Web Graphics." *Webreview.com*. <http://webreview.com/pub/97/07/25/feature/index4.html> [accessed 17 August 1999].

———. 1998. "Crafting the User Experience." *Webreview.com*. <http://webreview. com/wr/pub/web98east/21/webnav1.html> [accessed 21 August 1999).

———. 1998. "Designing for Users." *Webreview.com*. <http://webreview.com/ wr/pub/web98east/21/webnav3.html> [accessed 22 August 1999).

J. D. Williams Library. 1999. "EDLS101." *EDLS101*. <http://www.olemiss.edu: 8042/courses/EDLS101/> [accessed 29 December 1999].

———. 1997. "Library Instruction Homepage." *Library Instruction Homepage*. <http://www.olemiss.edu/depts/general_library/lip/home.html> [accessed 28 December 1999].

Jurist, Susan. 1996. "Top 10 Rules for Creating Graphics for the Web." *College and Research Libraries News* 57, no. 7: 418–21.

Luck, Donald D., and J. Mark Hunter. "Visual Design Principles Applied to World Wide Web Construction." Paper presented at the annual conference of the International Visual Literacy Association, Cheyenne, Wyoming, October 1996, ERIC, ED 408985, 1997.

Netomat. "Download Netomat." *Netomat.* <http://www.netomat.net/data/1.1/install.htm> [accessed 29 December 1999].

*The Matrix.* Dir. Wachowski Brothers, Warner Brothers, 1999, digital video disk.

Mitchell, William J. 1996. *City of Bits.* Cambridge, Mass.: MIT Press.

Potatoland. 1998. "Launch Shredder." *Shredder.* <http://www.potatoland.org/shredder/> [accessed 29 December 1999].

Small, Ruth V. 1997. "Assessing the Motivational Quality of World Wide Web Sites." ERIC ED 407930.

Summerville, Jennifer B. 1998. "The Role of Awareness of Cognitive Style in Hypermedia." Paper presented at the national convention of the Association for Educational Communications and Technology, St. Louis, Missouri, 18-22 ERIC, ED 423865.

Tipton, Mary H., Cindy L. Kovalik, and Mary B. Shoffner. "Visual Literacy." *Visual Literacy.* <http://www.educ.kent.edu/vlo/> [accessed 11 September 1999].

Z. Smith Reynolds Library. 1999. "Research: Putting the Pieces Together: An Interactive Tutorial." *Putting the Pieces Together: An Interactive Tutorial.* <http://www.wfu.edu/Library/referenc/research/index.html> [accessed 29 December 1999].

## Chapter 9: Building Bridges with Faculty through Library Workshops

MiraCosta College Library. "Guidelines for Library Assignments: California Clearing House for Library Instruction." <http://www.miracosta.cc.ca.us/library/Instruction/CCLI.html> [accessed 15 December 1998].

Mosley, Pixey Anne. 1988. "Creating a Library Assignment Workshop for University Faculty." *Journal of Academic Librarianship* 29, no. 1 (January): 33–41.

Stauffer Library, Queen's University. "Designing Library Assignments." <http://stauffer.queensu.ca/inforef/instruct/design.htm> [accessed 15 December 1998].

Sterling C. Evans Library, Texas A&M University. "Creating Successful Library Assignments: A Guide for Faculty." <http://library.tamu.edu/reference/instruction/libassig.html> [accessed 15 December 1998].

———. "Creating Successful Library Assignments: Quick Tips and General Guidelines." <http://library.tamu.edu/reference/instruction/assign.html> [accessed 15 December 1998].

Wilson Library, University of Minnesota. "Designing Assignments that Can Be Effectively Supported by the Libraries." <http://www.lib.umn.edu/reference/libassi.html> [accessed 15 December 1998].

## Chapter 21: New Learners, New Models

American Library Association, Presidential Committee on Information Literacy. 1989. "Final Report." Chicago: American Library Association. <http://www.ala.org/acrl/nili/ilit1st.html> [accessed 3 November 1999].

Bloom, B. S. 1984. "The Search for Methods of Group Intervention as Effective One-to-One Tutoring." *Educational Leadership* 41:14. Quoted in Patricia Senn Breivik, *Student Learning in the Information Age*, American Council on Education/Oryx Press Series on Higher Education. Phoenix, Ariz.: Oryx Press, 1998, 24.

Boyer Commission on Educating Undergraduates in the Research University. 1998. "Reinventing Undergraduate Education: A Blueprint for America's Research Universities." Albany, N.Y.: SUNY Press. <http://notes.cc.sunysb.edu/Pres/boyer.nsf> [accessed 4 November 1999].

Breivik, Patricia Senn. 1998. *Student Learning in the Information Age*. American Council on Education/Oryx Press Series on Higher Education. Phoenix, Ariz.: Oryx Press.

Bruce, Christine. 1997. *The Seven Faces of Information Literacy.* Adelaide, Australia: Auslib Press.

Gardiner, Lion. 1994. *Redesigning Higher Education: Producing Dramatic Gains in Students' Learning.* ASHE-ERIC Higher Education Report, No. 7. Washington, D.C.: Graduate School of Education and Human Development, George Washington University. Quoted in Breivik, *Student Learning in the Information Age*, 24.

Shapiro, Jeremy J., and Shelly K. Hughes. 1996. "Information Literacy as a Liberal Art: Enlightenment Proposals for a New Curriculum." *Educom Review* 31, no. 2 (March–April). <http://www.educause.edu/pub/er/review/Articles/31231.html> [accessed 21 October 1999].

## Chapter 30: Designed to Serve from a Distance

Adams, Joyce A. 1998. "Tips and Tools for Beginning Web Authors." *Online* 22 (March–April): 66–70, 72.

Abels, Eileen G., Marilyn Domas White, and Karla Hahn. 1997. "Identifying User-Based Criteria for Web Pages." *Internet Research* 7:252–62.

Abels, Eileen G., Marilyn Domas White, and Karla Hahn. 1999. "A User-Based Design Process for Web Sites." *OCLC Systems & Services* 15:35–44.

Casey, Carol. 1999. "Accessibility in the Virtual Library: Creating Equal Opportunity Web Sites." *Information Technology and Libraries* 18 (March): 22–25.

Clausen, Helge. 1999. "Evaluation of Library Web Sites: The Danish Case." *The Electronic Library* 17 (April): 83–87.

D'Angelo, John, and Sherry K. Little. 1998. "Successful Web Pages: What Are They and Do They Exist?" *Information Technology and Libraries* 17 (June): 71–81.

Dewald, Nancy H. 1999. "Transporting Good Library Instruction Practices into the Web Environment: An Analysis of On-Line Tutorials." *Journal of Academic Librarianship* 25 (January): 26–32.

Diaz, Karen. 1999. "The Role of the Library Web Site: A Step beyond Deli Sandwiches." *Reference and User Services Quarterly* 38: 41–43.

Gregory, Gwen, and M. Marlo Brown. 1997. "World Wide Web Page Design: A Structured Approach." *Journal of Interlibrary Loan, Document Delivery & Information Supply* 73: 45–59.

Head, Alison J. 1999. "Web Redemption and the Promise of Usability." *Online* 23 (November–December): 20–28, 30, 32.

Horton, William, et. al. 1996. *The Web Page Design Cookbook.* New York: Wiley.

King, David L. 1998. "Library Home Page Design: A Comparison of Page Layout for Front-Ends to ARL Library Web Sites." *College & Research Libraries News* 59 (September): 458–65.

Lingle, Virginia A., and Eric P. Delozier. 1998. "Policy Aspects of Web Page Development." *Internet Reference Services Quarterly* 3: 33-48.

Metz, Ray E., and Gail Junion-Metz. 1996. *Using the World Wide Web and Creating Home Pages: A How-To-Do-It Manual for Librarians.* New York: Neal-Schuman Publishers.

Mosley, Pixey Anne. 1998. "Making Library Instructional Handouts Accessible through the World Wide Web." *Research Strategies* 16: 153–61.

Nicotera, Cynthia L. 1998. "Information Access by Design: Electronic Guidelines for Librarians." *Information Technology and Libraries* 18 (June): 104–8.

Pyette, Sandra D., and Oya Y. Rieger. 1998. "Supporting Scholarly Inquiry: Incorporating Users in the Design of the Digital Library." *Journal of Academic Librarianship* 24 (March): 121–29.

Rowbotham, Julie. 1999. "Librarians—Architects of the Future?" *ASLIB Proceedings* 51 (February): 59–63.

Stover, Mark. 1999. *Leading the Wired Organization: The Information Professional's Guide to Managing Technological Change.* New York: Neal-Schuman Publishers.

Stover, Mark, and Steven D. Zink. 1996. "World Wide Web Home Page Design: Patterns and Anomalies of Higher Education Library Home Pages." *Reference Services Review* 24 (Fall): 7–20.

Tilton, Eric, et. al. 1996. *Web Weaving: Designing and Managing an Effective Web Site.* Reading, Mass.: Addison-Wesley.

## Chapter 31: Supporting and Educating Students at a Distance

Fisher, R. K. 1991. "Off-Campus Library Services in Higher Education in the United Kingdom." *Library Trends* 39, no. 4 (Spring): 479–94.

Carty, J., et al., 1996. "Towards a Strategy for Supporting Distance-Learning Students through Networked Access to Information: Issues and Challenges in Preparing to Support the Doctorate in Education." *Education for Information* 14:305–16.

The National Committee of Inquiry into Higher Education. 1997. *Higher Education in the Learning Society (Dearing Report)* (July): 467.

Raven, D. 1999. "Breaking the Campus Boundary." *Library Association Record* 101, no. 6 (June): 346–48.

## Chapter 32: Information Competency Continuum

American Library Association. 1998. *Information Power: Building Partnerships for Learning.* Chicago: American Library Association Editions.

American Association of School Librarians. 1999. *Information Literacy Standards for Student Learning.* Chicago: American Library Association Editions.

California Media and Library Educators Association. 1997. *From Library Skills to Information Literacy: A Handbook for the Twenty-First Century.* Castle Rock, Colo.: Hi Willow Research and Publishing.

Loertscher, David V., and Blanche Woolls. 1999. *Information Literacy: A Review of the Research: A Guide for Practitioners and Researchers.* Castle Rock, Colo.: Hi Willow Research and Publishing.

## Chapter 34: Web Technology and Evidence-Based Medicine

Brink, Tom, et al., 1998. *Usability First.* <http://www.usabilityfirst.com> [accessed 19 January 2000].

Chisman, Janet, Karen Diller, and Sharon Walbridge. 1999. "Usability Testing: A Case Study." *College & Research Libraries* 60, no. 6 (November): 552–69.

Head, Alison J. 1999. "Web Redemption and the Promise of Usability." *Online* 23, no. 6 (November–December): 20–23, 26–28, 30, 32.

Instone, Keith. 1996. *Usable Web.* <http://www.usableweb.com> [accessed 19 January 2000].

Nielsen, Jakob. *useit.com: Jakob Nielsen's site (Usable Information Technology)* <http://www.useit.com> [accessed 19 January 2000].

Sackett, David L., et al. 1997. *Evidence-based Medicine: How to Practice & Teach EBM.* New York: Churchill Livingstone.

Scherrer, Carol S., and Josephine L. Dorsch. 1999. "The Evolving Role of the Librarian in Evidence-Based Medicine." *Bulletin of the Medical Library Association* 87, no. 3 ( July): 322–28.

## Chapter 36: Improving Nurses' Access to and Use of Professionally Relevant Information in a BSN Completion Program

AACN Task Force on the Essentials of Baccalaureate Education for Professional Nursing Practice. 1998. "The Essentials of Baccalaureate Education." Washington, D.C.: American Association of Colleges of Nursing.

Commission on Collegiate Nursing Education. 2000. *CCNE Accreditation.* American Association of Colleges of Nursing [accessed January 4, 2000]. Available from <http://www.aacn.nche.edu/Accreditation/>.

Covey, Stephen R. 1991. *Principle-Centered Leadership.* New York: Summit Books.

O'Neill, E. H., and Pew Health Professions Commission. 1998. "Recreating Health Professional Practice for a New Century." San Francisco: Center for the Health Professions.

Pew Health Professions Commission. 1995. "Health Professions Education and Managed Care Challenges and Necessary Responses." San Francisco: UCSF Center for the Health Professions.

Pew Health Professions Commission. 1995. "The Third Report of the Pew Health Professions Commissions—Critical Challenges: Revitalizing the Health Professions for the Twenty-First Century." San Francisco: UCSF Center for the Health Professions.

## Chapter 40: Preassessment of Library Skills: Why Bother?

Addison Northeast Supervisory Union Tech Team. Faculty/Staff Information Technology Competencies Survey. <http://www.vetc.vsc.edu/anesu/techplan/survey.htm> [accessed 20 January 2000].

Akins, Maureen. Computer Skill Assessment Checklist for Faculty. Augusta State University. <http://www.aug.edu/instructional_services/Skills/checklists/past.htm> [accessed 20 January 2000].

Alexander, Linda B. 1944. "LIBS 1000: A Credit Course in Library Skills at East Carolina University." ERIC, ED 376 818.

American Library Association Assessment Links. <http://www.ala.org/aasl/learning/hotlinks/assessmentlinks.html> [accessed 19 January 2000].

Assessment Planning Committee, Indiana University Bloomington Libraries. An Assessment Plan for Information Literacy. May 1, 1996 (Final). <http://www.indiana.edu/~libreser/kris/assess-plan-info-lit.html> [accessed 20 January 2000].

Avery, Susan. Search Strategy Checklist. Staley Library, Millikin University <http://www.millikin.edu/staley/Instruction/cwrr/search.html> [accessed 20 Jan. 2000].

Baker, Mark. 1990. "What Do Your Students Know and When Do They Know It?" *Library Research Skills Workbook, Grades 7-12*. Worthington, Ohio: Linworth Publishing.

Brown, Lyn S., and Jeremiah G. Ryan. 1995. "The Relationship of Time to Effectiveness in Research Skills Instruction for Students at Philadelphia College of Bible." ERIC, ED 402931.

"Cal State L.A. Website on Information Competence." <http://web.calstatela.edu/academic/infocomp/> [accessed 20 January 2000].

Cameron, Lynn. 1993. "Assessment of Library Skills. What Is Good Instruction Now: Library Instruction for the '90s." Paper presented at the Twentieth National LOEX Library Instruction Conference 20th: 1992, at Eastern Michigan University, Ann Arbor. Published in *Learning Resources and Technologies*. Ann Arbor, Mich.: Pierian Press.

Chiang, Ching-hsin. 1991. "Learning COMCAT (Computer Output Microform Catalog): Library Training Program for Foreign Students at New York Institute of Technology." ERIC, ED 343613.

Clougherty, Leo, et al. 1998. "The University of Iowa Libraries' Undergraduate User Needs Assessment." *College and Research Libraries* 59, no. 6 (November): 573–84.

Coupe, Jill. 1993. "Undergraduate Library Skills: Two Surveys at Johns Hopkins University." *Research Strategies* 11, no. 4 (Fall): 188–201.

Delta College Library, University Center, Michigan. "How Competent I Feel about My Information Literacy Skills." <http://www.delta.edu/~library/html/how_competent_do_i_feel_about_.html> [accessed 20 January 2000].

———. "Library Preassessment Questions, Spring 1998." <http://www.delta.edu/~library/html/library_pre-assessment_questio.html> [accessed 20 January 2000].

———. "Assessment of Familiarity with Library Terms." <http://www.delta.edu/~library/html/assessment_of_familiarity_with.html> [accessed 20 January 2000].

———. "Information Literacy Outcomes and Assessment." <http://www.delta.edu/~library/html/information_literacy_outcomes_.html> [accessed 20 January 2000].

———. "Library Skills Assessment." <http://www.delta.edu/~library/html/library_skills_assessment.html> [accessed 20 January 2000].

Detroit Public Schools, Department of School Libraries and Detroit Public Schools, Department of Curriculum Development Services. 1982. The Middle School Library Media Center. "Instructional Units." ERIC, ED 231356.

Drake, Liselle, and Larry Rudner. "Assessment and Evaluation on the Net." <http://ericae.net/TOOLBAR.HTM> [accessed 19 January 2000].

Delta College Library, University Center, Michigan. "Examples of Good Assessments." <http://www.delta.edu/~library/html/examples_of_good_assessments.html> [accessed 20 January 2000].

Fenske, Rachel F., and Susan E. Clark. 1995. "Incorporating Library Instruction in a General Education Program for College Freshmen." *RSR: Reference Services Review* 23, no. 3:69–74.

Fernandez, Georgina. 1985. "Pretest-Posttest Evaluation of Course Integrated Library Instruction in a Community College: A Critique of an Experiment." ERIC, ED 293576.

Fields, Carolyn B. 1987. "Using Results of a Pretest to Determine Lecture Content: A Case Study." *Research Strategies* 5, no. 1 (Winter): 29–35.

Fowler, Rena. 1990. "Assessment of Library Skills and Traits of Entering and Lower English Students, Northern Michigan University, Olsen Library." ERIC, ED 339370.

Franklin, Godfrey, and Ronald C. Toifel. 1994. "The Effects of BI on Library Knowledge and Skills among Education Students." *Research Strategies* 12, no. 4 (Fall): 224–37.

Fry, Thomas K., and Joan Kaplowitz. 1988. "The English 3 Library Instruction Program at UCLA: A Follow-Up Study." *Research Strategies"* 6, no. 3 (Summer): 100–8.

Geffert, Bryn, and Beth Christensen. 1998. "Things They Carry; Attitudes toward, Opinions about, and Knowledge of Libraries and Research among Incoming College Students." *Reference & User Services Quarterly* 37, no. 3 (Spring): 279–89.

Geffert, Bryn, and Robert Bruce. 1997. "Whither BI? Assessing Perceptions of Research Skills over an Undergraduate Career." *RQ* 36, no. 3 (Spring): 409–17.

Hawaii State Department of Education, Honolulu. 1982. Office of Instructional Services. "Library/Study Skills Instruction in Hawaii's Schools: A Guide for Teachers and Librarians." ERIC, ED 232645.

Kaplowitz, Joan. 1986. "A Pre- and Posttest Evaluation of the English 3-Library Instruction Program at UCLA." *Research Strategies* 4, no. 1 (Winter): 11–17.

Krentz, Roger. 1989. "Library Literacy of Incoming College Freshmen." ERIC, ED 346886.

Kuhlthau, Carol. 1988. "Perceptions of the Information Search Process in Libraries: A Study of Changes from High School through College." *Information Processing & Management* 24, no. 4:419–27.

Kunkel, Lilith R., et al. 1996. "What Do They Know? An Assessment of Undergraduate Library Skills." *Journal of Academic Librarianship* 22, no. 6 (November): 430–34.

Lamm, Kathryn. 1995. *10,000 Ideas for Term Papers, Projects, Reports, and Speeches.* 4th ed. New York: Macmillan.

Langley, Linda B. 1987. "The Effects of a Credit Course in Bibliographic Instruction." *Technicalities* 7, no. 11 (November): 3–7.

Lawson, V. Lonnie. 1987. "Students' Preference for Bibliographic Instruction: Library Tour vs. a Computer-Assisted Instruction Program." ERIC, ED 335055.

———. 1989. "Using a Computer-Assisted Instruction Program to Replace the Traditional Library Tour: An Experimental Study." *RQ* 29, no. 1 (Fall): 71–79.

Lenn, Katy. Get Ready Tutorial. University of Oregon. <http://libweb.uoregon.edu/getready/handson/> [accessed 20 January 2000].

Library Instruction Committee, Cal State University, Sacramento. Library Instruction Assessment Plan. <http://www.csus.edu/indiv/g/goffl/libinst/assess.htm> [accessed 20 January 2000].

Libutti, Patricia O'Brien, ed. 1995. *Teaching Information Retrieval and Evaluation Skills to Education Students and Practitioners; A Casebook of Applications.* Chicago, Ill.: American Library Association, Association of College and Research Libraries, Education and Behavioral Sciences Section.

London Guildhall University. "Deliberations in Teaching and Learning in Higher Education: Assessment." <http://www.lgu.ac.uk/deliberations/assessment/index.cgi> [accessed 19 January 2000].

Lutzker, Marilyn. 1988. *Research Projects for College Students: What to Write across the Curriculum.* Westport, Conn.: Greenwood.

Michaelsen, Karen Lueck. Student Survey and Pretest, Introduction to Information Resources. Seattle Community College. <http://www.sccd.ctc.edu/~karenm/survey.html> [accessed 20 January 2000].

Neuman, Delia, and Rebecca Van Campen Jackson. 1990. "MAJIK/1: HyperCard Introduction to the Use of Periodicals. Final Report." ERIC, ED 323964.

Paterson, Ellen R. 1978. "An Assessment of College Library Skills." *RQ* 17, no. 3 (Spring): 226–29.

Platoff, Annie, Linda Shackle, and Orchid Mazurkiewicz, comp. "Univ 100 Library Projects: Library Skills and Research Skills." *Help Using the Library; Guides for Doing Term Papers.* Arizona State University Libraries. <http://www.asu.edu/lib/help/help2.htm> [accessed 20 January 2000].

Primack, Alice. Information Skills Minicourse. University of Florida. <http://web.uflib.ufl.edu/instruct2/mini/index.html> [accessed 20 January 2000].

Ragains, Patrick. "Assessment in Library and Information Literacy Instruction." <http://www.library.unr.edu/~ragains/assess.html> [accessed 19 January 2000].

Sheridan, Jean, ed. 1995. *Writing-Across-the-Curriculum and the Academic Library: A Guide for Librarians, Instructors, and Writing Program Directors.* Westport, Conn.: Greenwood.

Smith, Drew, ed. "Directory of On-Line Resources for Information Literacy." <http://www.cas.usf.edu/lis/il/index.html> [accessed 20 January 2000].

Stripling, Barbara. 1999. "Expectations for Achievement and Performance: Assessing Student Skills." *NASSP Bulletin* 83, no. 605 (March): 44–52.

Swanson, Judy. CSU Information Competence Tutorials. Cal Poly State University, San Luis Obispo, Calif. <http://www.lib.calpoly.edu/infocomp/modules/> [accessed 20 January 2000].

Vidmar, Dale J. 1998. "Affective Change: Integrating Presessions in the Students' Classroom Prior to Library Instruction." *Reference Services Review* 26, no. 3–4 (Fall–Winter): 75–95; see also: <http://www.sou.edu/library/dale/loex98/> (PowerPoint slides).

Viles, Ann. 1999. Appalachian State University Information Literacy Assessment, Fall 1999. <http://www.appstate.edu/~vilesea/literacy.html> [accessed 20 January 2000].

334 *Bibliography*

Whitmire, Ethelene. 1998. "Development of Critical Thinking Skills: An Analysis of Academic Library Experiences and Other Measures." *College and Research Libraries* 59, no. 3 (May): 266–73.

Wollter, Patricia. 1987. "Development and/or Furthering Library Research Skills for Local Junior and Senior High School Students." ERIC, ED 324025.

Zahner, Jane E. 1993. "Thoughts, Feelings, and Actions: Integrating Domains in Library Instruction." ERIC, ED 362215.

## Chapter 41: Implementing an Assessment Program for Student Information Competency at Appalachian State University

Association of College and Research Libraries. 1999. *Information Literacy Competency Standards for Higher Education—Revised Draft.* <http://www.ala.org/acrl/ilcomstan.html> [accessed 5 January 2000].

———. 1998. *Task Force on Academic Library Outcomes Assessment Report.* <http://www.ala.org/acrl/outcome.html> [accessed 5 January 2000].

Breivik, Patricia, and E. Gordon Gee. 1989. *Information Literacy: Revolution in the Library.* New York: American Council on Education.

Doyle, Christina S. 1999. *Development of a Model of Information Literacy Outcome Measures within National Education Goals of 1990.* Ann Arbor, Mich.: UMI Dissertation Services.

Feinberg, R. P., and C. E. King. 1992. "Performance Evaluation in Bibliographic Instruction Workshop Courses: Assessing What Students Do as a Measure of What They Know." *Reference Services Review* 20, no. 2:75–80.

## Chapter 42: Situated Learning at the Georgia Tech Library

Bonwell, Charles C., and Eison, James A. 1991. "Active Learning: Creating Excitement in the Classroom." The National Teaching and Learning Forum. <http://www.ntlf.com/html/lib/bib/91-9dig.htm> [accessed 20 January 2000].

Dijkstra, Sanne, Bernadette H. A. M. Van Hout Wolters, and Peter C. Van Der Sijde, eds. 1989. *Research on Instruction: Design and Effects.* Englewood Cliffs, N.J.: Educational Technology Publications.

Dills, Charles R., and Alexander J. Romiszowski, eds. 1997. *Instructional Development Paradigms.* Englewood Cliffs, N.J.: Educational Technology Publications.

Duffy, Thomas M., and Donald J. Cunningham. 1996. "Constructivism: Implications for the Design and Delivery of Instruction." In *Educational Communications and Technology,* ed. David H. Jonassen. New York: Simon & Schuster.

Duffy, Thomas M., Joost Lowyck, and David H. Jonassen, eds. 1993. *Designing Environments for Constructive Learning,* New York: Springer-Verlag.

Fardouly, Niki. 1998. "Learner-Centered Teaching Strategies." In *Principles of Instructional Design and Adult Learning,* University of New South Wales, Faculty of the Built Environment, 23 December 1998. <http://www.fbe.unsw.edu.au/learning/instructionaldesign/strategies.htm> [accessed 9 January 2000].

Grabinger, R. Scott. 1996. "Rich Environments for Active Learning." In *Educational Communications and Technology*, ed. David H. Jonassen. New York: Simon & Schuster.

Petraglia, Joseph. 1998. *Reality by Design: The Rhetoric and Technology of Authenticity in Education*. Mahway, N.J.: Lawrence Erlbaum Associates.

Wilson, Brent G., and Peggy Cole. 1996. "Cognitive Teaching Models." In *Educational Communications and Technology*, ed. David H. Jonassen. New York: Simon & Schuster.

Winn, William. 1993. "A Constructive Critique of the Assumptions of Instructional Design." In *Designing Environments for Constructive Learning*, ed. Thomas M. Duffy, Joost Lowyck, and David H. Jonassen. New York: Springer-Verlag.

Wood, Julie, and Anne Garrison. 1998. *Information Competencies: Students, Scholars,* and *Librarians*. Atlanta: Georgia Institute of Technology, Library and Information Center.

# Index

# Contributors

Susan Avery, assistant professor and reference and instruction librarian, Staley Library, Millikin University

Sandy Ballasch, team leader of database maintenance and special projects, University of Iowa Libraries, University of Iowa

Kathy Ballou, clinical instructor, Health Sciences Library, University of Missouri–Kansas City

Hope Barton, coordinator of collection management and materials processing, Hardin Library for the Health Sciences, University of Iowa

Susan Sykes Berry, instruction and reference librarian, Health Sciences Library, University of Missouri–Kansas City

Karla J. Block, assistant librarian and project coordinator/training manager for Health Information Access for Rural Nurse Practitioners, Biomedical Library, University of Minnesota

Stephanie Sterling Brasley, reference/instruction librarian and instructional outreach coordinator, College Library, University of California–Los Angeles

Alison Bremner, learner support librarian, Open University, United Kingdom

Joanna M. Burkhardt, head librarian, College of Continuing Education Library, University Library, University of Rhode Island

Sandy Campbell, reference and instruction librarian, Science and Technology Library, University of Alberta

Julie Chapman, reference librarian, Odum Library, Valdosta State University

Shelley Cudiner, reference librarian, Jeremy Richard Library, University of Connecticut

Leslie Czechowski, reference librarian and college archivist, Burling Library, Grinnell College

Diane Dallis, librarian for electronic instructional services, Undergraduate Library Services, Indiana University–Bloomington

Susan Deese-Roberts, director of Zimmerman Library Public Services, University of New Mexico

Nancy DeJoy, professor of English and professor of excellence in teaching, Staley Library, Millikin University

Stephen H. Dew, coordinator of Library Services for Distance Education, University of Iowa Libraries, University of Iowa

Barbara I. Dewey, dean of libraries, University of Tennessee; formerly director of Information and Research Services, University of Iowa

Lori A. DuBois, assistant undergraduate librarian for instruction, University of Illinois at Urbana–Champaign

Jim Duncan, coordinator of Information Commons and electronic services, Hardin Library for the Health Sciences, University of Iowa

Richard Eimas, curator of the John Martin Rare Book Room, Hardin Library for the Health Sciences, University of Iowa

James Elmborg, information technology librarian, Furman University/ Wofford College

Carole Ann Fabian, assistant educational technology librarian, University at Buffalo, State University of New York

Clarissa C. Fisher, administrative librarian, Hunter Library, Western Carolina University

Bruce Gilbert, director of library operations and technology, Cowles Library, Drake University

Rebecca S. Graves, educational services librarian, J. Otto Lottes Health Sciences Library, University of Missouri–Columbia

Oskar R. Harmon, associate professor of economics, University of Connecticut

Lisa Janicke Hinchliffe, library instruction coordinator, Milner Library, Illinois State University

Susan Hollar, technology support librarian and knowledge navigation center manager, Harlan Hatcher Graduate Library, University of Michigan

Maggie Houlihan, undergraduate outreach coordinator, Social Sciences and Humanities Library, University of California–San Diego

Jon R. Hufford, assistant head of Information Services for Library Instruction, TTU Library, Texas Tech University

Elizabeth O. Hutchins, assistant professor, St. Olaf College Library

Carolyn Johnson, information librarian and assistant professor, Owens Library, Northwest Missouri State University

Sally Kalin, associate dean for University Park, Penn State University Libraries, Pennsylvania State University

Mary L. Kinnaman, clinical instructor, Health Sciences Library, University of Missouri–Kansas City

R. Cecilia Knight, catalog librarian, Burling Library, Grinnell College

Melissa H. Koenig, assistant reference librarian and coordinator of library instruction, UIC Main Library, University of Illinois at Chicago

Mary C. MacDonald, reference/information literacy librarian, University Library, University of Rhode Island

Marybeth McCartin, head of Instructional Services, NYU Libraries, New York University

Virginia McQuiston, associate professor, reference and instruction librarian and head of Public Services, Staley Library, Millikin University

Patricia Mackstroth, reference librarian, Milner Library, Illinois State University

Joyce A. Meldrem, head librarian for collection management and assistant professor, Owens Library, Northwest Missouri State University

Marsha Miller, coordinator of library instruction, Indiana State University

Eleanor Mitchell, head of the College Library, University of California–Los Angeles

Dr. W. Bede Mitchell, university librarian, Georgia Southern University

Darlene Nichols, coordinator of Graduate Library Instruction, Harlan Hatcher Graduate Library, University of Michigan

Eric Novotny, reference librarian, UIC Main Library, University of Illinois at Chicago

Emily Okada, librarian for Instructional Services, Undergraduate Library Services, Indiana University–Bloomington

Afeworki Paulos, International Studies bibliographer, University of Iowa Libraries, University of Iowa

Andrée J. Rathemacher, reference and business bibliographer, University Library, University of Rhode Island

Randy Reichardt, reference and instruction librarian, Science and Technology Library, University of Alberta

Tom Rocklin, director of the Center for Teaching and professor of educational psychology, University of Iowa

Lynne Rudasill, assistant education and social science librarian, University of Illinois at Urbana–Champaign

Joan D. Ruelle, coordinator of User Services, Science and Engineering Libraries, University of Virginia

John Schacht, reference librarian, University of Iowa Libraries, University of Iowa

Susan E. Searing, Library and Information Science librarian, University of Illinois at Urbana–Champaign

Bonnie S. Sherman, associate professor of psychology, St. Olaf College

Janice Simmons-Welburn, director of Central Public Services, University of Iowa Libraries, University of Iowa

Loanne Snavely, head of instructional programs, Penn State University Libraries, Pennsylvania State University

Margaret Spinner, reference librarian, Lamar Soutter Library, University of Massachusetts Medical School

Carol Spradling, assistant professor of computer science and information systems, Owens Library, Northwest Missouri State University

Scott Stebelman, formerly of Gelman Library, George Washington University

Laurie Sutch, faculty exploratory manager, Harlan Hatcher Graduate Library, University of Michigan

Duffy Tweedy, instruction/outreach coordinator, Social Sciences and Humanities Library, University of California–San Diego

Robert Vander Hart, reference librarian and government documents specialist, Lamar Soutter Library, University of Massachusetts Medical School

Dr. Ann Viles, interim associate university librarian, Appalachian State University

Angela E. Weaver, performing and fine arts reference and liaison librarian, Fenwick Library, George Mason University

Michelle White, reference librarian, Odum Library, Valdosta State University

Lizabeth A. Wilson, director, University of Washington Libraries, University of Washington

Rick W. Wilson, assistant professor of physical therapy, Western Carolina University

Julie Wood, information consultant and instruction coordinator, Georgia Institute of Technology

Karen Zimmerman, formerly TWIST project coordinator, University of Iowa Libraries, University of Iowa